THE CAMBRIDGE COMPANION TO
C.S. LEWIS

A distinguished academic, influential Christian apologist, and best-selling author of children's literature, C.S. Lewis (1898–1963) is a controversial and enigmatic figure who continues to fascinate fifty years after his death. This *Companion* is the first comprehensive single-volume study written by an international team of scholars to survey Lewis's career as a literary historian, popular theologian and creative writer. Twenty-one expert voices from Oxford, Cambridge, Princeton and Wheaton, among many other places of learning, analyse Lewis's work from theological, philosophical and literary perspectives. Some chapters consider his professional contribution to fields such as critical theory and intellectual history, while others assess his views on issues including moral knowledge, gender, prayer, war, love, suffering and scripture. The final chapters investigate his work as a writer of fiction and poetry. Original in its approach and unique in its scope, this *Companion* shows that C.S. Lewis was much more than merely the man behind *Narnia*.

Robert MacSwain is Assistant Professor of Theology and Christian Ethics at the School of Theology, the University of the South, Sewanee, Tennessee. He is the co-editor, with Jeffrey Stout, of *Grammar and Grace: Reformulations of Aquinas and Wittgenstein* (2004), and, with Ann Loades, of *The Truth-Seeking Heart: Austin Farrer and His Writings* (2006).

Michael Ward is Chaplain of St Peter's College, University of Oxford. He is the author of *Planet Narnia: The Seven Heavens in the Imagination of C.S. Lewis* (2008) and the co-editor, with Ben Quash, of *Heresies and How to Avoid Them: Why it Matters What Christians Believe* (2007).

CAMBRIDGE COMPANIONS TO RELIGION
A series of companions to major topics and key figures in theology and
religious studies. Each volume contains specially commissioned chapters
by international scholars which provide an accessible and stimulating
introduction to the subject for new readers and non-specialists.

Other titles in the series

THE CAMBRIDGE COMPANION TO CHRISTIAN DOCTRINE
edited by Colin Gunton (1997)
ISBN 0 521 47118 4 hardback   ISBN 0 521 47695 x paperback

THE CAMBRIDGE COMPANION TO BIBLICAL INTERPRETATION
edited by John Barton (1998)
ISBN 0 521 48144 9 hardback   ISBN 0 521 48593 2 paperback

THE CAMBRIDGE COMPANION TO DIETRICH BONHOEFFER
edited by John de Gruchy (1999)
ISBN 0 521 58258 x hardback   ISBN 0 521 58781 6 paperback

THE CAMBRIDGE COMPANION TO KARL BARTH
edited by John Webster (2000)
ISBN 0 521 58476 0 hardback   ISBN 0 521 58560 0 paperback

THE CAMBRIDGE COMPANION TO CHRISTIAN ETHICS
edited by Robin Gill (2001)
ISBN 0 521 77070 x hardback   ISBN 0 521 77918 9 paperback

THE CAMBRIDGE COMPANION TO JESUS
edited by Markus Bockmuehl (2001)
ISBN 0 521 79261 4 hardback   ISBN 0 521 79678 4 paperback

THE CAMBRIDGE COMPANION TO FEMINIST THEOLOGY
edited by Susan Frank Parsons (2002)
ISBN 0 521 66327 x hardback   ISBN 0 521 66380 6 paperback

THE CAMBRIDGE COMPANION TO MARTIN LUTHER
edited by Donald K. McKim (2003)
ISBN 0 521 81648 3 hardback   ISBN 0 521 01673 8 paperback

THE CAMBRIDGE COMPANION TO ST PAUL
edited by James D.G. Dunn (2003)
ISBN 0 521 78155 8 hardback   ISBN 0 521 78694 0 paperback

THE CAMBRIDGE COMPANION TO POSTMODERN THEOLOGY
edited by Kevin J. Vanhoozer (2003)
ISBN 0 521 79062 x hardback   ISBN 0 521 79395 5 paperback

THE CAMBRIDGE COMPANION TO JOHN CALVIN
edited by Donald K. McKim (2004)
ISBN 0 521 81647 5 hardback   ISBN 0 521 01672 x paperback

THE CAMBRIDGE COMPANION TO HANS URS VON BALTHASAR
edited by Edward T. Oakes SJ and David Moss (2004)
ISBN 0 521 81467 7 hardback   ISBN 0 521 89147 7 paperback

Continued at the back of the book

THE CAMBRIDGE COMPANION TO

C.S. LEWIS

Edited by Robert MacSwain and Michael Ward

 CAMBRIDGE
UNIVERSITY PRESS

CAMBRIDGE UNIVERSITY PRESS
Cambridge, New York, Melbourne, Madrid, Cape Town, Singapore,
São Paulo, Delhi, Tokyo, Mexico City

Cambridge University Press
The Edinburgh Building, Cambridge CB2 8RU, UK

Published in the United States of America by Cambridge University Press, New York

www.cambridge.org
Information on this title: www.cambridge.org/9780521711142

© Cambridge University Press 2010

First published
Reprinted 2011

Printed in the United Kingdom at the University Press, Cambridge

A catalogue record for this publication is available from the British Library

ISBN 978-0-521-88413-6 Hardback
ISBN 978-0-521-71114-2 Paperback

To Simon Barrington-Ward

Contents

Contributors

Joseph P. Cassidy is Principal of St Chad's College, Durham University, and a non-residentiary canon of Durham Cathedral. His publications include 'Who's In and Who's Out' in Mark D. Chapman (ed.), *Living the Magnificat* (2008); 'Cultural and Spiritual Aspects of Palliative Medicine' with Douglas J. Davies in Derek Doyle *et al.* (eds), *Oxford Textbook of Palliative Medicine* (2005); 'The Post-Communion Prayer: Living Sacrifice', in Stephen Conway (ed.), *Living the Eucharist* (2001); 'Directing the Third Week', in David Fleming (ed.), *Ignatian Exercises. Contemporary Annotations: The Best of the Review 4* (1996); and 'The Is–OUGHT Problem and the Ground of Economic Ethics', in Masudul Alam Choudhury (ed.), *Ethics and Economics* (1995). Dr Cassidy, for many years a Jesuit before becoming an Anglican, has also published extensively in social ethics and Central American policy analysis.

Dennis Danielson is Professor of English at the University of British Columbia. His publications include *Milton's Good God: A Study in Literary Theodicy* (Cambridge University Press, 1982; repr. 2009); *The First Copernican: Georg Joachim Rheticus and the Rise of the Copernican Revolution* (2006); *The Cambridge Companion to Milton* (Cambridge University Press, 1989; 2nd edn 1999); and *The Book of the Cosmos: Imagining the Universe from Heraclitus to Hawking* (2000). Professor Danielson has also published articles in journals such as *Mind, Nature, American Journal of Physics, Journal for the History of Astronomy*, and *American Scientist*.

Mark Edwards is Tutor in Theology at Christ Church and Lecturer in Patristics for the Theology Faculty in the University of Oxford. His publications include *Catholicity and Heresy in the Early Church* (2009); *Culture and Philosophy in the Age of Plotinus* (2006); *John through the Centuries* (2003); *Origen against Plato* (2002); and *Neoplatonic Saints* (2000). Dr Edwards has also published articles in journals such as *Classical Quarterly, Journal of Theological Studies, American Journal of Philology, Downside Review*, and *Journal of Ecclesiastical History*.

Paul S. Fiddes is Professor of Systematic Theology in the University of Oxford, where he is also Principal Emeritus and Professorial Research Fellow of Regent's Park College. His publications include *The Promised End: Eschatology in Theology and Literature* (2000); *Participating in God: A Pastoral Doctrine of the Trinity* (2000); *Freedom and Limit: A Dialogue between Literature and Christian Doctrine* (1991); *Past Event and Present Salvation: The Christian Idea* *of Atonement* (1989); and *The Creative Suffering of God* (1988). He has served as Chairman of the Doctrine and Worship Committee of the Baptist Union of Great Britain. In 2005 he delivered the Bampton Lectures as *Seeing the World and Knowing God: Ancient Wisdom and Modern Doctrine*. Professor Fiddes serves as series editor of New Critical Thinking in Religion, Theology and Biblical Studies.

John V. Fleming is the Louis W. Fairchild Professor of English and Comparative Literature Emeritus at Princeton University. His publications include *The Roman de la Rose: A Study in Allegory and Iconography* (1969); *Reason and the Lover* (1984); *An Introduction to the Franciscan Literature of the Middle Ages* (1977); *Classical Imitation and Interpretation in Chaucer's "Troilus"* (1990); and *The Anti-Communist Manifestos: Four Books that Shaped the Cold War* (2009). Professor Fleming is the former President of the Medieval Academy of America, a Fellow of the American Academy of Arts and Letters, and a member of the Guild of Scholars of the Episcopal Church.

Malcolm Guite is Chaplain of Girton College in the University of Cambridge, and Associate Chaplain of the Church of St Edward King and Martyr, Cambridge. His publications include *Faith, Hope and Poetry: Theology and the Poetic Imagination* (2010); *What Do Christians Believe?* (2006; Dutch and Greek edns 2007; American edn 2008); 'Through Literature', in Jeremy Begbie (ed.), *Beholding the Glory: Incarnation through the Arts* (2000); and 'Our Truest Poetry is Our Most Feigning … Poetry, Playfulness and Truth', in Trevor Hart, Steven R. Guthrie and Ivan P. Khovacs (eds), *Faithful Performances: Enacting Christian Tradition* (2007). Dr Guite has also published poetry in *The Temenos Academy Review*, *Church Times*, *Second Spring*, *Mars Hill Review*, and *The Ambler*. His website is <www.malcolmguite.com>.

Stanley Hauerwas is the Gilbert T. Rowe Professor of Theological Ethics at the Divinity School of Duke University, North Carolina. His publications include *A Cross-Shattered Church: Reclaiming the Theological Heart of Preaching* (2009); *Christianity, Democracy and the Radical Ordinary*, with Romand Coles (2008); *The State of the University: Academic Knowledges and the Knowledge of God* (2007); *Matthew: A Theological Commentary* (2006); and *Performing the Faith: Bonhoeffer and the Practice of Non-violence* (2004). In 2001 he gave the Gifford Lectures at the University of St Andrews as *With the Grain of the Universe*. Professor Hauerwas is a founder member of the Ekklesia Project, an ecumenical think-tank.

Alan Jacobs is Clyde S. Kilby Professor of English at Wheaton College, Illinois. His publications include *Original Sin: A Cultural History* (2008); *Looking Before and After: Testimony and the Christian Life* (2008); *The Narnian: The Life and Imagination of C.S. Lewis* (2005); *A Theology of Reading: The Hermeneutics of Love* (2001); and *What Became of Wystan: Change and Continuity in Auden's Poetry* (1999). Professor Jacobs is currently completing a critical edition of W.H. Auden's poem *The Age of Anxiety*.

David Jasper is Professor of Literature and Theology at the University of Glasgow, and also Changyang Chair Professor at Renmin University of China. His publications include *The Sacred Body: Asceticism in Religion, Literature, Art and*

Culture (2009); *The Sacred Desert: Religion, Literature, Art and Culture* (2007); *The Oxford Handbook of English Literature and Theology*, co-edited with Andrew Hass and Elizabeth Jay (2007); *A Short Introduction to Hermeneutics* (2004); and *The Bible and Literature: A Reader*, co-edited with Stephen Prickett (1999). Professor Jasper is a Fellow of the Royal Society of Edinburgh and is the founding editor of the journal *Literature and Theology*.

Ann Loades is Honorary Professorial Fellow of St Chad's College and Professor of Divinity Emerita, Durham University, where she was the first woman to be awarded a professorial chair personal to herself. Her publications include *Feminist Theology: Voices from the Past* (2001); *Evelyn Underhill* (1999); *Dorothy L. Sayers: Spiritual Writings* (1993); *Searching for Lost Coins: Explorations in Christianity and Feminism* (1988); and *Kant and Job's Comforters* (1985). She has undertaken work for the Arts and Humanities Research Council since 1999, mostly in connection with the development of postgraduate awards. She edited the journal *Theology* from 1991 to 1997. Professor Loades is a former President of the Society for the Study of Theology (2005–06), and is currently a member of the Christian – Muslim Forum established by the Archbishop of Canterbury, Rowan Williams.

Stephen Logan is Lecturer in the Faculty of English at the University of Cambridge, having begun his academic career as a Research Fellow at St John's College, Oxford. His publications include 'Destinations of the Heart: Romanticism in Anglo-Welsh Poetry', *Planet: The Welsh Internationalist* 164 (2004); 'Hiraeth and the Recoil from Theory', *Planet: The Welsh Internationalist* 155 (2002); the best-selling *William Wordsworth: Everyman's Poetry Library* (1998); and 'In Defence of C.S. Lewis', *Times Literary Supplement* (21 Feb. 1997). He has lectured and published widely on Romantic English poetry (especially in relation to cultural change) and on the practicalities of criticism. Dr Logan has written three volumes of poetry and works also as a psychotherapist.

Robert MacSwain is Assistant Professor of Theology and Christian Ethics at the School of Theology of the University of the South, Sewanee, Tennessee. His publications include 'Imperfect Lives and Perfect Love: Austin Farrer, Stanley Hauerwas, and the Reach of Divine Redemption', in Natalie K. Watson and Stephen Burns (eds), *Exchanges of Grace: Essays in Honour of Ann Loades* (2008); *The Truth-Seeking Heart: Austin Farrer and His Writings*, co-edited with Ann Loades (2006); 'An Analytic Anglican: The Philosophical Theology of William P. Alston', *Anglican Theological Review* 88 (2006); and *Grammar and Grace: Reformulations of Aquinas and Wittgenstein*, co-edited with Jeffrey Stout (2004). He has also published articles, poems and book reviews in journals such as *New Blackfriars*, *Journal of Anglican Studies*, *Studies in Christian Ethics*, *Christianity and Literature* and *International Journal of Systematic Theology*. He is currently working on an intellectual biography of Austin Farrer, provisionally entitled *A Swift among Swallows*.

Gilbert Meilaender is Duesenberg Professor in Christian Ethics at Valparaiso University, Indiana. His publications include *Neither Beast Nor God: The Dignity of the Human Person* (2009); *The Way That Leads There: Augustinian Reflections on the Christian Life* (2006); *Faith and Faithfulness: Basic Themes* *in Christian Ethics* (1991); *Friendship: A Study in Theological Ethics* (1981); and *The Taste for the Other: The Social and Ethical Thought of C.S. Lewis* (1978; 2nd edn 1998, repr. 2003). Professor Meilaender served on the President's Council on Bioethics from 2002 to 2009.

Peter J. Schakel is Peter C. and Emajean Cook Professor of English at Hope College, Michigan. His publications include *Word and Story in C.S. Lewis: Language and Narrative in Theory and Practice*, co-edited with Charles A. Huttar (2007); *Imagination and the Arts in C.S. Lewis* (2002); and *Reason and Imagination in C.S. Lewis: A Study of 'Till We Have Faces'* (1984; online at <http://hope.edu/academic/english/schakel/tillwehavefaces/index.htm>). Professor Schakel also has interests in English literature of the Restoration and eighteenth century, especially verse satire and the work of Jonathan Swift. His publications in this field include *Critical Approaches to Teaching Swift* (1992) and *The Poetry of Jonathan Swift: Allusion and the Development of a Poetic Style* (1978).

T.A. (Tom) **Shippey** is now professor emeritus, having retired from the Walter J. Ong SJ Chair of Humanities at Saint Louis University, Missouri. His publications include *Roots and Branches: Selected Papers on Tolkien* (2007); *The Road to Middle-earth* (1982; revd and expanded edn 2005); *J.R.R. Tolkien: Author of the Century* (2001); *The Shadow-Walkers: Jacob Grimm's Mythology of the Monstrous* (2005) and *The Critical Heritage: Beowulf*, with Andreas Haarder (1998). Professor Shippey has also published extensively on medieval studies and modern fantasy.

Caroline J. Simon is John and Jeanne Jacobson Professor of Philosophy at Hope College, Michigan. Her publications include *The Disciplined Heart: Love, Destiny and Imagination* (1997); 'Friendship's Role in Coming to Know as We are Known', *Christian Reflections: A Series in Faith and Ethics* 27 (2008); 'What Wondrous Love is This? Meditations on Barth, Love and the Future of Christian Ethics', in George Hunsinger (ed.), *For the Sake of the World: Karl Barth and the Future of Ecclesial Theology* (2004); 'Seduction: Does How You Get to "Yes" Still Matter?', in Marya Bower and Ruth Groenhout (eds), *Philosophy, Feminism and Faith* (2003); and 'Inquiring After God through Our Neighbor', in Ellen T. Charry (ed.), *Inquiring After God* (2000). Professor Simon has also published extensively on the nature of Christian higher education.

Charles Taliaferro is Professor of Philosophy at St Olaf College, Minnesota. His publications include *Evidence and Faith: Philosophy and Religions since the Seventeenth Century* (Cambridge University Press, 2005); *Naturalism*, with Stewart Goetz (2008); *Contemporary Philosophy of Religion: An Introduction* (1998); and *Consciousness and the Mind of God* (Cambridge University Press, 1994; repr. 2004). He is also a contributor to *The Chronicles of Narnia and Philosophy: The Lion, the Witch, and the Worldview* (2005). Professor Taliaferro serves on the editorial board of *Religious Studies*, *Faith and Philosophy*, *American Philosophical Quarterly*, *Ars Disputandi* and *Philosophy Compass*.

Kevin J. Vanhoozer is Blanchard Professor of Theology at the Graduate School of Wheaton College, Illinois. His publications include *Remythologizing*

Theology: Divine Action, Passion, and Authorship (Cambridge University Press, 2010); *Pictures at a Biblical Exhibition: Theological Scenes of the Church's Worship, Witness, and Wisdom* (2010); *The Drama of Doctrine: A Canonical-Linguistic Approach to Christian Theology* (2005); *Is There a Meaning in This Text?: The Bible, the Reader, and the Morality of Literary Knowledge* (1998); *Biblical Narrative in the Philosophy of Paul Ricœur: A Study in Hermeneutics and Theology* (Cambridge University Press, 1990). Professor Vanhoozer serves on the editorial board of the *International Journal of Systematic Theology* and *Pro Ecclesia* and is the North American Consultant for the forthcoming edition of the *New Dictionary of Theology*.

Jerry L. Walls is a Senior Research Fellow in the Center for Philosophy of Religion at the University of Notre Dame, Indiana, where he is writing a book on Purgatory, to complete a trilogy begun with *Hell: The Logic of Damnation* (1992) and *Heaven: The Logic of Eternal Joy* (2002). Dr Walls's other publications include *The Oxford Handbook of Eschatology* (2007); *C.S. Lewis as Philosopher: Truth, Goodness and Beauty*, co-edited with David Baggett and Gary R. Habermas (2008); and *C.S. Lewis and Francis Schaeffer: Lessons for a New Century from the Most Influential Apologists of Our Time*, with Scott R. Burson (1998).

Michael Ward is Chaplain of St Peter's College in the University of Oxford. His publications include *Planet Narnia: The Seven Heavens in the Imagination of C.S. Lewis* (2008); *Heresies and How to Avoid Them*, co-edited with Ben Quash (2007); 'The Tragedy is in the Pity: C.S. Lewis and the Song of the Goat', in T. Kevin Taylor and Giles Waller (eds), *Christian Theology and Tragedy: Theologians, Tragic Literature, and Tragic Theory* (forthcoming 2011); 'C.S. Lewis', in Andrew Atherstone (ed.), *The Heart of Faith: Following Christ in the Church of England* (2008); and 'Christianity and Film', in Angus J.L. Menuge (ed.), *Christ and Culture in Dialogue* (1999). Dr Ward's work on Lewis's theological imagination was the subject of the BBC television documentary *The Narnia Code* (2009); a book of the same title followed (2010). His website is <www.michaelward.biz>.

Judith Wolfe is a Research Fellow at Wolfson College in the University of Oxford, and a post-doctoral fellow at the European College of Liberal Arts in Berlin. Her doctoral dissertation was on Heidegger's secular eschatology. Her publications include *C.S. Lewis and the Church*, co-edited with Brendan Wolfe (forthcoming, 2011); '"Hineingehalten in die Nacht": Heidegger's Early Appropriation of Christian Eschatology', in J.P. Manoussakis and N. DeRoo (eds), *Phenomenology and Eschatology* (2008); 'Salvation is in Suffering: Heidegger between Luther and Hölderlin', in George Pattison (ed.), *Heidegger and Religion: Colloquia of the Oxford Centre for Christianity and Modern European Thought* (2008); 'Acknowledging a Hidden God: A Theological Critique of Stanley Cavell on Scepticism', *The Heythrop Journal* 48 (2007); and '"Like this Insubstantial Pageant Faded": Eschatology and Theatricality in *The Tempest*', *Literature and Theology* 18 (2004). Dr Tonning is a former President of the Oxford University C.S. Lewis Society and is General Editor of the *Oxford Journal of Inklings Studies*, a peer-reviewed journal indexed in the MLA.

Abbreviations

Lewis's works are cited in the notes in the following editions and with the following abbreviations:

AGO	*A Grief Observed*. London: Faber & Faber, 1966.
AMR	*All My Road Before Me: The Diary of C.S. Lewis, 1922–1927*, ed. Walter Hooper. London: HarperCollins, 1991.
AOL	*The Allegory of Love: A Study in Medieval Tradition*. Oxford: Oxford University Press, 1958.
AOM	*The Abolition of Man*. Glasgow. Collins, 1984.
AT	*Charles Williams and C.S. Lewis, Arthurian Torso*. London: Oxford University Press.
CLI	*Collected Letters, Volume I*, ed. Walter Hooper. London: HarperCollins, 2000.
CLII	*Collected Letters, Volume II*, ed. Walter Hooper. London: HarperCollins, 2004.
CLIII	*Collected Letters, Volume III*, ed. Walter Hooper. London: HarperCollins, 2006.
CP	*The Collected Poems of C.S. Lewis*, ed. Walter Hooper. London: Fount, 1994.
DI	*The Discarded Image*. Cambridge: Cambridge University Press, 1964.
DT	*The Dark Tower and Other Stories*, ed. Walter Hooper. London: Collins, 1977.
EC	*Essay Collection*, ed. Lesley Walmsley. London: HarperCollins, 2000.
EIC	*An Experiment in Criticism*. Cambridge: Cambridge University Press, 1961.
EL	*English Literature in the Sixteenth Century, Excluding Drama*. Oxford: Clarendon Press, 1954.
FL	*The Four Loves*. Glasgow: Collins, 1991.
GD	*The Great Divorce: A Dream*. Glasgow: Collins, 1982.
GMA	*George MacDonald: An Anthology*. San Francisco: HarperCollins, 2001.
HHB	*The Horse and His Boy*. Glasgow: Fontana Lions, 1980.
LB	*The Last Battle*. Glasgow: Fontana Lions, 1981.
LTM	*Prayer: Letters to Malcolm*. London: Collins, 1983.

LWW	*The Lion, the Witch and the Wardrobe*. Glasgow: Fontana Lions, 1982.
M	*Miracles: A Preliminary Study, revised edn*. Glasgow: Collins, 1980.
MC	*Mere Christianity*. Glasgow: Collins, 1990.
MN	*The Magician's Nephew*. Glasgow: Fontana Lions, 1981.
NP	*Narrative Poems*, ed. Walter Hooper. London: HarperCollins, 1994.
OSP	*Out of the Silent Planet*. London: Pan, 1983.
OTOW	*Of This and Other Worlds*, ed. Walter Hooper. London: Collins, 1982.
PC	*Prince Caspian: The Return to Narnia*. Glasgow: Fontana Lions, 1981.
Per	*Perelandra*. London: Pan, 1983.
PH	E.M.W. Tillyard and C.S. Lewis, *The Personal Heresy: A Controversy*. London: Oxford University Press, 1965.
POP	*The Problem of Pain*. Glasgow: Collins, 1983.
PPL	*A Preface to Paradise Lost*. Oxford: Oxford University Press, 1984.
PR	*The Pilgrim's Regress: An Allegorical Apology for Christianity, Reason and Romanticism*. Glasgow: Fount, 1980.
ROP	*Reflections on the Psalms*. Glasgow: Collins, 1984.
SBJ	*Surprised by Joy: The Shape of My Early Life*. Glasgow: Collins, 1982.
SC	*The Silver Chair*. Glasgow: Fontana Lions, 1981.
SIL	*Spenser's Images of Life*, ed. Alastair Fowler. Cambridge: Cambridge University Press, 1967.
SIW	*Studies in Words*. Cambridge: Cambridge University Press, 1990.
SL	*The Screwtape Letters*. Glasgow: Collins, 1982.
SLE	*Selected Literary Essays*, ed. Walter Hooper. Cambridge: Cambridge University Press, 1980.
SMRL	*Studies in Medieval and Renaissance Literature*, ed. Walter Hooper. Cambridge: Cambridge University Press, 1966.
THS	*That Hideous Strength: A Modern Fairy-tale for Grown-ups*. London: Pan, 1983.
TST	*They Stand Together: The Letters of C.S. Lewis to Arthur Greeves (1914–1963)*, ed. Walter Hooper. London: Collins, 1979.
TWHF	*Till We Have Faces: A Myth Retold*. Glasgow: Collins, 1985.
UND	*Undeceptions: Essays in Theology and Ethics*, ed. Walter Hooper. London: Geoffrey Bles, 1971. Known as *God in the Dock* in the United States.
VDT	*The Voyage of the 'Dawn Treader'*. Glasgow: Fontana Lions, 1981.

C.S. Lewis: Chronology

1941   First talks to Royal Air Force; *The Screwtape Letters* serialized; preaches 'The Weight of Glory' in University Church, Oxford; gives BBC radio broadcasts on 'Right and Wrong'

1942   Becomes President of Oxford University Socratic Club; *A Preface to Paradise Lost*

1943   *Perelandra*; *The Abolition of Man*

1944   *The Great Divorce* serialized

1945   End of World War II; death of Charles Williams; *That Hideous Strength*

1947   On cover of *Time* magazine; *Miracles*

1948   Elected Fellow of the Royal Society of Literature

1950   Receives first letter from Joy Gresham, née Davidman; *The Lion, the Witch and the Wardrobe*

1951   Death of Jane Moore

1952   *Mere Christianity*; meets Joy Gresham

1954   Elected Professor of Medieval and Renaissance Literature and Fellow of Magdalene College, University of Cambridge; *English Literature in the Sixteenth Century*

1955   Takes up Cambridge chair; elected Fellow of the British Academy; *Surprised by Joy*

1956   Secretly marries Joy Gresham in Oxford Registry Office (Apr.); Joy hospitalized with cancer (Oct.); Lewis publishes news of their wedding (Dec.); *Till We Have Faces*; receives Carnegie Medal for *The Last Battle*

1957   Marries Joy Gresham in Christian ceremony at her hospital bedside; her cancer goes into remission

1958   *Reflections on the Psalms*

1960   *The Four Loves*; death of Joy Lewis; *Studies in Words*

1961   *A Grief Observed*; *An Experiment in Criticism*

1963   Resigns chair at Cambridge owing to ill-health; death of C.S. Lewis (22 Nov.)

1964   *Letters to Malcolm*; *The Discarded Image*

1 Introduction

ROBERT MACSWAIN

LEWIS AND THE CONTEMPORARY ACADEMY

C.S. Lewis is both a phenomenon and an anomaly.

He is a phenomenon in that, almost fifty years after his death, he remains one of the world's most popular and best-selling authors. And he remains so, not just in one genre but many: children's literature, science fiction, theology, philosophy, Christian apologetics, autobiography, essays, the novel, poetry. Remarkably, all of this output was incidental to his professional career as a highly respected scholar of medieval and Renaissance literature at Oxford and Cambridge. Despite enormous changes in the way literature in general is studied and despite substantial shifts in the scholarly landscape of his specific areas of expertise, his academic publications are still of considerable importance to students and specialists alike.

Rather oddly for such a literary and donnish figure, even his personal life is part of the phenomenon. Numerous biographies have been written about him. *Shadowlands*, the story of his late marriage and eventual bereavement, won popular and critical acclaim as a television film, a stage play, a radio-play, and a movie. His most famous children's book – *The Lion, the Witch and the Wardrobe* (the first of the Chronicles of Narnia) – also achieved success as a major motion picture, and became one of the top-grossing films of 2005. Lewis's close friendship with J.R.R. Tolkien (a similar figure in many ways whose fiction has also, of course, been adapted for the stage and screen) adds to the fascination. Both the individual personalities and the collective character of the 'Inklings' – their circle of literary friends – have, perhaps surprisingly, become legendary.[1]

But if Lewis is a phenomenon he is also an anomaly in that, while he has a vast and loyal readership, scholars are sharply divided over the value and significance of his work. This is especially true in theology and religious studies. While in evangelical circles Lewis's reputation is astonishingly high, most mainstream academic theologians do not consider him a 'serious' figure. For example, in 2000 the influential American evangelical magazine *Christianity Today* put Lewis's *Mere Christianity* on the very top of their list as the 'best' religious book of the twentieth century, with Karl Barth's massive *Church Dogmatics* following humbly at number 3, and other influential texts such as the documents of Vatican II, Gustavo Gutiérrez's *A Theology of Liberation*, Jürgen Moltmann's *The Crucified God*, William James's *The Varieties of Religious Experience* and Simone Weil's *Waiting for God* ranked even lower.[2] But anyone conversant with contemporary trends in academic theology would consider these ratings topsy-turvy.

Take the comprehensive multi-author reference work *The Modern Theologians: An Introduction to Christian Theology since 1918*, an excellent and authoritative survey of theological figures and movements in this period.[3] In this volume, Lewis's *Mere Christianity* is not discussed at all (not even in the chapters on Anglican or evangelical theology), and Lewis himself does not even make the index (although he is in fact mentioned once, as an example of someone who believed in miracles[4]).The editors undoubtedly have good reasons for their criteria of selection, but it is still fair to ask whether the importance of a figure is best judged by their standing in the academy or by influence outside of it. As I will argue further below, academic theology ignores Lewis at its peril.[5]

But Lewis is also anomalous in that evaluations and interpretations of his life and work do not simply fall within the 'enthusiastic evangelical' and 'apathetic academic' options noted above, but go far beyond them in each direction. Lewis often inspires extreme reactions, both positive and negative, with readers either devoting themselves to him with a passionate and uncritical acceptance that borders on the fanatical, or reacting with a loathing and contempt that is scarcely less intense. The positive extreme is largely associated with American evangelicals, and the negative extreme with British atheists, but the actual situation is rather more complex than that neat national/ideological dichotomy. His detractors are certainly not all British, and those who regard his thought as valuable and interesting can be found across the theological spectrum, including British and North American Anglicans, Roman Catholics and Eastern Orthodox.

In an article from the *Chronicle of Higher Education*, literary scholar James Como is quoted as saying that 'C. S. Lewis is one of those writers who takes hold of a person's intellect and imagination, and rearranges the furniture. … The inner landscape changes. With some readers, that experience leads to a kind of proprietary attitude, a feeling that "he's *mine*".[6] Accordingly, various schools of Lewis interpretation have developed on both sides of the Atlantic, some scholarly, some less so, each promoting its own version of the man: now more Catholic, now more evangelical, now more conservative, now more liberal; there has been a maelstrom of conspiracy theories; questions about the canon have been raised. And just as the proprietary voices are numerous and mixed in quality, so are the accusations of his critics: is Lewis to be condemned for sexism, racism, obscurantism, philistinism, Christianity, or all of these at once?

This may seem like a rather journalistic beginning to a Cambridge Companion, but it aptly expresses the challenge faced by anyone who wants to think intelligently about C.S. Lewis in the contemporary context. While all writers may hope for the result Como describes above, such a response inevitably makes scholarly assessment of Lewis's work difficult. He is not a simple topic – or target – to begin with; his immense popularity considerably complicates matters; and what may fairly be called 'Jacksploitation' makes the situation almost intractable.[7] Far from being a 'dead' figure whose place in the canon of British literature and Christian thought is 'fixed', or someone merely of interest to scholars and students, Lewis is the subject of intense concern and lively controversy that spills far outside the confines of normal academic discussions.[8]

He is, however, almost certainly the most influential religious author of the twentieth century, in English or any other language. For good or ill, literally millions of people have had their understanding of Christianity decisively shaped by his writings. Whether they respond positively or negatively, it is Lewis's vision of the Christian faith that they (for whatever reason) take as normative, and thus either accept as Saving Truth or reject as Pernicious Error. But why? Why has Lewis – a former atheist turned Anglican Christian, a literary scholar without formal theological training or church authority – assumed such a significant role as the interpreter of Christianity for so many? Theories abound, but there is no simple answer. Lewis is, as stated at the beginning of this introduction, both a phenomenon and an anomaly, and by definition such entities confound regular categories. But – again, for good or ill – he is too important to be ignored.

For, most surprisingly, he has been ignored, at least by the mainstream academic theologians mentioned above. It is not an exaggeration to say that many such theologians – even among his fellow Anglicans – have been hoping for over half a century that Lewis would quietly go away.[9] Obviously, he hasn't, but up to this point, with rare exceptions, the most substantial studies of Lewis's work have been from literary scholars.[10] Outside of evangelical Christian circles, theologians and specialists in religious studies have for the most part kept their distance.[11] While some prominent philosophers of religion have occasionally mentioned Lewis as an influence, and while the odd article on some aspect of his thought may appear in a major journal, there has been very little sustained engagement with or critique of him in the general academy. Indeed, aside from the late Paul Holmer (Yale Divinity School), Wesley Kort (Duke University), and Gilbert Meileander (Valparaiso University), it is difficult to think of any other mainstream scholar in theology or religious studies who has ever written a monograph on him.[12]

However, as stated above, academic theology can ill afford to disregard C.S. Lewis. If only because he is so influential, scholars and students need to be familiar with the specific content of his many books in order to know (and if necessary counter or correct) his impact on the masses. But, more positively, it is at least possible that Lewis – despite not being an academic theologian himself – might have something to teach academic theologians about their own subject. Among other things, this may have to do with the way in which Lewis harnessed his imagination, reason, historical knowledge, wit, and considerable rhetorical gifts in a sustained effort to communicate the substance of his convictions to as wide an audience as possible. In its commendable quest for disciplinary purity and intellectual integrity, academic theology is actually in great danger of sealing itself within a very small, self-enclosed echo chamber in which experts talk to other experts while losing all contact with the outside world. Meanwhile, Lewis continues to sell millions of books a year and to shape the religious faith of thousands.

CLIVE STAPLES ('JACK') LEWIS: 1898–1963

This is not the place for an extensive biographical portrait, and for several full-length treatments the reader is directed to the Bibliography at the end of this volume. However, it is important to establish the basic facts and thus present at least one 'version' of Lewis as more or less normative for this Companion.

Clive Staples Lewis was born on 29 November 1898 in Belfast, Ireland – partition was still decades off – and was baptized the following year in the (Anglican) Church of Ireland. His parents – Albert James Lewis and Florence Augusta Hamilton – were well-educated members of the middle class. Their only other child, Lewis's older brother Warren

(1895–1973), was to become Lewis's closest lifelong friend. At a young age, not liking his name, Lewis announced that he was 'Jack', and 'Jack' he remained to his family and friends for the rest of his life. He died on 22 November 1963, the day of John F. Kennedy's assassination.

Lewis's early childhood was happy, but his mother's death from cancer a few months before his tenth birthday had a devastating effect on him: not only did he lose his mother, but this also led to a growing emotional estrangement from his father. Perhaps unwisely, he was sent away to boarding school in England less than a month after her death. It was a horrendous experience, and Lewis also hated his subsequent educational experience at Malvern College (1913–14). In 1911 he became an atheist, although on 6 December 1914 he still accepted the Anglican rite of confirmation in the same church where he had been baptized. After leaving Malvern, Lewis was privately tutored by his father's former headmaster, William Kirkpatrick. He entered University College, Oxford on 29 April 1917.

Of course, the First World War was in full tragic spate, and almost immediately after arriving at Oxford Lewis joined the British Army. He travelled to France as a second lieutenant in the 3rd Somerset Light Infantry and arrived in the front line on his nineteenth birthday. On 15 April 1918, in the Battle of Arras, he was seriously injured by an exploding shell and spent the remainder of the war in hospital. In January 1919, he returned to Oxford to continue his formal education.

By any standard, Lewis was a brilliant student. He achieved three consecutive First Class qualifications: the first two in the Oxford 'Greats' course – Classical Honour Moderations (1920) and Literae Humaniores (1922) – and the third in English (1923). 'Greats' involved 'the study of Greek and Latin language and literature, philosophy and ancient history, and thus provided a threefold mental training: in precision of language, clarification of concepts and the weighing of historical evidence'.[13] In terms of twentieth-century philosophy, Lewis was educated in the metaphysical Hegelian tradition of British Idealism, then dominant in Oxford, but soon to suffer a dramatic eclipse by the more logically and linguistically oriented work of the Cambridge philosophers G.E. Moore, Bertrand Russell and Ludwig Wittgenstein.[14] He never formally studied theology.

Lewis's first position was teaching philosophy at his own college ('Univ'), but this was only a one-year sabbatical-replacement appointment. In 1925, he was elected to a fellowship in English at Magdalen College, Oxford. Although he was certainly a competent philosophy tutor and possessed considerable analytical and dialectical gifts, Lewis's first love was English literature and it became his area of professional expertise. He tutored at Magdalen and lectured at Oxford for almost thirty years, and it is in this context that most people think of him. However, in January 1955 he became the first occupant of the Chair of Medieval and Renaissance Literature at the University of Cambridge, where he was to remain for the rest of his career. In July of that year he was also elected a Fellow of the British Academy.

As stated above, Lewis became an atheist in 1911. This was not the passing phase of an angry and bereaved adolescent, but a sincere, thoughtful and indeed rather intense rejection of religious belief on moral and intellectual grounds. Lewis's diaries, letters and earliest writings all testify to the consistency and vigour of his atheism. However, as Lewis details at length in his autobiography, *Surprised by Joy*, his atheistic view of the universe was in constant tension with a recurring experience that he called 'Joy' and identified with the German Romantic concept of *Sehnsucht*: an 'unsatisfied desire which is itself more desirable than any other satisfaction'.[15] This persistent experience, combined with various philosophical difficulties over naturalism, alongside his growing friendship with Tolkien (a devout Roman Catholic), rendered Lewis increasingly – if reluctantly – open to the possibility of theism. And in 1929 he indeed became a theist, but only in abstract, impersonal, 'Idealist' terms. It was not until September 1931, after a long conversation with Tolkien and Hugo Dyson about metaphor and myth, that Lewis finally accepted Christianity as what he called 'a true myth: a myth working on us in the same way as the other, but with this tremendous difference that *it really happened*'.[16] Lewis eventually reaffiliated with the Anglican tradition of his childhood and – since he was already baptized and confirmed – simply began attending services in his local Church of England parish, Holy Trinity, Headington Quarry, outside Oxford.

Because he is now so strongly associated with American evangelicalism, it is important to stress Lewis's essentially Anglo-Irish and Anglican character. Culturally and socially, Lewis was very much the product of his middle-class Ulster childhood, Edwardian Britain, the trenches of the First World War, and the Oxford Greats School. And, in the preface to *Mere Christianity*, Lewis says: 'There is no mystery about my own [religious] position. I am a very ordinary layman of the Church of England, not especially "high", nor especially "low", nor especially anything else.'[17] Although he eventually adopted some 'High Church' practices – such as spiritual direction, confession and frequent communion – Lewis was never a member of the Anglo-Catholic wing of the Church of England, nor indeed of the evangelical or any other 'wing'. He remained committed to 'mere Christianity', which he found in the broad Anglican *via media*, with its attempt to fuse the Catholic and Protestant tendencies of Western Christendom, its long tradition of scholarship and literary expression, and its reluctance to define points of controversy among Christians. Although theologically traditional, doctrinally orthodox and generally conservative in his interpretation of the Bible, Lewis nevertheless accepted some form of cosmic and biological evolution, did not hold to the inerrancy of scripture, and was not committed to a specific theory of the atonement. Nor, on the other hand, did he accept papal infallibility, Marian dogmas, or the claims to primacy made by the Roman Catholic Church. These issues, for him, were not essential to mere Christianity.

If Lewis had not made this journey into Christian faith, he would still very likely have continued on his path toward academic eminence, and so would probably only be remembered today by a few specialists for some exceptionally erudite but obscure works of scholarship. However, Lewis's conversion set off an unanticipated secondary career while simultaneously releasing his powers of imagination, intellect and persuasion to an exceptional degree. In addition to his distinguished professional work at Oxford and Cambridge, for the next three decades Lewis wrote book after book in one genre after another, beginning with *The Pilgrim's Regress: An Allegorical Apology for Christianity, Reason and Romanticism* (1933) and ending with the posthumously published *Letters to Malcolm: Chiefly on Prayer* (1964).

The details of his life and career, along with various controversial interpretations of them, are provided in several biographies, and the themes of his books are surveyed in the chapters which follow this introduction. But to conclude this section it must be mentioned that in 1957 Lewis greatly surprised his colleagues – and himself – by marrying Joy Davidman, a terminally ill, divorced American (with two young sons) who was also an author, a former Marxist atheist, and an ethnically Jewish convert to Christianity: the story told in *Shadowlands*. Lewis thus became both a phenomenon and an anomaly, and so we arrive back at the beginning of this introduction.

THE CAMBRIDGE COMPANION TO C.S. LEWIS

It is not at all obvious that this volume should appear in the Cambridge Companions to Religion series, as opposed to the Cambridge Companions to Literature. As stated above, Lewis's professional work was literary rather than religious; much of his published output falls within various literary genres; and most of the best work on Lewis has been produced by literary scholars. A good case may thus be made that Lewis ought to be studied primarily as a literary figure himself, a writer of fiction and fantasy, satire and polemic, poetry and autobiography – in short, as a 'man of letters' rather than as a theologian or philosopher. This would help explain his almost total absence from texts such as *The Modern Theologians* and his general neglect within academic theology and religious studies, and might also suggest that a 'Cambridge Companion to C. S. Lewis' should focus primarily on his accomplishments from a literary angle.

However, it is part of Lewis's anomalous character to confound this expectation as well, and for two reasons. First, some of his professional writings do trespass into the territory of academic theology and philosophy, and his works of fiction and poetry are likewise often occupied with such matters. This, indeed, is one reason why Lewis is so often criticized or condemned by students of *literature*: he is, rightly or wrongly, perceived as someone who is not literary *enough*, but who is primarily engaged in a didactic or evangelistic purpose thinly veiled under fairy-tales or science fiction. He is, they say, not a real writer, but only a closet theologian – precisely the opposite to the charge the theologians bring against him! Hence, for better or worse, even Lewis the 'man of letters' is inevitably read as a religious man of letters, and so any serious study of his writing at least needs to take this element into account. This present volume will thus, we hope, be of use to those whose interest in Lewis is indeed primarily literary rather than religious.

But second, and more positively, it may also be the case that Lewis should rightly be considered in this particular series because he has, in fact, expanded the genre of theology to include the imaginative works for which he is so famous. Thus, instead of an amateur, dilettante theologian who cannot possibly be considered in the same league as, for example, Barth, Gutiérrez or Moltmann, Lewis might rather be seen (*à la* Kierkegaard) as a deliberately 'indirect' theologian, as one who works by 'thick description' or evocative images, operating in multiple voices and genres, through which a single yet surprisingly subtle and complex vision emerges. Yes, of course it is ludicrous to compare Lewis's *Mere Christianity* to Barth's *Church Dogmatics* – but perhaps it is equally ludicrous to let Barth define the character of all theology. And when Lewis's entire output is considered as a whole, the comparison might not be so ridiculous after all. Lewis cannot possibly count as a theologian on the Barthian model, but he may nevertheless offer a model of theological expression which needs to be appreciated on its own terms.

This Cambridge Companion is therefore an intentional and perhaps risky experiment. First of all, it is impossible adequately to cover every aspect of Lewis's accomplishment in a single volume, although we have at least aimed at comprehensiveness. Although this text belongs in the Cambridge Companions to Religion series and so will probably be read mostly in that context, we have still included introductory chapters on Lewis's literary scholarship and other professional interests. This is an essential aspect of his career and those who want to understand him must at least be familiar with it. The other chapters are also written by a more interdisciplinary team than usual for such a volume, but all have still been intentionally composed for inclusion in a Cambridge Companion to Religion.

Second, in a deliberate attempt to widen the discussion of Lewis's legacy beyond 'the usual suspects', we have invited a number of contributors who have not hitherto participated in these debates, or at least not at this public level. While several of the contributing scholars are indeed already well known for their work on Lewis, all are experts drawn from various areas to which Lewis himself contributed (intellectual history, literary criticism, theology, philosophy). They include some of the most prominent contemporary practitioners in these fields. Feeling that the current situation in Lewis scholarship represented something of an impasse, we wanted to bring some fresh voices to the conversation. Some are evangelicals; some are not. Some offer their chapter as a first-order contribution to theology or philosophy; some as an academic essay on the interpretation of Lewis's work. And we have deliberately sought out some provocative figures to interact with well-known aspects of Lewis's thought.

However, in all cases, the contributors to this volume fall somewhere between the two polarized communities of interpretation mentioned earlier. Despite many disagreements and differences of opinion, we all believe that Lewis has made some genuinely important contributions to a wide range of disciplines and genres: literary, historical, philosophical, ethical, theological, spiritual, narrative, and poetic. He is, beyond doubt, a major twentieth-century voice – particularly when the full range of his work is considered as a whole – who does not deserve to be ignored, dismissed, or even vilified by today's intelligentsia. However, he also does not occupy the place of unique, privileged and untouchable significance that some of his followers have attributed to him. Hence, his legacy both deserves and requires careful commentary and critical analysis. Our goal here is not to offer the definitive treatment of C.S. Lewis, nor conclusively to answer either his defenders or his detractors. Rather, our goal is to stimulate conversation about Lewis in academic theology and religious studies, and to facilitate a greater understanding of his work. We hope this volume will contribute to that end.

Notes

1   See Humphrey Carpenter, *The Inklings: C.S. Lewis, J.R.R. Tolkien, Charles Williams, and Their Friends* (London: HarperCollins, 2006; 1st publ. 1978).

2   'Books of the Century', *Christianity Today* 44:5 (24 Apr. 2000). The magazine compiled its list of the hundred best and most influential religious books of the twentieth century by asking one hundred of its regular contributors and evangelical church leaders each to nominate ten titles. The preface states: 'By far, C.S. Lewis was the most popular author and *Mere Christianity* the book nominated most often. Indeed, we could have included even more Lewis works, but finally we had to say, "Enough is enough, give some other authors a chance."' They do, however, include the Chronicles of Narnia in the unranked list of 90 books that follow the top ten. This article and list is available online at <www.christianitytoday.com/ct/2000/april24/5.92.html>.

3   David F. Ford (ed.) with Rachel Muers, *The Modern Theologians: An Introduction to Christian Theology since 1918*, 3rd edn (Malden, MA: Blackwell, 2005).

4   See Ford (ed.), *The Modern Theologians*, 346.

5   Although they are both British theologians, Ford and Muers are forthright about the decisive emphasis in their volume on the 'German-language tradition of academic theology' as it developed in the nineteenth and twentieth centuries. It is arguably, they say, 'the best single tradition through which to be introduced to what it means to do Christian theology in intelligent engagement with modern disciplines, societies, churches, and traumatic events' (see the preface, pp. viii–xi, especially p. ix). And this explains why Lewis is not treated – and is indeed barely mentioned – in that book, for he was not a professional academic theologian, nor a modern one, nor did he seriously engage with the tradition of German-language theology. Thus, according to those criteria, it is no surprise that he is not discussed in *The Modern Theologians*, since he wasn't one. Lewis is also entirely absent from Colin E. Gunton (ed.), *The Cambridge Companion to Christian Doctrine* (Cambridge: Cambridge University Press, 1997). Paul Fiddes, however, considers the extent to which Lewis may indeed still be considered a theologian, and even a significant one, in Chapter 7 of the present volume.

6   Scott McLemee, 'Holy War in the Shadowlands: A New Book Revives Old Allegations and the Struggle for the Intellectual Legacy of C.S. Lewis', *Chronicle of Higher Education*, 20 July 2001 (http://chronicle.com/article/Holy-War-in-the-Shadowlands/19700).

7 Obviously a pun on the term 'blaxploitation' and Lewis's nickname 'Jack'. I would define 'Jacksploitation' as a work related to Lewis that has no scholarly substance or originality whatsoever, produced by someone whose only credential is that the work is related to Lewis. The world is awash in Jacksploitation. In a wider (and less culpable) sense, Jacksploitation may also refer to works which may indeed have scholarly merit or legitimate credentials, but whose primary purpose is still to 'cash in' on Lewis's popularity rather than to advance significantly our understanding of his work. My concern about Jacksploitation is not mere academic snobbery: I think it is a genuine problem that inhibits objective appreciation of his legacy.

8 Another complication is that the rights to Lewis's work are not yet in the public domain, but are currently still shared by several British and American publishers who are, naturally, more interested in sales than in Lewis's academic reputation. Accordingly, his essays are constantly being repackaged in a bewildering array of new combinations and titles. What Lewis desperately deserves and needs is a proper, multi-volume, critical edition of his work from start to finish – but this will not appear for many years.

9 See e.g. Norman Pittenger, 'Apologist versus Apologist', *Christian Century* 75 (1958), 1104–07, and Lewis's response, 'Rejoinder to Dr Pittenger', *Christian Century* 75 (1958), 1359–61; repr. in UND 177–83.

10 See, for example, Bruce L. Edwards (ed.), *The Taste of the Pineapple: Essays on C.S. Lewis as Reader, Critic and Imaginative Writer* (Bowling Green, OH: Bowling Green State University Popular Press, 1988); C.N. Manlove, *C.S. Lewis: His Literary Achievement* (London: Macmillan, 1987); Doris T. Myers, *C.S. Lewis in Context* (Kent, OH and London: Kent State University Press, 1994); Peter J. Schakel (ed.), *The Longing for a Form: Essays on the Fiction of C.S. Lewis* (Kent, OH: Kent State University Press, 1977); and George Watson (ed.), *Critical Essays on C.S. Lewis* (Aldershot: Scolar Press, 1992). The recent volume by my co-editor, Michael Ward, primarily fits into this category as well, although he draws out various implications for Lewis's thought more generally: *Planet Narnia: The Seven Heavens in the Imagination of C.S. Lewis* (New York: Oxford University Press, 2008).

11 There is a huge secondary literature on Lewis from an American evangelical perspective, far too sizeable even to begin to cite here. Much of it is good, solid scholarship, but for the most part it is content to expound or summarize what Lewis wrote rather than engage critically with it (in the positive, constructive, scholarly sense of 'critical'). For some exceptions to this rule, see the volumes edited by Baggett, Habermas and Walls; Menuge; Mills; Travers; and Walker and Patrick (all cited in the Bibliography at the end of this volume). For a study of Lewis from a Roman Catholic perspective, see Joseph Pearce, *C.S. Lewis and the Catholic Church* (San Francisco: Ignatius Press, 2003).

12 The books by Holmer, Kort and Meilaender are listed in the Bibliography. Note that all three of these authors are Americans. Readers may

well object that my term 'mainstream scholar' is both imprecise and demeans the excellent evangelical works referred to in n. 11, but I am not intending to be contentious. I simply mean the work of scholars who, whatever their religious convictions, are writing primarily for a *general* (academic) audience *outside* the evangelical Christian community and not *primarily* for their fellow-believers. An evangelical may also be a 'mainstream scholar' in this sense, and many are (some, indeed, have contributed to this volume). My point is that, aside from the sort of literary work cited in n. 10, very little 'mainstream scholarship' in this sense has been written on Lewis. Two leading philosophers of religion, however, have cited Lewis as an influence or inspiration; see William P. Alston, *Divine Nature and Human Language: Essays in Philosophical Theology* (Ithaca, NY and London: Cornell University Press, 1989), 212 n. 18, and Alvin Plantinga, *Warranted Christian Belief* (New York: Oxford University Press, 2000), *passim*.

13   Basil Mitchell, 'Introduction', in Brian Hebblethwaite and Douglas Hedley (eds), *The Human Person in God's World: Studies to Commemorate the Austin Farrer Centenary* (London: SCM Press, 2006), 2. Farrer, who later became one of Lewis's closest friends, went through the Greats course just a few years afterwards, so this description holds for Lewis's experience as well.

14   For an account of the philosophical milieu in which Lewis was educated and in which he later operated, see James Patrick, *The Magdalen Metaphysicals: Idealism and Orthodoxy at Oxford, 1901–1945* (Macon, GA: Mercer University Press, 1985). It may well be the case that – like British Idealism at the hands of Moore, Russell and Wittgenstein – Lewis's various metaphysical arguments do not translate well into the idiom of contemporary Anglo-American philosophy. This claim is made extensively by John Beversluis, but contested by Victor Reppert, both of whom are philosophers rather than theologians. Another philosopher, Erik Wielenberg, comes down somewhere in the middle (see the Bibliography for references). The debate partly turns on what is meant by 'reason' and 'rationality', and our capacity as humans to exercise and/or participate in them.

15   SBJ 20.

16   Letter to Arthur Greeves, 18 Oct. 1931 (CLI 977).

17   MC p. vi.

Part I

Scholar

2 Literary critic

JOHN V. FLEMING

The professional medievalist must be somewhat bemused by the fact that the literary scholarship and criticism of C.S. Lewis is so little known among his general readership and to some not known at all. After all, teaching literature was Lewis's 'day job' and he expended much energy and talent in writing about it. Following a brief stint as a teacher of philosophy,[1] he spent the first three decades of his career (1925–54) as a Fellow and Tutor in English at Magdalen College, Oxford, and most of the last decade at the University of Cambridge as the first occupant of the Chair in Medieval and Renaissance Literature, a professorship that had been created in large part deliberately to lure him there.

All aspects of Lewis's voluminous writings were influenced by the conditions and associations of the academic world in which he worked, but for his scholarly writing they were in a sense determinative. Though on occasion he wrote essays about authors and topics across the whole range of English literature, including even the contemporary scene,[2] it was the old Oxford English teaching curriculum – which privileged Old and Middle English texts (roughly from the years 1000 to 1400) and in which even early modern authors were often read from a primarily philological point of view – coupled with a special interest in Spenser from the sixteenth century and Milton from the seventeenth, that defined his principal scope of activity and that I will therefore focus on in this chapter.

The British literature faculties of eighty years ago were very different in spirit from what they are today. What might be called the 'American academic model' of a faculty credentialled with doctoral degrees and evaluated principally on the basis of the quantity and quality of published research was then unknown at Oxford. Many dons, including some of the most brilliant and most learned, published little or even nothing. The word 'amateur', meaning the lover of a subject, was still a benign term; and amateurism had not yet been trounced by 'professionalism'. Individual works of scholarship were often widely admired, but 'publication' itself was tolerated rather than required. It is in no way surprising, therefore, that Lewis was approaching forty when he published his first major work, *The Allegory of Love*, in 1936; nor is it remarkable that throughout his career competing 'amateur' interests (the philosophy, theology, fiction and poetry treated in Parts II and III of this Companion) reduced a potentially stupendous scholarly output to one that is merely astonishing.

THE ALLEGORY OF LOVE

The Allegory of Love begins with a substantial chapter on courtly love, the concept that dominates Lewis's approach to love allegory. He was by no means a pioneer here, but his book was very influential in validating the concept. 'Courtly love' is not a medieval term. It was first used in the late nineteenth century by a French medievalist to describe an artificial 'code' of behaviour discernible in the relations between male lovers and the female object of their desires as presented in a large body of European amatory poetry. 'Every one has heard of courtly love,' Lewis writes, 'and every one knows that it appears quite suddenly at the end of the eleventh century in Languedoc.'[3]

Characteristically the courtly lover must 'serve' a woman, always a paragon of beauty and usually of virtue, who is remote, aloof, and unavailable to him. The great love affairs of the Middle Ages, whether in fact or in fiction – the loves of Dante and Petrarch not less than those of Lancelot and Troilus – conform to greater or lesser extent to the 'conventions' of courtly love. Lewis finds the 'system' actually codified in the *De amore* of Andreas Capellanus, which has been widely distributed in English as *The Art of Courtly Love*. There is a poetic version in the elaborate 'ten commandments' given by the god of Love to the Lover in the *Romance of the Rose*.

Since Lewis's day the very concept of courtly love has been the subject of lively controversy. Some scholars (among whom I must in candour announce myself) have rejected it as unhelpful and misleading. Many others find it a useful way of approaching medieval love poetry so long as its purely literary and imaginative character is acknowledged. Comparatively few still believe, as Lewis did, that courtly love reflects an actual social reality and an important shift in the history of human consciousness and sentiment.

Courtly love, an essentially figural phenomenon, naturally tended toward literary allegory, according to Lewis, so he himself turns there in a stunning second chapter that remains perhaps the very finest comprehensive and succinct presentation of the varieties of medieval literary allegory. He may undervalue the importance of the allegorical mode in patristic biblical exegesis, but he is learnedly aware of it. Indeed, his chapter ends with the allegorists of the School of Chartres, who 'in an age of wilful asceticism and wilful *Frauendienst* ... asserted the wholeness of the nature of man'.[4] He now arrives at his real subject, which is the fusion of antique Latin erudition and courtly love in major poets of the later Middle Ages and into the Renaissance: Guillaume de Lorris, Jean de Meun, Chaucer, Gower, Usk and Spenser.

The inescapable text is the thirteenth-century French *Roman de la Rose*, in the study of which Lewis must forever be honoured as a pioneer. Given the fact that the *Roman*, 'as a germinal book ... ranks second to none except the Bible and the *Consolation of Philosophy*',[5] its neglect by earlier scholars can be explained only in terms of the work's great length and, at times, excessive strangeness. The *Roman* had two authors. The first, Guillaume de Lorris, left a love allegory of about four thousand lines, apparently unfinished, around 1240. Sometime around 1280 a Parisian intellectual, Jean de Meun, wrote a continuation and conclusion of eighteen thousand lines more. The two parts of the poem, though they pursue the same 'plot', are markedly different in style. Lewis was of the opinion that Jean was either indifferent or positively hostile to Guillaume's psychological delicacies.

The chapter devoted to Chaucer was in a number of ways revolutionary. Lewis begins with the claim that 'for all general readers, the great mass of Chaucer's work is simply a background to the *Canterbury Tales*'.[6] That was probably true at the time, and if it is no longer true it is only because Chaucer no longer has many 'general readers'. Lewis suggests a very different approach, which is to examine the 'early works' without reference to the *Canterbury Tales*: 'Chaucer is a poet of courtly love, and he ceases to be relevant to our study when he reaches the last and most celebrated of his works.'[7] He is aware that there will be loss as well as gain in his procedure, but it has the advantage of demonstrating Chaucer's 'work of assimilating the achievements of French poetry, and thus determining the direction of English poetry for nearly two hundred years'.[8]

Lewis establishes a 'reading' of Chaucer's earlier work, and especially of *Troilus and Criseyde*, founded in various more or less casual comments of a number of Chaucer's contemporaries or admirers: John Gower, Thomas Usk and John Lydgate. 'Their Chaucer was the Chaucer of dream and allegory, of love-romance and erotic debate, of high style and profitable doctrine.'[9] This statement is questionable, though one is unlikely to question it while being swept along on the cascading white water of Lewis's prose. The technique legitimates an interpretation of Chaucer that is romantic root and branch and that disallows a very great deal that most of us see in Chaucer: 'Not many will agree with the critic who supposed that the laughter of Troilus in heaven was "ironical"; but I am afraid that many of us now read into Chaucer all manner of ironies, slynesses, and archnesses, which are not there, and praise him for his humour where he is really writing with "ful devout corage".'[10]

What followed in *The Allegory of Love* was no less revolutionary. Lewis unleashed his remarkable powers of invigilation and illumination on two poets – Gower and Usk – who at the time were mainly footnotes in medieval English literary history. In a chapter entitled 'Allegory as the Dominant Form' he took up writers yet more obscure, like Guillaume de Deguilleville, investing them by his serious and detailed attentions with a critical dignity they have never relinquished. His book ends with a long, rich and brilliant chapter on Spenser and the *Faerie Queene*. If there is a happier concord between poet and critic than that between Spenser and Lewis, I have yet to discover it.

Lewis's scintillating 'Study in Medieval Tradition', as *The Allegory of Love* was subtitled, had an immediate dramatic effect in the world of letters. Nevill Coghill, who was Lewis's close contemporary, colleague and friend, once in conversation compared its publication to a powerful explosion, wholly unanticipated, that staggered literature faculties throughout Britain: 'When we recovered and shook off the dust, we began to look around to see whether any of the comfortable old landmarks were still standing.' By 'comfortable old landmarks' he meant the informal consensus of ideas about medieval English literature that had emerged in the literature faculties at Oxford, Cambridge and London in the previous half century. Some of the landmarks were indeed still there, in fact most of them. However, things were utterly changed. Chaucer was there, but he was not exactly the Chaucer of old. This was not Chaucer the Londoner, but Chaucer the European.

Up until the time of this 'explosion' the study of medieval literature in Britain had developed in a somewhat peculiar way, as an adjunct to or implication of the study of philology. The great scholarly achievement of the nineteenth century, so far as literary study was concerned, was the New English Dictionary, now usually called the Oxford English Dictionary (OED). It was a stupendous achievement. To produce a dictionary 'based on historical principles' demanded first of all access to a huge corpus of words from all periods of English linguistic history. From this need was born the Early English Text Society (EETS). It was in EETS editions that most of our medieval texts found their first, and in many instances their only, appearance in print. An EETS edition aimed for a philological apparatus rather than a critical or interpretive introduction. And of course the emphasis was on the English language and therefore 'Englishness' generally. Even Chaucer's great nineteenth-century editor, W.W. Skeat, a man well versed in the medieval Latin theological literature and possessed of a competent command of Chaucer's French and Italian sources, produced a scholarly apparatus much influenced by the English philological model.

As a matter of fact, however, there is not very much in Chaucer's work that he would have written differently had no one before him even penned a single line of English poetry. Lewis does not say that explicitly, but the context of his discussion of Chaucer in *The Allegory of Love* returns 'the father of English poetry' to his proper context as great cosmopolitan European, like Jean de Meun, Dante and Boccaccio. Chaucer knew these authors, two of them well, and he sought to engage with them in making new and fresh the classical tradition in its Latin and its Continental vernacular expressions.

It is perhaps the greatest achievement of *The Allegory of Love* that Chaucer studies have more or less remained where Lewis put them in 1936.[11] What Lewis probably thought of as his more major contributions – his discussions of medieval allegory and of medieval love – have not stood up so well.

A PREFACE TO PARADISE LOST

Lewis's critical masterpiece is probably *A Preface to Paradise Lost* (1942), which typifies his best criticism in two important ways. First, it found its origins in a series of lectures and retains much of the tone of a vivacious and intimate pedagogy. Second, it is a monument to a fecund intellectual friendship, that with Charles Williams, who shared with Lewis, among many other things, a passionate interest in Milton. Lewis's essay performs beautifully the true office of criticism, which is to effect a respectful introduction between a reader and a work, to clarify the text and encourage the reader without attempting to supplant either, and then leave text and reader, if not too dazzled, to get further acquainted on their own. It does assume an interested and intelligent student with at least the fundamentals of a literary education.

At first blush, the idea that John Milton, an English Puritan of the seventeenth century and a man of stern morality and learned piety, would write an epic poem in which Satan is the hero and God Almighty perforce the villain, might seem unpromising. The further historical fact that for the first two centuries after its publication *Paradise Lost* occupied a central position in the literary culture of English-speaking Christians does little to redeem that idea. But what William Blake had written as paradox in the eighteenth century – 'Note the reason Milton wrote in fetters when he wrote of Angels & God, and at liberty when of Devils & Hell, is because he was a true Poet and of the Devil's party without knowing it'[12] – had become, with the New Criticism, something like literary orthodoxy. Satan has too many of the great lines in the poem. The autocracy of divine government is tedious in its pronouncements. On the other hand the devils' debates in Pandemonium are lively, spirited and adversarial in the best traditions of Westminster or even on occasion Washington. It was Lewis's task to help readers to discover that Milton had not merely intended but achieved something rather different from what the post-Romantic sensibility was so willing to find.

There was of course a large irony in Lewis's project. He had only recently participated in the debate with E.M.W. Tillyard (a famous Milton scholar and intellectual historian) published under the title *The Personal Heresy: A Controversy*, in which he appeared to advance the position ('just nonsense' according to Bateson[13]) that great poetry is the product of a special consciousness for which the particularities of a historical authorial 'personality' are irrelevant. Yet the point of the *Preface* was to provide a reader with information about the history of literature and the history of theology and above all about the history of ideas deemed essential preparation for an approach to Milton. Indeed Lewis's *Preface* very closely resembles Tillyard's *Elizabethan World Picture* in its aspiration. Lewis begins with a typically memorable sentence: 'The first qualification for judging any piece of workmanship from a corkscrew to a cathedral is to know *what* it is – what it was intended to do and how it is meant to be used.'[14]

The answer to the implied question 'What is *Paradise Lost*?' is that it is an epic; and this answer is the occasion for several dazzling and original chapters on epic – here characterized, with a useful binary division typical of the man's mind, as 'primary' and 'secondary' epic. By 'primary epic' he seems to mean the epic before, or untouched by, Virgil. Lewis claims that the received opinion about epic *subject* (the 'great matter') is not in fact a literary essential, but an accidental historical implication of Virgil's response to the Augustan moment. Lewis seems to believe that the first set of difficulties to be overcome by the reader of Milton inhabits the realm of poetic manner rather than that of theological matter. So he devotes two of his longest chapters to 'The Style of Secondary Epic' and 'Defence of this Style'.

If it is true that there recurs in Lewis's criticism an unresolved tension between the demands of history required by his erudition and a romantic subjectivity masquerading as a deference to the exceptionalism of 'great' poetry, the chapter on 'The Doctrine of the Unchanging Human Heart' makes an unequivocal case for historical criticism, for reading 'each work of wit | with the same spirit that its author writ'.[15] In response to a critic who wanted to separate the 'lasting originality of Milton's thought' from its 'theological rubbish,' Lewis writes: 'This is like asking us to study *Hamlet* after the "rubbish" of the revenge code has been removed, or centipedes when free of their irrelevant legs, or Gothic architecture without the pointed arch. Milton's thought, when purged of its theology, does not exist.'[16]

The second half of Lewis's book is mainly serious theology approached in anything but a solemn or deadening fashion. Arresting apothegms adorn nearly every page. Its two main contributions from the doctrinal point of view are its discussion of assumptions concerning hierarchy – so essential to Milton's universe and so repellent to modern modes of thought based in dynamically interacting polarities – and the meaning of the sin of pride and its catastrophic role in the Fall. ('The Stock response to Pride, which Milton reckoned on when he delineated his Satan, has been decaying ever since the Romantic Movement began,' Lewis writes; '– that is one of the reasons why I am composing these lectures.'[17]) His delineation of Augustine's presentation of the tropological meaning of the Fall is so lucid and learned that I am left grieving all the more that he could have missed its relevance to the *Roman de la Rose*.

The three single most fascinating pages in the essay, perhaps, form the very short chapter entitled 'Unfallen Sexuality'. Anyone who has taught Milton to undergraduates knows that the sleepiest among them wake up to the quasi-pornography of the ninth book. But that is our familiar *fallen* sexuality. Lewis notes that Augustine's discomfort (*De civitate dei* 14) in speculating about the bliss of unfallen sexuality, which he knew must have been splendid, is the effect of a postlapsarian constitution to which what was once gratuitous nourishment is now mortal danger: 'This is a warning to Milton that it is dangerous to attempt a poetical representation of something which is unimaginable, not in the sense of raising no images, but in the more disastrous sense of inevitably raising the wrong ones. This warning he defied. He has dared to represent Paradisal sexuality. I cannot make up my mind whether he was wise.'[18] If there is anything more astonishing than that Milton could be titillating about sex, it is that C.S. Lewis could be even more titillating. The reader who reaches these late pages in the *Preface* is almost guaranteed to move swiftly to the poem.

THE DISCARDED IMAGE

Lewis has another stunning essay as a literary critic, and it must be mentioned here even at the cost of a chronological violation and of trespassing into Dennis Danielson's territory in Chapter 4 of this Companion. *The Discarded Image* (1964), though published only posthumously, codifies ideas he was developing during the length of his career. Strictly speaking it is not so much a work of literary criticism as an essay in intellectual history. Yet it is appropriately subtitled 'An Introduction to Medieval and Renaissance Literature', for it succinctly and brilliantly lays out before the interested student the principal features of that alterity to be discovered on the other side of the Enlightenment and the triumph of the Copernican model. It would be hard to say whether it is more impressive in its erudition or in the artful manner in which the erudition is masked lest it intimidate a beginner.

If literary art is 'imitation' in the sense used by Aristotle, to understand literature, let alone to judge it, requires of its reader some prior knowledge of the world it imitates. Lewis was a pioneer in what later French historians would call *l'histoire des mentalités* – the shifting history of human mental structures. The 'image' that we have 'discarded' is precisely the pre-modern understanding of the structure of the universe with the Earth as its centre, and with human beings the central reality of an Earth created by an omnipotent and immanent God. It is this universe, and not ours of infinite galaxies randomly distributed in an infinite space, that is reflected in medieval and Renaissance literature.

This 'old' world was perhaps created and was certainly sustained by certain classic texts, and Lewis introduces his reader to the small library of ancient and early medieval writers (such as Claudian, Macrobius and Boethius) most influential in its delineation and transmission. A consistent theme of *The Discarded Image* is textual power, the tenacity and longevity of ideas once accepted as authoritative, the cohesion but also the constrictions of a worldview which 'everybody' believed. Textual power often involved textual paradox. Lewis points out, for example, that our ancestors' belief in marvellous beasts, a fairy world, and ranks of unseen angels and demons was caused by the same thing that has caused us to disbelieve in them: literacy. Intellectual history is not history's only branch, but I know of no better introduction to the fundamental assumptions undergirding the medieval and Renaissance literature of Christian Europe than *The Discarded Image*.

ENGLISH LITERATURE IN THE SIXTEENTH CENTURY

The greatest single monument to Lewis's astonishing literary erudition is his *English Literature in the Sixteenth Century, Excluding Drama*, a contribution to the multi-volume Oxford History of English Literature. (Lewis, exasperated by the length of time it took to write – a full fifteen years – nicknamed it his 'O hell!' volume.) This is described on the title page as 'the completion of the Clark Lectures' given at Trinity College, Cambridge in 1944, and now a decade later, considerably revised and much expanded, published in Oxford in 1954. It is in every sense a very large work.

Lewis loved binary patterns, and two important binaries structure his book, though he begins by questioning a bifurcation long cherished by literary historians. He was a pioneer in a scholarly trend, now very widely accepted, that seeks to describe the cultural and especially literary developments of Europe in the period from 1300 to 1700 in terms of gradual developments, continuities and new initiatives as opposed to a dramatic and revolutionary movement from the 'Middle Ages' to the 'Renaissance'. So he began his book with a long and brilliant introduction, called 'New Learning and New Ignorance', which is probably a permanently valuable contribution to intellectual history, in which with great subtlety he painted the backdrop necessary to understand the peculiarities of insular humanism that define much of the British sixteenth century.

One background chapter demanded another, a long essay of a hundred pages on late medieval literature, but here divided between the cultural history of Scotland and that of England. The implicit priority of Scotland was intentional and innovative, and his essay anticipates another current scholarly trend that looks beyond the 'Scottish Chaucerians' to examine a rich literature in its fullness.

Another structural binary, perhaps more questionable, is his stylistic division between 'drab' and 'golden' (the quotation marks being authorial and essential). This was doubtless a clever and useful distinction when he introduced it in one of the Clark Lectures. It is a consistent principle of his criticism that literary style can never be wholly separated from literary content, and his terminology makes a confrontation with the stylistic inescapable. But what was perhaps a brilliant device for a single lecture may become coercive over the length of a book of seven hundred pages. At times it may be unclear whether there is much distinction between golden/drab and good/bad, or what C.S. Lewis really likes and what he likes less.

A second possible problem, this one fully anticipated by the author, concerns scale and proportion. The sixteenth century was opulent of literary genius in Britain, but it was opulent also of literary mediocrity. One has the impression that Lewis had read, and read with care, his way completely through the *Short Title Catalogue*. My memory of first reading this book as a graduate student is of my dismay at being over-whelmed with an avalanche of authors' names and book titles of which I had never heard. One suspected that John Colet's commentaries on the Pauline epistles were more important than John Rastell's *Book of Purgatory*, but absolute certainty was wanting. In a brief prefatory apo-logia Lewis writes thus: 'Good books which are remote from modern sympathy need to be treated at greater length than good books which everyone already knows and loves. Bad books may be of importance for the history of taste and if they are passed over too briefly the student's picture of a period may be distorted.'[19]

Lewis's knowledge of the religious literature of the second half of the sixteenth century – much of it controversial and polemical – was extraordinary. It must have been a challenge to the imaginative, cheer-ful and charitable Christian apologist to try to read with sympathetic understanding so much in his 'own' genre that was leaden, cheerless and vitriolic. But the review of that vast literature was not simple duty. It provides the intellectual and ideographic backdrop against which a few authors and works of unquestioned genius can stand out in their authentically noble profiles. His third section (entitled 'Golden') begins with the *tour de force* of a lengthy chapter on Sidney and Spenser. One has the impression that the author arrived at this chapter as a thirsting Bedouin might arrive at an oasis. The reader who has attended every page of the second book ('Drab') will feel no less refreshed.

Lewis was a brilliant reader of Spenser, a great poet who today com-mands too few readers of any stripe. It is arguable that the best chapter of *The Allegory of Love* is the final chapter devoted to Spenser, and Lewis's skill as a Spenserian is again on display in *English Literature in the Sixteenth Century*. He is not entirely unsparing of the 'faults that Spenser never quite outgrew; we call him a Golden poet because there is so much gold, not because there is so little Drab, in his work'.[20] But he was enamoured of Spenser's allegory and had a rare understanding of its symmetrical analogies, which were so loved by and so typical of medieval and Renaissance artists of all kinds. A remark he made at the beginning of the *Preface* concerning Milton is probably even more apt for his view of Spenser: 'when the old poets made some virtue their theme they were not teaching but adoring, and ... what we take for the didactic is often the enchanted'.[21] Space does not allow me to discuss his various essays on Spenser in *Studies in Medieval and Renaissance Literature*,[22] nor his unfinished *Spenser's Images of Life*, posthumously edited by Alastair Fowler and published in 1967.

ASSESSMENTS

Though it fills several volumes, Lewis's formal literary scholarship is but a small part of his published corpus, and much of it had to be wrenched from his unwilling hands so to speak or gathered from the papers he left at his death. Even so, given the fecundity of his mind and the energy of his constitution, it is impossible in an essay of this length to do more than try to characterize some of his most important contributions. Even harder is it to offer a synoptic summary of his achievement as medieval and Renaissance literary critic, as I must now attempt to do.

A preliminary issue demands attention. Lewis was a Christian, and he naturally wrote as a Christian. The question of the degree to which Lewis the Christian *apologist* and Lewis the *critic* were the same man could command a study of its own, but several times he states his awareness of the difference between a pulpit and a lectern.[23] In his approach to acknowledged Christian masters like Dante, Spenser and Milton he exhibits and sometimes explicitly states a warm sympathy with their most fundamental religious ideas. On the other hand he was strangely content to identify 'courtly love', an extra-Christian if not anti-Christian substitute for the foremost of the theological virtues, as the mainspring of medieval European poetry. It is my opinion, expressed elsewhere,[24] that in his pursuit of 'courtly love' in the *Roman de la Rose* he became the corrupting Aristotle who misled a generation of readers in understanding the supremely important poem he had done so much to rescue from oblivion.

The student of Lewis the critic must immediately be struck by the *social* context of his literary thought. He was a man of deep intellectual friendships, and he enjoyed the good fortune of having friends who were great in more senses than one, men who shared broad sympathies and imaginative powers: Owen Barfield, J.R.R. Tolkien, Charles Williams and many others. The Inklings were a donnish coterie in the old and admiring sense of that word, and Lewis began as a coterie critic even as Chaucer began as a coterie poet.

His generosity of spirit is evident in the warmth of his praise of colleagues and friends like Williams and Tolkien, but no less so in the stance adopted toward his adversaries – of whom he had quite a few. The 'controversy' with Tillyard, though neither combatant pulled many rhetorical punches, leaves an impression of erudite high jinks rather than intellectual rancour. His disagreements with Eliot, which were numerous and deeply felt, were (in public at least) kept in proportion: 'I agree with him about matters of such moment that all literary questions are, in comparison, trivial.'[25] He appears to have been actually offended by Denis Saurat's *La pensée de Milton* (*Milton, Man and Thinker*), but what he says just before making that almost clear is that 'Milton studies owe a great debt to Professor Saurat'.[26] Perhaps the only time Lewis approaches genuine scorn for a fellow literary critic is in his handling of Derek Traversi.[27]

C.S. Lewis the literary scholar commanded three powerful tools. The first was a remarkable erudition. He knew about as much as it is possible to know from reading the primary sources in his field. Next, he had a supremely supple imagination and historical sympathy that allowed him to make surprising, illuminating connections among the numerous categories of his vast learning. Finally, he had to a remarkable degree that capacity defined by Pope as 'true wit' – the power to put into felicitous language 'what oft was thought but ne'er so well expressed'.[28]

His erudition was founded in his knowledge of languages, beginning with his native English, which he commands with a powerful mixture of reverence and audacity, but extending also into the European vernaculars in their various historical periods and, especially, classical Latin and Greek. Lewis lived perhaps at the very end of the age when nearly all European literary scholars knew their Virgil and their Horace, and probably also their Homer and their Theocritus; but Lewis's classicism went far beyond textual familiarities. Familiarity with a text is not always the same thing as familiarity with a language. He had internalized the languages, and not only the texts. In *Surprised by Joy* he writes that he early learned that upon encountering the word 'naus' (*navis*) he should summon to mind not the word *ship* but a ship itself with its sails and creaking ropes, or its ranks of oars.[29] In his criticism Lewis allows us – perhaps forces us – to see old texts in the vivacity with which he saw them.

To be able to imagine in detail and with coherence a large physical, social or intellectual system that might exist in some time or world other than our own is of the same genre of capacity as to be able to imagine a vanished past within the time scheme of our own world. In Lewis there was no large distance between the primary and secondary imaginations of Coleridge. He is hardly less imaginative in the expression of his thought as in the thought itself.

Readers of Lewis do not need a professor to tell them in a Cambridge Companion that he was a remarkable prose stylist. The style is there for all to enjoy: his range of cadences, the perfect word plucked from a vast vocabulary, the mixture of the learned and the homely, the striking analogy likely to cause a reader to stop to admire or to rebel in the middle of a page, the tone of authority that never becomes the tone of the bully. What a professor *can* point out, perhaps, is that Lewis's prose is probably most confident and also most magnificent when he is addressing an audience most like himself: an audience admiring of and widely read in the earlier periods of English literature. Hence I would argue that his literary scholarship is, from the point of view of writing skill alone, his greatest work. Why do we 'like' Milton's Satan? Anyone who has read *Paradise Lost* knows why, in some impressionistic and usually unarticulated sense, a sense that 'oft was thought'. But Lewis is able to tell us in a single sentence of wide critical applicability, halfway to being an epigram: 'It is a very old critical discovery that the imitation in art of unpleasing objects may be a pleasing imitation'.[30]

Notes

1   See the essays by Taliaferro and Meilaender in this volume (Chapters 8 and 9) for a discussion of two of Lewis's principal philosophical concerns.
2   These essays, which include studies of Bunyan, Austen, Scott, Kipling, Orwell, 'four-letter words' and science fiction, are to be found in SLE and EC.
3   AOL 2.
4   AOL 110.
5   AOL 157.
6   AOL 161.
7   AOL 161.
8   AOL 161.
9   AOL 162.
10   AOL 163–64.
11   Another important contribution to Chaucer studies was his essay 'What Chaucer Really Did to *Il Filostrato*' (1932), repr. in SLE 27–44. It was this essay of Lewis's perhaps more than any other that inspired D.W. Robertson to write his own classic 'The Concept of Courtly Love as an Impediment to the Understanding of Medieval Texts' (1968). According to Lewis, what Chaucer had 'really done' to the *Filostrato*

of Boccaccio was to 'have corrected certain errors that Boccaccio had committed against the code of courtly love'. His chief means of correction was to 'medievalise' the story of Troilus. It is a demonstrable fact, however, that Chaucer makes a much more rigorous attempt than ever Boccaccio did to be 'classical', that is, to write a historical novel in which his ancient pagan characters act like ancient pagans. The love conventions within the poem certainly do constitute a 'code' of sorts, but the codification is that of Ovid in his *Ars amatoria* as stylistically modernized by two great medieval Ovidians, Guillaume de Lorris and Jean de Meun.

12 William Blake, *The Marriage of Heaven and Hell*, pl. 5; see *The Complete Writings of William Blake*, ed. Geoffrey Keynes (London: Oxford University Press, 1966), 150.
13 F.W. Bateson, reviewing *The Personal Heresy* in the *Review of English Studies* 16 (1940), 488.
14 PPL 1.
15 Alexander Pope, *Essay on Criticism*, ll. 233–34, the epigraph to ch. 1 of PPL.
16 PPL 65. Lewis is responding to Denis Saurat, *Milton, Man and Thinker* (London: Jonathan Cape, 1924), 111.
17 PPL 56.
18 PPL 122.
19 EL p. v.
20 EL 368.
21 PPL p. v.
22 The collection includes a few gems – particularly some pieces on Dante, with whom one can but wish he had engaged more fully – but also some unpolished work.
23 See e.g. PPL, ch. 12,'The Theology of *Paradise Lost*'.
24 John V. Fleming, *The Roman de la Rose: A Study in Allegory and Iconography* (Princeton, NJ: Princeton University Press, 1969), *passim*.
25 PPL 9.
26 PPL 82.
27 SIL 62–63.
28 Alexander Pope, *Essay on Criticism*, ll. 297–98: 'True Wit is Nature to advantage dress'd, | What oft was thought, but ne'er so well express'd'.
29 SBJ 115.
30 PPL 94.

3 Literary theorist

STEPHEN LOGAN

The claim that C.S. Lewis was a literary theorist is, from one point of view, uncontroversial. If literary theory is understood as the practice of reflecting philosophically on the nature and function of literature, then there seems little doubt that Lewis made a contribution to literary theory. In this sense, Aristotle's *Poetics*, Horace's *Ars Poetica*, Sidney's *Apology for Poetry*, Coleridge's *Biographia Literaria* and the *Selected Essays* of T.S. Eliot are all works of literary theory. Several of Lewis's books may be said to contain, or consist of, literary theory so understood: *An Experiment in Criticism* most obviously and explicitly, but also *The Discarded Image*, his side of the debate with E.M.W. Tillyard in *The Personal Heresy*, the chapters on the concept of the Renaissance in his *English Literature in the Sixteenth Century*, and the discussion of primary and secondary epic in *A Preface to Paradise Lost*. In this reckoning of Lewis as a literary theorist, we should include, moreover, a large body of essays, such as 'De Audiendis Poetis', 'De Descriptione Temporum', 'On Three Ways of Writing for Children', 'On Period Tastes in Literature', 'The Genesis of a Medieval Book', 'The Parthenon and the Optative' and 'Bluspels and Flalansferes: A Semantic Nightmare'. By no means does all such work fall within the realm of English studies. 'Modern Theology and Biblical Criticism', for instance, is theoretical in that it argues that what passes for literary criticism in theology is often insufficiently literary. Perhaps even more important in terms of their cumulative effect are the more scattered discussions – such substantial, if topical, items as the sequence of three essays gathered by Walter Hooper under the title 'Christianity and Literature', or even the statements sent to *Delta* (a Cambridge undergraduate magazine) in response to the imputation of a patronizing pedantry of critical approach. There are also the innumerable remarks in Lewis's published letters which demonstrate the consistency with which his mind was trained upon matters of literary theory. The range of theoretical concerns represented by this large body of work is remarkable: semantics, etymology, prosody, metaphysics, theology, *Quellenforschung*, psychoanalysis, philology – all these subjects are touched on; some are comprehensively investigated. It becomes difficult, indeed, to specify the point at which Lewis's interest in literary theory ends, or to name a discursive writing on a literary subject which has no relevance to it.

It is when we attempt some rather more exacting definition of the term 'literary theorist' – especially in the modified sense entailed by the rise and fall of 'Theory'[1] – that its application to Lewis becomes doubtful, even preposterous. If literary theory is a matter of trying to say what literature is, how it differs from other kinds of writing (if it does), and how we form a sense of what a literary text means; if it is a matter of considering the assumptions involved in that use of the word 'we', or of examining how the conception of literature is affected by the institutional contexts in which literature is most widely studied, of gauging the effect on a critic of her gender, nationality, race, sexual orientation or political affiliation, of wondering why it should be that, in my last clause, I used the feminine pronoun 'her' instead of the more conventional masculine one; if this heightened (or exacerbated) degree of self-consciousness about metaphysical, cultural and hermeneutical matters to do with literature is what distinguishes a literary theory; then the claim that Lewis was, except incidentally, a theorist involves a bit of a stretch. His essays 'The Anthropological Approach' and 'Psychoanalysis and Literary Criticism' anticipate trends which, in the post-structuralist era, ramified wildly. But the difficulty over whether or not to call Lewis a literary theorist in this second sense is a product of recent cultural history. In the first, more general sense, literary theory is almost as old, one might suppose, as literature. In the West, it is at least as old as Aristotle. In the second, more specialized, sense, literary theory is a mere child, having assumed its distinctive forms in the period immediately after Lewis's death in 1963. As you might expect from this difference in historical (and cultural) span, the varieties of new-style literary theory exist between much narrower limits, being determined by the ideological tendencies of a group of European intellectuals between the late sixties and the turn of the millennium. Old-style literary theory, by contrast, though often treated as a simple counterpart to its newer variants, has a history spanning more than twenty-four centuries and a corresponding extent of linguistic and cultural diversity.

The significance of the contrast between the traditional and contemporary forms of literary theory is ultimately moral and metaphysical.

Although post-structuralist literary theory was a localized, academic phenomenon, the causes of its emergence lie deep in our cultural history. The relativistic – and in many cases nihilistic – tendencies of 'Theory' are the expression of trends which originated much further back in time. According to Lewis, literary criticism in the aftermath of Modernism was part of 'the whole tradition of educated infidelity from Arnold to *Scrutiny*'.[2] Characteristically, he saw this period between Victorianism and Modernism in a context which reduced it from self-proclaimed historical pre-eminence to just 'one phase in that general rebellion against God which began in the eighteenth century'.[3] While still a young man and an atheist he already recognized the same decisive shift. Rather than treating it as a matter of religious dispute merely, he located it deep in ideological history: 'It will be a comfort to me all my life to know that the scientist and the materialist have not the last word: that Darwin and [Herbert] Spencer [1820–1903] undermining ancestral beliefs stand themselves on a foundation of sand; of gigantic assumptions and irreconcilable contradictions an inch below the surface.'[4] Accordingly, in his inaugural lecture as Professor of Medieval and Renaissance Literature at Cambridge, Lewis posited a moral chasm, originating in Enlightenment rationalism but decisively deepening at a point 'somewhere between us [in 1954] and *Persuasion* [published in 1818]'.[5] Austen, for Lewis (as for Alasdair MacIntyre), was 'the last great effective imaginative voice' of foundationalist morality.[6] It is perhaps for this reason that Austen is not readily imagined as a Romantic writer, since Romantics are assumed to be morally subversive. Yet she was a contemporary of Wordsworth's.

The Romantic movement, by seeking to restore a supernatural dimension to popular conceptions of reality, suggests how far a secularizing materialism had, by the late eighteenth century, taken hold. A further resurgence of this secularizing trend occurred with the growth of scientism in the Victorian period, though, once again, the depth of enthusiasm for Wordsworth (among such progressive intellectuals as John Stuart Mill and George Eliot) suggests how strongly it was being resisted. By the early twentieth century, however, the dethronement of Christianity in favour of a scientistic, materialistic epistemology was beginning to look, in many Western European cultures, increasingly secure and the anti-Romantic triumvirate of Darwin, Marx and Freud had come to represent the era in which Lewis lived his life. We should remember, however, two important qualifications. First, that Lewis was Irish, not English, and his early years were spent in a cultural environment in which Christian traditions remained (as they still remain) comparatively secure. Second, while recognizing with Lewis the extent to which the character of a sensibility may be related to historical trends,[7] we should be wary of abandoning the uniquely personal determinants of Lewis's experience in favour of intellectual abstractions.

CHARACTERISTIC EMPHASES

Lewis was a philosopher before he was a literary scholar and a poet before either. He therefore has certain characteristic emphases which put him implicitly at odds with the theoretical (second sense) dimensions of modern academic literary studies.

He treats old books as a potential source of wisdom.[8] He sees the present as a period, with its 'characteristic mistakes'.[9] He sees the whole phenomenon of modernity in a cultural and philosophical perspective that reaches back to Homer and embraces two ancient languages as well as the literatures of Italy and France (and, less assuredly perhaps, of Germany and Spain). He insists on a high level of literary competence and the priority of adequate literary experience as bases for sound critical judgement.[10] As a poet, he gave a degree of attention to the auditory properties of poetry which, among critics, now seems rare.[11] Thus equipped and disposed, he was extremely sensitive to ideological disparities as the source of critical disagreement, saying of F.R. Leavis on Milton's verse, for example, 'we differ not about the nature of Milton's poetry, but about the nature of man'.[12] On the negative side, he may be said to have had what will strike a modern academic as too homogeneous a conception (in terms of class, gender and literary experience) of his students. And his disregard of 'practical criticism' may have proceeded in part from a literary confidence which enabled him to dispense with it as an explicit procedure. His distaste for biographical and psychological interpretation may also (to modern students interested in both) seem evidence that Lewis was too completely enclosed within his own period preferences. Yet on both these linguistic and psychological matters, the reality is more complex.

Lewis, as a young man, often professed himself at odds with T.S. Eliot on points of poetic and literary theory, though by the time that they came to collaborate on a revision of the Psalter, it was perhaps evident to both men that their disagreements belied their affinities. In 1919, when he was thirty-one, Eliot published 'Tradition and the Individual Talent', an essay which includes the celebrated claim that 'the more perfect the artist, the more completely separate in him will be the man who suffers and the mind which creates; the more perfectly will the mind digest and transmute the passions which are its material'.[13] This is philosophically akin to Lewis's claim, in the three essays which compose his share of *The Personal Heresy* (1939), that 'when we read poetry as poetry should be read, we have before us no representation which claims to be the poet, and frequently no representation of a *man*, a *character*, or a *personality* at all'.[14] The over-emphasis of 'at all' there resembles Eliot's insistence that the personality of the poet will be not merely *distinct* from the character of the poem, but 'completely separate'.

Though Lewis continued to deflect his attention, as a matter of principle, from the personalities of poets, these essays, written in his mid-to-late thirties, contain passages of dialectical bluster which smack of desperation. Quoting a famous poem in which Robert Herrick rhymes 'goes' with 'clothes',[15] Lewis comments:

> I can learn from reading these lines that the pronunciation 'clo'es' for *clothes* is at least as old as the date at which the poem was written. That piece of philological knowledge is a result of the poem; but clearly philological truths do not make part of the poem, nor do I encounter them so long as I am apprehending it with my imagination, but only when I come to reflect upon it, later … The problem, therefore, is whether my perception of the poet's character is part of my direct experience of the poem, or whether it is simply one of those later and unpoetical results … In other words, my idea of the poet presupposes that the poem has already had its effect on my imagination, and cannot, therefore, be part of that effect.[16]

The sensitivity to sound here is entirely characteristic and entirely salutary. What is less salutary is describing the inference about Herrick's pronunciation as a piece of 'philological knowledge' which does not properly belong to our experience of the poem. The poem is not merely its text, but the sequence of sounds of which the text is a symbolic representation. The sounds which scholarly research and literary sensitivity may recover are the very substance of the poem. Later, in *Studies in Words* (1960), Lewis would insist that scholarship could guard us against misapprehension of the senses in which words are used in old books. In *An Experiment in Criticism* (1961), and elsewhere, he insists that the sound of words is not a quality superadded to their meaning but is the medium in which their meaning inheres.[17] And once we have made this effort to reconstitute the original sound of a poem, the effect upon our senses inevitably contributes to that vague, shifting, rudimentary yet distinct notion of the poet's personality which the poet's name ('Herrick') symbolically suggests. Once this notion exists, it can be modified, but it cannot be eliminated.

Yet elimination of the personal is what Lewis seems, in this early book, intent upon: 'It is absolutely essential that each word should suggest not what is private and personal to the poet, but what is common, impersonal, objective.'[18] In order to enforce this point, however, Lewis has quoted a famous passage of Keats which he seeks to characterize by quoting a list of words dissociated from what makes them inalienably Keatsian: 'summer, night, wood, oak, stars, gust, air'.[19] These, he rightly comments, are the names of 'familiar *sensibilia*'; yes, but the 'summer' and the 'night', for instance, are by Keats compounded as a 'summer night' (adjective and noun, not noun and noun) and this night, moreover, is 'trancèd'; the oaks are 'branch-charmèd by the earnest stars' and 'dream all night without a stir'. It is indeed necessary that the words mean in Keats essentially what they mean in Lewis; but what the word 'Keats' means is a matter of how *he* modifies the mood and movement of common words so as to make them distinctively his own. When Lewis quotes a passage from *The Prelude* in which Wordsworth writes of shaking off 'That burthen of my own unnatural self',[20] there is perhaps not only a revelation of Wordsworth's personality (by means of his poetic character) but also of Lewis's. Owen Barfield remarked that reading a poem of Lewis's produced an impression 'not of an "I say this", but of a "This is the sort of thing a man might say"'.[21] Barfield was noticing an impulse in Lewis towards self-abnegation which, paradoxically, but in a way fully consistent with Christian teaching, became a distinctive feature of his literary personality.

An Experiment in Criticism, written right at the end of Lewis's life, benefits from that softening and moderation of tone observable across the whole range of his writings. The book is a primer in the principles of good reading which offers advice in the spirit of respectful collaboration. The book originated in opposition to pro-Modernist presumptions about the nature of poetry and to a critical peremptoriness associated with Leavis (by this time Lewis's Cambridge colleague). The writing, exemplary in its grace and verve, often demonstrates a willingness to examine sympathetically even critical developments which Lewis deplored:

> To read the old poetry involved learning a slightly different
> language; to read the new involves the unmaking of your mind,
> the abandonment of all the logical and narrative connections
> which you use in reading prose or in conversation. You must

achieve a trance-like condition in which images, associations, and sounds operate without these. The common ground between poetry and any other use of words is reduced almost to zero. In that way poetry is now more quintessentially poetical than ever before.[22]

That reading Modernist poetry might involve 'the unmaking of your mind' is a notion which Lewis examines patiently and curiously. But an experienced reader of Lewis will recognize in that use of 'poetical' a premonition of revolt. It soon arrives: 'Unfortunately, but inevitably, this process is accompanied by a steady diminution in the number' of those who read poetry.[23] Here, as generally, Lewis is honourably elitist in that he affirms the importance, for a reader, of acquiring appropriate forms of historical and linguistic knowledge; but he is profoundly pro-democratic in wanting to extend the benefits of genuine literary experience to the largest possible number of readers.

The incidental strengths of *An Experiment in Criticism* are innumerable, chief among them its combination of a capacity for philosophical generalization and attention to the minutiae of 'rhythm and vocalic melody' in poetry.[24] Yet the overall argument of the book is perhaps dubious in a way that recalls *The Personal Heresy*. The common view of F.R. Leavis in the 1960s was that he encouraged students to restrict their attention to those writers whom he judged supreme. Actually this was a misconception which resulted from confusing Leavis's general convictions about what it was valuable to read with his particular recommendations about what a student might be expected to read in the course of studying for a degree. To counteract the narrowness of a strictly selective canon and the danger of presuming on the authority of one's own selective criteria, Lewis proposed that, instead, a reader should try to give any work the same quality of attention which might be elicited by the best. An inferior work would reveal itself by being unable to sustain the best quality of attention the reader was capable of. As a strategy for counteracting critical dogmatism and as a counsel of critical humility, this is admirable. Lewis (very much at odds with his earlier critical persona, perhaps) declares roundly that 'we must, and should, remain uncertain' about our critical judgements.[25] However, just as it is impossible to obliterate one's developing idea of an author's identity, it is impossible to avoid implicit recourse to one's sense of 'the best that has been known and thought'. Lewis's plea for greater humility, generosity and adaptability in reading does not require the support of a systematic theory.

As may by now be apparent, a major point of difference between Lewis as a theorist and all but the ablest proponents of literary theory is his relation to his own language. Most post-structuralist theory is read in translation; some written in English reads as though it were a translation. Lewis works as a poet both when engaged in metaphysical speculation and when analysing the minutiae of poetic style. His theory, that is to say, is nuanced by the same awareness of the potentialities of language as his comments on, for example, Dorothy Sayers's translation of Dante, the poetry of Charles Williams, or the *Faerie Queene*. What other critic writing in English whose work encompasses literary theory has a comparable range and height of achievement? He was conscious from the outset of his career of a wish to perfect his prose. He encouraged others to think of writing as a highly exacting art. He reads poetry from the inside out – as one who, at a lower order of achievement, knew how to write it.[26] The usual lack of consonance between literary and critical discourse is thereby much reduced. Lewis writes about literature as a practitioner; but a practitioner whose erudition and powers of analysis find few parallels.

ROMANTICISM

Lewis, I would argue, is thus a poetico-philosophical writer whose orientation is profoundly Romantic. He fulfils Coleridge's counsel of perfection: that a literary critic should attend to 'the moral or metaphysical Inherencies' of style.[27] The fact that Lewis is so succinct, orderly and elegant a writer may have obscured for many his profound Romantic affinities. He is, indeed, assiduously intent upon the 'Inherencies' of what he reads: 'Those who are not interested in an author's matter can have nothing of value to say about his style or construction.'[28] Yet he conceives of the substance by strict attention to the words in which it is embodied; for it is only through attending to verbal minutiae that a writer's meaning can be accurately apprehended. Wordsworth's comment on Shelley that he is 'the best artist of us all – I mean in workmanship of style' asserts the importance (for writer and reader) of attending to 'innumerable minutiae' as a necessary, but not sufficient, condition of full artistic excellence. It was a surprise to me to discover the fervour of Lewis's dedication to Shelley. ('He loved Shelley particularly'.[29]) Aspects of his style which I would have expected Lewis to dislike – its 'unplanned' quality, its local indeterminacies of meaning, its headlong, propulsive, wandering syntax and its general opalescence – are actually qualities he loves and defends. They are conducive to the evocation of a view of the world Christian in its moral preoccupations, but pagan in its supernatural expansiveness. Indeed, there are qualities in Spenser which are, in these terms, distinctly (or indistinctly) Shelleyan. Lewis was a Romantic reader of Spenser, reading him with vastly more learning than Keats did, but with an adoring delight in the faerie-ness of *The Faerie Queene* that Keats, *mutatis mutandis*, shared. Because Lewis's literary personality ostensibly conforms, in many ways, to his description of himself as a 'rationalist', readers are easily persuaded (as if colluding with Lewis's own defences) to ignore the depth of his preoccupation with the sub-, supra- and trans-rational.

Lewis's interest in the world beyond the world – in those forms and aspects of reality which elude but entice our senses – will be obvious to everyone who reads the Narnia Chronicles or *Surprised by Joy*. Both of these writings and, in some respects, virtually everything he wrote are informed by what Lewis came to regard as the single most influential experience of his imaginative life. This experience he signified by the word 'joy', used in the special sense of *Sehnsucht*, or 'an unsatisfied desire which is itself more desirable than any other satisfaction'.[30] Lewis has put this in a characteristic way. He seems both clear and elegant. But the elegance of the paradox deflects attention from certain important and puzzling stray potentialities of its meaning. The sentence compares neither two desires, nor two satisfactions, but a desire and all other satisfactions. It implies, therefore, that the unsatisfied desire for the world beyond the world is itself more satisfying than any other satisfied desire. But what it *says* is not that the unsatisfied desire is more satisfying, but that it is more *desirable*. The effect of the sentence is to simulate a yearning to transcend the limits of sensory experience, by making us wish for the clarification that lies beyond strict logic. Here, even within the limits of a beautifully chiastic sentence, we see Lewis straining beyond the bounds of rationality.

Lewis's commitment to Romanticism has two important corollaries: one metaphysical, the other epistemological. Metaphysically, his romanticism is expressed in a sacramental view of reality. He thinks that reality may be said to have within its natural dimension supernatural inherencies. His insistence that readers should understand this about the world of medieval romance arises from a belief that it remains true, despite the coercive materialism of modernity.[31]

The process by which the inherently supernatural world of romance is translated into a system of occult symbolism resembles the modern habit, much opposed by Lewis, of treating myth as allegory. That he shared with Wordsworth and Traherne a conception of reality in which the natural and the supernatural are coinherent is most magnificently demonstrated by a passage from his sermon, 'The Weight of Glory' (1941):

> It is a serious thing to live in a society of possible gods and goddesses, to remember that the dullest and most uninteresting person you can talk to may one day be a creature which, if you saw it now, you would be strongly tempted to worship, or else a horror and a corruption such as you now meet, if at all, only in a nightmare. All day long we are, in some degree, helping each other to one or other of these destinations. It is in the light of these over-whelming possibilities, it is with the awe and the circumspection proper to them, that we should conduct all our dealings with one another, all friendships, all loves, all play, all politics. There are no *ordinary* people. You have never talked to a mere mortal. Nations, cultures, arts, civilizations – these are mortal, and their life is to ours as the life of a gnat. But it is immortals whom we joke with, work with, marry, snub, and exploit – immortal horrors or everlasting splendours.[32]

Would it be possible to choose a passage more vulnerable to attack – more at odds with the prevailing assumptions of contemporary culture – than this? Lewis assumes, with Blake and contrary to the beliefs of many natural scientists, that reality is not coterminous with the evidence of our senses, however magnified, and that imagination supplies a means of access to its supernatural dimensions. Yet for all the sharpness of its divergence from the ideological norms of today, Lewis expresses here a vision of reality with which Chaucer, Spenser, Shakespeare, Milton, Wordsworth and Eliot might find themselves metaphysically in agreement. It is thus one of Lewis's most creative functions as a literary scholar to enter fully into possession of a moral and metaphysical outlook corroborated by many canonical writers but powerfully discountenanced by much contemporary criticism and theory. He repopulates the empty universe and suggests what it feels like to think of morality not as contingent, but as built into the structure of reality.

Just as Lewis knows that there is more to reality than what our senses can get at, epistemologically he knows that there is more to the mind than ratiocination. Its other modes of operation may help us become aware of the supernatural elements of experience. As a poet, Lewis realizes that 'thought' is a complex term. Of thought in poetry he urges us to 'understand that "thought" here carries no specially *intellectual* connotation'.[33] Writing of Spenser, a poet whose reputation never stood higher perhaps than in the Romantic period, Lewis declares an interest in the unconscious activities of the mind:

> Spenser, with his conscious mind, knew only the least part of what he was doing, and we are never very sure that we have got to the end of his significance. The water is very clear, but we cannot see to the bottom. That is one of the delights of the older kind of poetry: 'thoughts beyond their thoughts to those high bards were given'.[34]

Thoughts of the kind generally operative in critical prose may have often only a tenuous relation to the depths of a person's psyche. In 'Shelley, Dryden and Mr. Eliot' (1939), Lewis asserts that a poet should follow his imagination because our imaginations are *'constrained by deepest necessities'*.[35] Poetry can take us beyond or beneath the ratiocinative thinking Lewis was all too good at, into the depths of such reverie as Shelley commends in his essay 'On Life'. Thus we may enter depths of our being that ratiocination barricades us out of, proffering subtlety as an illusory earnest of depth.

But these emphases are rendered uniquely personal – are given the quality that peculiarly attracts or repels us – by their relation to the personality behind them.

CONCLUSION

In vociferously asserting the importance of the predominantly political issues which traditional literary theory was ignorant about, theory in the second sense – 'Theory' (and post-structuralist theory in particular) – often seemed inadequately attentive to its own moral and metaphysical presuppositions. One of these was the priority of the political as the principal domain within which literary theorists should be active. Since politics is, in our own era, largely secularized, any activity which defines itself in political terms will be liable to exclude religion or religious considerations. The chief ground of distinction between post-structuralists and traditionalists was, in fact, not their respective attitudes towards nationality, race and gender, but their respective attitudes towards morality and religion: in short, towards the supernatural. It would be far too crude to say that most post-structuralists were materialists and most traditionalists were supernaturalists. Nonetheless, it was rare to find a Theorist who was also a Christian; and, if there were still few Christians among the traditionalists, that was not because the nature of their critical practice made faith impossible. From the seventeenth century until the twentieth, most anglophone literary theorists were Christian. And most of their European predecessors, from Aristotle to Cicero, had treated the notion of the supernatural with respect. What distinguished Lewis as a literary theorist was that he was fully intimate with the older and far longer metaphysical tradition at a time when it was beginning to come under attack – when the cultural changes were occurring which would result in the emergence of an aggressively secular and materialistic form of literary theory.

Because Lewis recognized that the real grounds of disagreement in many critical disputes were ultimately metaphysical – and because he had so keen a sense of the moral contrast between the pre- and the post-Modernist eras – he soon accustomed himself to addressing the metaphysical issues implicit in literary disputes. An early example of this is the series of essays on 'Christianity and Literature' (especially the passage about originality[36]: not addressed to post-structuralists, of course, but to a strain in literary criticism and theory which, once fully elaborated, would issue in post-structuralism). From these he went on to write the passage on 'Stock Responses' in *A Preface to Paradise Lost* (1942),[37] 'The Poison of Subjectivism' (1943) and *The Abolition of Man* (1943). What motivated him was the depth and strength of his attachment to a view of the world transfigured by the presence of a loving and omniscient Creator. He experienced this world directly (Joy). But his experience was corroborated most profoundly by the work of poets, chiefly those writing in the English language (that not being, as it is for many of Lewis's modern successors, the only language in which he could fluently read poetry). Behind this literary experience there was, I believe, a deep and harrowing personal need, which some would take as discrediting its authority, though I do not.

Lewis's work in literary theory is distinguished by a unique combination of literary and philosophical virtues. From the standpoint of traditional Christian morality he can reasonably be described as one of the most important literary theorists of the twentieth century, provided we remember that literary theory continually modulates – as in the work of Raymond Williams – into cultural analysis. Lewis's achievements in the field of literary theory are unique. He is the writer who most incisively and insistently comments on the moral and metaphysical infrastructure of literary and critical art, while having the most exuberantly appreciative appetite for literary artistry. He sees the metaphysics in a metaphor and feels the ache or the exhilaration encompassed in a cadence. Most of all, he suffers an existential loneliness for which, in the personal but self-transcending worlds of literature, he sought vivid reassurances of a final cure. The examination of Lewis as a literary theorist takes us a long way from the practicalities of literary appreciation. That is what is distinctive about him as a theorist. We see his attempts to achieve an almost unachievable personal unity, first as a poet, then by means of a conception of the world embraced and secured by the natural law, finally by means of a Christian sacramental vision. He glimpses within the particularities of literary experience a destiny beyond space and time where all pain will be assuaged eternally in the love of God.

Notes

1 The textbook that explained 'radical' literary theory to two generations of undergraduates was Terry Eagleton's *Literary Theory: An Introduction* (Oxford: Basil Blackwell, 1983; revd 1996). The sequel to the second edition of this book was not a further revision, but a (characteristically engaging) recantation: *After Theory* (London: Allen Lane, 2003). See my review in the *Times Higher Education Supplement* (14 Nov. 2003, 28).

2 'Christianity and Culture', EC 78. *Scrutiny* was a critical journal, edited mainly by F.R. Leavis and his wife, Q.D. Leavis, from 1932 to 1953, which for many students had acquired a quasi-religious authority.

3 'Christianity and Culture', EC 78.

4 Letter to his father, 14 Aug. 1925 (CLI 649).

5 '*De Descriptione Temporum*', SLE 7.

6 The parallel with MacIntyre is noted by Basil Mitchell, 'C.S. Lewis on the Abolition of Man', in *C.S. Lewis Remembered*, ed. Harry Lee Poe and Rebecca Whitten Poe (Grand Rapids: Zondervan, 2006), 181.

7 'One cause of misery and vice is always present with us in the greed and pride of men, but at certain periods in history this is greatly increased by the temporary prevalence of some false philosophy': 'The Poison of Subjectivism', EC 657.

8 SL 140.

9 'On the Reading of Old Books', EC 439.

10 'Fern-Seed and Elephants', EC 242–54.

11 See e.g. 'The Alliterative Metre', SLE 15–26.

12 PPL 130.

13 T.S. Eliot, *Selected Essays*, 3rd edn (London: Faber & Faber, 1951), 18.

14 PH 4.

15 'Upon Julia's Clothes'. A more accurate text than the one Lewis quotes is given in *The Poetical Works of Robert Herrick*, ed. L.C. Martin (Oxford: Clarendon Press, 1956), 261.

16 PH 5–6.

17 EIC 90.

18 PH 19.

19 PH 18.

20 PH 7.

21   *Light on C.S. Lewis*, ed. Jocelyn Gibb (London: Geoffrey Bles, 1965), p. xi.
22   EIC 97.
23   EIC 97.
24   EIC 29.
25   EIC 111.
26   See Malcolm Guite's essay in this volume (Chapter 21).
27   Letter to Sir George Beaumont, 1 Feb. 1804 (*Collected Letters of Samuel Taylor Coleridge*, ed. Earl Leslie Griggs, 6 vols (Oxford: Clarendon Press, 1956–71), II, 1054).
28   Letter to George Watson, 9 Oct. 1962 (CLIII 1375).
29   Derek Brewer, 'The Tutor: A Portrait', in *Remembering C.S. Lewis: Recollections of Those Who Knew Him*, ed. James T. Como (San Francisco: Ignatius Press, 2005), 127.
30   SBJ 20.
31   'The Anthropological Approach', SLE 310.
32   'The Weight of Glory', EC 105–06.
33   PH 147.
34   'Edmund Spenser, 1552–99', SMRL 143.
35   'Shelley, Dryden, and Mr. Eliot', SLE 207 (my emphasis).
36   'Christianity and Literature', EC 413–18.
37   PPL 54–58.

4 Intellectual historian

DENNIS DANIELSON

According to late-nineteenth-century German philosopher Wilhelm Dilthey, the historian shares with the poet a capacity to apprehend and re-enact a complex of thoughts, feelings, circumstances and characters in such a way that readers may re-live or experience (*nacherleben*) a world from which they would otherwise be quite cut off. Dilthey offers the example of his own encounter with Luther:

> Within my own existence, as in that of most people today, the possibility of experiencing religious states of mind is narrowly restricted. Yet when I make my way through the letters and other writings of Luther, ... I experience a religious event of such eruptive force, of such energy – such a matter of life and death – that it transcends the possible lived experience of anyone today. ... This event thus opens up for us in Luther and his early-Reformation contemporaries a religious world that stretches our horizon of lived human possibility otherwise inaccessible to us. ... In short, we humans, limited and determined by the realities of life, are set free not only (as often asserted) by art, but also by historical understanding.[1]

C.S. Lewis never claimed to be an intellectual historian. Despite his continuous immersion in historical writings and themes, he set himself the scholarly role of stitching what he called 'a backcloth for the arts',[2] especially literature. And this he did with conspicuous success. What is just as conspicuous, however, is his lack of an audience among late-twentieth- and early twenty-first-century students of intellectual history – which is a pity. For few intellectual historians of this period have proven as skilled as Lewis in evoking, exuding and exemplifying the kind of *Nacherlebnis* described by Dilthey and still sought by intellectual historians both amateur and professional.

In offering a case for Lewis as intellectual historian, I shall limit myself to four of his works, focusing on them in varying degrees and not worrying much about the chronology of their publication. The outward clothing of these works is predominantly literary, an appearance (as already hinted) that may obscure, rather than readily disclose, the body of notable and stimulating, if not totally irreproachable, intellectual history they incorporate.

'DE DESCRIPTIONE TEMPORUM'

Perhaps the most self-conscious and pithy example of Lewis's practice of intellectual history is '*De Descriptione Temporum*' (1954),[3] the inaugural lecture he gave upon assuming the Chair of Medieval and Renaissance Literature at Cambridge, of which he was the first occupant. The very name of the chair evoked periodization; and in his lecture Lewis did not neglect the opportunity for tackling the necessity and yet pitfalls of our habitual division of history into epochs, nor for pondering how such habits offer insight into the minds of the habits' practitioners. Indeed, such reflection is always part of Lewis's project: a two-way process in which his historical analysis places the 'now' as well as the 'then' in a revealing and critical – even satirical – light.

In his lecture Lewis professes to interpret the establishment of a Chair of Medieval and Renaissance Literature as a sign that mid-twentieth-century Cambridge, at least, might have got over the antithesis that often characterizes the distinction between those two epochs. He cites J.M. Berdan's *Early Tudor Poetry* to exemplify the flavour of the antithesis: 'We begin with twenty-nine pages ... of unrelieved gloom about grossness, superstition, and cruelty to children, and on the twenty-ninth comes the sentence, "The first rift in this darkness is the Copernican doctrine"; as if a new hypothesis in astronomy would naturally make a man stop hitting his daughter about the head'.[4] Pressing the view that 'the barrier between those two ages [medieval and Renaissance] has been greatly exaggerated', and urging that 'all lines of demarcation between what we call "periods" should be subject to constant revision', Lewis nonetheless admits that historians cannot dispense with periods altogether. Indeed, in the rest of the lecture he seeks an overarching categorization of periods that would identify a 'Great Divide' between all periods that precede it and all that come after. If this divide does not fall between medieval and Renaissance, then where does it fall?

Returning to his title, '*De Descriptione Temporum*' ('On the description of 'ages', or 'periods') – borrowed from a chapter in Isidore of Seville's early-seventh-century *Etymologies* – Lewis considers the contenders for 'Great Divide', and never conceals the fact that he is inclined to place it relatively recently. Among the contenders, of course, is the division between 'Antiquity' and 'the Dark Ages', or (not the same thing) between pagan and Christian. But Lewis, without minimizing the differences, proposes that whereas our ancestors saw history falling on two sides of the watershed formed by the advent of Christianity, we must recognize *three* large periods: the pre-Christian, the Christian, and the post-Christian. Lewis clearly thinks of the division between the last two as more radical than that between the first two. For 'the gap between those who worship different gods is not so wide as that between those who worship and those who do not'[5] – an aphorism that sums up a great deal of Lewis's view of philosophy and culture. Thus he proposes that 'the gap between Professor [Gilbert] Ryle and Thomas Browne is far wider than that between Gregory the Great and Virgil'; and 'surely Seneca and Dr. [Samuel] Johnson are closer together than [Robert] Burton and [Sigmund] Freud'.[6]

Lewis then considers, and makes short work of, the divides that fall in the early twelfth century (between 'the Dark and Middle Ages') and in the late seventeenth century ('with the general acceptance of Copernicanism, the dominance of Descartes, and [in England] the foundation of the Royal Society'). Of course the latter transition is associated with the rise of science, a momentous enough series of events. But Lewis – typically aphorizing that 'science was not the business of Man because Man had not yet become the business of science' – suggests that it was later, technological applications of science in the form of steam engines and their progeny, along with other applications in biology, psychology and economics, that 'liberated' science to play a role in our daily lives and worldview.

The weakness of these candidates having been exposed, the way is prepared for Lewis to place his leading candidate for Great Divide somewhere (allowing for the arbitrariness of any attempt at precision) this side of the early nineteenth century, roughly after the work of novelists Jane Austen (1775–1817) and Walter Scott (1771–1832). He then outlines four markers of the mighty change, in ascending order of importance, beginning with politics – or what has become 'government by advertisement'. Whereas before, people prayed that they might 'live "a peaceable life in all godliness and honesty" [1 Timothy 2.2]' we now demand campaigns and initiatives from charismatic *leaders* rather than expecting justice and clemency from incorruptible *rulers*. Even more so in the arts, it is change that is demanded, novelty, and an unprecedented abandonment of in-principle agreed-upon meanings. Lewis offers the sweeping claim that from Gilgamesh and Homer to the nineteenth century, there was no change in the development of literature comparable to the shift to radical ambiguity evident in the poetry of T.S. Eliot and his contemporaries. And the third category of evidence that Lewis cites in favour of his proposed Great Divide relates to the already-mentioned religious shift from Christian to post-Christian. He dismisses any claim that the latter can be equated with paganism: 'The post-Christian is cut off from the Christian past and therefore doubly from the Pagan past.'[7] This development too, then, represents an entirely new thing.

What Lewis calls his 'trump card', however, is 'the birth of the machines'. It is they that have radically altered man's place in nature, produced the assumption that 'recent' means 'better' – 'that everything is provisional and soon to be superseded' – and rendered the word 'primitive' a pejorative term (in contrast to its once positive meanings: first, pure, pristine, permanent). The machines have not only shaped our surroundings and ways of life; they have also imprinted our assumptions concerning what life is for. Our premise 'that the attainment of goods we have never yet had, rather than the defence and conservation of those we have already, is the cardinal business of life, would most shock and bewilder' our ancestors if they could visit our world.

The implicit thought-experiment involved in imagining a visitor arriving from beyond the Great Divide is one that, strikingly, Lewis presents himself as enacting. There is no hiding *his* shock and bewilderment at the state of the world into which he speaks; and in a powerful sense, he *is* the ancestor who has come to expound his world and in so doing help us taste the poverty of our own. He lightly cloaks this role in self-deprecation: 'I would give a great deal to hear any ancient Athenian, even a stupid one, talking about Greek tragedy.'[8] Yet, despite his half-jocular claim to be an authentic 'dinosaur', a useful 'specimen', there is no deeper tone of apology in his claim to speak as a native of the 'Old Western order'. It is a bold and impressive stance, and perhaps a fitting one for a professor of medieval and Renaissance literature. Lewis embodies the very otherness to which he, as an intellectual historian, offers access. He makes the historical contemporaneous. In Dilthey's terms, his performance of *Nacherlebnis* is particularly vivid because, for Lewis, it is actually *Erlebnis*.

This exposition of the past, however, almost always entails in Lewis's writing a critique of the present. His styling himself a citizen of another world certainly lends his writing energy, but it also runs the risk that *qua* foreigner he will be rejected or resented by much of his potential readership. Without using the word 'modernism' anywhere in his inaugural lecture, Lewis yet makes it abundantly clear that his project is no mere exposition of the norms and literature of earlier ages; it is also, even overwhelmingly, a critique of modernism. Rather than contemporary post-modernism, however, Lewis offers a pre-modern perspective. The relationship between Lewis and his modern audience, if only for reasons of their cultural distance from each other, will thus almost inevitably be tinged with something akin to mutual xenophobia.

'NEW LEARNING AND NEW IGNORANCE'

In the same year as his inaugural lecture, Lewis contributed to the Oxford History of English Literature series a volume titled *English Literature in the Sixteenth Century*. His introduction to this work, 'New Learning and New Ignorance',[9] is among the richest and most concentrated pieces of intellectual history he ever produced.

The task of hoisting a properly instructive 'backcloth for the arts' in part entails covering over or tearing down other backcloths, deliberately erected or not, that serve to distort perceptions of the arts or the history with which the arts are interwoven. Lewis is a critic who openly loves the English literature of the sixteenth century, especially the last quarter of it, which displays 'almost a new culture', characterized by 'fantasy, conceit, paradox, colour, incantation ... youth'.[10] Yet he just as openly deplores scholarly humanism, with its 'recovery of Greek and ... substitution of Augustan for medieval Latin', to whose influence many have tended to attribute this burgeoning of English literature in the late sixteenth century. Some of Lewis's principal manoeuvres, accordingly, are intended to put such humanism in its place, to rebrand (negatively) the reputation of the 'Renaissance', and to associate it with 'new ignorance'. In short, 'the more we look into the question, the harder we shall find it to believe that humanism had any power of encouraging, or any wish to encourage, the literature that actually arose'.[11]

Lewis also has many provocative reflections to offer concerning science, especially cosmology, to which he would turn again later in *The Discarded Image*. However, we may wonder in this connection whether Lewis's pugnacious tendencies might not occasionally weaken his overall argument or alienate his audience. The reader willing to ponder his unfavourable judgement of humanism is nonetheless taken up short when he claims that humanism 'tended to be on the whole indifferent, if not hostile, to science'.[12] Perhaps the problem is one of definition. 'Science', as we use the term today, may be largely anachronistic when applied to the sixteenth century; 'humanism', even then, admitted of degrees and subspecies. Still, to take a most obvious counterexample, Copernicus by education and temperament was certainly a humanist, in fact the first scholar in Poland to publish his own Latin translation of a Greek author.[13] Similarly, as a natural philosopher, he sought to translate and interpret the 'text' of the creation, the 'book of God's works'. One of Copernicus's deepest motivations for developing his sun-centred cosmological model was his belief that earlier interpreters of nature had produced a 'translation' that was incoherent and aesthetically unappealing – one that did not do justice to the skill of the original Author/Creator. And it is hard to see this application of humanism's emphasis on (literally or figuratively) recovering and rereading ancient texts as involving anything like the hostility to science of which Lewis accuses it.

More effective and enlightening is Lewis's sketch of Florentine Neo-platonism, particularly in the persons of Ficino and Pico. Not surprisingly, Lewis emphasizes this school's syncretism, its 'conviction that all the sages of antiquity shared a common wisdom and that this wisdom can be reconciled with Christianity'. He does not adjudicate this effort a success, however. Indeed,

> though the Florentine Platonists were wholly pious in intention, their work deserves the epithet *pagan* more than any other movement in that age. ... One has the suspicion that though [Ficino] and Pico doubtless believed Christianity to be true, they valued it even more for being lofty, edifying, and useful. They have the air of men rallying the forces of 'religion' or even of 'idealism' in general against the danger of naturalistic philosophies that deprive man of his dignity and freedom; a danger represented for them not by the new real sciences but by astrological determinism. The title of Pico's *De Dignitate Hominis* would really have served as the title for all their works.[14]

Lewis's account of Ficino and Pico serves his purposes in at least two other ways. It provides an opportunity to undercut yet another common modern misconception, which reads back into the sixteenth century an antithesis between superstition and enlightenment, with great Renaissance figures (of course) allied with the latter. A writer like Pico, however, was an opponent of astrology and a proponent of magic, both of which we now tend to place on the side of superstition. Lewis tellingly avers that 'the new *magia*, far from being an anomaly in that age, takes its place among the other dreams of power which then haunted the European mind'.[15] Startlingly, Lewis yokes such interest in magic with the kind of knowledge sought by Bacon – which has, since the inception of the Royal Society, been routinely associated with the rise of science (read 'enlightenment'). Yet Bacon himself openly avows affinity with the magicians, for they alike 'seek knowledge for the sake of power (in Bacon's words, as "a spouse for fruit" not a "curtesan for pleasure")'.[16]

The other thesis implicit in Lewis's exposition is that, in the sixteenth century, freedom and determinism arise as twin plagues once the 'earlier doctrine of Man' – which 'had guaranteed him, on his own rung of the hierarchical ladder, his own limited freedom and efficacy' – is abandoned in favour of an uncertainty whereby 'perhaps Man can do everything, perhaps he can do nothing'. Both thoughts are often seen to coexist within a single mind. For example, Paracelsus writes that 'if we rightly knew our owne spirite no thing at all would be impossible to us on earth'; yet he also elsewhere offers a completely passive picture of humans' relationship to nature, whereby 'man is related to the elements as the image in a mirror is related to a real object'.[17]

The sharp paradoxes of freedom and necessity form a current that continues to flow through Lewis's account of sixteenth-century intellectual thought. As part of his critique of humanism – perhaps as a counterbalance to the cheerleading tone that dominated nineteenth-century historians of the Renaissance such as Jakob Burkhardt – Lewis emphasizes the extent to which the humanists were *not* champions of capacious creativity. People now read their writings, with the rare exception of More's *Utopia*, only to find out about the humanists, not for their inherent beauty or philosophy or edification. Humanism's influence on literature, in short, was a baleful one, and 'Racine and Milton are perhaps the only poets who thoroughly followed out the humanistic ideal of style and were not destroyed by it'.[18]

The relentless partisanship of Lewis's account of the sixteenth century is both a strength and a weakness. Together with his obvious, delighted immersion in the works of the period – including his habit of translating quotations from Latin into the authentic-looking idioms and spellings of the period – his partisanship helps convey to his readers the lived vibrancy of sixteenth-century thought in a way that Dilthey himself would surely approve of. Nor can one deny the necessity of Lewis's campaign against (in this case) the humanists' own campaign against all things medieval, especially medieval literature and philosophy. For their caricatures of the former as 'barbarous and silly', and of the latter (especially scholasticism) as trivial and hair-splitting, even now continue to obscure and devalue the rich medieval legacy. Even the words and (implicit) oppositions – 'medieval' and 'Renaissance', 'scholastic' and 'humanist' – with which we conduct our historical thinking are implicitly partisan. Lewis's contrary partisanship may accordingly be applauded as a much-needed corrective. The danger, however, is that the critic may counter caricature with caricature, oversimplification with oversimplification. Of the humanists' approach to medieval philosophy, Lewis tellingly declares: 'They jeer and do not refute'.[19] One can add only that Lewis's own critique of humanism might be even more persuasive if he himself had placed greater emphasis on detailed refutation and resorted less to jeering epithets such as 'Philistine' and 'obscurantist'.[20]

The other sixteenth-century movement of which Lewis provides a vivid sketch is Puritanism (which he spells in lower case), and here his aim is similarly corrective, if less openly adversarial, perhaps because fewer among his potential twentieth-century audience would align themselves with Puritanism than with humanism. Lewis rightly insists that, to start with, 'puritan' was predominantly 'a hostile term', which its objects then often accepted. Moreover, they 'were so called because they claimed to be purists or purifiers in ecclesiastical polity: not because they laid more emphasis than other Christians on "purity" in the sense of chastity. Their quarrel with the Church of England was at first rather ecclesiastical than theological'.[21]

Lewis valuably paints a startling but undoubtedly true picture of the exhilaration experienced by the first English Protestants, who enjoyed – and were criticized for enjoying – their election to salvation by grace. For the Roman Catholic Thomas More, as Lewis points out, 'a Protestant was one "dronke of the new must of lewd lightnes of minde and vayne gladnesse of harte". Luther, More said, 'had made converts precisely because "he spiced al the poison" with "libertee."' Thus 'Protestantism was not too grim, but too glad, to be true … Protestants are not ascetics but sensualists'.[22] Lewis offers an impressive series of quotations from the sixteenth century to support the claim that early Protestants, contrary to modern stereotypes of them (stereotypes perhaps reinforced by later developments of certain strains of Protestantism), formed an enthusiastic, non-austere, and life-affirming movement within Christianity.

If Lewis's approach to the Reformation itself again savours of partisanship, it is a partisanship on behalf of the Church as a whole and *against* the centrifugal partisanships that so characterized the debates of the sixteenth century. In a passage that typifies his verve and talent for analogy, Lewis sees the Protestant and Puritan emphasis on faith as legitimate – but sadly devolving into unseemly disputes. The issues at stake, he says, could have been fruitfully debated only between mature and saintly disputants in close privacy and at boundless leisure. Under those conditions formulae might possibly have been found which did justice to the Protestant ... assertions without compromising other elements of the Christian faith. In fact, however, these questions were raised at a moment when they immediately became embittered and entangled with a whole complex of matters theologically irrelevant, and therefore attracted the fatal attention both of government and the mob. ... It was as if men were set to conduct a metaphysical argument at a fair ... under the eyes of an armed and vigilant police force who frequently changed sides. Each party increasingly misunderstood the other and triumphed in refuting positions which their opponents did not hold.[23]

Redirecting his gaze from the Continent to England, Lewis offers a further arresting analogy to convey the flavour of the influence there of John Calvin. While conceding that modern parallels are always to some extent misleading, yet, he goes on,

it may be useful to compare the influence of Calvin on that age with the influence of Marx on our own; or even of Marx and Lenin in one, for Calvin had both expounded the new system in theory and set it going in practice. This will at least serve to eliminate the absurd idea that Elizabethan Calvinists were somehow grotesque, elderly people, standing outside the main forward current of life ... Unless we can imagine the freshness, the audacity, and (soon) the fashionableness of Calvinism, we shall get our whole picture wrong.[24]

Moreover, to round out his analogy with a fearsome prospect, Lewis suggests that readers of Calvin *then* were 'troubled by the fate of predestined vessels of wrath just about as much as young Marxists in our own age are troubled by the approaching liquidation of the bourgeoisie'.[25]

One of Lewis's outstanding skills is his discernment of affinities between apparently disparate elements within a period. For example, as to the temperament of the Puritans and humanists, Lewis comments, 'both felt themselves to be in the vanguard, both hated the Middle Ages, and both demanded a "clean sweep". The same youthful intransigence characterised both. The eagerness to smell out and condemn vestiges of popery in the Church and the eagerness to smell out and condemn vestiges of "barbarism" in one's neighbour's Latin had, psychologically, much in common'.[26] A perhaps even more telling set of affinities, as

Lewis points out, appears in regard to matters of freedom and necessity. The Calvinist declaration of humans' dependence upon God's sovereign will not only found a political counterpart in the 'doctrine of Divine Right' that was rising 'over the horizon'; it also highlighted the extreme subject-positions that the age seemed to render more thinkable than ever before: 'In the magician and the astrologer we saw a readiness either to exaggerate or to minimise the power and dignity of Man.' But 'Calvinism perhaps satisfies both inclinations by plunging the unregenerate man as deep as the astrologers and exalting the elect as highly as the magicians. Similarly the new politics embody limitless power and freedom in the prince, and make the subjects his (as they were the stars') tennis balls'.[27]

It is a remarkable summing up, pulling together some of the great themes Lewis has drawn out in the process of weaving a sixteenth-century backcloth; and it offers conceptual furniture that his reader, whether principally interested in literature or in intellectual history, can put to good use in his or her further reading within the period and beyond.

MILTON'S THEOLOGY

In Lewis's much earlier work *A Preface to Paradise Lost* (1942), likewise an aid to literary study but also a piece of intellectual history in its own right, we again catch glimpses of Lewis's striking breadth of knowledge, of his capacity to enter into the thought-world of an epoch, and also perhaps of his tendency to let a certain partisanship obscure subtleties that a reader or historian of a period should wish to examine and possibly treasure.

There is no doubt at all but that Lewis treasures Milton. His *Preface* repeatedly offers itself as something of a fervent rescue attempt. The dedication to Charles Williams praises the latter's own preface to Milton (1940) as 'the recovery of a true critical tradition after more than a hundred years of laborious misunderstanding'[28] – a judgement reiterated in Lewis's concluding pages: 'After Blake, Milton criticism is lost in misunderstanding'.[29] Lewis has in mind not only the Blakean 'pro-Satan' reading of *Paradise Lost*, but also the disparaging of Milton by influential (and disparate) critics such as Walter Raleigh, T.S. Eliot and F.R. Leavis. Moreover, Lewis praises Milton both as a poet and as a fellow-Christian. The stakes could thus hardly be higher. For example, as Lewis famously writes, 'Many of those who say they dislike Milton's God only mean that they dislike God'.[30] In this connection one sees

again, as in '*De Descriptione Temporum*', Lewis's conception of himself
as 'specimen': 'But for the student of Milton my Christianity is an
advantage. What would you not give to have a real, live Epicurean at
your elbow while reading Lucretius?'[31]

A Preface to Paradise Lost is indeed a potent, compelling and
eloquent piece of writing, probably among the three most influential
studies of Milton to appear in the mid-twentieth century. However, perhaps its principal weakness is precisely its manner of doing intellectual
history. The criticism may be put simply: in his eagerness to transport
readers out of their modern spiritual and intellectual landscape and into
that of an earlier, more devout and more doctrinally rigorous age, Lewis
over-generalizes the beliefs of that age in a way that can occlude the
particularities of the very text he sets out to illuminate.

Lewis asserts, at the beginning of chapter 10, that 'Milton's version
of the Fall story is substantially that of St Augustine, which is that
of the Church as a whole'.[32] He then lays out eleven features of that
doctrine, accompanied by 'proof-texts' from *Paradise Lost*. Although
highly informative and relevant, the process is nonetheless severely
deductive. For example, in his eleventh point – that 'disobedience of
man's organism to man is specially evident in sexuality as sexuality
now is but would not have been but for the Fall' – Lewis says that 'this
is why Milton places a scene of sexual indulgence immediately after
the Fall'. Lewis, who is truly attentive to what Milton actually wrote,
adds however that Milton '*doubtless intended* a contrast between this
and the pictures of unfallen sexual activity in [books] IV and VIII (500–
520). But he has made the unfallen already so voluptuous and kept
the fallen still so poetical that the contrast is not so sharp as it *ought
to have been*'.[33] Suffice it to say that intellectual history is best con-
ducted by examining what a poet such as Milton actually wrote (rather
than what he 'doubtless intended'), and that if he did not in fact por-
tray the contrast between pre- and postlapsarian sexuality in keeping
with Augustine's prescription or Lewis's expectations, then the difference is better examined and explained than merely explained away.

The problem transcends Milton's portrayal of unfallen sexuality.
Lewis also imposes on Milton the Augustinian assumption that Adam's
'mental powers ... surpassed those of the most brilliant philosopher
as much as the speed of a bird surpasses that of a tortoise'.[34] Yet, if
such were the case (Milton seems to have realized), how unaccount-
able would seem Adam's decision to disobey? Accordingly, in shaping
his narrative of the Fall, Milton portrays an unfallen Adam and Eve
who do indeed display elements of uncertainty and inexperience, even

childlikeness – qualities that Lewis explicitly states we must remove 'from our imaginations'.[35] Such an approach both underestimates the variety of views to be found within even mainstream Christian interpretation and creates problems for Milton's own project of justifying 'the ways of God to men'.[36] For Milton, more important than reproducing the abstract doctrines of Augustine is the requirement that the narrative of the Fall be coherent and that the motivations and deliberations of its two main characters be intelligible, even though tragically skewed.

THE MEDIEVAL MODEL

The Discarded Image, published posthumously in 1964, once again presents Lewis in the role he described for himself in '*De Descriptione Temporum*': that of a 'specimen'. The result is perhaps his most successful and accessible effort to give readers an inside glimpse, even a Diltheyan *Nacherlebnis*, of what it might have been like to think as a real inhabitant of the thought-world of the Middle Ages and Renaissance. This book, based on lectures Lewis had given to undergraduates, has the energy and sweep evident in some of his other intellectual-historical writing but without the sometimes distracting polemical edge. Here, he is an unabashed and in one sense hopeless lover of a world gone by, and most readers will find themselves charmed both by Lewis's open affection for it and by that world itself.

Lewis's deep immersion in ancient, medieval and Renaissance writings of all kinds enables him to weave a remarkable synthesis while acknowledging the almost wildly eclectic nature of thought in the European late Middle Ages and early modern period. He acknowledges the tensions, for example, between medieval cosmology and religion, recognizing (as many medievals seemed not to) that Aristotelian physics and Christian theology were no easy match.[37] Nonetheless, in *The Discarded Image*, his notable accomplishment as an intellectual historian is to offer a clear if simplified glimpse of the old worldview that bypasses and subverts the condescending stereotypes prevalent in popular history from the eighteenth century onward. For example, from Chalcidius (a fourth-century commentator on Plato) he illustrates the persistent understanding (one only emphasized, not invented, by Copernicus) that 'the Earth is infinitesimally small by cosmic standards', and from Alain de Lille (late twelfth century) the belief that the visible spatial order of the universe is a reversal of the spiritual, so that the central earth of medieval cosmology is, within the framework of deeper realities, marginal and 'merely suburban'. Thus, as Lewis memorably declares, the medieval model is not anthropocentric but 'anthropoperipheral'.[38] Does this picture comport with the teachings of Christianity, according to which divine incarnation and human redemption are anything but peripheral? It may not, Lewis concedes. And yet again, perhaps it may. For one 'may say that the Good Shepherd goes to seek the lost sheep because it is lost, not because it was the finest sheep in the flock. It may have been the least'.[39]

However, such sympathetic advocacy of the coherence of the model does not cause Lewis to defend its truth. Instead, he wants his audience to grasp its fascination and value as an object of thought: 'Other ages have not had a Model so universally accepted as [the medievals'], so imaginable, and so satisfying to the imagination.'[40] Again, then, Lewis functions as a 'native', a 'specimen', in order to present as vividly as possible a framework within which to understand the arts, especially literature. Yet, in his very use of the term 'model', he at the same time invites a critical awareness of the provisional and constructed nature of all systems of human thought, modern ones as well as medieval. Accordingly, it would be 'subtly misleading to say, "The medievals thought the universe to be like that, but we know it to be like this". Part of what we now know is that we cannot, in the old sense, "know what the universe is like" and that no model we can build will be, in that old sense, "like" it'.[41] But these, for Lewis, are counsels of humility, not scepticism or despair. His conclusions might be called, to echo the great medieval philosopher Nicolaus Cusanus, exercises in *docta ignorantia*, learned ignorance, entailing a deep enough understanding of human knowledge that the knower refuses to idolize or absolutize the knowledge.

In this sense, for all its gentleness, *The Discarded Image* too – like the other works considered in this chapter – serves as not only an imaginative support and stimulant for readers of medieval and Renaissance literature but also a general caution against the potentially stifling smugness of modernism, or what Lewis memorably dubbed 'chronological snobbery'.[42] In an age that increasingly values the kind of interdisciplinary work that he unostentatiously embodied, Lewis merits a more careful hearing than ever before – for both the imaginative and critical sides of his impressive endeavour. Even if he did not call it intellectual history, his contribution as an historian of ideas deserves high recognition along with other, better-known aspects of his extraordinary œuvre.

Notes

1 Wilhelm Dilthey, 'Plan der Fortsetzung zum Aufbau der geschichtlichen Welt in den Geisteswissenschaften', in *Gesammelte Schriften*, VII (Stuttgart: Teubner, 1958), 215–16.
2 DI 14.
3 Reprinted SLE 1–14.
4 SLE 1.
5 SLE 5.
6 SLE 5.
7 SLE 10.
8 SLE 13.
9 EL 1–65.
10 EL 1.
11 EL 2.
12 EL 2.
13 The author was Theophylactus Simocatta. On Copernicus's translation of his *Letters*, see Edward Rosen (ed.), *Nicholas Copernicus: Minor Works* (Baltimore and London: Johns Hopkins University Press, 1992), 19–24.
14 EL 11.
15 EL 13.
16 EL 14.
17 EL 14.
18 EL 25.
19 EL 30.
20 EL 31.
21 EL 32.
22 EL 34.
23 EL 37.
24 EL 42–43.
25 EL 43.
26 EL 46.
27 EL 49–50.
28 PPL p. v.
29 PPL 129.
30 PPL 126.
31 PPL 64.
32 PPL 65.
33 PPL 68–69, emphasis added.
34 PPL 113.
35 PPL 114.
36 See for example N.P. Williams, *The Ideas of the Fall and of Original Sin* (London: Longmans, Green, 1927), *passim* and Dennis Danielson, *Milton's Good God: A Study in Literary Theodicy* (Cambridge: Cambridge University Press, 1982), ch. 6.
37 For example, Aristotle's teaching concerning the eternity of the world seems inconsistent with the Christian doctrine of creation

out of nothing. For further examples related to the much-debated 'Condemnation of 1277', see Edward Grant, *A History of Natural Philosophy* (Cambridge: Cambridge University Press, 2007), 202–11.

38 DI 54–58.
39 DI 120.
40 DI 203.
41 DI 218.
42 'The uncritical acceptance of the intellectual climate common to our own age and the assumption that whatever has gone out of date is on that account discredited': SBJ 167.

5 Classicist

MARK EDWARDS

Classics is the study of Greek and Latin and of the literature that was written in those languages before Christianity won its ascendancy in the Roman Empire. Up to the time of Lewis's death in 1963 (and for some years after) instruction in Latin at least was mandatory in public schools.[1] As these were the schools that fed the universities in Lewis's time, it was seldom possible and never prudent to go up to Oxford or Cambridge without some competence in the pagan tongues. Lewis, as we shall see, acquired more than a mere competence in Classics before he was admitted to University College, Oxford in 1917.

The majority of colleges at Oxford and Cambridge had been founded when Latin was still the common dialect of philosophers, theologians and scientists in the great European nations; after the Reformation of the sixteenth century, Greek was considered a necessary acquirement for every minister of the gospel in the established Church of England. By the end of the nineteenth century, the more compelling arguments for the study of the classics were pedagogic and plutocratic. The pedagogic argument maintained (and not without cogency) that a knowledge of the great poets of Greece and Rome was an indispensable preparation for the study of English literature, that the ancient canon furnished a more enduring standard of excellence than any modern vernacular, and that the practice of translating into a language that did not admit of word-for-word conversion forced the student to reflect upon his own meaning and to prune his thoughts of verbiage.[2] The very fact that the ancient gods were dead could be turned to advantage, as it permitted one to canvass the political and metaphysical theories of their devotees with a freedom and detachment that could not be sustained in living controversies. For the plutocrat, on the other hand, the pursuit of this manifestly useless discipline was a testimony to one's membership of a class which could afford to maintain its children in idleness throughout adolescence. There was profit as well as pride in such display, for in all societies those most likely to obtain lucrative employment are those who have learned to use both leisure and wealth with dignity. Sly contemporaries of Lewis noted that, while teachers might propound unworldly reasons for the perpetuation of classical studies, pupils (or their parents) were more likely to be enticed by the 'positions of considerable emolument'[3] that accrued to this venerable expertise.[4]

It cannot be said that Lewis's education in the literature of Greece and Rome either formed his tastes or circumscribed his judgement. Yet he came to feel that, by virtue of this schooling, he was the child of an epoch other than the one to which the majority of his contemporaries belonged. At the same time, his transition from Classics to English and his espousal of Christianity estranged him from custodians of the older tradition in Oxford, the majority of whom regarded English as a spare-time study and Christianity as a school of barbarism. Having been both unbeliever and churchman, having mastered both the classical and the vernacular, Lewis was uniquely placed to see that the Christian empires which succeeded Rome had added new classics to the Latin language, and conversely that many a work of the Middle Ages or the Renaissance owes its durability to a pagan residue. It was not the decrepitude of ancient literature, but the waning of our power to appreciate it, that he lamented when he said of himself in a famous lecture, 'There are not going to be many more dinosaurs'.[5]

LEWIS'S READING IN THE CLASSICS

At his first school, where he never 'got in sight of a Roman author',[6] Lewis none the less spent two years, from 1908 to 1910, in the composition of Latin exercises. At Malvern College he was touched by the *Odes* of Horace, the fourth book of the *Aeneid* and the *Bacchae* of Euripides, but continued to think the gods of Greece insipid by comparison with those of northern Europe.[7] Under the private tuition of the retired headmaster William Kirkpatrick, he learned to think in Greek and his teacher pronounced Lewis 'the most brilliant translator of Greek plays I have ever met'.[8] During childhood he had made the acquaintance of the *Iliad* and the *Odyssey* in translation, and when he embarked on the study of Homer in Greek he professed to 'worship' him.[9] He read the two great historians Thucydides and Herodotus, the former only to please Kirkpatrick,[10] the latter with genuine delight.[11] At an early age he was familiar with the best orators in both languages, whom he regarded as 'great bores'.[12] In adult life it was the philosophers who engaged him most, and as a tutor he read Plato and Aristotle with eminent classical scholars such as W.R.F. Hardie and J.A. Smith,

his Magdalen colleagues.[13] Having made a conscious resolution to read
Aristotle's *Politics*,[14] he completed the task alone, and carried away a
distinction between servility and obedience in freedom which he used
to explain Paul's teaching on the relation of man and wife.[15] On the
other hand, having once subscribed to Aristotle's doctrine that the
object of work is to make us fit for leisure, he came to regard this as
an excuse for indolence.[16] In one of his few unsolicited observations on
Homer, Lewis ranks the *Odyssey* with *The Worm Ouroboros* and *The
Lord of the Rings*, together with the works of the Irish poets Yeats and
Stephens, as a specimen of imagination healthily exercised and free of
artificial sentiment.[17] The admission of the work to this circle of latter-
day romantics shows that Lewis prized it chiefly for its fantastic elements, and that he derived that evergreen pleasure from the perusal of it
which he took to be the surest mark of greatness in literature. There is
nothing else in his letters, however, to indicate that he took it up as frequently as he took up his English favourites, and he nowhere confesses
to reading it with the passion that was excited in him by the study of
ancient Norse.

CLASSICAL AUTHORS IN LEWIS'S CRITICISM

The study of medieval and Renaissance literature introduces one
to a different canon of classical literature. It was in Cicero's *Dream
of Scipio*, in Lucan, Statius and Apuleius, that Lewis saw the founda-
tions of the medieval superstructure – the 'Model' – which he delineated in *The Discarded Image*. In handling works that he might have
neglected to read but for his conversion, Lewis tends to accentuate
those points which, in his apologetic writings, he could summon to
the defence of the Church against charges of ignorance and parochial-
ism. Thus we are told that the Middle Ages learned from Lucan and
Cicero that the Antipodes are peopled[18] (which implies, of course,
that the world is a sphere) and that, far from putting this planet and
its denizens at the centre of God's purposes, the geocentric theory
makes the Earth inferior to the moving stars in position, magnitude
and purity of matter.[19] Lewis maintains that only Christianity could
give rise to a vivid personification of Nature, who achieves no more
than a silhouette of womanhood in Statius and his forebears:[20] some
remarks on the figure of Wisdom in scripture would be in order here,
and also of the eloquence which Nature achieves in the *Enneads*
of Plotinus, the Roman Platonist.[21] This chapter of *The Discarded
Image* also illustrates the ubiquity of the ban on suicide in pagan and

Christian moralizing;[22] to Lewis this was no anachronism, nor did he think that modern thought had necessarily invalidated even the teaching of Apuleius on the constitution of intermediate spirits.[23] In *The Screwtape Letters* he warns that it is as perilous to deny the existence of these airy neighbours as it is to take an unhealthily excessive interest in them.[24]

The first author whom Lewis allots to the 'seminal period' of antiquity is Chalcidius, a mediocre philosopher of the fourth century, whose commentary on the *Timaeus* of Plato often displaced the original in medieval libraries.[25] This is followed by Macrobius's commentary on the *Dream of Scipio*, a work of similar date and calibre, which traces each kind of vision to its origin.[26] Pseudo-Dionysius (*c.* 500) is the one undoubted Christian of this epoch: after noting the ubiquity of the Triad in the most fecund of his works, the *Celestial Hierarchy*, Lewis complains of the 'degradation' of angels after Milton.[27] He reserves his longest paraphrase for the five books of the *Consolation of Philosophy*, traditionally ascribed to the Christian senator Boethius. This exhortation to singleness of heart amid vicissitude, with its masterly excursus on the relation of time to eternity, was described by Edward Gibbon as a 'golden volume';[28] Lewis endorsed the eulogy,[29] but there is no echo of it in his correspondence. The classical texts that he took from his study to the fireside were in general those that every schoolboy was supposed to know.

To judge by his frequent use of ancient touchstones in his essays, Lewis never perceived that the reader of modern literature is likely to have been an indifferent student of the classics. He was scandalized (as Classicists still are) by the inability of native-speaking students of English literature to master the rules of prosody in their own language.[30] After the trial of *Lady Chatterley's Lover*, he produced a catena of passages from Greek and Latin authors (without translating the rare vocabulary) to show that their Muses countenanced only a comic or satirical use of the scatological terms to which Lawrence tried to give a more elevated function.[31] He rebukes the 'provincialism' of critics who fail to see that tropes in Shelley which they trace to Godwin are anticipated in Plato, Aeschylus and Aristotle.[32] Ovid (seldom praised by Lewis, but quarried more often than any author but Cicero and Horace in *Studies in Words*) is mentioned without an introductory notice in an essay on the models of Chaucer's *Troilus and Criseyde*, though short glosses are provided for Sidonius Apollinaris, Ennodius and Venantius Fortunatus.[33] Even occasional pieces are coloured by his erudition: thus the Herodotean jibe at the end of 'Xmas and Christmas' delights the

Classicists but will baffle many a reader who has hitherto been conscious of humour, but not of parody.[34]

When he has to expound a simile from Dante, he assumes (conventionally, though not inevitably) that Homer is the exemplar of the 'primeval' style in epic, and Virgil 'imitation for the sake of imitation'.[35] Homer, he explains, pursues the details of a simile for his own pleasure, whereas Virgil in developing his takes care that every detail which does not reveal similarity should accentuate the unlikeness in the comparison. There was nothing novel in this, but in *A Preface to Paradise Lost* he reforms the terms of the antithesis, pronouncing Homer primary rather than natural, and Virgil secondary not through excess of art, but on account of a natural shift in sensibility.[36] The Greeks, says Lewis, inaccurately,[37] were content to record one great affair, were indifferent to chronology and never traced the fortunes of a city back to its origins. The Romans, on the other hand – and this is true enough – were always looking beyond the past to the primordial, and their epic poets therefore faced the 'problem' (as Lewis styles it) of combining Homer's unity of vision with the long perspective of a chronicle. Virgil's solution was to hold present and past in counterpoint throughout the poem: Aeneas is at once the Trojan fugitive and the founder of Rome, uniting in one soul the gains and losses of his descendants and the tribulation of all humanity. If he seems to lack the unreflective and three-dimensional vigour of Achilles, that is not because Virgil is the weaker spirit: it is because, whereas Achilles is a boy who lives for himself alone, Aeneas is a man who leads other men to their ineluctable destiny.[38] If we substitute Adam and Satan for Aeneas and Achilles, we have an answer to those who argue that the devil is the true hero of *Paradise Lost*.

To study the universal in the particular is not the same thing as allegory, which Lewis defines in *The Allegory of Love* as a reification of the abstract, less congenial to the classical and the modern reader alike than symbolism, which ennobles or enriches the common ingredients of our own world.[39] The book is by no means a consistent vindication of allegory, and even palliatives are in short supply in Lewis's chapter on its classical antecedents. Prudentius, a Christian poet of the fourth century, built one of his three short epics, the *Psychomachia*, round a battle between the vices and the virtues for dominion in the soul. Few conceits have proved more fertile, but in Lewis's view Prudentius is a feeble poet who happened to be the first to do what would have been done in any case.[40] His work is marred by his failure to honour the logic of his own allegory: his combatants do not gain in integrity what they lose in animation, while his virtues, even the meekest, are as bellicose as their adversaries, and no less given to taunting. The infelicities of the Christian poet are no more original than his few merits, for the 'drift' began with the epic poet Statius in the first century AD[41] and the 'decline of mythology into allegory' can be observed in the panegyrics of Claudian, a pagan of the same epoch.[42] Lewis writes more briefly, though no less caustically, on authors after Prudentius who at best created models for the later 'allegorist'.[43] At the same time, the exsanguination of the Homeric gods in late antiquity is not wholly to be lamented: it was the by-product of a maturing in the theology of the Roman world, a universal acknowledgement that nothing but God is god. A Christian can praise with fervour only the sublimity, the solitude, the immutable serenity of the divine; a single passage in Homer and another in the 'atheist' Lucretius were, by Lewis's reckoning, all that survived to show that classical poetry could accommodate this loftier metaphysic.[44]

LEWIS ON MYTH

An Experiment in Criticism includes a chapter on myth as a perennial form whose ability to move the reader or hearer is independent of its literary garb. Aristotle's paraphrase of the *Odyssey* is juxtaposed with a skeletal account of the story of Orpheus and Eurydice, composed, according to Lewis, in the 'first words that come to hand'. The first he pronounces too jejune to move us without some further contrivance on the part of the author; the second, by contrast, loses none of its potency in synopsis, because it elicits sorrow, not for the tribulations of any one character but for the human condition at large.[45] It is typical of myths, he adds, to be solemn and fantastic, to awaken awe and to shun such characteristic tools of the novelist as suspense and surprise. The genre appears to be one in which the Greeks excelled, for they furnish four of Lewis's seven examples on a single page,[46] and on the next page the six digests named as possible mediators of 'the same myth' are all compiled from classical sources. Lewis's judgements here are so peremptory as to savour of polemic. The first surviving version of the tragedy of Orpheus is an episode in the fourth book of Virgil's *Georgics*: had this not been an incomparable masterpiece, we cannot be sure that others would have thought the tale worth retelling. In Virgil's time (*c.* 30 BC) two accounts of the adventure were current, only one of which demonstrably ends with the loss of Eurydice.[47] It is possible, therefore, that the ending in Virgil's narrative would have surprised the first readers; the *Odyssey*, on the other hand, eschews suspense, as the victory of the hero is prefigured by numerous omens. Nor is it clear to all scholars that Odysseus is a less mythical figure than Orpheus: ancient philosophers construed his wanderings as a parable of the good soul's peregrinations on Earth, while Robert Graves, whose *Greek Myths* is among the anthologies cited by Lewis, puts Homeric matter cheek by jowl with tales that never found a literary patron.[48]

Plato would have contested Lewis's view that the greatness of the Homeric narratives lies in the execution rather than in the bare content: in the *Republic* Socrates inveighs against the mimetic style in tragedy and epic, and sets out to prune the *Iliad* of its vices by the substitution of spare, third-person narrative.[49] There can be little doubt that Lewis is also drawing a bow against Freud when he omits the story of Oedipus from his catalogue of myth and goes on to deny in a subsequent chapter that it is even a probable fiction. He explains in an appendix that 'it is not a story simply about a man who married his mother, but about a man cruelly destined to marry his mother, unknowingly and unwillingly, in a society where such marriages were regarded as abominable'.[50] Now this is in fact the premise of Freud's argument that Oedipus personifies desires which, because they are dangerous but universal, are universally forced into the subconscious. If Lewis had granted this – and one could argue that the sphinx and Freud are only stating the doctrine of original sin in another guise – he would have been forced to admit that Oedipus owes his notoriety not so much to the art of Sophocles but to the trepidation inspired in all spectators by his unintended crimes. At the same time, whatever it lacks in cogency, his discussion of this topic in *An Experiment in Criticism* reveals his erudition, for the passage which he cites from Apollodorus to show that marriages between close kin were believed by the Greeks to be lawful in some societies[51] is not one that a typical student of Classics at Oxford would have encountered, even in the successful pursuit of a First.

CREATIVE USE OF CLASSICAL THEMES

Lewis composed a number of poems on classical subjects, most of them imitative, none of them servile or untouched by his prepossessions as a critic and a Christian. 'After Aristotle'[52] is an extended paraphrase of a poem ascribed to the great philosopher, the first line of which is quoted in *Till We Have Faces* as Orual remembers her lessons in literature with the Fox. 'Pindar Sang'[53] is a skein of passages translated from the greatest lyric poet of antiquity: since snatches of different works are interwoven where they narrate the same episode or express the same sentiment, it is difficult to separate the original from Lewis's own pastiche.

In 'A Cliché Came Out of Its Cage',[54] Lewis wonders archly whether the resurrection of paganism that some of his contemporaries foretold would take the form of a Nordic Götterdammerung or a Greek submission to the invisible stewards of cosmic order. Two of these stewards, Athene and Demeter, are contrasted in 'Reason'[55] as maid and mother, one representing the heaven-born power of intellect, one the visceral imagination: only when these rivals are at one can the poet 'wholly say, that I BELIEVE'. In ancient philosophy Venus or Aphrodite embodies the universal principle of love which draws the elements together and quickens the procreative capacity in animals: this sublimated myth and the opening chapter of Genesis coalesce in Lewis's 'Le Roi S'Amuse',[56] where the rising of this goddess from the deep is followed by that of 'stern Athene' with a train of fabulous creatures. In making contemplation and laughter the instruments of creation, Lewis mingles one of Plato's best-known texts with the esoteric philosophy of the ancients. The treacherous fecundity of imagination appears to be the theme of 'Vitrea Circe',[57] in which the sorceress who was said to have turned Greek mariners into animals protests that she enthralled them only by remaining innocent of their passions, until she in turn succumbed to the resolute passion of Odysseus. The nameless hero of 'The Landing'[58] follows the Odysseus of Dante and Tennyson to the west, though it transpires that the 'true and utter west' lies beyond the painted anchorage that they at first mistake for Eden. It may be that they forget that the world is round; it may be that the vision of Joy will always mock our powers of approximation on this Earth.

Lewis's first extensive work of fiction, *The Pilgrim's Regress*, is his valediction to pagan thought and literature. Each of its ten books is introduced by a page of epigraphs. The first of them all is a testimony from Plato, to the soul's inkling of an unseen beatitude.[59] The second of three mottoes to the second book is a passage in which Plato (or his imitator) laments the soul's incapacity to discover an object worthy of her longing.[60] Lewis adds in a footnote, truly enough, that many deny the ascription of the text to Plato; whether or not it is genuine, this text, like its predecessor, exemplifies what Lewis called the Romantic strain in Greek philosophy. The first epigraph to book 3 is an obituary on virtue from Thucydides.[61] Pindar and Aeschylus warn us against false paths at the beginning of book 5.[62] Book 6 commences with Aristotle's strictures on those who fail to imitate the *megalopsychos*, or great-souled man, who embodies the highest order of practical virtue.[63] Book 7 has a longer preface: an extract from the *Aeneid*, in which the crew of Aeneas are tempted to burn their boats and put an end to their labours even if this entails the renunciation of a higher destiny.[64] The last ancient tag, on the threshold of book 8, is a counsel of prudence from the *Works and Days* of Hesiod, a didactic poet contemporary with Homer.[65] In this sequence, lofty unease gives way to spurious virtue, then to sloth, and the end of all is an acquiescence in conventional wisdom. As the protagonist arrives bodily at the goal that Plato had glimpsed through the refracting lens of myth, a final quotation from him supplies the first epigraph to book 10: it describes, however, not the illumination of the philosopher but the mockery which he suffers on returning to common affairs.[66] The use of Latin chapter headings throughout the book suggests that Lewis did not wish Classics to lose its cardinal place in the education and esteem of the reading public; at the same time the majority of these rubrics are derived from Christian rather than classical sources, as though to intimate that, as Virgil could lead Dante out of hell but not to heaven, so a classical schooling cannot play more than a propaedeutic or ancillary role in the consummation of the soul's quest for God. The one character whose speech is peppered with Latin aphorisms (also the only one to speak Greek) is Mr Sensible, whose philosophy is discovered to be 'parasitic' and 'precarious'.[67] When, close to the end, the pilgrim skirts the land of Pagus, he learns that its inhabitants have perished because they went on trying to reproduce the pictures that they ought to have used as signposts, and allowed desire to wither into lust.[68]

Greek and Roman myths are seldom harvested in the Chronicles of Narnia, though the country teems with naiads, fauns and satyrs. Bacchus, the god of wine, and his acolyte Silenus join the carnival of misrule that follows the victory of the hero in *Prince Caspian*.[69] The bather who turns to gold in *The Voyage of the 'Dawn Treader'* has inverted the fate of Midas.[70] The ass dressed as a lion in *The Last Battle* is enacting a fable from Aesop, while the murder of a dryad recalls an episode from Ovid.[71] The Professor's expostulation in the same book – 'It's all in Plato! All in Plato: bless me, what do they teach them at these schools?' – alludes to a passage in Plato which foretells the translation of souls after death to a world in which all that is best in ours persists except that the lines are bolder and the colours more intense.[72]

Classical motifs are equally rare in Lewis's science fiction, with the exception of one short story in which a visitor to a strange planet finds no life but a landscape strewn with petrified figures. Too late he becomes aware of a feminine presence, which the reader is left to identify as the Medusa from the final sentence, when 'his eyes met hers'.[73] Rider Haggard and Andrew Lang, Euripides and Rupert Brooke are the sponsors of another tale, 'Ten Years After', which recounts the tribulations of Menelaus after the fall of Troy has reunited him with his ageing wife.[74]

LEWIS AND APULEIUS

Lewis's one sustained adaptation of a classical prototype is *Till We Have Faces*. The source is not a myth (as Lewis defined that term) but a literary fable which the Latin sophist Apuleius embeds in his picaresque novel, *The Golden Ass*. While Lewis names this work among the masterpieces of fantasy in *An Experiment in Criticism*,[75] he will also have met the tale of Cupid and Psyche as a poem in William Morris's *Earthly Paradise*, a chapter in Walter Pater's novel *Marius the Epicurean*, and a *tour de force* of versification, *Eros and Psyche*, divided into twelve cantos and 365 stanzas by Robert Bridges, sometime laureate and a favourite of the young Lewis.[76] None of these interpretations had unlocked the hidden sense of the original, which can be summarized as follows. Psyche (whose name means 'soul') is, for Apuleius, an earthly counterfeit of Venus, the goddess of beauty and love; it is when the world begins to confuse the mortal image with its heavenly archetype that Venus commissions her own son Cupid, or Love, to procure the death of the impostor. The enamoured god, however, takes her secretly to his own abode and becomes her lover, dissembling both his face and his identity. When Psyche's wicked sisters learn of her happiness, they persuade her that her paramour is a monster, and she resolves to take him by surprise at night. Overwhelmed by his beauty she wakes him inadvertently, whereupon she is driven forth and falls at once under the dominion of Venus. Miraculous aid enables her to perform a series of tasks above her strength, and when at last she is reconciled to her persecutor, the birth of her child Voluptas (Pleasure) cements her marriage with Cupid.

In the original, Venus perhaps represents the inexorability of natural law, to which the soul is subject during periods of embodiment; Cupid stands for the beauty of the supercelestial realm (as Plato styles it[77]) from which erring souls descend and to which they are not allowed to return until they have suffered the appointed term of exile. To grasp prematurely at beauty is to incur a second fall, after which the soul will experience discipline as bondage, nature as fate. In this account, the soul saves herself; in Lewis's revision it is Orual, the ugly sister of Psyche, who expiates her crime. In the second half of the book she becomes a queen but hides her features under a veil, which causes some to credit her with an ineffable beauty. Cupid in the original is taken for a monster because he concealed his divinity; Orual, who in Lewis's story failed to see the palace that was visible to Psyche, is doomed to see but go unseen. As Psyche means 'soul', one might interpret Orual as an emblem of the body, which occludes the soul's perceptions and tempts her to fall but delivers her by bearing the tribulation that accrues from her captivity in this world.

CONCLUDING OBSERVATIONS

Is Lewis's Christianity 'all in Plato'?[78] Lewis seems to grant Plato an intimation of the joy beyond love, of the numinous beyond what we now call knowing. We have seen, on the other hand, that in his critical works Lewis denies this incipient vision to the majority of the ancients, that in his letters he extols their guidance only in mundane affairs, and that his judgement on the pagan world – allegorically expressed in *The Pilgrim's Regress*, and symbolically in *Till We Have Faces* – is that, because it lingered in a perpetual adolescence, it was bound to die at last of that which nourished it. The Fathers of the Church believed that the cross marks an indelible caesura in human history; all the more curious, then, that Lewis barely grants Augustine a passing mention in *The Discarded Image*,[79] that in his preface to a translation of Athanasius he confesses a meagre knowledge of Christian Greek,[80] and that the medieval Christians whom he cites in Latin are commonly philosophers and poets, not divines. It is almost as though he believed that there had been no Pentecost for the pagan languages, that (in contrast to the vernaculars that succeeded them) they were destined to remain what Homer, Plato and Virgil had made them under the prompting of the Spirit – vessels of clarity but not instruments of light.

Notes

1   'Public schools', in Lewis's time as today, were in large part the cocoons of the male professional class, though the majority of their students are financed by private means. Both 'public schools' and 'private schools' are part of what, in the United Kingdom, is known as the 'independent sector' in education, as opposed to the 'state sector', the latter being funded by the government through the tax system.

2   See further E.C. Mack, *British Schools and Public Opinion 1780–1860* (New York: Columbia University Press, 1939), 172–79.

3   Attributed to Dean Thomas Gaisford of Christ Church and quoted in William Tuckwell, *Reminiscences of Oxford*, 2nd edn (London: Smith, Elder, 1907), 271.

4   See A.N. Whitehead, *The Aims of Education* (1929, repr. London: Benn, 1962), 94.

5 'De Descriptione Temporum', SLE 14.
6 SBJ 26.
7 SBJ 93.
8 TST 158 n. 1.
9 Letter to Arthur Greeves, 12 Oct. 1915 (CLI 145).
10 Letter to Arthur Greeves, 12 Oct. 1915 (CLI 145).
11 Letters to Arthur Greeves, 28 Feb. 1917 (CLI 284), 27 June 1920 (CLI 498).
12 SBJ 114–18 (on Cicero and Demosthenes).
13 AMR *passim*.
14 Letter to Arthur Greeves, 22 June 1930 (CLI 909).
15 Letter to Mary Neylan, 18 Apr. 1940 (CLII 395), referring to Aristotle, *Politics* 1259a–1260a and 1 Corinthians 11.
16 Letter to Dom Bede Griffiths, 16 July 1940 (CLII 422).
17 Letter to Jane Gaskell, 2 Sept. 1957 (CLIII 881).
18 DI 28, 31, citing Cicero, *Somnium* 20; Lucan, *Pharsalia* 9.877; Dante, *Convivio* 3.5.12.
19 DI 24–25, 32–34.
20 DI 37–39.
21 *Enneads* 3.8.4, overlooked at SIW 38.
22 DI 25.
23 DI 42–44.
24 SL 9.
25 DI 49–60.
26 DI 60–65.
27 DI 75.
28 Edward Gibbon, *The History of the Decline and Fall of the Roman Empire*, ed. J.B. Bury (London: Methuen, 1896–1900), IV, 201.
29 DI 90.
30 'Metre', SLE 285.
31 'Four-Letter Words', SLE 169–74.
32 'Shelley, Dryden and Mr Eliot', SLE 195, citing Aristotle, *Nicomachean Ethics* 1169a.
33 'What Chaucer Really Did to *Il Filostrato*', SLE 38–39.
34 'Xmas and Christmas', EC 735–37.
35 'Dante's Similes', SMRL 64–66.
36 PPL 20–51.
37 He overlooks Polybius, Dionysius of Halicarnassus, and a clutch of lesser writers.
38 PPL 37–8.
39 AOL 45–46, conscripting Plato's theory of forms as the first example of symbolism. Lewis is discreetly making common cause with Plato against the poets throughout this chapter.
40 AOL 67.
41 AOL 48–56, still one of the most illuminating criticisms of Statius in English, as well as one of the first.
42 AOL 74–76.
43 AOL 85 (on Fulgentius).

44   AOL 83, quoting Homer, *Odyssey* 6.41ff. and Lucretius, *De rerum natura* 3.18; cf. 6.68–70.
45   EIC 40–44.
46   EIC 42.
47   Virgil, *Georgics* 4.453–527; Plato, *Symposium* 179b–c; Euripides, *Alcestis* 357.
48   Robert Graves, *The Greek Myths* (Harmondsworth: Penguin, 1955).
49   Plato, *Republic* 393c–394a.
50   EIC 142.
51   EIC 162, citing Apollodorus, *Bibliotheca*, ed. and tr. J.G. Frazer (London: W. Heinemann, 1921) II, 373–74.
52   CP 94.
53   CP 29.
54   CP 17.
55   CP 95.
56   CP 37.
57   CP 39, more pungent than the early and Keats-like 'Circe: A Fragment', CP 241.
58   CP 41.
59   PR 27.
60   PR 45, quoting Plato, [Letter] 2, 312e–313a.
61   PR 63, quoting Thucydides, *Peloponnesian War* 3.83.
62   PR 96, quoting Pindar, *Pythian* 10.29–30 and [Aeschylus,] *Prometheus* 545–48.
63   PR 121, quoting Aristotle, *Nicomachean Ethics* 1124b.
64   PR 143, quoting Virgil, *Aeneid* 5.626–35.
65   PR 173, freely rendering Hesiod, *Works and Days* 293–97.
66   PR 221, quoting Plato, *Republic* 516e–517a.
67   PR 109, 112, 113, 115, 120.
68   PR 195–99; cf. Plato, *Republic* 517c, 596d–597a.
69   PC 169–74; cf. 136–38.
70   VDT 98–100; cf. Ovid, *Metamorphoses* 11.142–43.
71   LB 21; cf. Ovid, *Metamorphoses* 8.770–76.
72   LB 160; cf. Plato, *Phaedo* 110b–c.
73   'Forms of Things Unknown', EC 881–88.
74   'After Ten Years', EC 864–81; cf. Euripides, *Helen*; H. Rider Haggard and Andrew Lang, *The World's Desire* (London: Longmans, Green, 1890); Rupert Brooke, 'Menelaus and Helen', in *Collected Poems* (London: 1916), 79–80.
75   EIC 50.
76   William Morris, *The Earthly Paradise: May* (London: n.p., 1868); Walter Pater, *Marius the Epicurean* (London: n.p., 1865), ch. 5; Robert Bridges, *Eros and Psyche* (London: George Bell and Sons, 1885).
77   *Phaedrus* 247c; cf. also *Symposium* 180d–181c on the two forms of Aphrodite or Venus, heavenly and pandemic.
78   A question pursued by Andrew Walker in 'Scripture, Revelation and Platonism in C.S. Lewis', *Scottish Journal of Theology* 55 (2002), 19–35.

79 DI 49, 50, 107 n., 121 n., 155–56, 168, 175. He read *The City of God* in 1937 (letter to Arthur Greeves, 28 Mar. 1937, CLII 214), and discusses the relation between Augustine and Milton in PPL 66–72.

80 Preface to *St Athanasius On the Incarnation of the Word of God*, repr. as 'On the Reading of Old Books', EC 443. He read the Greek in 1942 (letter to Sister Penelope, 29 July 1942, CLII 526).

Part II

Thinker

6 On scripture

KEVIN J. VANHOOZER

Tolle, lege! ('Take up and read!'). These overheard sing-song words prompted Augustine to take up and read Romans 13.13, a lectionary event that led to his conversion to Christianity.[1] The differences and similarities between Augustine and C.S. Lewis, both avid readers who came to faith in Jesus Christ as adults, are many and striking. As regards similarities, both were well acquainted with the pagan philosophical options of their day; both were skilled in the art of ancient rhetoric, though neither knew Hebrew; both initially regarded the style of biblical texts to be somewhat lowbrow and unseemly. As regards differences, one contrast will have to suffice: whereas Augustine felt compelled to repudiate as false the Manichaean gnostic myths in which he used to believe, Lewis's conversion led him to recognize the biblical story of Jesus as 'myth become fact'. This phrase has puzzled both critics and admirers as to its implications for his view of scripture. It also places Evangelicals, perhaps the group most responsible for Lewis's popularity, in something of a quandary when it comes to scripture, for Evangelicals warm to 'fact' but sound the alarm over 'myth'.[2]

Lewis was not terribly troubled over his Evangelical credentials or lack thereof. He was neither a biblical scholar nor professional theologian but a 'mere Christian' and scholar of medieval and Renaissance English literature. He was a person of 'books' before he became a person of 'the book'.[3] While others may trace how his profession of faith shaped his professional work, the present essay sets out in the opposite direction, enquiring how Lewis the reader and scholar approached the literature of the Bible. It is difficult to extract a 'doctrine' of scripture from Lewis's occasional writings, for Lewis was less interested in critical approaches to, or doctrines of, scripture than he was in the realities about which scripture speaks.

A reader once wrote a letter to Lewis explaining her reservations about the Virgin Birth, doubts confirmed by some members of the clergy who were under the influence of a certain strand of biblical criticism. His response serves as a fitting introduction to the present chapter: '*Your* starting point about this doctrine will not, I think, be to collect the opinions of individual clergymen, but to read Matthew Chap. I and Luke I and II.'[4] Lewis did not intend by this to denigrate church tradition; elsewhere he accords it the highest respect. Yet he considered the matter of Christian faith too important to be left to the clergy, or the theologians. Rather, the Bible itself, read in the right spirit, is a form of holy and imaginative reasoning that orients and speeds pilgrims on their way.

BETWEEN FUNDAMENTALISM AND MODERN BIBLICAL CRITICISM

Lewis acknowledged the Bible as more than literature, but not less. As with all literature, the purpose of the Bible is not to call attention to its own originality but to embody a truth, goodness and beauty from elsewhere. Lewis was quick to distance himself from fundamentalists and modern biblical critics alike, for neither came to scripture with ears to hear what God was saying through biblical literature and myth.

Lewis has no scruples about calling either the fall of Adam or the story of Job or of Jonah 'myth': 'a particular kind of story which has a value in itself – a value independent of its embodiment in any literary work'.[5] Myths are therefore 'extra-literary' – storied accounts 'of what *may have been* the historical fact'.[6] They are addressed primarily to the imagination rather than the intellect and mediate, in Cunningham's words, 'an immediate nonconceptual apprehension of reality'.[7] Not just any story can take on mythic proportions, only those that make us feel 'as if something of great moment had been communicated to us'.[8] Lewis had a lifelong love affair with myth: 'I have the deepest respect even for Pagan myths, still more for myths in Holy Scripture.'[9] Indeed, his conversion coincided with his coming to believe that the story of Jesus Christ was *true* myth: myth made fact.[10]

Lewis's view of scripture is inseparable from his view of myth. Christians must 'both assent to the historical fact and also receive the myth (fact though it has become) with the same imaginative embrace which we accord to all myths'.[11] He therefore distinguished himself from fundamentalists, who lose the 'myth' (imagination), and from modern biblical critics, who eliminate the 'became fact' (history).[12] He takes aim at the latter in a 1959 essay, written in the heyday of demythologizing, where he archly comments that no matter what modern liberal theologians may be as biblical scholars, they are no *critics*: 'They seem to me to lack literary judgment, to be imperceptive about the very quality of the texts they are reading.'[13] They claim to see fern-seed but miss the elephant in the room of the text. Rudolf Bultmann, for example, claims that the New Testament is indifferent to the personality of Jesus even though the Jesus 'of peasant shrewdness, intolerable severity, and irresistible tenderness'[14] stands out from all the other characters in Western literature. One need not be a professional biblical critic, merely a literary historian, to know that the Gospels do not read like legends.

Lewis objects to the biblical critics' chronological snobbery – the implicit assumption behind every new theory that all previous interpreters got it wrong – and to their presupposition that miracles do not and cannot happen: 'the rejection as unhistorical of all passages which narrate miracles is sensible if we start by knowing the miraculous in general never occurs'.[15] He goes for the critical jugular by demonstrating the high improbability of source- and form-critical attempts to reconstruct the genesis of the texts under investigation. His scepticism concerning such critical reconstructions was fuelled by the repeated experience of having critics in his own time fail so badly to discover the composition history of his own writings: 'These critics ... have every advantage which modern scholars lack in dealing with Scripture ... In spite of this, when they tell us how the books were written they are all wildly wrong! After that, what chance can there be that any modern scholar can determine how Isaiah or the Fourth Gospel ... came into existence? ... They don't know the *smell*, as a real critic does, the difference in myth, in legend, and a bit of primitive reportage.'[16] The critics are looking *at* but not *along* the texts, to turn a Lewisian phrase.[17] We can respect their learning perhaps, but not their judgement.[18]

Lewis could do neither, however, as concerns fundamentalists, and towards the end of his essay he states matter-of-factly, 'We are not fundamentalists.'[19] He recognizes, for example, that passages almost verbally identical, such as many in the synoptic Gospels, cannot be independent; hence a little redaction criticism may not be a dangerous thing. His main concern with fundamentalists, however, is essentially the same as what worries him about modern critics: *neither party displays good literary sense*. With regard to identifying literary genre, each is all thumbs. Discussing this point with a correspondent, Lewis explains:

> My own position is not Fundamentalist, if Fundamentalism means accepting as a point of faith at the outset the proposition 'Every statement in the Bible is completely true in the literal, historical sense.' That would break down at once on the parables. All the

same commonsense and general understanding of literary kinds
which would forbid anyone to take the parables as historical statements, carried a very little further, would force us to distinguish
between (1.) Books like *Acts* or the account of David's reign, which
are everywhere dovetailed into a known history, geography, and
genealogies (2.) Books like *Esther*, or *Jonah* or *Job* which deal with
otherwise unknown characters living in unspecified periods, &
pretty well *proclaim* themselves to be sacred fiction.[20]

Fundamentalism and modern biblical criticism alike mistakenly talk
'about' scripture, thus keeping it at a safe distance, instead of experiencing from head to toe the reality for which it serves as means and
medium. It is the particular virtue of myth that we come nearest 'to
experiencing as a concrete what can otherwise be understood only as an
abstraction'.[21] Fundamentalist and critic alike try each in his own way
to distil the truth from the reality. In the process, each lets the reality
which truth is about slip through his fingers – two different species of
inept readers, each dropping 'the sacred Fish'.[22]

TRANSLATIONS

As the biblical texts mediate truth, so translations of the Bible are
in their own way 'transpositions' from a higher medium (the original)
into a lower (the vernacular of ordinary life).[23] Lewis was very much
in favour of seeking up-to-date translations of the Bible and lamented
his countrymen's attachment to the venerable but often antiquated and
sometimes unintelligible prose of the Authorized (King James) Version.
The Bible's language ought not to create an obstacle between its subject matter and the reader. When its *thee*s and *thou*s conjure up solemn
ecclesial ceremonies rather than historical realities, however, the language gets in the way. Lewis wants thoroughly to disabuse us of the
notion that the Bible was written in a grand style. On the contrary: 'The
same divine humility which decreed that God should become a baby
at a peasant-woman's breast, and later an arrested field-preacher in the
hands of the Roman police, decreed also that He should be preached in
a vulgar, prosaic and un-literary language.'[24] There is a pastoral point
to Lewis's musings. The beauty of the Authorized Version's language
may dull our appreciation of what it says: 'we may only sigh with tran-
quil veneration when we ought to be burning with shame or struck
dumb with terror or carried out of ourselves by ravishing hopes and
adorations'.[25]

What kind of influence does the Authorized Version wield? It is first a source: 'A Source gives us things to write about; an Influence prompts us to write in a certain way.'[26] The Bible is an important font of much English literature, though it is the content of the Authorized Version rather than its style that has counted most. Lewis recognizes a strictly literary impact as well, best seen in the way the Authorized Version has left traces on English vocabulary. That Lewis cares more for the influence of substance than style, however, is evident from his remark on John Bunyan: 'Without the Bible he would not have written the *Pilgrim's Progress* at all, for his mind would have been utterly different; but its style might have been much the same without the Authorised Version.'[27]

The purpose of a good translation is to let as much of the original through as possible. Words and literary genres are the media, not the matter; only when the sacred subject matter of the Bible is acknowledged will the literature of the Bible continue to have an impact. Strictly speaking, 'the Bible as literature' does not exist: 'Now the New Testament has nothing at all to tell us of literature.'[28] When the church assembled the various writings into the canon it did not have literary principles in mind, only a desire to hear the word of God and learn the mind of Christ.

Lewis looked askance at the new trend to teach 'the Bible as literature'. What may seem to be the 'second coming' of the Bible in Western culture, after its first coming as sacred scripture, looked to Lewis like a false start: 'those who read the Bible as literature do not read the Bible'.[29] In a secular age that has little taste for the numinous, stories like that of Moses at the Burning Bush hold little relish: 'Unless the religious claims of the Bible are again acknowledged, its literary claims will, I think, be given only "mouth honour" and that decreasingly. For it is, through and through, a sacred book.'[30] The relentlessly theological nature of its subject matter excludes a merely aesthetic approach: 'You can read it as literature only by a *tour de force*. You are cutting the wood against the grain, using the tool for a purpose it was not intended to serve ... I predict that it will in the future be read as it always has been read, almost exclusively by Christians.'[31]

Lewis held that for literature in general, but perhaps for scripture especially, both author and the author's language are not masters but ministers of the text's subject matter. The prophets and apostles had no desire to be creative or original, only to let the reality of Christ take their thought, and imaginations, captive: 'an author should never conceive himself as bringing into existence beauty or wisdom which did not exist before, but simply and solely as trying to embody in terms of his own art some reflection of eternal Beauty and Wisdom'.[32]

THE MYTHOPOEIC REVELATION OF SCRIPTURE

Lewis never explicitly set forth a 'doctrine' of scripture in his published works, though he explains how he understands the Bible to be the word of God in a brief chapter in *Reflections on the Psalms*. There are also valuable discussions in his letters, especially in response to Evangelicals eager to co-opt him for their cause. Yet Lewis himself clearly values the 'primary language' of faith – sacred myth made fact – more than second-order theological articulations. Doctrinal formulations pass away, but the myth-made-fact endures for ever.

We know God, says Lewis, because God has first chosen to make himself known. To be precise: God has chosen to be 'mythopoeic': to reveal himself through metaphors and myths – stories about mighty acts, shed blood, death and rebirth. The Bible conveys a taste of God's reality through its myth-like history of Jesus Christ.[33]

In a letter written in 1931 on the brink of his conversion, Lewis explains how he was coming to regard the Gospels as 'God's myth': 'The "doctrines" we get out of the true myth are of course less true: they are translations into our concepts and ideas of that which God has already expressed in a language more adequate, namely the actual incarnation, crucifixion, and resurrection.'[34] The myth made fact of Jesus Christ is merely the end of a long divine mythic pedagogy that includes much of the Old Testament:

> Myth in general is not merely misunderstood history ... nor
> diabolical illusion ... not priestly lying ... but at its best, a
> real though unfocused gleam of divine truth falling on human
> imagination. The Hebrews, like other people, had mythology: but
> as they were the chosen people so their mythology was the chosen
> mythology – the mythology chosen by God to be the vehicle
> of the earliest sacred truth, the first step in that process which
> ends in the New Testament where truth has become completely
> historical.[35]

Lewis sets forth a unique mythic variation on the theme of progressive revelation: 'If you take the Bible as a whole, you see a process in which something which, in its earliest levels ... was hardly moral at all, and was in some ways not unlike the Pagan religions, is gradually purged and enlightened till it becomes the religion of the great prophets and Our Lord Himself. That whole process is the greatest revelation of God's true nature.'[36]

THE INSPIRATION OF SCRIPTURE

As to the Bible's inspiration – the manner in which it is both human and divine – Lewis acknowledges some ambivalence. The primary thing is that of which the Bible speaks; our speaking about the Bible is secondary by comparison.[37] However, though the theory of inspiration may have been a matter of some indifference to him, the fact of inspiration was not: 'That the over-all operation of Scripture is to convey God's Word to the reader (he also needs His inspiration) who reads it in the right spirit, I fully believe.'[38]

Scripture itself refutes the idea of dictation. Paul distinguishes between what he says 'of himself' and what 'the Lord' says, yet both are scripture. At least on one occasion Lewis sounds neo-orthodox: 'It is Christ Himself, not the Bible, who is the true word of God. The Bible, read in the right spirit and with the guidance of good teachers will bring us to Him.'[39] This impression that Lewis owes a debt to perhaps the pre-eminent name in modern theology is, however, misleading: 'Barth I have never read, or not that I remember.'[40]

Some may nevertheless detect quasi-Barthian overtones when Lewis likens biblical inspiration to the incarnation: 'I myself think of it as analogous to the Incarnation – that, as in Christ a human soul-and-body are taken up and made the vehicle of Deity, so in Scripture, a mass of human legend, history, moral teaching etc. are taken up and made the vehicle of God's Word.'[41] In both cases, God lifts up a creaturely vehicle, sanctifying it as a medium of his self-communicative activity: 'Thus something natural – the kind of myth that is found among most nations – will have been raised by God above itself, qualified by Him and compelled by Him to serve purposes which of itself it would not have served.'[42] Every literary form in the Bible has thus been 'taken into the service of God's word'.[43] Lewis opines: 'If every good and perfect gift comes from the Father of Lights then all true and edifying writings, whether in Scripture or not, must be *in some sense* inspired.'[44] One commentator dubs Lewis's position on scripture 'literary inspiration': 'To understand Scripture, we should look beyond the language to what is represented ... We respond not to the Bible per se but to the realities conveyed through the Bible by the power of the Holy Spirit.'[45]

Books in the Bible have natural histories then, yet their authors were also subject to various kinds of 'divine pressure'. God ultimately guides the composition of the Bible, even while the 'human qualities of the raw materials show through'.[46] To be sure, 'it will always be possible to ignore the up-grading and see nothing but the lower'.[47] Yet, to those with eyes to see and ears to hear, the literature of the Bible is the vehicle of God's word.[48] Scripture 'carries' the Word of God, but we receive it as such 'not by using it as an encyclopedia or an encyclical but by steeping ourselves in its tone or temper and so learning its overall message'.[49] Indeed, we are not fundamentalists.[50]

AUTHORITY AND INTERPRETATION

Where, then, does Lewis stand *vis-à-vis* other Christians on the question of biblical truth? He occupies that sparse territory between fundamentalists and modern critics that is contiguous to but does not coincide with Evangelicalism.

Scripture has supreme authority in matters of faith and practice for Lewis not least because, when taken as a whole and rightly interpreted, it is true: 'I take it as a first principle that we must not interpret any one part of Scripture so that it contradicts other parts.'[51] For example, the nihilism of Ecclesiastes gives us a cold picture of life without God: 'That statement is itself part of God's word.'[52] Christian thinking must therefore be according to the scriptures, as Lewis implies in a letter to a friend: 'Yes, Pascal does directly contradict several passages in Scripture and must be wrong.'[53] Yet 'we must not use the Bible (our fathers too often did) as a sort of Encyclopedia out of which texts (isolated from their context and read without attention to the whole nature & purport of the books to which they occur) can be taken for use as weapons'.[54]

Lewis never regarded any narrative as unhistorical 'simply on the ground that it includes the miraculous'.[55] If he questioned the absolute historical and scientific accuracy of the scriptures, it was not because he doubted God's ability to speak the truth or to do what the text said he did, but rather because he was not convinced that every biblical text makes historical and scientific claims. The truth of a literary form such as Jesus' parables, for example, does not depend upon the factuality of the events it recounts. Conservative Evangelicals, in their zeal for historical truth, so strain at the gnats that they sometimes cannot see the camel standing in front of them.

Lewis places himself in the company of Jerome, who remarked that Moses described creation in Genesis 'after the manner of a popular poet', and Calvin, who questioned 'whether the story of Job were history or fiction'.[56] Lewis considers Job unhistorical simply because it does not *read* or *feel* like history: it begins with no genealogy, is set in a country about which the Bible nowhere else has anything to say, and concerns a man unconnected with Israel's history. Lewis concludes: 'the author quite obviously writes as a story-teller not as a chronicler'.[57] We might have preferred our Bible to be straight history or systematic theology or even science – 'something we could have tabulated and memorised and relied on like the multiplication table'[58] – yet, since this is not what God has done, we must conclude it was best to use just these literary forms, humble though they be.

What are often deemed errors in the Bible may actually be errors in interpretation.[59] Furthermore, not every statement in scripture has to be historically true for the simple reason that not every statement claims to be historical. This becomes clear in a particularly important letter on scripture addressed to Clyde Kilby. Lewis writes that the question 'Is Ruth historical?' does not even occur to him as he is reading, and that it would still act on him as the word of God even if it were not: 'All Holy Scripture is written for our learning. But learning *of what*? I should have thought that the value of some things (e.g., the Resurrection) depended on whether they really happened: but the value of others (e.g., the fate of Lot's wife) hardly at all. The ones whose historicity matters are, as God's will, those where it is plain.'[60]

Not every statement in scripture must be true, or inspired, in the same way. Lewis therefore rules out the view 'that any one passage taken in isolation can be assumed to be inerrant in exactly the same sense as any other: e.g., that the numbers of O.T. armies … are statistically correct because the story of the Resurrection is historically correct'.[61] Errors of minor fact remain, though one must remember 'that our modern & western attention to dates, numbers, etc. simply did not exist in the ancient world. No one was looking for *that* sort of truth.'[62] Indeed, 'the very *kind* of truth we are often demanding was, in my opinion, never even envisaged by the Ancients'.[63] And this is the central point. Inerrancy without right interpretation is at best but a pyrrhic victory.

It is more important to read the Bible correctly than to know things 'about' it: 'What flows into you from the myth is not truth but reality (truth is always *about* something, but reality is that *about which* truth is).'[64] The doctrine of inerrancy does not teach one to taste and see that the Lord is good. In the final analysis, one must be the kind of reader who can receive what is written, losing oneself in love, virtue and the pursuit of understanding to the issue of the biblical text. To catch the 'sacred Fish' is not necessarily the same thing as affirming the historicity of the great fish that swallowed Jonah: 'the whole *Book of Jonah* has to me the air of being a moral romance, a quite different *kind* of thing from, say, the account of K. David or the N.T. narratives, not *pegged*, like them, into any historical situation'.[65] Sound – which is to say, *believing* – critical reading 'reveals different *kinds* of narrative in the Bible', hence it would be 'illogical to conclude that these different kinds should all be read in the same way'.[66]

Lewis once famously argued that Christ is either what he claimed to be or else a liar or lunatic.[67] Curiously, he fails to argue something similar on behalf of the prophets and apostles, and this despite their frequent claims to speak not of themselves but upon divine authority. Still, everything Lewis does say about the Bible encourages us to read its authors in such a way that they are neither liars nor lunatics, but rather as men whose writings the Spirit takes up to reveal things into which even angels long to look (1 Pet. 1.12).

CONCLUSION: RE-ENCHANTING BIBLICAL THINKING

To look 'at' rather than 'along' Lewis's view of scripture is as mistaken a strategy as is the critics' tendency to look at rather than along scripture itself. For Lewis was less interested in formulating a doctrine of scripture than he was in looking through scripture into the truths and mysteries of the faith. The Bible is the medium by which human beings taste and see the goodness of God, the power of the gospel. As such, engaging with scripture involves one's whole being – cognitive, volitional and affective capacities alike: 'The most valuable thing the Psalms do for me is to express the same delight in God which made David dance.'[68] Lewis wants to take every thought, and imagination, captive to the word of God about the God-made-man.

Lewis was qualified to tutor in philosophy and was a widely read amateur theologian, yet neither philosophy nor theology ultimately rules his life and thought. No, the reshaping of life and thought that Christianity requires happened to Lewis not through logical argument alone but rather 'by having his thought-life formed and accommodated to the flow of [secular] literature and what it is about ... on the one side, and to the New Testament and what it is about, on the other'.[69]

What Lewis offers us is not a novel doctrine of scripture but a new way of thinking biblically, a new way of understanding what it is to be biblical. Lewis pronounces a pox on both interpretive houses – fundamentalist and liberal – insofar as they fail to read the Bible with appropriate literary sensitivity. Lewis cared with heart, mind and soul more for the substance of the gospel – the thing itself as it is inextricably and irreducibly mediated to us through the literature of the Bible in all its generic diversity – than for any theory of biblical inspiration or school of criticism.

Scriptural interpretation is for Lewis a matter of reading the whole Bible with one's whole being. For the Bible is much more than 'mere' literature: 'Those who talk of reading the Bible "as literature" sometimes mean, I think, reading it without attending to the main thing it is about; like reading Burke with no interest in politics, or reading the *Aeneid* with no interest in Rome.'[70] Being biblical in one's theological outlook means being rational, not in a single and univocal way – that way the Enlightenment lies – but analogically, thinking the subject matter of scripture along its diverse literary grains. To read scripture in faith is not to repack the first-order discourse of the Bible in second-order theoretical terms but to receive 'an imaginative extension'[71] of our being as the words and worlds of the biblical text enter into our world with inspired enchantment. *Tolle, lege!*: take, read (with literary sensitivity), and be transformed.

Notes

1 For a complete account, see Augustine, *Confessions*, book 8.
2 See, for example, Duncan Sprauge, 'The Unfundamental C.S. Lewis: Key Components of Lewis's View of Scripture', *Mars Hill Review*, 2 May 1995, 53–63; Lyle W. Dorsett, *Seeking the Secret Place: The Spiritual Formation of C.S. Lewis* (Grand Rapids, MI: Brazos Press, 2004), ch. 3.
3 David Lyle Jeffrey describes Lewis as a 'reader' rather than a 'critic': a reader is a servant to the text and is committed to recovering the author's intention; a critic is the text's judge and master. In this sense, Lewis *reads* the Bible 'like any other book' ('C.S. Lewis, the Bible, and Its Literary Critics', *Christianity and Literature* 50 (2000), 95–109). However, Clyde S. Kilby writes: 'It would be a bad mistake to infer ... that Lewis regarded the Bible as simply another good book. He repeatedly calls it "Holy Scripture," assures us that it bears the authority of God, sharply distinguishes even between the canon and the apocrypha, presses the historical reliability of the New Testament in particular, and often assures us that we must "go back to our Bible," even to the very words' (*The Christian World of C.S. Lewis* (Grand Rapids, MI: Eerdmans, 1968), 156).
4 Letter to Genia Goelz, 13 June 1959 (CLIII 127).
5 EIC 41.
6 POP 64 n. 1.
7 Richard B. Cunningham, *C.S. Lewis: Defender of the Faith* (Philadelphia: Westminster Press, 1967), 74: see also 87–102.
8 EIC 44.

9   POP 59.
10 'Myth Became Fact', EC 138–42.
11 'Myth Became Fact', EC 141.
12 Cunningham comments that Lewis's biblical hermeneutics is 'a strange hybridization which fully satisfies hardly anybody', combining as it does a belief in miracles with a willingness to affirm both mythic and historical elements (C.S. Lewis, 84).
13 'Modern Theology and Biblical Criticism', repr. as 'Fern-Seed and Elephants', EC 242–54. See also SL 116–20 (letter 23).
14 'Fern-Seed and Elephants', EC 246.
15 'Fern-Seed and Elephants', EC 247.
16 Letter to Francis Anderson, 23 Sept. 1963 (CLIII 1459).
17 'Meditation in a Toolshed', EC 607–10.
18 Cunningham comments that, while Lewis offers a middle ground between radical criticism and literalism, his 'refusal to acquaint himself with responsible Biblical criticism is almost inexcusable' (C.S. Lewis, 94).
19 'Fern-Seed and Elephants', EC 252.
20 Letter to Janet Wise, 5 Oct. 1955 (CLIII, 652–53).
21 'Myth Became Fact', EC 140.
22 ROP 100. Mark Edwards Freshwater complains that, for all his apologetic work, Lewis never provided the necessary basis for his assertion that the gospel is 'myth made fact' (C.S. Lewis and the Truth of Myth (Lanham, MD: University Press of America, 1988), 126).
23 'Transposition', EC 267–78.
24 'Modern Translations of the Bible', EC 473. For Lewis's opinions about sixteenth- and seventeenth-century English translations of the Bible, see EL 204–15.
25 'Modern Translations of the Bible', EC 473.
26 'The Literary Impact of the Authorised Version', SLE 133.
27 'The Literary Impact of the Authorised Version', SLE 140.
28 'Christianity and Literature', EC 411.
29 'The Literary Impact of the Authorised Version', SLE 142.
30 'The Literary Impact of the Authorised Version', SLE 144.
31 'The Literary Impact of the Authorised Version', SLE 144.
32 'Christianity and Literature', EC 416.
33 See his letter to Gracia Bouwman, 19 July 1960 (CLIII 1173). In Mere Christianity, Lewis identifies four modes of divine revelation: conscience, the history of Israel as God's chosen people, pagan myths, and the incarnation (MC 51). In The Problem of Pain he includes the sense of the numinous (POP 4–9).
34 Letter to Arthur Greeves, 18 Oct. 1931 (CLI 977).
35 M 138 n. 1.
36 Letter to Mrs Johnson, 14 May 1955 (CLIII 608). For an alternative, Platonizing account of Lewis's view of revelation, see Andrew Walker, 'Scripture, Revelation, and Platonism in C.S. Lewis', Scottish Journal of Theology 55 (2002), 19–35.
37 See his response to a request for his evaluation of the Wheaton College Statement Concerning Inspiration of the Bible: letter to Clyde Kilby, 7 May 1959 (CLIII 1044).

38 Letter to Clyde Kilby, 7 May 1959 (CLIII 1046).

39 Letter to Mrs Johnson, 8 Nov. 1952 (CLIII 246).

40 Letter to Corbin Scott Carnell, 13 Oct. 1958 (CLIII 980). Cf. PR 18; EL 449.

41 Letter to Lee Turner, 19 July 1958 (CLIII 960–61).

42 ROP 111.

43 ROP 111.

44 Letter to Clyde Kilby, 7 May 1959 (CLIII 1045).

45 Michael J. Christensen, *C.S. Lewis on Scripture: His Thoughts on the Nature of Biblical Inspiration, the Role of Revelation, and the Question of Inerrancy* (Nashville: Abingdon, 1989), 80.

46 ROP 111.

47 ROP 116.

48 Lewis also argued for the inspiration of scripture on the basis of Jesus' attitude towards the Old Testament (ROP 117).

49 ROP 112.

50 See his letter to Janet Wise, 5 Oct 1955: 'Of course I believe the composition, presentation, & selection for inclusion in the Bible, of all the books to have been guided by the Holy Ghost. But I think He meant us to have sacred myth & sacred fiction as well as sacred history' (CLIII 652–53). Garry L. Friesen agrees with Lewis's own estimate that his doctrine of scripture was 'tentative' and identifies Lewis's failure to discuss the Bible's own claims for itself as particularly egregious ('Scripture in the Writings of C.S. Lewis', *Evangelical Journal* 1 (1983), 23). Will Vaus expresses similar regrets (*Mere Theology: A Guide to the Thought of C.S. Lewis* (Downers Grove, IL and Leicester: InterVarsity Press, 2004), 40–41).

51 Letter to Emily McLay, 3 Aug. 1953 (CLIII 354). Lewis is alluding to Article XX of the Thirty-Nine Articles of Religion in the Anglican Book of Common Prayer.

52 ROP 115.

53 Letter to Dom Bede Griffiths, 28 May 1952 (CLIII 195).

54 Letter to Mrs Johnson, 8 Nov. 1952 (CLIII 246).

55 ROP 109.

56 ROP 109.

57 ROP 110.

58 ROP 112.

59 Lewis stipulates that any account of biblical authority will have to 'make room for' apparent inconsistencies such as that between the genealogies of Matthew 1 and Luke 3 and the accounts of Judas' death in Matt. 27.5 and Acts 1.18–19 (letter to Clyde Kilby, 7 May 1959 (CLIII 1045)).

60 Letter to Clyde Kilby, 7 May 1959 (CLIII 1044–45).

61 Letter to Clyde Kilby, 7 May 1959 (CLIII 1046).

62 Letter to Lee Turner, 19 July 1958 (CLIII 960–61).

63 Letter to Clyde Kilby, 7 May 1959 (CLIII 1046).

64 'Myth Became Fact', EC 141.

65 Letter to Corbin Scott Carnell, 5 Apr. 1953 (CLIII 319).

66 Letter to Corbin Scott Carnell, 5 Apr. 1953 (CLIII 319). Christensen's notion that Lewis's example 'proves that one can be a dedicated evangelical, accept the full authority of Scripture, yet disbelieve in inerrancy' (*C.S. Lewis on Scripture*, 91) seems, in retrospect, to be rather optimistic. What Lewis offers evangelicals is a standing challenge to interpret the Bible with hearts, minds and imaginations attuned to the ways in which the Bible's literary genres mediate the reality of faith's mystery – the divine things themselves.

67 MC 52.

68 ROP 45.

69 Paul L. Holmer, *C.S. Lewis: The Shape of His Faith and Thought* (New York and London: Harper & Row, 1976), 96.

70 ROP 2–3.

71 Holmer, *C.S. Lewis*, 107–08.

7 On theology

PAUL S. FIDDES

> At the beginning I said there were Personalities in God. Well, I'll go further now. There are no real personalities anywhere else. Until you have given up your self to Him you will not have a real self.[1]

So writes C.S. Lewis towards the end of his book of broadcast talks, *Beyond Personality*, which later became the last part of *Mere Christianity*. He regarded this small book as his attempt at communicating (or as he later puts it, 'translating[2]') Christian theology for the non-theologian, and even more for the non-Christian. This is his sustained effort at Christian doctrine. Elsewhere in *Mere Christianity* he assumes the role of apologist, evangelist and Christian ethicist, but here he puts on the mask of the theologian, though with some hesitancy, and it is in this role that I want to assess him in this chapter.

THE HEART OF THE MATTER – THE MAKING OF PERSONS

In the short passage I have quoted above, Lewis brings together the doctrines of God, human nature and salvation in a concise way. I hope to show both how they hit the very centre of Christian belief, and yet how they also, ironically, raise some disturbing questions about Lewis's approach.

Here Lewis is focusing on the theme of 'being a person' in order to bring together a Christian understanding of both God and humanity. He calls the book *Beyond Personality*, and this is a deliberately ambiguous phrase, applying both to God and to human beings. *God* is infinitely personal, and so 'beyond' any human personality we know. With the vision of God as Trinity, says Lewis, Christians offer an idea of what a God who is 'beyond personality' might be like. Indeed, he claims, 'the Christian idea is the only one on the market'.[3] Human beings in turn become truly personal only in this God, going 'beyond' the personalities they have been given by nature. A supremely personal God is a Trinitarian God, a God who begets God, and so this is a vision of the Trinity as a deeply 'practical' doctrine, concerned with human transformation: 'I warned you that theology is practical. The whole purpose for which we exist is to be thus taken into the life of God.'[4] As we are 'drawn' into God's Trinitarian life, we become truly persons or – as Lewis puts it – become real selves.

Lewis has excellent theological instincts here. If one is looking for the heart of Christian theology, for 'mere Christianity', this is right on target. He has anticipated a great deal of modern Christian doctrine which has stressed the making of persons through participation in the triune God; I need mention in passing only Jürgen Moltmann, Wolfhart Pannenberg and Hans Urs von Balthasar as representative theologians. Moreover, like them he does not consider this personal engagement in God to be a mere individualism. Using the image of a telescope for seeing something which will otherwise be unknown, he proposes that the instrument through which we see God is the whole Christian community: 'Christian brotherhood [*sic*] is, so to speak, the technical equipment for this science'.[5] Lewis does not explicitly take the step that recent theology has done, to affirm that we are involved in a God of communion *through* human community, that we are immersed in a God of relations through being persons in relation; however, he might be thought to imply it since he follows his introduction to the doctrine of the Trinity immediately by his thoughts about Christian believers as one body, united in love.[6] The Christian concept of a tri-personal God is, he admits, complicated, but then 'we cannot compete, in simplicity, with people who are inventing religions ... of course anyone can be simple if he has no facts to bother about'.[7]

THE DIVINE DANCE

To elucidate this complex doctrine, Lewis uses argument, humour, passionate prose – but above all he employs images and metaphors. A little later I want to assess some of these, but for now I want to draw attention to one of them. To illustrate being 'drawn' into God, he uses the image of a divine dance:

> In Christianity God is not a static thing – not even a person – but a dynamic, pulsating activity, a life, almost a kind of drama. Almost, if you will not think me irreverent, a kind of dance ... The whole dance, or drama, or pattern of this three-Personal life is to be

played out in each one of us: or (putting it the other way round) each one of us has got to enter that pattern, take his place in that dance.[8]

In recent theology, the image of the divine life as a drama has also become prominent,[9] but most striking here is the image of the dance, which has become increasingly popular in the last thirty years. Though it is increasingly common for present-day theologians to refer to the *perichoresis* or interweaving of persons in God with the image of the dance,[10] it is difficult to find an unambiguous reference to the Trinity as a dance in earlier Christian thinking.[11] There are certainly references to the *angels* and other created beings as forming a dance around the still centre of God, moving around a God who is himself unmoving in a Platonic stasis; this, for example, is the picture of the first rank of angels in Pseudo-Dionysius' treatise on *The Celestial Hierarchy*,[12] to which Lewis himself draws attention in *The Discarded Image*.[13] There is something similar in Dante.[14] The activity of *Christ* on Earth is depicted as a dance in several texts, among them the Gnostic *Hymn of Jesus*[15] and the medieval English carol 'Tomorrow will be my dancing day'. But I await the finding of an instance earlier than Lewis for the picturing of the *Trinity* as a dance. Perhaps it is Lewis himself who has extended the image in Pseudo-Dionysius, thereby criticizing the Neo-platonic and Aristotelian concept of an unmoving mover.

Lewis returns to the image at the end of *Perelandra*, with Ransom's vision of the Great Dance. It is quite difficult here to be certain whether the Trinity *itself* is moving in a dance, or whether all things are simply sharing in a dance around the centre where God is, a centre – Lewis affirms – where all created beings equally are.[16] However, Ransom sees that God's 'love and splendour flow forth like a strong river ... [making] new channels'; the dance is like ribbons or circles of light *in* which millions of entities live and die;[17] and 'all which is not itself the Great Dance was made in order that he might come down into it'.[18] This last phrase distinguishes the created world we know from the dance itself, perhaps then identifying the dance in essence as God; but the dance which pre-exists *our* creation, which is the site of the incarnation, could include the angels as in Pseudo-Dionysius. As he looks upon the Dance, Ransom hears a voice declaring, 'He is his own begotten and what proceeds from Him is Himself',[19] with the implication that this eternal generation is, or is part of, the dance. One could then read all this as meaning that the patterns of the dance are the patterns of God's love, and so are the movement of the Trinity itself.

I have laid stress on this evocative image, as it underlies a key point that Lewis makes about theological language. The image of dance or drama is an image of participation, and it is the *experiential* aspect of talking about God that interests Lewis.[20] He admits that language about the Trinity is difficult; indeed a three-personal God cannot be imagined or pictured in the mind even with the help of analogies. This Lewis sees not as a disadvantage but a positive advantage, writing:

> You may ask, 'If we cannot imagine a three-personal Being, what is the good of talking about him?' Well, there isn't any good talking *about* him. The thing that matters is actually being drawn into that three-personal life, and that may begin any time – tonight if you like.[21]

He goes on to explain that it is in the experience of prayer above all that we find ourselves involved with God, and so 'the whole threefold life of the three-personal Being is actually going on in that ordinary little bed-room where an ordinary man is saying his prayers'.[22] By speaking of God as 'beyond personality' but not as impersonal Lewis is recognizing a necessary apophaticism or negative way in all theological language. We might say that the very elusiveness of the picture of the divine dance in *Perelandra*, for all Lewis's efforts, illustrates that the dance cannot be observed or even imagined but only participated in.

BEGOTTEN, NOT MADE

Fundamental to the concept of the Trinity is the belief that the Father eternally generates the Son; the Son is 'begotten, not made', as the Creed of Nicaea affirms. Now, since human beings are to become truly persons by being drawn into the Trinity, it seems that the generation of the Son must also be relevant to the becoming personal of created beings. Lewis thus draws the conclusion that, since Christ is begotten and not made, human beings can themselves move on from the state of being 'made' to that of being 'begotten'. If the Son in the Trinity is begotten and not made, then by entering the Trinity we cease in effect to be 'made' and become 'begotten', as sons and daughters of God. This is the 'next step' in human history, which Lewis generously allows us to call 'evolution' if we want to; it is 'a change from being creatures of God to being sons of God'.[23]

Lewis's proposal here is essentially in accord with the Christian tradition. The New Testament shows several variations on the theme of becoming 'sons' of God. The apostle Paul regards this as a kind of adoption, where we are accepted into God's family alongside the true Son, Jesus.[24] The Fourth Gospel pictures regeneration as being 'born from above', a second birth after our natural birth.[25] Athanasius explains salvation as *theosis*, or divinization, in which 'Christ became man so that we might become gods', and he understands this transformation (following Heb. 2.10) as 'bringing many sons to glory'.[26] Lewis seems to have acquired a closer acquaintance with Athanasius shortly before preparing this third series of broadcast talks, through reading Sister Penelope's translation of *De incarnatione* and writing an introduction to it. He had already spoken of becoming 'gods and goddesses' in, for example, his sermon 'The Weight of Glory' (1941),[27] perhaps deriving this theme from his earlier reading of Augustine; but while he speaks in the sermon of 'passing beyond nature', it is only in this last series of talks that he explicitly contrasts 'being creatures' with 'becoming sons'.

Lewis's thought is thus generally in line with Christian ideas about salvation. However, the concise formulation that becoming sons and daughters of God means transferring from a state of being 'made' to one of being 'begotten' by God is not so usual. It *can* be found, as for example in another work of Athanasius, who comments that 'we are not begotten first, but made',[28] but it can hardly be called 'mere' or 'common' Christianity. Further, Lewis's contrast between two sorts of *life* – a life which is 'made' and a life which is 'begotten'[29] – appears to be without precedent, though it is arguably an extension of the same idea. His somewhat uncommon, though not unorthodox, definitions are perhaps indicative of a theological struggle that engages Lewis throughout his writings and of which he was very well aware: that is, how to discern the proper continuities and discontinuities between a state of 'nature' and a state of 'grace'.

In *Mere Christianity* Lewis is captivated by an imaginative image which tends to tip the balance one way, towards discontinuity. The image is that of statues coming to life, derived from the Pygmalion myth, and used by Shakespeare in *The Winter's Tale*. In the Pygmalion myth the sculptor falls in love with the statue of a beautiful woman he has made, and the gods bring her to life for him. In *The Winter's Tale*, Hermione, who has been thought to be dead for twenty years, pretends to be a statue and apparently comes miraculously to life for Leontes. Elsewhere Lewis makes reference to both these sources.[30] So Lewis proposes that human beings can similarly come to life, and be changed from being mere statues to being children of God. The progression of his thought is this: 'What God begets is God ... what God creates is not

God'.[31] So God has *begotten* Christ, and only *made* human beings. They may be like God in certain respects, but they are not things of the same kind. They are, says Lewis, 'more like statues or pictures of God'.[32] If we are to become *gods*, then like Christ we shall have to be *begotten* not made. When we become sons in this true sense we are like statues that have come alive: 'This world is a great sculptor's shop. We are the statues and there is a rumour going round the shop that some of us are some day going to come to life'.[33]

For Lewis, all human beings are created in the image of God, but in their natural life – which he calls *Bios* – they are mere statues of the divine. As created, they are lifeless as far as spiritual life – *Zoe* – is concerned. Christ gives us this *Zoe* life which, Lewis says, is 'the spiritual life which is in God from all eternity and which made the whole natural universe'.[34] It is as if we are the creatures in the White Witch's courtyard in *The Lion, the Witch and the Wardrobe*, turned by her magic into stone statues;[35] like them, we need the breath of Aslan to come to life. So we become *begotten* and not just *created* 'sons', coming to spiritual life just as Christ is alive. Christ is made incarnate and dies to natural life in order to make it possible for human beings to come alive as sons. Lewis sums up:

> We are not begotten by God, we are only made by him: in our natural state we are not sons of God, only (so to speak) statues. We have not got *Zoe* or spiritual life: only *Bios* or biological life which is presently going to run down or die. The whole offer which Christianity makes is this: that we can, if we let God have his way, come to share in the life of Christ. If we do, we shall then be sharing a life which was begotten, not made, which always has existed and always will exist.[36]

Perhaps, as in the ribbons of light and love in the vision of *Perelandra*, Lewis thinks of this *Zoe* life as the very pattern of the dance of the Trinity. By being taken into this 'life which is begotten' and not made we – mere statues – come to life as sons, or as gods.

This is touching doctrine with the glow of imagination. Lewis's fundamental insight is that, by entering the dance or drama of the Trinity, we truly become sons and daughters of God; we truly become persons. This is mainline Christian doctrine, expressed in an imaginative form. The supplementary image of statues coming to life is a vivid one, and effective in a particular literary context. But there always remains the danger of opening up too large a gulf between a life which is created (*Bios*) and a life which is begotten (*Zoe*).

A modern Eastern Orthodox theologian, John Zizioulas, similarly writes about two kinds of personality – a biological hypostasis we possess by nature and an 'ecclesial hypostasis', derived from Christ. For Zizioulas the biological is 'adapted' to, changed into, or conformed to the ecclesial in a new birth, without losing its natural forms of love, whether *erōs* or *agapē*.[37] For Lewis, writing much later than *Mere Christianity* on the nature of love, divine Gift-love (*agape*) also summons all natural loves 'to become modes of Charity while ... remaining the natural loves they were', and yet the divine Love which God shares with us is still 'different from the Gift-loves He has built into [our] nature'.[38] Between the summoning and the difference there lies the tension which Lewis experienced, which he found both problematic and enriching, and which he tried to capture in a succession of images which he recognized must always remain provisional.

THE NATURAL AND THE SPIRITUAL

I have been suggesting that Lewis's use of a certain image, the statues, may have led him into a stronger discontinuity between natural and spiritual than he intends. The image has captured his imagination and shaped the doctrinal concept. This is now underlined by another image – that of tin soldiers or toy soldiers:

> Imagine turning a tin soldier into a real little man. It would involve turning the tin into flesh. And suppose the tin soldier did not like it. He is not interested in flesh; all he sees is that the tin is being spoilt.[39]

This image inevitably magnifies the difference between being created and re-created, opening an ontological gap (tin and flesh, parallel to flesh and spirit), and so depreciating the state of natural existence. There can be no continuity between tin and flesh, no basis for the one in the other. The simile presents nature as a phase to be superseded by something else, which can only come into nature wholly 'from outside'.[40] It also leaves nature as a space which can be occupied by the Dark Power, and in which Christ is an invader. Here is another potent image, drawn from the contemporary experience of war in Europe, that of invasion. The rightful king has landed in enemy-occupied territory 'in disguise and is calling us all to take part in a great campaign of sabotage'.[41] Dualism, states Lewis, is closer to Christianity than people think: Christianity agrees that the universe is at war, but it is occupied by a Dark Power which was created by God and has rebelled. The image of a secret invasion here is telling. For theologians like Gustaf Aulén and Karl Barth, the decisive grand battle against evil has been already won in the cross of Jesus, and all that is left is a mere mopping-up operation.[42] For Lewis, the last battle has not yet happened, but there are soldiers of the resistance dotted all over the world. Perhaps Lewis's sense of the power of evil is truer to its reality as we experience it, but the image again tends to relegate nature to something less than real.

Of course, a Christian theologian must agree with Lewis that we can only attain *full* personality in Christ. We must be summoned to go 'beyond personality', transcending our human-beingness in the life of God. But our biological personality (to use both Lewis's and Zizioulas's term) is liable to be undermined as a creation of God when Lewis writes: 'what I so proudly call myself [is] merely the meeting-place for trains of events which I never started and I cannot stop', a matter of 'heredity and upbringing and surroundings' and with desires 'thrown up by my physical organism ... or even suggested to me by devils'.[43] In his spoken version of the extract with which this chapter begins, Lewis glosses the phrase 'there are no real personalities anywhere else' than in God with the phrase 'I mean no full, complete personalities', which gives the respect to human nature that he certainly intends. In the written version this is unfortunately omitted, leaving only the qualifier 'real', implying that our *Bios* life is somehow unreal.

When thinking more philosophically about the status of nature, Lewis defends himself here against the process theologian Norman Pittenger,[44] who criticizes Lewis for supposedly regarding miracles as a 'violation of the laws of nature'. Lewis points to his study on *Miracles*, which makes clear that supernatural events 'interrupt nature' but do not break the laws of nature, since nature always has the capacity to adjust to new events.[45] Nature, he affirms, is partly good and partly evil, and will be redeemed.[46] Lewis affirms the resurrection of the body, and celebrates the value of the human senses in his poem 'On Being Human', with its memorable line 'an angel has no nose'.[47] In *Mere Christianity*, reflecting on the sacraments, he rejoices that 'God likes matter. He invented it'.[48] In *Miracles*, he insists that God is the God of wheat and wine and oil; he is Bacchus, Venus and Ceres all rolled into one.[49] In *The Allegory of Love* he writes that he distrusts 'that species of respect for the spiritual order which bases itself on contempt for the natural'.[50]

For all this, when Lewis comes to speculate on the resurrection body in *Letters to Malcolm*, he envisages the sensuous life as being inside the soul,[51] so that a new world could be created out of the spirit alone, which carries the sensations created by matter within it. Rather like the 'image-body' of the philosopher H.H. Price,[52] he writes that 'in the sense-bodies of the redeemed the whole New Earth will arise'. Vividly, he writes, 'I can now communicate to you the vanished field of my boyhood – they are building sites today – only imperfectly by words. Perhaps the day is coming when I can take you for a walk through them'.[53] The idea here is not the transformation of the physical universe into a new kind of bodiliness, but the survival of 'the sensuous life'. There is continuity between nature and spirit in the redemption of sensations or sense-memories. Thus far has Lewis moved away from his beginnings in Idealist philosophy, but no further. Lewis can refute Pittenger, but he might have found it more difficult to deal with the verdict of his friend Austin Farrer, who writes after Lewis' death that 'Lewis was raised in the tradition of an idealist philosophy which hoped to establish the reality of the mental subject independently of, or anyway in priority to, that of the bodily world. Though he moved some way from such positions he was still able to overlook the full involvement of the reasonable soul in a random and perishable system.'[54]

INVASION AND IMMERSION

Lewis tells us that he had never wanted to be 'interfered' with,[55] and so when he yielded and confessed that 'God was God' – i.e. that the Absolute Spirit of Idealism was a personal God to whom he could relate – it seems apt that he came to conceive of this God as an 'invader' of the world. Nature must suffer an invasion or interference (or 'interruption') from its creator. For Lewis the former Idealist philosopher, even the rational spirit of human beings has a 'super-natural' element to it, as 'something which invades, or is added to, the great interlocked event in space and time, instead of merely arising from it',[56] although this sort of spirit is actually created and so is still another kind of nature. How much more, then, will the 'absolutely supernatural' invade the natural world, and it is this very life (*Zoe*) which the human mind can become.[57] So the incarnation for Lewis is the Grand Miracle; it is the supreme invasion of nature to which all other invasions are related, and because of which they are not just 'arbitrary raids'. Statues and tin soldiers can become persons because their world has been invaded.

Lewis thus argues that we begin to see how God can become man at all when we see that every human being is already the site of an invasion: a supernatural creature – the mind – is united with a natural creature – the physical organism. In Jesus not a supernatural *creature* but the supernatural *Creator* himself becomes united with a natural creature. So, as Lewis puts it, 'our own composite existence is … a faint image of the divine Incarnation itself – the same theme in a very minor key'.[58] In Christ the divine spirit dwells within a human spirit just as the human spirit dwells within any human body.[59] We need not explore here the similarity of this Christology to the 'Logos–Sarx' (Word–body) Christology of fourth-century Alexandria, and especially that of Athanasius.[60] Nor need we explore the way that Lewis's accompanying idea of a *warfare* between the body and the rational mind in every human being[61] is surprisingly like the Christology of a less orthodox Alexandrian – Apollinaris.[62] I simply want to underline that the metaphor of invasion is bound to lead to some discontinuity between the natural and the spiritual.

Of course, Lewis stresses that the invasion – whether in the many miracles of the Old and New Testaments, or in the incarnation itself, is not the invasion of an alien power.[63] Nature is being invaded by her own King, and so her laws are not being broken. Nature is not an illusion, though she is infected with evil and depraved by the fall of humanity. She 'has the air of a good thing spoiled'.[64] We can thus still see within her some poor reflections of God's own patterns of activity, and, for Lewis, one is the pattern of God's descent into death and re-ascent to life. As expressed in myths of the dying and rising corn-king, the process of death and rebirth is written large into all levels of the natural world. In Christ this myth becomes fact; he is the reality to which all myths of a dying and rising god refer.[65] In Christ, God goes down into the very depths of time and space, like a diver plunging to the bed of the sea, to the very roots of the nature he has himself created, in order to bring the whole ruined world up with him to new life. He must, says Lewis, 'stoop in order to lift'.[66] I suggest that this image of immersion into the depths is a more potent metaphor than 'invasion', and that it avoids opening a gap between nature and spirit in the same way.

This image of redemption connects with Lewis's stress in *Mere Christianity* that what matters is the suffering and death of Christ in order to expiate our sins and destroy the power of death, not any particular *theory* of atonement. The central Christian belief is that 'Christ's death has somehow put us in the right with God', and if we could produce a theory to explain it, 'it would not be the thing from beyond nature'.[67] In so far as he has any preference for a theory (and he is hesitant about this), he is impressed by the idea of Christ as the perfect penitent. The only way out of our dilemma of sin and rebellion is that of repentance, which means killing part of ourselves. But we find it impossible to repent; we can only turn away from ourselves if we are helped to do so, and this is the effect of Christ's death. God becomes human in order to make a perfect penitence, and 'you and I can go through this process only if God does it in us';[68] we will only die to ourselves, and so make death our enemy into our servant, if we share in God's own dying.[69] Lewis has probably taken this idea of perfect penitence from R.C. Moberly's book *Atonement and Personality*, which he had read,[70] but he has made it much more empathetic than in Moberly, where it remains a vicarious penitence.[71] Lewis proposes that God puts his own penitent spirit into us,[72] just as he draws an analogy with the adult mind descending into sympathy with children, and humans into sympathy with animals.[73] Thus the plunging of God into human life is interpreted as empathy which has a transforming effect.

The image of the 'descent' of God into the world has a long history in Christian tradition, and while it *can* be pictured as an invasion, it can also be pictured as someone diving 'down through increasing pressure into the death-like region of ooze and clime and old decay; then up again, back to colour and light ...'[74] This picture of immersion belongs with that of entering the dance, since they are both images of participation rather than intervention. It is not surprising then that, in describing the effect of the Grand Miracle on a nature which is totally interlocked, Lewis returns to the image of the dance:

> The partner who bows to Man in one movement of the dance receives Man's reverences in another. To be high or central means to abdicate continually: to be low means to be raised: all good masters are servants: God washes the feet of Men.[75]

GETTING INTO GOD

We have been reflecting on Lewis's portrayal of the movement from being merely creatures of nature to being sons through receiving the spirit of Christ, a life (*Zoe*) which is not created but begotten. While statues, tin soldiers and invasion are images of discontinuity in this process, immersion, sympathy and dancing are images that express continuity. But the question then arises: how does the life of Christ enter us?

In book II of *Mere Christianity* Lewis enquires how the new life can be 'put into us',[76] and in book IV he speaks of its being 'injected' into us in order to turn the tin soldier into a live man.[77] How can this happen, he asks? Lewis appears somewhat perplexed by this question. In book II he comments that we receive our natural life, our *Bios*, in a way that is 'a very curious process, involving pleasure, pain and danger'. He means sex, and remarks that he does not blame children for not believing it when they are first told about it, since it is 'very odd'. So then, the God who arranges *that* process is the same God who arranges how the new kind of life, the Christ life, is to be spread, and 'We must prepare for it being odd too'.[78] His answer in part II is that the three ordinary methods of spreading the Christ life are baptism, belief and the Lord's Supper. They may seem odd, but we believe on the authority of Christ that the new life is to be communicated in this way.

The image of injection is, however, rather mechanical, and later in book IV Lewis places alongside it a more dynamic image: the new life is to be caught as we catch an 'infection'. This new life is not carried on, he writes, by sexual reproduction and heredity as in the process of evolution. Christ transmits the new life by 'good infection'.[79] We are infected by being in the company of Christ, and by other people who are 'carriers' of Christ to other people, sometimes without being infected themselves: 'People who were not Christians themselves helped me to Christianity,' recalls Lewis.[80] We catch the good infection from the presence of the invisible Christ alongside us, helping us.

At base, then, we are catching the new life by being caught up into the dance of the Trinity. As we take our place in the dance, we come close to a 'great fountain of energy and beauty spurting up at the very centre of reality', and we are bound to become wet with its spray.[81] But then, another question arises: how do we get into this dance? Lewis answers that it is by sharing in Christ's life, and then explains this participation in activist terms of 'laying ourselves open' or 'handing over our whole self to Christ', or 'shoving back' all our own wishes and hopes at the beginning of each day, in order to let the new life 'rush in'. Is it possible to say more about the act of God in drawing us in or 'infecting' us? Many modern theologians will want to affirm that all human beings are by their creation *already* immersed into the triune life, already participating in the dance of the threefold personal God. Even the human rebellion against God is within God, a distortion and a breaking of the steps of the dance.[82] Through that engagement in God's dynamic life persons are enabled to trust in Christ and so make their participation in God *deeper* and more transforming. They can move, in the title of the penultimate chapter of Lewis's last Chronicle of Narnia, 'further up and further in'.

Lewis is wary of anything that might be construed as pantheism, associating this with the Idealism of Hegel, from which he wants to distance himself, despite still being in some debt to his Idealist heritage.[83]

However, in his account of the Great Dance in *Perelandra*, he does offer something like the vision of God I have been suggesting, and which might be called not pantheism but 'panentheism' (or 'everything in God'):

> [Ransom] could see wherever the ribbons or serpents of light intersected, minute corpuscles of momentary brightness: and he knew somehow that these particles were the secular generalities of which history tells – peoples, institutions, climates of opinion, civilisations, arts, sciences and the like – ephemeral coruscations that piped their short song and vanished. The ribbons or cords themselves, in which millions of corpuscles lived and died, were things of some different kind.[84]

The ribbons of light are the more 'lasting' things, including some created persons who endure and some universal truths or qualities which are eternal, but these also interweave with 'a far vaster pattern in four dimensions' whose centre draws Ransom with 'the cords of infinite desire'. This is a vision of interpenetration (*perichoresis*) which is finally in God, occupying space in the midst of the dance of the Trinity. It is an image of continuity between nature and grace which, together with the images of immersion, sympathy and infection, is held in tension with the images of discontinuity – the statues, tin soldiers, invasion and injection.

Lewis is struggling on behalf of us all with this tension in the making of persons. His distrust of evolution as continuous improvement of humanity (while he accepts it as a scientific mechanism of change) and his vivid sense of human fallenness mean that he will always be urging us to leave the womb of 'our great mother' nature behind.[85] But on the other side there is his vision of the Great Dance, his perception that once immersed in the world 'Christ will not *go out of* nature again'[86] and his own experience of having caught the infection of Christ from those who are not Christians. His images, provisional as they are, reflect this tension: immersion is placed against invasion, infection against injection, dance against the vivifying of statues. He is doing theology by inviting us to indwell these images, to find our own resolution there, and so finally to dwell in God.

Notes

1 MC 188.
2 'Rejoinder to Dr Pittenger', UND 183.
3 MC 137.

4   MC 138.

5   MC 141.

6   MC 140. In this period he is also critical of Martin Buber's 'I–Thou' personalism for what he discerns as an excessive individualism: see his letter to Sister Penelope, 29 July 1942 (CLII 526).

7   MC 141.

8   MC 148–49.

9   See Hans Urs von Balthasar, *Theo-Drama: Theological Dramatic Theory. Vol. I: Prolegomena*, tr. G. Harrison (San Francisco: Ignatius Press, 1994), esp. 89–134.

10 Making a play on words between *perichoreo* (to interpenetrate) and *perichoreuo* (to dance around): e.g. Edmund Hill, *The Three-Personed God* (Washington, DC: University of America Press, 1982), 272; Catherine M. LaCugna, *God For Us: The Trinity and Christian Life* (San Francisco: HarperCollins, 1991), 271; Elizabeth Johnson, *She Who Is: The Mystery of God in Feminist Theological Discourse* (New York: Crossroad, 1993), 220–21; Paul S. Fiddes, *Participating in God: A Pastoral Doctrine of the Trinity* (London: Darton, Longman and Todd, 2000), 72–81.

11 Though it is to be found earlier in Lewis's own work. He uses the image of dance for the generation of the Son from the Father at POP 141.

12 Pseudo-Dionysius, *The Celestial Hierarchy*, 209d–212b; cf. 205b–c.

13 DI 71.

14 Dante, *Paradiso* 28.133–35.

15 *The Gnostic Hymn of Jesus*, tr. and ed. G.R.S. Mead (London and Benares: Theosophical Publishing Society, 1907), set to music by Gustav Holst.

16 Per 198.

17 Per 201, 203.

18 Per 199.

19 Per 202.

20 For more on participation, see his 'Meditation in a Toolshed' (EC 607–10), where he distinguishes between 'looking at' and 'looking along' things, the latter being a matter of 'stepping inside'.

21 MC 139, my italics.

22 MC 139.

23 MC 172.

24 Gal. 4.5; Rom. 8.15, 23; cf. Eph. 1.5.

25 John 3.3–6.

26 Athanasius, *De incarnatione* 10.

27 'The Weight of Glory', EC 105.

28 Athanasius, *Contra Arianos*, 2.59.

29 MC 150.

30 Letter to Arthur Greeves, 5 Sept. 1931 (CLI 968); POP 132; 'William Morris', SLE 224; 'Hermione in the House of Paulina', CP 32.

31 MC 135.

32 MC 135.

33 MC 136.

34 MC 136.
35 LWW 152–56.
36 MC 150.
37 John Zizioulas, *Being as Communion: Studies in Personhood and the Church* (London: Darton, Longman and Todd, 1985), 53.
38 FL 122, 117.
39 MC 151–52.
40 MC 183.
41 MC 47.
42 Gustaf Aulén, *Christus Victor*, tr. A.G. Hebert (London: SPCK, 1937), 58–60; Karl Barth, *Church Dogmatics*, tr. and ed. G.W. Bromiley and T.F. Torrance (Edinburgh: T. & T. Clark, 1936–77), III/3, 366–67. Lewis had read Aulén, with approval: see letter to H. Morland, 19 Aug. 1942 (CLII 529).
43 MC 187–88.
44 'Rejoinder to Dr Pittenger', UND 177–83.
45 M 65–66.
46 M 125ff.
47 CP 49.
48 MC 62.
49 M 118.
50 AOL 267.
51 LTM 121.
52 H.H. Price, 'Survival and the Idea of "Another World"', in John Donnelly (ed.), *Language, Metaphysics and Death* (New York: Fordham University Press, 1978), 176–95. Price was a colleague of C.S. Lewis at Magdalen College, and a frequent speaker at the Socratic Club, of which Lewis was for many years president.
53 LTM 121.
54 Austin Farrer, 'The Christian Apologist', in Jocelyn Gibb (ed.), *Light on C.S. Lewis* (London: Geoffrey Bles, 1965), 41.
55 SBJ 182.
56 M 173.
57 M 174.
58 M 115.
59 M 115.
60 According to the Logos–Sarx model, the divine Logos either replaced the human soul in the person of Christ, or effectively took over its functions as director of the body: see J.N.D. Kelly, *Early Christian Doctrines*, 4th edn (London: A. & C. Black, 1958), 153–58, 284–95.
61 M 131.
62 See R.A. Norris, *Manhood and Christ* (Oxford: Oxford University Press, 1963), 112–22.
63 M 136.
64 M 125.
65 M 115–20. For further exploration of myth 'becoming fact', see Lewis's 'Myth Became Fact', EC 138–42, and Paul S. Fiddes, 'Lewis the Myth-Maker', in Andrew Walker and James Patrick (eds), *A Christian for*

All Christians: Essays in Honour of C.S. Lewis (London: Hodder and Stoughton, 1990), 132–55.

66 M 115.
67 MC 55.
68 MC 57.
69 M 133–34.
70 See letters to Arthur Greeves, 25 May 1941 (CLII 487) and H. Morland, 19 Aug. 1942 (CLII 529).
71 R.C. Moberly, *Atonement and Personality* (London: John Murray, 1924), 80–92.
72 MC 53–58.
73 M 115.
74 M 116.
75 M 128.
76 MC 59.
77 MC 159.
78 MC 59.
79 MC 146–50.
80 MC 160.
81 MC 150.
82 See Hans Urs von Balthasar, *Theo-Drama: Theological Dramatic Theory. Vol. IV: The Action*, tr. G. Harrison (San Francisco: Ignatius Press, 1994), 330.
83 MC 40.
84 Per 202–03.
85 MC 185.
86 M 127.

8 On naturalism

CHARLES TALIAFERRO

'Naturalism' may be loosely defined as the thesis that *nature alone exists*. This is a good start, so long as we then define 'nature' but, unfortunately, at this point self-described naturalists differ dramatically. Forms of naturalism sometimes called *strict* or *scientific* see nature as, ultimately, that which may be described and explained in terms of a complete physics. This is very strict indeed, for lots of things like consciousness itself, desires, and values do not appear to be likely items in a complete physics. This form of naturalism (also described as *puritanical naturalism* because of its severity) differs from broader naturalistic accounts of nature that both privilege the natural sciences and also allow for whatever is identified by the social sciences. Broad naturalists often allow for the emergence of consciousness among humans and some non-human animals, they certainly accept the types of realities identified in evolutionary biology, and so on. The biologist Richard Dawkins is representative of a broad form of naturalism whereas the philosopher Richard Rorty is a strict naturalist.[1]

The one thing that all broad and strict naturalists agree on is that there is no God, no souls or afterlife, and no irreducible, objective moral values. A moral value is 'reducible' if you can reduce it to claims that do not involve moral truths, as, for example, if one were to claim that the assertion 'Murder is wrong' is really only to assert that 'I hate murder' – the latter is simply a state of emotional revulsion and not an objective moral truth. Another way to reduce or eliminate objective values would be to take the route of cultural relativism and treat moral claims as reflecting culturally embedded judgements so that to claim 'Murder is wrong' becomes 'In my society, murder is condemned.'[2]

C.S. Lewis was a worthy opponent of both of these forms of naturalism. Lewis had considerable philosophical training and actually began his teaching career at Oxford in philosophy. Although his professional academic interests eventually shifted towards literature, his work continues to interest, inspire, irritate or provoke contemporary philosophers in equal measure and has received a surprising amount of attention over the years. In this chapter, I consider and assess two of Lewis's major arguments against naturalism: the argument from reason and the argument from morality. I then turn to Lewis's reflections on the soul and life after death over against the naturalist portrait of death. Finally, I conclude with some reflections about the role of imagination in the assessment of rival worldviews such as naturalism and Christian theism.

THE ARGUMENT FROM REASON

Lewis developed a significant argument that naturalists could not account for reasoning. If successful, this is a devastating objection, because naturalists themselves advance their position on rational grounds. I present the argument in what I believe is its most effective form, which is a critique of strict naturalism as opposed to the broader forms of naturalism.

As noted earlier, strict naturalists only allow for ideal physics to be the final arbiter of what is true. Here is Rorty's version of strict naturalism:

> Every speech, thought, theory, poem, composition and philoso-
> phy will turn out to be completely predictable in purely natural-
> istic terms. Some atoms-and-the-void account of micro-processes
> within individual human beings will permit the prediction of
> every sound or inscription which will ever be uttered. There are no
> ghosts.[3]

Lewis does not think that reason requires ghosts (!), but he does think that a view like Rorty's has a problem with the normativity of reason. Lewis explains:

> All possible knowledge ... depends on the validity of reasoning. If
> the feeling of certainty which we express by words like *must be*
> and *therefore* and *since* is a real perception of how things outside
> our own minds really 'must' be, well and good. But if this certainty
> is merely a feeling in our own minds and not a genuine insight
> into realities beyond them – if it merely represents the way our
> minds happen to work – then we can have no knowledge. Unless
> human reasoning is valid no science can be true.[4]

Lewis is here making the point that in any reasoning our beliefs are related to each other so that one belief *makes evident* or *provides reasons* for our accepting another belief such as the conclusion of an argument. To illustrate Lewis's point, consider this question: what is the smallest perfect number? In formulating an answer, a person must ascertain which is the smallest number that is equal to the sum of its divisors, including 1, but not itself. We answer the question with '6' because we reason that 6 *is* $1 + 2 + 3$. We perceive or understand that the conclusion *must* follow. (Such a mathematical equation is actually an identity claim: $6 = 1 + 2 + 3$ because $1 + 1 + 1 + 1 + 1 + 1$ equals $1 + 1 + 1 + 1 + 1 + 1$.) But now consider Rorty's strict naturalism. None of the micro-processes in the human body involves any beliefs or powers of reason. In fact, none of the elementary particles posited by contemporary physics has any beliefs or reasons. If Rorty is correct, then the explanation of why you answered the original question '6' was perfectly predictable by non-reasoning forces; 6 was not a conclusion you reached in virtue of (or because of) your mathematical reasoning. Lewis drives his point home against those who wish to trust reason while at the same time believing that reasoning itself is a product of chance events:

> If Nature when fully known seems to teach us (that is, if the sciences teach us) that our own minds are chance arrangements of atoms, then there must have been some mistake; for if that were so, then the sciences themselves would be chance arrangements of atoms and we should have no reason for believing in them. There is only one way to avoid this deadlock. We must go back to a much earlier view [than naturalism]. We must simply accept it that we are spirits, free and rational beings, at present inhabiting an irrational universe and must draw the conclusion that we are not derived from it. We are strangers here. We come from somewhere else. Nature is not the only thing that exists.[5]

IS LEWIS'S ARGUMENT PERSUASIVE?

Three points are worth noting in reply. First, Lewis's argument is best seen as exposing a problem with reasoning, not with truth. In the passage cited earlier when Lewis concludes that if naturalism is true, then 'no science can be true', I think his point would be better phrased in terms of claiming that if naturalism is true, *then we are unable to account for the normativity of science or for the phenomenon of reasoning itself*. If strict naturalism is true, the final portrait of a complete physics would, in fact, be true and offer an exhaustive account of reality. The problem lies in whether we may still recognize the normativity of reasoning, not in whether (as a matter of truth and falsehood) naturalism might be correct. Second, Lewis's conclusion might be qualified somewhat. Rather than conclude 'we are not derived from Nature', he might better conclude that there must be more to us than strict naturalism allows. Finally, I believe Lewis's argument works against *strict naturalism*. It is no serious objection to Lewis that we have calculating machines that we might describe as adding or subtracting even though their micro-processes do not have reasons or beliefs. Calculating machines are only devices we use to enable us to engage in mathematics; your calculator does not answer '6' by virtue of (literally) *understanding* and *thinking* about the sum of the divisors of 6. But broad naturalism is a different story. Broad naturalists often employ the term *emergence* to describe the appearance of novel, even radically new powers and qualities in the natural world. Some broad naturalists thereby simply posit that at a certain point in our evolutionary history, consciousness appears and (eventually) we are able to engage in normative reasoning.[6]

It is not possible to examine in detail whether broad naturalists are entitled to posit such radical emergence. I have argued elsewhere that they are not.[7] One of the problems facing broad naturalism is that if one posits that humans (and possibly some other animals) develop through biological processes the ability to reason, it seems that they need to posit the emergence of a substantial subject (the reasoner) and not just posit the emergence of a new property. The problem they face may be appreciated if you consider any whole physical object made of parts, such as a wheel. The whole object may have properties not had by any of its parts, e.g. the wheel is round and weighs 20 pounds, but perhaps none of its parts is round and each, taken separately, weighs less than 20 pounds. But the wheel as a whole inherits or derives all its properties (it is able to travel at a certain speed when attached to a car or chariot, and so on) from its parts and their relationship to other physical objects and their parts. In the case of reasoning, however, it appears that we have a novel, different order of explanation that is *not at all at work in the parts of our bodies or in the micro-processes of the physical world*. Reasoning is a *teleological* (that is, purposive) activity that proceeds on the basis of grasping beliefs and their entailments and is not at all captured by a purely mechanical, non-purposive activity.[8] There is not space to extend this argument here. For the present, I suggest that the best way to look at Lewis's argument is that Lewis has given us some reason to challenge strict naturalism. Perhaps naturalism can simply posit radical emergence (or perhaps not), but the more that broad naturalists recognize certain human functions or attributes as emerging (consciousness, normative reasoning powers, moral and aesthetic judgments, and so on), the more difficult it will be not to look beyond the natural world in order to account for the existence and continuation of the world itself.

Lewis's argument from reason is widely discussed today, with a range of significant advocates.[9] His argument directly challenges Darwin's own thinking about the emergence of thought. Darwin held that thinking was not itself a matter of normativity but the result of impersonal forces: just as the movements of inanimate objects are determined by non-purposive forces, so too are our thoughts. Darwin wrote: 'Shake ten thousand grains of sand together & one will be uppermost: – so in thoughts, one will rise according to law.'[10] Darwin worried about this deeply, for he thought his own theory might undermine the trustworthiness of reasoning.[11] (After all, a false theory might have all sorts of evolutionary advantages, so the mere fact that evolution might favour a theory does not *ipso facto* show it to be true. It may, for example, be an evolutionary disadvantage to be a sceptic about our senses, but that alone would not demonstrate that scepticism is false.)

One illustration that presses home the problem facing Darwin – or a Darwinian trusting her faculties if she believes that those faculties are the result of chance – is introduced by Richard Taylor (a theist, but also opposed to all actual religions as the outcome of immature fear). Taylor asks us to entertain the following. Imagine you are on a train and see on a neighbouring hill what appears to be a sign saying that you are entering Wales. Imagine, also, that you have compelling reasons to believe that the apparent sign is made up of rocks that formed these words through a completely random process; from a volcanic eruption, for example, or perhaps from workers simply throwing stones off the track. Under those circumstances, even if it turns out that you are in Wales, it would (so argues Taylor) be unreasonable for you to trust the 'sign', for it was not produced by way of reasons or teleology. Given that we know the rock formation is utterly a chance product, we might question whether it is at all proper even to refer to the formation as a sign in the first place.[12]

THE ARGUMENT FROM MORALITY

A good way to appreciate Lewis's argument from morality is to continue with some observations about Darwin's own naturalism. Darwin was personally a man of conscience concerning many of the issues of his day; for example, he was deeply opposed to slavery and the slave trade. Moreover, Darwin argued that human beings who developed sympathy for others and the virtues of civil responsibility will tend to survive as opposed to those who are cruel:

> When two tribes of primeval man, living in the same country, came into competition, if ... the one tribe included a greater number of courageous, sympathetic, and faithful members, who were always ready to warn each other of danger, to aid and defend each other, this tribe would without doubt succeed best and conquer the other.[13]

Darwin even makes the following claim in *On The Origin of Species*: 'Natural selection is daily and hourly scrutinising, throughout the world, every variation, even the slightest; rejecting that which is bad, preserving and adding up all that is good; silently and insensibly working, whenever and wherever opportunity offers, at the improvement of each organic being.'[14] The problem is that there is no guarantee that evolution will favour what *we* think of as good or just. Darwinian naturalism simply leaves us with an account of what does or does not survive; nowhere does it have an account of why some act is good or not.[15] This is especially troubling given Darwin's views about the inevitability of racial extermination in human evolutionary theory.[16]

Lewis may be seen as directly addressing the strict naturalism of Darwin when he writes:

> Let us begin by supposing that Nature is all that exists. Let us suppose that nothing ever has existed or ever will exist except this meaningless play of atoms in space and time: that by a series of hundredth chances it has (regrettably?) produced things like ourselves – conscious beings who now know that their own consciousness is an accidental result of the whole meaningless process and is therefore itself meaningless ...
> In this situation there are, I think, three things one might do:
> 1. You might commit suicide ...
> 2. You might decide simply to have as good a time as possible. The universe is a universe of nonsense, but since you are here, grab what you can ...
> 3. You might defy the universe ...
>
> I suppose that most of us, in fact, while we remain materialists, adopt a more or less uneasy alternation between the second and the third attitude ... All Naturalism leads us to this in the end – to

a quite final and hopeless discord between what our minds claim to be and what they really must be if Naturalism is true.[17]

Lewis's choices above may seem less than exhaustive; in fact, elsewhere he notes how difficult it is for naturalists *not* to act still on the grounds that there are objective, moral values:

> The Naturalist can, if he chooses, brazen it out. He can say ... 'all ideas of good and evil are hallucinations – shadows cast on the outer world by the impulses which we have been conditioned to feel.' Indeed, many Naturalists are delighted to say this. But then they must stick to it; and fortunately (though inconsistently) most real Naturalists do not. A moment after they have admitted that good and evil are illusions, you will find them exhorting us to work for posterity, to educate, revolutionise, liquidate, live and die for the good of the human race ... They write with indignation like men proclaiming what is good in itself and denouncing what is evil in itself, and not at all like men recording that they personally like mild beer but some people prefer bitter.[18]

I suggest that Lewis's position does seem right: unless one goes with broad naturalism and simply accepts that at a certain stage in our evolution, objective moral (and aesthetic and other) values emerged and came into being as new realities, then it does appear that naturalism undermines not only the normativity of reason but also the normativity of morality. Lewis writes:

> When men say 'I ought' they certainly think they are saying something, and something true, about the nature of the proposed action, and not merely about their own feelings. But if Naturalism is true, 'I ought' is the same sort of statement as 'I itch' or 'I'm going to be sick'.[19]

Indeed, some naturalists today explicitly embrace this conclusion. Michael Ruse maintains that moral judgements may appear objective but this is only the 'illusion of objectivity'.[20] The strict naturalism of Ruse and E.O. Wilson lead them to conclude that 'ethics as we understand it is an illusion fobbed off on us by our genes in order to get us to cooperate'.[21] If we have good reason to believe ethics is *not* an illusion, as Lewis thinks we do in human experience, then we have reason to reject strict naturalism.[22]

Lewis also seems right about the difficulty of actually living with the idea that morality is not normative, but he may have underestimated the way that some strict naturalists can be led away from promoting what we normally take to be just and good. Having noted earlier Darwin's positive views about sympathy and courage, we should remember the haunting ways in which Darwin also seemed not just to countenance racial extermination but (despite his horror over slavery in his day) to recognize what he saw as the past evolutionary advantage of slavery.

I do not want, in any way, to argue against the theory of evolution or against Darwin specifically on the grounds that Darwinian evolution promotes racism and genocide, even though (historically) one can document some Nazi use of evolutionary theory.[23] (I should add, parenthetically, that I personally do accept evolutionary biology, though I simultaneously oppose Darwin's naturalistic philosophy.[24]) But what should be appreciated is that from the standpoint of Darwin's own naturalism, there is nothing objectively immoral or unjust about any acts, even slavery or genocide; there are just some beliefs and practices that promote survival and some that do not. Values do not enter Darwinian naturalism and, on that point, I suggest Lewis's line of reasoning needs to be taken very seriously.

As for his positive case, in which Christian theism can provide a better account of the moral life than secular naturalism, Lewis does not give us a fully developed theory. Lewis's position seems most at home with what is called a divine command theory of ethics, but it can also be articulated in light of a general form of theism in keeping with Augustine, Aquinas and Anselm, according to which God is intrinsically good and the source of all good. This position is especially in keeping with Platonic forms of Christianity which identify God with goodness itself.[25] The contrast with naturalism could not be greater insofar as Christian theism treats goodness as a core, essential constitutive part of reality.[26]

While Lewis has located a problem (in my view) for strict naturalism, the broad naturalist is still able to affirm that objective, irreducible values simply emerged in human history. I know of no uncontroversial, successful broad naturalist account of such emergence, but it has to be said that Lewis has not demonstrated that such an account is impossible.[27]

NATURALISM, LIFE AND DEATH

Some contemporary naturalists such as Daniel Dennett claim to love evolution and its glory. In one passage from *Breaking the Spell*, Dennett even feels the need to make sure his readers do not think that his devotion to evolution is akin to a religion.[28] But one thing that naturalism (broad and strict) does conclude is that there is no afterlife for individuals. Biological destruction involves the annihilation of the individual person and, as most cosmologists believe, the long-range forecast for our planet is also not good: with the collapse of our sun in 4.5 billion years, the Earth will disintegrate. Lewis appreciated the implications of naturalism on this front:

> Nature does not, in the long run, favour life. If Nature is all that exists – in other words, if there is no God and no life of some quite different sort somewhere outside Nature – then all stories will end in the same way: in a universe from which all life is banished without possibility of return. It will have been an accidental flicker, and there will be no one even to remember it.[29]

Actually, Darwin himself appreciated just this sort of implication for his naturalism and, at times, it led him to despair.[30]

Lewis's further case against naturalism is less of a rigorous, formal argument and more of an appeal to fittingness. At the end of the day, in deciding between naturalism and (for example) Christian theism, which better accounts for the human condition and the natural world as a whole?[31] Lewis reasoned that the kind of longing we have not to perish but to live abundantly is itself a sign that we are not so made as to perish:

> If you are really a product of a materialistic universe, how is it you don't feel at home there? Do fish complain of the sea for being wet? Or if they did, would that fact itself not strongly suggest that they had not always been, or [would] not always be, purely aquatic creatures? Notice how we are perpetually surprised at time. ('How time flies! Fancy John being grown-up & married! I can hardly believe it!') In heaven's name why? Unless, indeed, there is something in us which is not temporal.[32]

Lewis is not engaging in wish-fulfilment here, or at least I suggest that is not his line of reasoning ('I wish that *X*, therefore *X*'). His position is best seen as an appeal to the fact that we are not reducible to material processes alone, that we do seem to possess a moral awareness that hints at a higher power (or at least a moral awareness that is not accounted for by strict naturalism), and that we have such a nature that seems only to be fulfilled in a realm that passes beyond this one.

Perhaps to bring out this point, consider the following line of reasoning. It normally makes sense for you to claim that you have exhausted the goodness of all kinds of events, from reading a book to playing a game to engaging in a great conversation or even to making love. Maybe not the lattermost, but in most other cases you will want to end the event and turn to others. And in the case of human bodies, it seems difficult to deny that they have a natural ending, a time when the good of the body simply seems exhausted. But if you imagine that a person you love has been endowed (whether by magic or a miracle or a new biology) with a body that is imperishable, could you ever come to conclude that the good of this person is exhausted or used up? Imagine that you even have the power of life or death over this person; can you further imagine ever willing that such a person should perish? This kind of reasoning helps support the view that a powerful, loving God who is able to save the soul of his beloved creature would in fact do so. And in making us for God, God would also will that creatures do in fact have a longing for an eternal good that may begin in this world but be finally fulfilled in the next.

Some philosophers, such as Bernard Williams, have questioned the goodness of an afterlife.[33] Wouldn't we ultimately find eternity boring? Samuel Johnson famously said that 'the man who is tired of London is tired of life', but wouldn't even London lose its charms after a billion years? However, it is safe to say that the vast bulk of Lewis's fiction (especially the stunning work *Perelandra*) is suffused with a sheer delight in *being* and the inexhaustible, awesome splendour of divine love as manifested not only in creation but also beyond it. The repeated refrain in the final Chronicle of Narnia, *The Last Battle*, is 'Further up and further in!'[34]

In his sermon 'The Weight of Glory', Lewis offers a profoundly positive view of the natural world and yet testifies to our longing for that which lies beyond this world:

> If we take the imagery of Scripture seriously, if we believe that God will one day give us the Morning Star and cause us to put on the splendour of the sun, then we may surmise that both the ancient myths and the modern poetry, so false as history, may be very near the truth as prophecy. At present we are on the outside of the world, the wrong side of the door. We discern the freshness and purity of the morning, but they do not make us fresh and pure. We cannot mingle with the splendours we see. But all the leaves of the New Testament are rustling with the rumour that it will not always be so. Some day, God willing, we shall get in. When human souls have become as perfect in voluntary obedience as the

inanimate creation is in its lifeless obedience, then they will put on its glory, or rather that greater glory of which nature is only the first sketch.[35]

Of course, the overcoming of death and the finding of new life beyond this one (and thus overturning Darwinian despair) would take a miracle. But then that is at the heart of Lewis's philosophy and religion: we are in the hands of an omnipotent, loving Creator who has endowed us with reason, morality, desire, and who, through the incarnation ('the Grand Miracle', as Lewis terms it), calls us to a deeper union and arena for fulfilment.

FURTHER REFLECTION

The philosophical debate over the arguments from reason and morality is very much alive today, as is the debate over the arguments from religious experience and desire, and the whole question of naturalism versus Christian theism versus other non-Christian alternatives to naturalism. Lewis deserves a rightful place in considering the arguments pro and con, not only because of the merits of his own arguments, but because he offers us a valuable lesson in assessing any theory. It is important imaginatively to explore such theories as whole accounts with their own interconnected structures and mutually supportive reasoning.

Lewis's case for Christianity (and thus his case against naturalism) may be characterized as an argument for an expanded framework or point of view. Lewis positioned Christianity as affirming the reality of the natural world, its physical laws, the facts of life and death (as we see them), but then he invites us imaginatively to conceive of a broader framework from which to view nature and sensory data. To entertain a Christian philosophy is not (as Richard Dawkins claims) a shutting down of the imagination and intellect, a sort of narrowing of our sights and ideals, but rather an embracing of a broader framework of coherence, intelligence and awesome wonder. Without actively entertaining this broader framework, naturalism seems like the only philosophy of choice. 'We all have Naturalism in our bones,' writes Lewis, 'and even conversion does not at once work the infection out of our system. Its assumptions rush back upon the mind the moment vigilance is relaxed.'[36] Lewis's own vigilant use of both reason and imagination in his case against naturalism allows one to relish and deeply appreciate the natural world. In Lewis's view, recognizing the supernatural actually enhances a love of the natural, rather than diminishing it, and helps us to see it rightly for what it really is:

> You must have tasted, however briefly, the pure water from beyond the world before you can be distinctly conscious of the hot, salty tang of Nature's current. To treat her as God, or as Everything, is to lose the whole pith and pleasure of her. Come out, look back, and then you will see ... this astonishing cataract of bears, babies, and bananas: this immoderate deluge of atoms, orchids, oranges, cancers, canaries, fleas, gases, tornadoes and toads. How could you ever have thought that this was the ultimate reality?[37]

Notes

1 For a survey of different forms of naturalism, see Stewart Goetz and Charles Taliaferro, *Naturalism* (Grand Rapids: Eerdmans, 2008).
2 A classic naturalist elimination of ethics as an objective, normative domain is J.L. Mackie's *Ethics: Inventing Right and Wrong* (New York: Penguin, 1977).
3 Richard Rorty, *Philosophy and the Mirror of Nature* (Oxford: Blackwell, 1980), 387.
4 M 18.
5 'On Living in an Atomic Age', EC 364–65.
6 This is Peter Unger's position in *All the Power in the World* (New York: Oxford University Press, 2006).
7 See Goetz and Taliaferro, *Naturalism*.
8 See both Goetz and Taliaferro, *Naturalism*, and Charles Taliaferro, *Consciousness and the Mind of God* (Cambridge: Cambridge University Press, 1994). For one heroic effort by a broad naturalist to accommodate reasoning and freedom of the will, see John Searle's *Freedom and Neurobiology* (New York: Columbia University Press, 2007). For an incisive critique, see J.P. Moreland's 'Searle's Rapprochement between Naturalism and Libertarian Agency: A Critique', *Philosophia Christi* 11 (2009), 189–99.
9 See especially Victor Reppert's *Lewis's Dangerous Idea: In Defense of the Argument from Reason* (Downers Grove, IL: InterVarsity Press, 2003). Reppert notes that something like Lewis's argument appears in an updated form in Alvin Plantinga's *Warrant and Proper Function* (New York: Oxford University Press, 1993), and Plantinga accepts the comparison (see 237 n. 28). A useful overview of Plantinga's work is available in James Beilby (ed.), *Naturalism Defeated? Essays on Plantinga's Evolutionary Argument against Naturalism* (Ithaca: Cornell University Press, 2002).
10 Paul Barrett *et al.* (eds), *Charles Darwin's Notebooks, 1836–1844: Geology, Transmutation of Species, Metaphysical Enquiries* (Ithaca: Cornell University Press, 1987), notebook M: 27, 31, 526–27.

11 See Darwin's letter to William Graham (3 July 1881) in Francis Darwin (ed.), *The Life and Letters of Charles Darwin*, 2nd edn (London: John Murray, 1887).

12 See Richard Taylor's *Metaphysics* (Englewood Cliffs, NJ: Prentice-Hall, 1974), 114–15. Lewis's original version of the argument from reason was famously criticised in a February 1948 meeting of the Socratic Club in Oxford, a club that regularly hosted philosophical presentations on religious beliefs. G.E.M. Anscombe distinguished between irrational and non-rational causes, and argued that while irrational causes undermine reason, non-rational causes do not. Lewis revised his position in the second edition of *Miracles* to make clear that, in his opinion, reason's normativity is undermined by non-rational as well as by irrational causes, and by any process that explains reasoning without appeal to beliefs, evidence and inference. For Anscombe's later assessment of the debate, see the introduction to her *Collected Philosophical Papers. Vol. II: Metaphysics and the Philosophy of Mind* (Minneapolis: University of Minnesota Press, 1981); her initial response – 'A Reply to Mr C. S. Lewis's Argument that "Naturalism" is Self-Refuting' – is included on pp. 224–32.

13 Charles Darwin, *The Descent of Man and Selection in relation to Sex* (New York: D. Appleton and Co., 1909), 130 (part I, ch. 5).

14 Charles Darwin, *The Origin of Species* (Harmondsworth: Penguin, 1982), 133.

15 See Lewis's satirical poem, 'Evolutionary Hymn' (CP 69), which includes the verse:

Far too long have sages vainly
Glossed great Nature's simple text;
He who runs can read it plainly,
'Goodness = what comes next.'
By evolving, Life is solving
All the questions we perplexed.

16 *The Descent of Man*, part I, ch. 6, 200–01.

17 'On Living in an Atomic Age', EC 363.

18 M 40–41.

19 M 40.

20 Michael Ruse, *Taking Darwin Seriously* (Amherst, MA: Prometheus Press, 1998), 253.

21 E.O. Wilson and Michael Ruse, 'The Evolution of Ethics', *New Scientist*, 1478 (17 Oct. 1985), 51.

22 See AOM for Lewis's extended use of the argument from morality.

23 For an overview, see Benjamin Wiker, *The Darwin Myth* (Washington, DC: Regnery Publishing, 2009), ch. 8.

24 Some of the problems with Darwinian evolution are highlighted in Jerry Fodor and Massimo Piatelli-Palmarini, *What Darwin Got Wrong* (London: Profile Books, 2009).

25 I survey different theistic accounts of value in my *Contemporary Philosophy of Religion* (Oxford: Blackwell, 1998).

26 For a new and excellent look at Lewis's moral argument, see Mark Linville, 'The Moral Argument', in W.L. Craig and J.P. Moreland (eds),

The Blackwell Companion to Natural Theology (Oxford: Wiley-Blackwell, 2009).

27   For scepticism about broad naturalism, see Goetz and Taliaferro, *Naturalism*.

28   Daniel Dennett, *Breaking the Spell* (New York: Viking, 2006), 268.

29   'On Living in an Atomic Age', EC 362. Lewis's point is developed in an excellent chapter, 'Naturalism as Bad News for the Many', in John Hick, *The Fifth Dimension* (Oxford: Oneworld Publications, 2004).

30   See John C. Greene, *Debating Darwin: Adventures of a Scholar* (Claremont, CA: Regina Books, 1999), 53–54.

31   There are of course many other alternatives to naturalism besides Christian theism, but I limit myself to contrasting just these two both for reasons of space and because of the present focus on Lewis's thought.

32   Letter to Sheldon Vanauken, 23 Dec. 1950 (CLIII 76).

33   See Bernard Williams, 'The Makropulos Case: Reflections on the Tedium of Immortality', in *Problems of the Self: Philosophical Papers 1956–1972* (Cambridge: Cambridge University Press, 1973), 82–100.

34   It is the title of ch. 15. See my 'Why We Need Immortality', *Modern Theology* 6 (1990), 367–79.

35   'The Weight of Glory', EC 104.

36   M 168.

37   M 70.

9 On moral knowledge

GILBERT MEILAENDER

In *The Magician's Nephew*, sixth in the Chronicles of Narnia, we learn how Aslan created the land of Narnia. As a culminating point of that creation, Aslan selects some of the animals to be Talking Beasts. To them he says:

> I give to you forever this land of Narnia. … I give you the stars and I give you myself. The Dumb Beasts whom I have not chosen are yours also. Treat them gently and cherish them but do not go back to their ways lest you cease to be Talking Beasts.[1]

It is possible, in other words, for Talking Beasts to give up their privileged position and cease to view themselves as anything other than Dumb Beasts, understanding themselves only 'from below'.

They *can* do that; however, in so doing they turn from their created nature. That is why, in the great scene of judgement at the end of the Chronicles of Narnia, the Talking Beasts who look on the face of Aslan with hatred rather than love cease in that moment to be Talking Beasts and become just ordinary animals.[2] A freely chosen abolition of their nature occurs.

The vision here depicted in the Chronicles is more systematically developed by Lewis in other writings, most centrally in *The Abolition of Man*.[3] It is especially important in his understanding of moral knowledge – what we know about our moral duties, and how we know it. We can develop the main elements in his view by examining, first, the structure of morality as he understands it, and, second, the remarkably prescient manner in which that understanding focused his attention on what we now call biotechnology.

THE STRUCTURE OF MORAL KNOWLEDGE

To develop Lewis's understanding of morality, we have to distinguish three elements: (1) *what* moral truths we know, (2) *how* we know them, and (3) how we *become able* to know them. The difference between the second and third of these may not be immediately apparent and, indeed, may not always have been clear to Lewis himself, but I think it will become clear as we make our way through the argument of *The Abolition of Man*.

What do we know when we know moral truth? Most fundamentally, according to Lewis, we know the maxims of what he calls 'the Tao' (the Way). These 'primeval moral platitudes' (as Screwtape once terms them[4]) constitute the human moral inheritance. They are, Lewis believes, the creation of no one, not even – though this is complicated – of God.[5] Because these maxims are so basic to all moral reasoning, even those who defend quite different moral theories are likely to agree about much of the content of virtue and vice, right and wrong.

In the essay 'On Ethics', the content of which is closely akin to *The Abolition of Man*, Lewis denies that he is 'trying to reintroduce in its full Stoical or medieval rigour the doctrine of Natural Law'.[6] That is surely true; nevertheless, we would not be wrong to characterize these maxims, the human moral inheritance, as the basic principles of natural law: the requirements of both general and special beneficence; duties both to parents and children; requirements of justice, truthfulness, mercy and magnanimity. These are the starting point for all moral reasoning, deliberation and argument; that is, they are to morality what axioms are to mathematics. They are not conclusions, but premises.[7] Begin from them and we may get somewhere in thinking about what we ought to do. Try to stand outside the Tao on morally neutral or empty ground, and we will find it impossible to generate any moral reasoning at all.

Lewis provides an illustration of the Tao in *That Hideous Strength*, the third and last volume in his Ransom Trilogy. He subtitled the story 'A Modern Fairy-Tale for Grown-Ups', and in the short preface he wrote for the book, he says: 'This is a "tall story" about devilry, though it has behind it a serious "point" which I have tried to make in my *Abolition of Man*'.[8] We can follow his hint and illustrate the Tao by referring to the scene in *That Hideous Strength* in which Frost (a suggestive name, as is that of his cohort Wither) begins to give Mark Studdock a systematic training in what Frost calls 'objectivity'. This is a training designed to kill in Mark all natural human preferences.

Mark is placed into a room that is ill-proportioned; for example, the point of the arch above the door is not quite in the centre. On the wall is a portrait of a young woman with her mouth open – and the inside of the mouth full of hair. There is a picture of the Last Supper, distinguished especially by beetles under the table. There is a representation of a giant mantis playing a fiddle while being eaten by another mantis, and another of a man with corkscrews instead of arms. Mark himself is asked to perform various obscenities, culminating in the command to trample upon a crucifix.

Gradually, however, Mark finds that the room is having an effect on him which Frost had scarcely predicted or desired: 'There rose up against this background of the sour and the crooked some kind of vision of the sweet and the straight'.[9] This was for Mark all interwoven with images of Jane (his wife), fried eggs, soap, sunlight, and birds singing. One might say, therefore, that Mark was not thinking in moral terms, but one might also, as the story puts it, think of him as 'having his first deeply moral experience. He was choosing a side: the Normal'[10]:

> He had never known before what an Idea meant: he had always thought till now that they were things inside one's head. But now, when his head was continually attacked and often completely filled with the clinging corruption of the training, this Idea towered up above him – something which obviously existed quite independently of himself and had hard rock surfaces which would not give, surfaces he could cling to.[11]

He is experiencing the Tao, no one's creation and certainly not his. He does not construct these moral truths; on the contrary, they claim him. The world around him is not neutral ground; it is from the start shot through with moral value.

We can, of course, criticize one or another of these moral maxims, or, at least, particular formulations of them, Lewis argues. But we will inevitably call on some other principle of the Tao when we do so. Thus, for example, we may think Aristotle's magnanimous man insufficiently merciful and a bit too concerned about his own nobility, using thereby one principle of the Tao (mercy) to refine another. In pursuit of our duties to posterity we may be willing to sacrifice the weak and vulnerable on the altar of medical research, but then we will have to ask whether we have transgressed the requirement of justice – every bit as much an element of the Tao as our duty to posterity. But to step, or try to step, outside the Tao entirely is to lose the very ground of moral reason itself.

It should be clear that the principles of the Tao do not solve moral problems for us; on the contrary, they create, frame, and shape those problems. They teach us to think in full and rich ways about them, as we recognize various claims the Tao makes upon us: as Lewis remarks,

'Who could ever have supposed that by accepting a moral code we should be delivered from all questions of casuistry? Obviously, it is moral codes that create questions of casuistry, just as the rules of chess create chess problems.'[12]

Indeed, if there is a query we might want to address to Lewis at this point, it would be something like the following. It is clear, to take an example, that Lewis himself thinks it would be better that posterity suffer than that we do injustice now in order to relieve that future suffering. What he does not give us is the full argument to explain why the duty of justice should be more fundamental than our duty to posterity. And, in fact, when he does give us a reason, it turns out to depend on certain distinctively Christian beliefs. Even if the maxims of the Tao themselves presuppose no specifically Christian beliefs, the way a prudent person deals with moral problems shaped by conflicting maxims will depend on a whole range of background beliefs. Thus, Lewis's sense that it would be better that posterity suffer than that we do present injustice is grounded in his belief that the second coming of Christ will one day bring down the curtain on our history. Duties to posterity cannot, therefore, be overriding; for 'the whole life of humanity in this world' – that is, the entirety of human history – is 'precarious, temporary, provisional'.[13] It is the demon Screwtape, his fellow-tempters, and their 'Father Below' who 'want a man hag-ridden by the Future – haunted by visions of an imminent heaven or hell upon earth – ready to break [God's] commands in the present if by so doing we make [the man] think he can attain the one or avert the other – dependent for his faith on the success or failure of schemes whose end he will not live to see'.[14]

Another example (one that has troubled and engaged many thinkers besides Lewis) is the question whether it could ever be right to lie (perhaps a seemingly harmless 'white lie' that avoids or eases social friction, or, more seriously, a lie necessary to protect someone in danger). Lewis's brother Warren recounts in his diaries an occasion when he 'had an argument with [Jack] on the ethics of social lying, he maintaining that a lie must not be told, even in indifferent matters, as a conversational counter in talking with a fool, I denying this strenuously'.[15] Almost a quarter century later, in a letter written to Sheldon Vanauken, Lewis found the question more complicated:

> I've often puzzled over the question of the obligatory lie – for I am sure wherever it is permissible it is obligatory. The case I am clear about is where an impertinent question forces you *either* to lie *or*

to betray a friend's secret (for to say 'I won't tell you' is often tanta-
mount to answering 'Yes') ... It is hardly possible ever to predict with
certainty that a lie will not be discovered some day to have been a
lie. I shd. be afraid lest that discovery might undo all the good it had
done and even aggravate the evil it was designed to remove.[16]

There may be no general rule by which to resolve such difficulties;
certainly the Tao itself does not provide one. The wisdom needed to see
where our duty lies in such circumstances depends on one's character
having been shaped in particular ways by those who are themselves
morally exemplary. Thus, we can see both the essential contribution of
the Tao to moral deliberation and its limits.

If this is *what* we know, *how* do we know it? If the world around
us is shot through with value, then to recognize a moral duty – to see it
as something other than our own choice or decision – is to see a truth.
Lewis thinks we just 'see' those primeval moral platitudes of the Tao.[17]
They cannot be proven, for it is only by them that we can prove or
defend any other moral conclusions we reach. It is, as Lewis puts it at
the very end of *The Abolition of Man*, 'no use trying to "see through"
first principles. ... To "see through" all things is the same as not to
see'.[18] We might say, as Lewis does in *Miracles*, that these first principles of moral reasoning are 'self-evident'.[19] One can argue *from* but not
to the maxims of the Tao.

This is, however, one place where we need to gloss Lewis's discussion just a bit, for he is not entirely consistent in his writing. If we look
at what I take to be Lewis's best expression of his view, in *The Abolition
of Man*, we will immediately see – for reasons to which I will come in
just a moment – that 'self-evident' cannot mean 'obvious'. It cannot
mean that any rational person, giving the matter some thought, will see
that the maxims of the Tao are the moral deliverances of reason itself.
Yet, consider a passage such as the following from *Mere Christianity*:

> This law was called the Law of Nature because people thought that
> every one knew it by nature and did not need to be taught it. They
> did not mean, of course, that you might not find an odd individual
> here and there who did not know it, just as you find a few people
> who are colour-blind or have no ear for a tune. But taking the race
> as a whole, they thought that the human idea of decent behaviour
> was obvious to every one. And I believe they were right.[20]

This is a different formulation, and a less satisfactory one, than that
of *The Abolition of Man*. The precepts of the Tao constitute a kind of

natural law not because everyone knows them without being taught, but because they express fundamental truths – which we may or may not learn – about human nature. Those of us who do learn them will, to be sure, just 'see' them. There will be no process of reasoning by which they are proven, but, at the same time, there is no reason to assume we all can or will easily discern these first principles of natural law.

Why not? In part – although Lewis does not put it this way in *The Abolition of Man*, a decidedly non-theological piece of writing – because human reason and desire are disordered by what Christians have called sin. The disorder is apparent even apart from any theological explanation. In 'opening our eyes', Iris Murdoch (reflecting Plato's thought, even as Lewis does) has written, 'we do not necessarily see what confronts us. We are anxiety-ridden animals. Our minds are continually active, fabricating an anxious, usually self-preoccupied, often falsifying *veil* which partially conceals the world.'[21] Indeed, if Lewis really held that the precepts of the Tao were 'obvious', the central theme of *The Abolition of Man* could make little sense; for it is a book about our need for moral education.

That brings us to the third element in Lewis's understanding of morality. If we ask *what* moral truths we know, the answer is: the maxims of the Tao. If we ask *how* we know them, the answer is: we just 'see' them as the first principles of all moral reasoning. And now, if we ask how we *become able to* 'just see' these maxims, the answer is: only as our character is well formed by moral education. Without such education we will never come to know the human moral inheritance. We may be very bright and very rational, but we will be 'trousered apes'.[22] Lacking proper moral education, our freedom to make moral choices will be a freedom to be inhuman in any number of ways. The paradox of moral education is that all genuine human freedom, a freedom that does not turn out to be destructive, requires that we be disciplined and shaped by the principles of the Tao.

Our appetites and desires may readily tempt us to set aside what moral reason requires. Hence, from childhood our emotions must be trained and habituated, so that we learn to love the good (not just what seems good for us). And only as our character is thus shaped do we become men and women who are able to 'see' the truths of moral reason. Moral insight, therefore, is not a matter for reason alone; it requires trained emotions and moral habits of behaviour inculcated even before we reach an age of reason. 'The head rules the belly through the chest'.[23] Reason disciplines appetite only with the aid of trained emotions. It turns out, then, that moral education does more than simply enable us to 'see' what virtue requires. It also enables us, at least to some extent, to *be* virtuous. For the very training of the emotions that makes insight possible will have produced in us traits of character that incline us to love the good and do it.

To think through this shaping of character is to appreciate how deeply Aristotelian are the roots of Lewis's understanding of morality. Moral education can never be a private matter, and Lewis follows Aristotle in holding that 'only those who have been well brought up can usefully study ethics'.[24] Hence, the process of moral education, if it is to succeed, requires support from the larger society. Ethics is, in that sense, a branch of politics. Thus, for instance, to take an example that Lewis could not have anticipated precisely, consider the problem of protecting children from Internet pornography. True as it may be that this protection should be the primary responsibility of parents, they face daunting obstacles and almost inevitable failure without a supportive moral ecology in the surrounding society. Moral education, if it is to be serious, requires commitment to moral principles that go well beyond the language of personal freedom – principles that are more than choice and consent alone.

We should not think of this moral education as indoctrination but, rather, as initiation. It is initiation into the human moral inheritance: 'men transmitting manhood to men'.[25] We initiate rather than indoctrinate precisely because it is not we but the Tao that binds those whom we teach. We have not decided what morality requires; we have discovered it. We transmit not our own views or desires but moral truth – by which we consider ourselves also to be bound. An acceptance of the objective reality of the Tao is, therefore, a moral prerequisite for what we might think of as democratic equality among the generations of humankind. It is 'necessary to the very idea of a rule which is not tyranny or an obedience which is not slavery'.[26] Genuine moral education – initiation rather than indoctrination – is not an exercise of power over future generations. To see what happens when it becomes an exercise of power by some over others, when we attempt to stand outside the Tao, we can look briefly at two ways in which Lewis's discussion of morality in *The Abolition of Man* takes shape in *That Hideous Strength*, his '"tall story" of devilry'.

WISDOM VERSUS POWER

At the centre of the plot in *That Hideous Strength* is the plan of the National Institute of Co-ordinated Experiments (N.I.C.E.) to take the

last step in the control and shaping of nature. Having gradually con-
quered the world of nature external to human beings, the goal of the
N.I.C.E. is now to treat human beings also as natural objects – in particular, to take control of birth, breeding and death. The project that
Lewis fancifully imagined in his 'fairy-tale for grown-ups' has made
considerable progress in the decades since he wrote, as the following
example may illustrate.

Consider the following sentences from Ernest Hemingway's *The
Old Man and the Sea*:

> He looked down into the water and watched the lines that went
> straight down into the dark of the water. He kept them straighter
> than anyone did, so that at each level in the darkness of the stream
> there would be a bait waiting exactly where he wished it to be for
> any fish that swam there ... I have no understanding of it and I am
> not sure that I believe in it. Perhaps it was a sin to kill the fish ...
> He urinated outside the shack and then went up the road to wake
> the boy. He was shivering with the morning cold ... Then he was
> sorry for the great fish that had nothing to eat and his determination
> to kill him never relaxed in his sorrow for him. How many people
> will he feed, he thought. But are they worthy to eat him? ... That
> was the saddest thing I ever saw with them, the old man thought.
> The boy was sad too and we begged her pardon and butchered her
> promptly ... The boy did not go down. He had been there before and
> one of the fishermen was looking after the skiff for him.[27]

Hemingway's prose is, of course, generally regarded as clear and straight-
forward, and I suspect that any single sentence in the passage above is
probably simple and transparent to readers. I also suspect that, taken as
a whole, the passage makes almost no sense. There's a reason for that.
The sentences in the passage are drawn from pages 29, 104–05, 22, 74,
48 and 123 of my edition – *in that order*.

Consider now the image of the human being at work in the following frequently quoted passage from Thomas Eisner, a biologist from
Cornell University:

> As a consequence of recent advances in genetic engineering,
> [a biological species] must be viewed as ... a depository of genes
> that are potentially transferable. A species is not merely a hard-
> bound volume of the library of nature. It is also a loose-leaf book,
> whose individual pages, the genes, might be available for selective
> transfer and modification of other species.[28]

I have tried to provide a humble illustration of this by splicing together sentences from different pages of just one book – producing thereby something unintelligible. And, letting our imaginations roam just a bit, I might also have spliced in sentences from *Anna Karenina* and *A Christmas Carol* – producing thereby an artefact we could scarcely name. This train of thought was first suggested to me by one of the findings of the Human Genome Project, a finding that received quite a bit of attention in news articles announcing (in February 2001) the completion of that project by two groups of researchers. We were told that the number of genes in the human genome had turned out to be surprisingly small. Thus, for example, we were informed that human beings have, at most, perhaps twice as many genes as the humble roundworm (a number downsized even more with new findings in 2004 that human beings and roundworms have about the same number of genes). Considering the complexity of human beings in relation to roundworms, it seemed surprising that, relatively speaking, a much less complex organism does not have far fewer genes than human beings.

Why, one might ask, should that seem surprising? It will be surprising if one assumes that the complexity of a 'higher' being is somehow built up from, and explained in terms of, 'lower' component parts (which serve as 'resources'). If we explain the higher in terms of the lower, it makes a certain sense to suppose that a relatively complex being would need lots of component parts – at least by comparison with a less complex being. And, of course, one might argue that the Human Genome Project is the ultimate product of such a reductionist vision of biology.

Thinking about human beings that way is, in a sense, just the last stage in a long movement of Western thought. First we learned to think that qualities of objects were not really present in the object but were supplied by the knowing subject. Then some philosophers suggested that the objects themselves – and not just their qualities – were simply constructs of the knowing subject. But what happens when even that subject disappears? When this reductive process is applied to the human subject, we get, as Lewis noted in a witty passage,

> a result uncommonly like zero. While we were reducing the world to almost nothing we deceived ourselves with the fancy that all its lost qualities were being kept safe (if in a somewhat humbled condition) as 'things in our mind'. Apparently we had no mind of the sort required. The Subject is as empty as the Object. Almost nobody has been making linguistic mistakes

about almost nothing. By and large, this is the only thing that has ever happened.[29]

In *The Abolition of Man* Lewis powerfully depicts the movement by which things came to be understood simply as parts of nature, objects that have no inherent purpose or *telos*, which therefore become resources available for human use. Hence, the long, slow process of what we call conquering nature could more accurately be said to be reducing things to 'mere nature' devoid of purpose or value. 'We do not', Lewis writes,

> look at trees either as Dryads or as beautiful objects while we cut them into beams: the first man who did so may have felt the price keenly, and the bleeding trees in Virgil and Spenser may be far-off echoes of that primeval sense of impiety ... Every conquest over Nature increases her domain. The stars do not become Nature till we weigh and measure them: the soul does not become Nature till we can psychoanalyse her. The wresting of powers *from* Nature is also the surrendering of things *to* Nature. As long as this process stops short of the final stage we may well hold that the gain outweighs the loss. But as soon as we take the final step of reducing our own species to the level of mere Nature, the whole process is stultified, for this time the being who stood to gain and the being who has been sacrificed are one and the same.[30]

In that final step of this reductive process, the human being becomes an artefact, to be shaped and reshaped. One way to describe this is to say that we take control of our own destiny. But the other way to describe it is the way Lord Feverstone puts it in *That Hideous Strength*: 'Man has got to take charge of Man. That means, remember, that some men have got to take charge of the rest.'[31] That is what happens, Lewis thinks, when we step outside the Tao and regard even morality as a matter for our own choice and free creation.

From this angle, developments in biotechnology are likely to affect most our attitudes toward birth and breeding. But there remains still the fact of death, and once we take free responsibility for shaping our destiny, we can hardly be content to accept without challenge even that ultimate limit. When Mark Studdock is asked to trample on a crucifix as the final stage in his training in 'objectivity', he is – even though he is not a Christian – reluctant to obey. For it seems to him that the cross is a picture of what the Crooked does to the Straight when they meet and collide. Mark has chosen the side of what he calls simply the Normal.

He has, that is, begun to take his stand within the Tao. Suppose, he now finds himself wondering for the first time, that the side he has chosen turns out to be, in a sense, the 'losing' side. 'Why not', he asks himself, 'go down with the ship?'[32]

For those who stand within the Tao, *how* we live counts for more than *how long*. There are things we might do to survive – or to help our species survive or advance or even just suffer less – which it would none the less be wrong or dishonourable to do. Indeed, we do not have to look very far in our own world to see how strongly we are tempted to regard as overriding the claims of posterity for a better and longer life. 'We want', Screwtape writes, 'a whole race perpetually in pursuit of the rainbow's end, never honest, nor kind, nor happy *now*, but always using as mere fuel wherewith to heap the altar of the Future every real gift which is offered them in the Present.'[33]

We can see, then, that life within the structure of the Tao is, for Lewis, a way of wisdom rather than a way of power. It is the task of moral education to set limits to what we will do in search of the rainbow's end – to set limits, lest that desire should lead to the abolition of man. 'For the wise men of old,' Lewis writes, but clearly with an eye toward what wisdom still means today, 'the cardinal problem had been how to conform the soul to reality, and the solution had been knowledge, self-discipline, and virtue'.[34] When, by contrast, freedom becomes not initiation into our moral inheritance but the freedom to make and remake ourselves, the power of some people over others, then it becomes imperative to remind ourselves that moral education is not a matter of technique but, rather, of example, habituation and initiation. And, as Lewis says, quoting Plato, those who have been so educated from their earliest years, when they reach an age of reason, will hold out their hands in welcome of the good, recognizing the affinity they themselves bear to it.[35]

Notes

1   MN 109.
2   LB 146.
3   Originally the Riddell Memorial Lectures delivered at the University of Durham, February 1943.
4   SL 118.
5   See 'The Poison of Subjectivism', EC 664. Lewis suggests there that it may be 'permissible to lay down two negations: that God neither *obeys* nor *creates* the moral law. The good is uncreated; it never could have been otherwise; it has in it no shadow of contingency'. Lewis

consistently holds that we can make sense of morality only if we see that what lies 'behind the universe is more like a mind than it is like anything else we know. That is to say, it is conscious, and has purposes, and prefers one thing to another' (MC 30). The argument is theistic but not specifically Christian. In any case, however we think of God as 'lying behind' the moral law, it cannot be in the sense of one who arbitrarily creates it. Rather, that law reflects something about the nature of this divine being.

6   'On Ethics', EC 312. In 'The Poison of Subjectivism' Lewis says that anyone who takes the trouble to investigate the ethical principles of different cultures will 'discover the massive unanimity of the practical reason in man' and 'will no longer doubt that there is such a thing as the Law of Nature' (EC 662). In *The Abolition of Man* he writes that what he calls the Tao 'others may call Natural Law' (29), and his appended illustrations of the Tao's maxims begins, 'The following illustrations of the Natural Law' (49).

7   AOM 27.

8   THS 7.

9   THS 299.

10   THS 299.

11   THS 310.

12   'On Ethics', EC 313.

13   'The World's Last Night,' EC 52.

14   SL 78–79.

15   Clyde S. Kilby and Marjorie Lamp Mead (eds), *Brothers and Friends: The Diaries of Major Warren Hamilton Lewis* (New York: Ballantine Books, 1982),168.

16   Letter to Sheldon Vanauken, 15 Dec. 1958 (CLIII 1000).

17   He seems to deny, however, that he is offering an 'Intuitionist' moral theory. See 'On Ethics', EC 312.

18   AOM 48.

19   M 39.

20   MC 17.

21   Iris Murdoch, *The Sovereignty of Good* (London: Routledge & Kegan Paul, 1970), 84.

22   AOM 11, 12.

23   AOM 19.

24   AOM 31.

25   AOM 18.

26   AOM 44.

27   Ernest Hemingway, *The Old Man and the Sea* (New York: Charles Scribner's Sons, 1952), 29, 104–05, 22, 74, 48, 123.

28   Thomas Eisner, 'Chemical Ecology and Genetic Engineering: The Prospects for Plant Protection and the Need for Plant Habitat Conservation', Symposium on Tropical Biology and Agriculture, Monsanto Company, St Louis, 15 July 1985; quoted in Mary Midgley, 'Biotechnology and Monstrosity', *Hastings Center Report* 30 (Sept.–Oct. 2000), 11.

29 'The Empty Universe', EC 364.
30 AOM 43.
31 THS 42.
32 THS 337.
33 SL 79.
34 AOM 46.
35 AOM 15.

10 On discernment

JOSEPH P. CASSIDY

The Screwtape Letters, published in 1942,[1] is a satire written from the perspective of a highly experienced devil, Screwtape, instructing his younger nephew, Wormwood, in the art of temptation, as Wormwood tries to turn a young human 'patient' away from the Enemy (God) towards the dark side. The letters are concerned with those temptations most typical of recent converts (indeed, the 'patient' turns to Christianity after the first letter) and blend ironic humour with indirect wisdom, the latter evidently stemming from Lewis's own hard-won self-knowledge and from his familiarity with the tradition of spiritual writing in the West (for example, though different in style, similar concerns can be found in such spiritual classics as St John of the Cross's *The Dark Night of the Soul*[2]). Not surprisingly, the inexperienced Wormwood is himself tempted to try to turn his patient via blatant and obvious temptations while the wiser Screwtape everywhere extols the 'virtue' of deceit and confusion. It is in the exposure of such guile that the book excels, for the basically good 'patient' (he is never named) can best be undermined by his own spiritual vanity, as moral self-blinding becomes ever more subtle and complex even if transparently (from our point of view) self-defeating.

Letters to Malcolm: Chiefly on Prayer was published posthumously in 1964, in Lewis's own voice but to an imaginary correspondent. As the subtitle indicates, these letters are mainly concerned with prayer, although they also touch on controverted doctrinal questions and even on matters of theological and liturgical taste. The book is obviously similar to *Screwtape* in form, but also – not so obviously – in content. As it reflects the older Lewis's personal struggle to pray, it could be said that *Letters to Malcolm* unwraps self-deceit as it was discovered and played out both in Lewis's own prayer life and as observed in the life of the wider church.

This dual concern with unmasking self-deceit and growing in discernment through prayer suggests a 'way into' these texts – at least for this chapter. A commentary on a selection of the various letters in *Screwtape* and *Malcolm* is provided and comparisons made with Ignatius of Loyola's approach to discernment, a comparison prompted by Lewis's mention of Ignatius in chapter 16 of *Malcolm*.[3] In addition to underlining some similarities and differences between Lewis and Ignatius, several other themes will emerge, key among which are Lewis's emphasis on the importance of the will and his (perhaps related) wrestling with God's relationship to time.

COMMENTARY: *THE SCREWTAPE LETTERS*

Letter 4 of *Screwtape* takes aim at the prayer novice's attempts to manufacture particular feelings or 'consolations'. The temptation is well known: those who are in the early days of more meditative or contemplative prayer will often experience powerful consolation through a sense of divine presence. However, as Lewis observes, to focus on those consolations or to pray in order to feel such consolations is to be self-absorbed rather than focused on God. But Lewis is also commending the *duty* of prayer, no matter what feelings or desires are present. This theme of duty, of the priority of will over affect in the face of the affective unattractiveness of prayer, is one of many themes in Lewis's work: it is emphasized here because the comparison with Ignatius highlights it, and because the theme becomes most evident in the later, and perhaps more mature, chapters of *Malcolm*.

Letter 8 focuses on obedience and freedom, and Lewis points out that God does not use irresistibility or irrefutability to overwhelm human souls. This is an important insight, for many Christians will have prayed to be 'possessed' by God. But in the Christian tradition, only Satan can 'possess' and God, in contrast, maximizes freedom by calling us to choose, even if we would prefer not to. In terms of principles of discernment this is crucial: any sense of compulsion arising in prayer does not come from God, no matter how good the object of compulsion may seem. As Screwtape says of the Enemy, 'He cannot ravish; He can only woo.' And though the early experience of God can seem almost overwhelming in intensity (Lewis himself said in *Surprised by Joy* that he was converted largely *against* his will, so compelling was God's approach[4]), still it is characteristic of God eventually to withdraw, requiring the soul to 'carry out from the will alone duties which have lost all relish'. Both here and in *Malcolm*,[5] Lewis says that prayer during such periods of dryness, even forsakenness, is most pleasing to God.

Lewis has a lively sense of the divine authorship of pleasure, but also a keen sense of the need for order in all things. Thus the strategy of hell is to rob pleasure of its natural context and to re-contextualize it unnaturally. This focusing on 'ordered and disordered affections' is a theme shared with Ignatius, though Lewis and Ignatius seem to operate with slightly different psychologies. For Lewis, it is the spiritually surrendered will that orders the affections, but for Ignatius order is achieved by first achieving sufficient freedom so that desires order themselves according to the promptings of the Spirit.[6]

Letter 13 reflects on the value of attending to the actual nature of any pleasure (or pain). Such attention keeps one's affections ordered away from mere appearance towards a real good (or real evil). Simplicity is thus key to avoiding deception: even something as simple as a satisfying walk can suffice to ground oneself, so that the walk is enjoyed disinterestedly, for its own sake. This insight reinforces both the theme of 'ordered' affections and also of the prime (and only) weapon of Satan: namely, deception (and concomitant secrecy). In so doing it underlines a key principle for all discernment of spirits – the reality test – and this explains Lewis's disdain for what he calls 'the Romantic method', which elevates affected pathos above real pain. As mentioned above, there may be a particular psychology at play here, one that appears to decouple desires and passions from the will – a psychology that at first sight seems to owe more to Kant than to Aquinas. But also present is a sense of hierarchy and of sublimation, where desires and passions are not entirely rejected but rather redirected away from implemental goods towards higher-order goods, where what might appear to be merely natural stirrings are revealed as part of a larger, supernatural longing. Lewis's goal was integration with one's final purpose, so that our elemental desires have an ultimately worthy object.

Letter 14's theme of humility as self-forgetfulness solves a riddle for anyone who has prayed for greater humility only to become endlessly self-preoccupied. Lewis's discussion of humility is insightful but abstract: this contrasts with Ignatius's treatment, where Jesus is presented as the exemplar of all virtue, and where *Jesus'* humility is more important than Jesus' *humility*. Lewis's concern with order is apparent in this letter, and it is noteworthy that the preoccupation shifts now to the moral order. This also contrasts somewhat with Ignatius, for whom spiritual discernment is never concerned with morality *per se*, but rather with discerning God's will. For Ignatius, although God of course *wants* us to do the good, God also *invites* us to do more than the good (the *magis* or *greater good*) – a matter not of moral requirement but invitation. Thus, for Ignatius, discernment is principally concerned with developing an acute sensitivity to anything that smacks of compulsion (including moral compulsion) so that the quite different graciousness of divine invitation can be discerned.

Letter 15 reminds us of de Caussade's[7] 'sacrament of the present moment'. Lewis is suspicious of focusing too much on the future because the future does not yet exist: it is unreal. Again the importance of being grounded in 'the real' is reinforced. Ignatius commends the same: his *examen*, which is done once or twice a day, keeps his followers focused very particularly on how God is moving them on a daily, even an hourly, basis. Lewis's advice is prompted by much the same concern as Ignatius's: too much focusing on the future leaves little room for providence.

Letter 16 will be especially interesting to Anglicans. Here Lewis takes clever shots at what are contrasting and still typical divides within Anglicanism. He eschews party churches – churches established according to particular doctrinal preferences – because the important thing is the duty to worship and to do so among those with whom one lives, rather than waiting until one finds a more comfortable church in another location. His preference for the parochial over the associational model of church and his desire for familiar and relatively stable liturgical forms would thus exclude him from some sorts of churches on various sides of the several Anglican divides. More importantly, for this context, this also practically applies his keen theological sense of the priority of grace over nature and provides an example of the deception that can rise when this priority is reversed.

Letters 18 and 19 contain some adroit insights into 'falling in love' (made especially comic owing to Screwtape's inability to perceive what love is all about). Lewis has wholly positive things to say about love and sex, but Letter 19 also reveals an important aspect of discernment. Screwtape, when pressed to say whether falling in love is good or bad in itself, says, 'Nothing matters at all except ... to move a particular patient at a particular moment nearer to the Enemy or nearer to us.' In terms of discernment of spirits this is key: experiences are to be judged not only on their own peculiar merits, but on whether they are part of a larger pattern of moving us closer to – or further from – God.

Letter 22 has a wonderful diatribe on divine hedonism. Perhaps not so noticeable, however, is Lewis's take on the Fall. He is no proponent of the utter depravity of the post-lapsarian universe: 'Out at sea, out at His sea, there is pleasure, and more pleasure.' This reflects a more Catholic perspective, where the challenge is not to deny the goods that remain in creation, but to allow God's grace to reorder our use of those goods towards divine ends.

Letter 23 starts by denouncing the search for the historical Jesus, as if we could detach ourselves from our history to gain a privileged point of view to rediscover the pristine Jesus of history. The caution is worth hearing: our reconstructions are always ideological, because we are ideological. Still, Lewis is too dismissive (even for his time) of historical-critical methods of reading scripture: too many scholars and pray-ers have received too much benefit in their academic struggles with the sacred texts to discount such methods so summarily (even within a satire such as *Screwtape*). Moreover, can we ever avoid attempting to rediscover the 'real' Jesus given the quite different testimony of the four Gospels? And yet Lewis is surely right to note that the 'earliest converts were converted by a single historical fact (the Resurrection) and a single historical doctrine (the Redemption) … The "Gospels" came later and were written not to make Christians but to edify Christians already made.'

Here Lewis makes two significant claims. First, the church pre-dates the New Testament – an obvious point, but one too easily forgotten. Second, true conversion is not owing to an historical and therefore quite fallible reconstruction of Jesus, but to direct encounter with the Holy Spirit. True, we would not know of the resurrection were it not for the accounts written later, but the role of the accounts is to point away from themselves towards an event: the biblical records, in the words of Bernard Lonergan, 'mediate immediacy'.[8]

In letter 27, Lewis relies on Boethius's[9] *ever-present-now* notion to explain God's omniscience and particularly God's foreknowledge. Lewis is careful to say that God never foresees people doing anything before it happens, 'but *sees* them doing so in His unbounded Now'. This classical approach is important for Lewis's understanding of the problem of evil (it leaves room for God's permissive will), but it is less theologically and philosophically satisfying than it first appears. For one, the collapsing of time into a single *now* does away with duration, and with the loss of duration goes sequentiality, and with the loss of sequentiality the intelligibility of the universe disappears. It is much better to affirm the intelligibility grasped by human beings, which includes our ability to grasp the not-yet-ness of an indeterminate future, and to affirm that God is wholly capable of grasping this very same sequential intelligibility. This does not rule out an infinitely greater divine grasp of reality, but it does allow God to grasp finite creation as truly finite and temporal. Moreover, the incarnation arguably ought to challenge the classic

Boethian solution to foreknowledge: the Second Person of the Trinity had and still has a created, finite human nature; and this nature cannot be separated from his divine person. However else we solve the thorny theological problems of predestination, any abstract notion that has God utterly outside of time ought to reckon with the Trinity's actual embracing of time in the incarnation.

Letter 29 can be compared to Ignatius's First Week of the *Exercises*, as both deal with sin. Lewis's insight into sin, especially the sin of despair, is useful, and it provides a glimpse into the problem of scruples, which is more a sin of pride than of false humility, for it holds that our sinfulness is beyond forgiveness, setting our wickedness up against God's mercy.

The last letter, 31, will be left without comment: revealing too much will spoil the experience for the new reader. Suffice it to say that this chapter is strangely moving and consoling.

COMMENTARY: *LETTERS TO MALCOLM*

To begin with a controversial topic, chapter 3 of *Malcolm* raises the issue of praying with, or to, the saints. Lewis here exhibits one of the chief characteristics of his Anglicanism: he is quite open to people praying *to* saints, even though he thinks it can lead to curious practices. He is also quite open to *not* praying to saints, and doesn't plan to adopt the practice himself. Yet he doesn't see in such differences any justification for divided churches. It is as though his discernment principle about the object of a practice leads him more towards a prudent personal opinion of its usefulness for spiritual progress than to an exclusionary dogmatic judgement.

Chapter 4 concerns petitionary prayer. His advice that we ought not 'to ask God with factitious earnestness for A when our whole mind is in reality filled with desire for B' is perfect. 'We must', as he says, 'lay before Him what is in us, not what ought to be in us' – even if the matter is sinful. Petitionary prayer, no matter what we think about its efficacy, is a sort of 'unveiling' or truth-telling before God. Chapter 5 provides some thoughts on the Lord's Prayer. The comments on the common petition '*encore*' remind us of Lewis's continuing concern for those who have just left behind the first 'fervours of their conversion'.

Chapter 7 discusses determinism in relation to petitionary prayer. There are some good insights into the existence of regularities alongside the non-systematic particularities and irrelevancies that make the universe indeterminate. For Lewis, petitionary prayer exists because of

indeterminacy. That said, Lewis is under no illusion that we will necessarily get what we pray for. In chapter 8 he cites, as his prime example,
Jesus' prayer at his passion. And, for Lewis, Jesus did not even have
the consolation of experiencing a God who, though he didn't answer
the prayer, was none the less present, for he takes Jesus' experience of
being forsaken as real – not merely apparent, as some would have it.
He explains it in terms of creation being both divinely authored and
yet not being divine. An experience of this necessary distinction or separation is a sort of 'dark night' that is part of the reality of God's creative act. Lewis goes on to suggest that 'perhaps there is an anguish, an
alienation, a crucifixion involved in the creative act' – something others
have referred to as 'metaphysical' as opposed to 'moral' evil.

Chapter 9 returns to petitionary prayer, and again Lewis's Boethian
approach is front and centre: 'if our prayers are granted at all they are
granted from the foundation of the world. God and his acts are not in
time'. Though a conventional thought, and though appealing appropriately to the need to trust in God's infinite wisdom and oversight, this
cannot easily be reconciled with Chalcedon or later ecumenical coun-
cils. For instance, even if there are two wills in Christ, one divine and
one human, there is still but one divine person who is the subject of all
of Christ's human acts. The incarnation clearly implies that God acts
in time.

Lewis also deliberates on agency, on whether *we* can act upon God,
and how that relates to traditional notions of God's impassibility. Lewis
insists that we can so act: without our sinning, he says, there would
be no cause for God's forgiveness. But he wiggles around the larger
impassibility problem by again appealing implicitly to Boethius, stating
that 'from before all worlds His providential and creative act (for they
are all one) takes into account all the situations produced by the acts of
his creatures'. However, as Lewis continues to wrestle with petitionary
prayer in chapter 10, he sensibly acknowledges that divine impassibility
is not a doctrine carefully grounded in scripture. He suggests that the
object of petitionary prayer is to be heard, rather than to have the prayer
request fulfilled. At the same time, he is unsympathetic towards those
who would make excuses for God. He especially rejects the view that
God cannot answer our prayers because God operates on the level of
grand design and not of the particular, that on the level of the particular
we (and God) are stuck with the unintended side-effects of our decisions
and of otherwise good processes that none the less produce curses as
well as blessings. Lewis ends the chapter by considering the value of
prayer as an end and not just as a means.

By way of contrast, this whole topic does not figure in Ignatius. Though there are all kinds of petitions in the *Exercises*, the petitions are chiefly concerned with discerning and doing God's will. The idea that prayer might be about persuading God to do *our* will does not occur. That is not to say that Ignatius did not pray assiduously for particular things, but the caveat (so crucial in Lewis's thought too) that 'Thy will, not mine, be done' governs all Ignatian prayer. Here, however, the genius of Lewis still shines. Lewis wants to wrestle with such seemingly simple problems as his overlong prayer list. He does not want to espouse a theology that undermines his need to pray for those on that list with real authenticity. Such determination raises real questions for real theology.

In chapter 11, Lewis faces the problem of the 'lavish' and unqualified promises of answers to our prayers that can be found in the New Testament. Lewis notes that, intellectually, we know that not all prayers can be answered: so many of our prayers contradict other prayers – our own and others'. He does not find the refusal of answers difficult; but he does wonder about the promise of answers. Lewis's answer to these dilemmas is much the same as Ignatius's: the kind of perfect faith that is spoken of in scripture 'occurs only when the one who prays does so as God's fellow-worker, demanding what is needed for the joint work'. Though Lewis is not a fan of Ignatian exercises (for reasons we will come to below), this is ironically one of the most apt descriptions of the goal of all Ignatian prayer.

The next chapter offers some thoughts on mysticism and on the need to distinguish Christian mysticism from other forms. Reading this chapter, one might be tempted to question Lewis's denial that he was in any way a mystic.[10] Though many of his insights into prayer can be found elsewhere, and though people *can* write seemingly knowingly about prayer without first-hand knowledge, Lewis's economy of style suggests that he knew the heart of the matter intimately. How could he have gained such insight into the subtle movements of the soul, how could he worry about being too distracted by Ignatian-style meditation, without having profound and relatively immediate experiences of God? One wonders whether his sense of duty and his devotion to the ordinary practices of the faith (prayer lists, etc.) mentioned in this same chapter led him to the humble, but perhaps mistaken, view that his prayer life was utterly dissimilar to that of the great medieval mystics.

In chapter 13, we find what might best be called Lewis's theology of prayer and discernment, albeit a thoroughly Pseudo-Dionysian one.[11] His focus on how our prayer arises from the depth of our being sits uncomfortably with any notion of the utter depravity of fallen human nature or of a solely forensic justification before God. Lewis writes:

> [God] is the ground of our being. He is always both within us and over against us. Our reality is so much from His reality as He, moment by moment, projects into us. The deeper the level within ourselves from which our prayer, or any other act, wells up, the more it is His, but not at all the less ours.[12]

The goal is 'a union of wills which, under Grace, is reached by a life of sanctity'. In terms of a theology of discernment, the goal is to learn to recognize disjunctions between our will and God's, because these disjunctions will exist within our very being. Lewis does not dwell on precisely how one accomplishes such discernment, but his theology lays the groundwork for at least recognizing the need to do so.

At the end of chapter 13, Lewis acknowledges that because of the incarnation one can say, 'Heaven drew earth up into it, and locality, limitation, sleep, sweat, footsore weariness, frustration, pain, doubt and death, are, from before all worlds, known by God from within'. Though the *ever-present-now* is still espoused, here the *ever-present-now* contains time and finiteness to such an extent that to distinguish eternity from duration seems but a vain attempt to get some purchase on God's experience of time – something we simply cannot do.

In chapter 14, Lewis distances himself from Neoplatonic and Origenist notions of creation-as-emanation as well as from pantheism. In a lovely few lines, he turns Neo-Platonism on its head via a paradox: 'The higher the creature, the more and also the less God is in it; the more present by grace, and the less present (by a sort of abdication) as mere power. By grace He gives the higher creatures power to will His will … the lower ones simply execute it automatically'. The chapter ends with some words of caution to those who may be attracted to a watered-down Christianity that seems to offer only pure consolation.

Chapter 15 discusses the challenges of placing oneself in the presence of God. Here Lewis reveals why he has been so intent on 'the real' in prayer and how the efficacy of the simple awareness of a walk in nature (as in *Screwtape*) could somehow ground him. In prayer, Lewis tries to become aware of the reality of his present situation, of what is himself and what is not himself. To be in touch with one's real situation, with one's real condition, via a sort of introspection that allows him to construct his 'me' – this opens him to the possibility that 'this situation itself is, at every moment, a possible theophany'. To counteract all this effort, Lewis reminds his correspondent that 'Only God

Himself can let the bucket down to the depths in us. And, on the other side, He must constantly work as the iconoclast. Every idea of Him we form, He must in mercy shatter.' If Lewis did not regard himself as practising mystical prayer, this sounds rather close.

In the next chapter, Lewis admits difficulty with the *compositio loci* (composition of place), which is a prelude to Ignatian prayer where the one making the *Exercises* is urged to imagine visually the place where a particular event from Jesus' life took place. Lewis found it less than useful to use the imagination in this way: he thought it would be too distracting to deal with the archaeological naïveté such a practice would seem to require. Moreover, he thought that such a use of the visual imagination might be at the expense of true Imagination, as he called it, with the risk that 'the picture would go on elaborating itself indefinitely and becoming every moment of less spiritual significance'.

But Lewis's comments here seem to turn on a caricature of the *Exercises*, perhaps evidencing familiarity with the text, but without the benefit of actually experiencing the *Exercises* as 'exercises' – things done, not read. The composition of place usually takes a short period of time (sometimes only a few minutes) within the typical hour of Ignatian prayer. Lewis was quite wrong to think that the *Exercises* were best for people with limited visual imagination. On the contrary, before widespread reading and other media, people were arguably much better at visualization – even if they did so without all the factual information we have today. Indeed, Lewis is not far from Ignatius when he speaks of different levels of imagination. In the fifth exercise of each day, during the 'application of the senses', those making the *Exercises* are urged to apply their senses analogically, so that they taste the sweetness of the divine – not the imagined saltiness of someone's sweat.

Chapter 17 is largely to do with ordering one's pleasures towards adoration. Tellingly, Lewis notes that 'the simplest act of obedience is worship of a far more important sort ... (to obey is better than sacrifice)'. Again, he distances himself from more Evangelical Protestant views: 'something tragic may, as I think I've said before, be inherent in the very act of creation'. He also reveals his view of heaven: 'to be utterly spontaneous; to be the complete reconciliation of boundless freedom with order – with the most delicately adjusted, supple, intricate, and beautiful order'. One must not underestimate the power of this vision of 'order' and its connectedness to some fundamental theological and spiritual instincts in Lewis, such as his espousal of natural law and of a universal moral sense (taught, he said, by all the major religions and moral traditions). For Lewis, were there not any such order, there would be no question of a fallen creation: there would simply be no creation at all.

Chapter 18 has useful things to say about anger and forgiveness. There is a qualified defence of the use of gothic imagery to describe one's moral corruption – good examples of which can be found also in Ignatius's *Exercises*.[13] While Lewis does not think that such images need be kept constantly in view, he does think them a useful tonic. It might be mentioned that, in the *Exercises*, such images co-exist with the exquisite joy of being forgiven without any merit whatsoever: they are designed not so much as to elicit loathsome self-regard as to set the stage for appreciating grace.

Chapter 19's discussion of Holy Communion is a devilishly simple restatement of the traditional Anglican view of the 'real presence' of Christ in the sacrament: devilish because he dares use the term 'magic' to describe this position (thus employing the very word so often used to criticize the Roman Catholic doctrine of transubstantiation); and 'simple' because he refuses to reduce the mystery of the Eucharist, saying only that it has 'an objective efficacy which cannot be further analysed'. Lewis thought that no definitions of the Eucharist were truly necessary and that none should ever have been allowed to divide Christians from one another.

Chapter 20's defence of prayers for the dead ('Of course I pray for the dead ... at our age the majority of those we love best are dead') is again simple, though Lewis does tackle Protestant objections more directly here, hinting at a possible transformative element in heaven, and defending the need for post-death purgation. He perfunctorily distances himself from some particular Roman Catholic notions of purgatory with but four words ('No nonsense about merit'), but he holds space for the soul's wholly appropriate desire to be cleansed before entering into the light.

In the final chapter, Lewis defends belief in a bodily resurrection as an essential link between ourselves in the here-and-now and a longed-for glorified existence. This is not just a matter of feeling: it is a matter of the total spiritual orientation of our physically embodied lives. The longing for heaven is a vector that directs all else towards God, that interprets all else in the only light that can possibly reveal who we are meant to be and thus who we really are. 'Who we are meant to be' is, in the end, not the motive for a dryly conceived sense of duty, but a motive for a different type of personal response – a profound and practical 'yes' to a God whose wondrous future order has already been inaugurated in a grace-filled creation that is itself longing for consummation.

SUMMARY

In terms of unmasking self-deceit and developing our powers of discernment, there is no explicit theology in Lewis of following Jesus quite as literally as there is in Ignatius. The human good is good only when it is aligned with God's will, but for Ignatius the question was a practical and immediate one: how am I to discern God's particular will for me individually? In *Screwtape* and *Malcolm*, the focus on order and nature and duty, which allows Lewis to appeal to the widest possible audience, might also have prevented him from being more precise: human nature is, after all, an abstraction, and a study of human and divine natures leads to general rather than historically specific claims on us. Thus it is no accident, nor grounds for criticism, that discernment in Lewis is more universal and strategic than situational and tactical, more of a clinical examination of any earnest soul than a practical element in concrete decision-making in a particular life of discipleship.

For Lewis, the temptations he wrote of were typical of the novice (though which Christian isn't still prone to them all?). For Ignatius, the temptations that concerned him most were typical of someone who had been at it a while (the Second Week rules): those whose lives are more and more orientated towards God are still deceived, though less by exploiting a moral vulnerability than by being offered a false good that plays on actual, if imperfect, virtue. Perhaps there is room for a sequel to *Screwtape*, one that shows with equal insight and humour just how the holiest are misled not by veiled evils, but by seeming goods.

Although his struggles with God in prayer were real, and at times acutely so, these two works also have Lewis wrestling with a God whose *nature* presents conceptual problems (as exemplified in the recurrence of the *ever-present-now* device in his discussion of petitionary prayer, the problem of evil, and prayers for the dead). This hardly exhausts Lewis's insight, nor is it the best window into his soul (other works provide much better glimpses), but Lewis's focus on philosophically informed problems contrasts with Ignatius's philosophically reckless God, who is bending over backwards in time, 'working' in our world.[14] For Ignatius, such wrestling with theological problems might have been considered distractions in prayer, but for Lewis they evidently emerge from very practical concerns that simply and honestly had to be brought into his praying.

The differences between Lewis and Ignatius on duty and love are also worth noting. To be sure, in *Screwtape* and *Malcolm*, Lewis uses modes of discourse other than dutifulness to represent the Christian's relationship to Christ, most notably in the experience of sweet desire. Equally, to be sure, Ignatius uses a sense of duty to motivate people to respond to Christ (as, say, in the Kingdom Exercise[15]), but there is a clear movement within the *Exercises* from acting out of reasonable duty towards acting out of mutual love, with the latter being generated by gratitude and suffused 'with great affection'. It is almost as though loving desire would eventually compel the will. But for Lewis, even though the attraction to God's glory emanates from the deepest chords of our being, and even though our fundamental duty coincides with our perfect joy, there is always work, even irksome work, to be done this side of heaven.

In his famous sermon 'The Weight of Glory', Lewis writes movingly of the divine glory Christians are destined to share, but he is constrained to end with the reminder that 'the cross comes before the crown' and that 'the load, or weight, or burden of my neighbour's glory should be laid daily on my back'.[16] This is an example of a compellingly honest and supremely humble spirituality that we also find (ironically expressed) in *The Screwtape Letters* and (more directly) in *Letters to Malcolm*. No watered-down Christianity for Lewis: the real thing is so much better.

Notes

1 Compiled and edited by Lewis from 31 letters previously published in *The Guardian*, a religious newspaper that ceased publication in 1951.
2 See especially chs 1–7 of book 1. St John of the Cross (1542–1591) was a Spanish mystic and Carmelite priest, best known for this poem and his commentary thereon.
3 St Ignatius of Loyola (c. 1491–1556) founded the Society of Jesus (the 'Jesuits') and is the author of the *Spiritual Exercises*, a manual chiefly concerned with discernment, especially with vocational discernment.
4 SBJ 182–83.
5 LTM 113–17.
6 For more on Lewis's understanding of the importance of virtuously habituating the will, see *The Abolition of Man* and ch. 7 of *The Problem of Pain*.
7 Jean-Pierre de Caussade (1675–1751), a French Jesuit probably best known for his *The Sacrament of the Present Moment*.
8 See Bernard Lonergan, *Method in Theology* (Toronto: University of Toronto Press, 1990), 29.
9 Anicius Manlius Severinus Boethius (c. 480–c. 525), best known for his *The Consolation of Philosophy*. Its reflections on divine timelessness (see especially book V) became important for later Christian theology.

10 For more on this, see David C. Downing, *Into the Region of Awe: Mysticism in C.S. Lewis* (Downers Grove, IL: InterVarsity Press, 2005).

11 Pseudo-Dionysius was a Neoplatonic mystical writer from the late fifth or early sixth century, whose writing is perhaps best known for its emphasis on the apophatic and more generally on levels of interiority.

12 LTM 71.

13 See, for instance, Ignatius's First Week meditations, where he encourages us to imagine ourselves as an open wound, a source of contagion, etc.

14 See Ignatius's Fourth Week. Here God is portrayed as a labourer, literally working on our behalf throughout creation, and our response is to cooperate.

15 The Kingdom Exercise separates the First from the Second Weeks of the *Exercises*, and Ignatius frames that exercise in terms of dutiful expectations.

16 'The Weight of Glory', EC 105.

CAROLINE J. SIMON

An obvious place to start in exploring C.S. Lewis's views on love is *The Four Loves* (1960). The book's major lesson is a theme that Lewis reiterated throughout his long career: natural loves are God-given goods, yet are also prone to distortions – distortions so severe that Lewis calls them demonic – unless they are transformed by Charity. *The Four Loves* is a slim volume that grew out of a series of radio talks prepared for the Episcopal Radio-TV Foundation of Atlanta, Georgia. Its conversational style and relative brevity give it an appearance of simplicity. This appearance is deceptive. As one commentator has observed, 'As an author of nonfiction [Lewis] is a demanding writer … If reading Lewis can be compared to the hikes that he loved famously then the reader must know ahead of time that he will at times outpace you with his thinking … *The Four Loves* is not easily "hiked" through in one reading.'[1] While casual familiarity with *The Four Loves* yields many insights and edifying pricks of conscience, even a second or third reading may leave the book's overall structure a mystery.

In this essay I will clarify Lewis's views on love, concentrating on some of the more puzzling aspects of his theoretical work, reflecting on the cultural contexts of his ideas, and briefly examining his literary depictions of love and its distortions.

HOW MANY LOVES?

Christians in certain circles will have heard repeatedly from the pulpit that there are three types of love – friendship (*philia*), romantic or desiring love (*erōs*) and Christian love, God's love, or love of neighbour (*agapē*). Lewis adds to this list affection (*storgē*), thus equipping himself for the four-fold analysis of love forecast by the book's title. However, while the title creates an expectation of a four-category exposition of types of love, the reader is first confronted with a discussion of the strengths and limitations of dividing loves into *two* categories: Need-love and Gift-love. More than a brief warm-up act that soon gives way to the main subject of the book, the discussion of Need-love and Gift-love is an early clue that love is not a simple subject and that Lewis has not written a simple book.

It would be tempting, Lewis says, to think that godly love is always Gift-love and that Need-love may be too self-centred to qualify as love at all. Lewis, however, rejects a sharp dichotomy between Need-love and Gift-love, pointing out that Need-love is a genuine love that binds humans to one another and is also a fitting creaturely response to God: 'It would be a bold and silly creature that came before its Creator with the boast "I'm no beggar. I love you disinterestedly"'.[2] After acknowledging that Gift-love is nearer to God 'by resemblance', Lewis observes that Need-love brings us nearer to God 'by approach'. In our journey to God, the closer we come the more we feel the profoundness of our need for God. God draws us through Need-love, all the while working to transform us into lovers who can love with a Gift-love that is selfless and unofficious, and transcends the need to be needed. By the end of *The Four Loves*, Lewis makes it clear that this work of transformation must begin in this life, but will only be completed in the next.[3]

After discussing the nature of Need-love and Gift-love, Lewis launches into an examination of loves of the sub-personal (including love of nature and love of country). This discussion in turn introduces a third major category of love – Appreciative Love. Thus, by the time chapter 3 (which is on Affection) starts, we already have been given a fifty-page excursion through what seems to be an alternative three-category taxonomy. Yet chapter 3 starts with the sentence, 'I begin with the humblest and most widely diffused of the loves, the love in which our experience seems to differ least from that of the animals.' Lewis's 'I begin with …' is, in its context of page 53, startling, raising sharply the question of what the first two chapters were doing if they were *not* the beginning of what Lewis wanted to say about love.[4]

Did Lewis write two books, a shorter one on the three loves (Need, Gift and Appreciative Love) and a somewhat longer one on the four loves (Affection, Friendship, Romance and Charity) and merely choose to have them bound together? No. While Lewis might have usefully given his readers more help in understanding the overarching shape of his project, his strategy is to use the tripartite analysis of love into Need-love, Gift-love and Appreciative Love and the four-fold analysis of love as Affection, Friendship, Romantic Love and Charity as mutually illuminating schemata. The two schemes serve as the warp and woof of his exposition, allowing more depth and complexity than either taxonomy could provide alone. He triangulates each of the four loves within the tripartite schema. This triangulation helps explain each natural love's particular excellence, each natural love's characteristic proneness to distortion, and Charity's role in redeeming and elevating each of the natural loves.

ANALYSING WITHOUT 'MURDERING TO DISSECT'

Within certain Christian circles, Lewis's reputation as an authority, a reverence for the Greek language, and the title '*The Four Loves*' have too often led to the assumption that love has, in its very essence, four species. Yet Lewis's exposition within the book undercuts this sort of essentialism. Depending on our purposes, it may be useful to divide love by its motivations, its characteristic feelings, its sources, its objects, or its characteristic results. Lewis himself, sometimes explicitly and sometimes more subtly, divides loves along at least four different parameters: (1) Love for the Sub-personal versus Love for Finite Persons versus Love for God; (2) Natural Love versus Supernatural Love; (3) Need-love versus Gift-love versus Appreciative Love; (4) Affection versus Friendship versus Eros versus Charity. If the multiplicity of these taxonomies is not enough to make us take taxonomies somewhat lightly, Lewis gives us an explicit admonition, drawn from Wordsworth: 'We murder to dissect'.[5]

As actually lived out, human love for one particular thing or person is more often than not a mix. Need, gift and appreciation mingle. Friendship and Eros can exist toward the same person at the same time. Affection can 'enter into other loves and colour them all through'.[6] Moreover, 'language is not an infallible guide' to how to understand concepts and not all languages distinguish among types of love in the same way.[7] Lewis gives little indication that he himself sees Greek as a canon before which other languages must bow. Looking either to Greek or to what the majority of languages and cultures have to give us by way of stored insight and experience is a starting point, not a destination.

Another starting point is experience. Lewis places so much confidence in our capacity to grasp the rudiments of love from lived experience that he never gives us an explicit definition of the genus of which Affection, Friendship, Eros and Charity could be considered candidate species. Though at one point he calls love 'mere feeling',[8] this is not a serious attempt at definition, even of the natural loves. Gilbert Meilaender's careful consideration of the whole corpus of Lewis's work uncovers a much more useful and illuminating implicit definition of love. For Lewis, says Meilaender, love is 'a relation among persons which – overcoming the recalcitrant claims of self – can generate and maintain a community of vicariousness and reciprocity'.[9] Meilaender concludes that *self-giving* is at the heart of Lewis's understanding of love.

Two caveats to Meilaender's explication of Lewis's definition are warranted. First, while Meilaender's definition concerns love between *persons*, Lewis also recognizes the important place of love for *non-persons*. Lewis's vision for a community of vicariousness and reciprocity embraces the whole of Creation together with the Trinity, Creation's empyrean. Love for non-persons is vital. Lewis reports that in his own case experiences of nature were pivotal to his love of God. If he had not given himself over to nature's imperative to 'Look. Listen. Attend',[10] he suspects that he would never have been taught the meaning of *glory*. Second, Meilaender identifies self-giving as love's core. But Lewis repeatedly points out that healthy, humble *need* is essential for a community of reciprocity. Humans' love for one another and for God must include the 'joy of dependence' that allows us to welcome our Need-love for others. Before God we are always, when clear-eyed, beggars; supernatural Need-love allows us to be 'jolly beggars'.[11] Supernatural Need-love also allows us to be willing to be loved with the self-giving Charity of others.[12]

Though taxonomies of love should not be venerated or ossified, Lewis puts them to good use in *The Four Loves* in making trenchant observations about the human heart. In discussing Affection, he uses the distinction between Need-love and Gift-love to acknowledge that loving others out of need (as when children love their parents) is natural to vulnerable social creatures such as human persons and that the Gift-love of parents for their children often reaches breathtaking levels of self-sacrifice. He makes even more illuminating use of the distinction when observing how entangled Gift-love and Need-love can become in our fallen state. Lewis offers multiple vignettes which draw our attention to our proneness to *need* our Gift-love to be *perpetually needed* by those whom we love, a perversion of St Francis's exhortation that it is in giving that we receive. Although Gift-love may seem more noble and godlike on the surface than Need-love, particular instances of affectionate 'selflessness' are all too often an assertion of ego and control.

One hallmark of Friendship, according to Lewis, is that it is centrally an Appreciative Love, not just because we are drawn to our friends by their admirable qualities but because friendships are always 'about something'. What each friendship is about is some particular subject of mutual admiration. To find a fellow nature-lover, fantasy-fiction-lover, or wine-lover (of just one's own particular sort) is to find a friend. Although we will go to our friends when in need and help them when they are in need, neither Need-love nor Gift-love has the major role in Friendship that they have in Affection. The role of Appreciative Love in Friendship is both the source of its particular excellence (making it the most spiritual and 'independent' of the natural loves[13]) and the source of its characteristic temptations. Though friendships are founded on shared admiration for some perceived good, this perception may be a false and destructive one. Being mutually drawn to 'torture, cannibalism or human sacrifice' cannot be excluded as bases for perverse friendships.[14] While our misapprehension of the admirable makes for bad friendships, here as elsewhere Lewis's more urgent warning is that Friendship, like each natural love, when at its *best*, can still succumb to their characteristic disease. Friendships founded on admiration of what is genuinely admirable are all too prone to become self-appointed aristocracies that see themselves on a higher plane than the rest of humanity.[15]

In Erotic Love, lovers so identify with their beloveds that this love plants 'the interests of another in the centre of our being'.[16] A large part of the grandeur of Eros is its obliteration of the distinction between giving and receiving; moreover, 'in Eros, a Need, at its most intense, sees the object most intensely as a thing admirable in herself, important far beyond her relation to the lover's need'.[17] In Eros, then, the distinctions among Need-love, Gift-love and Appreciative Love collapse, fuelling the transcendence of self-regard and willingness to sacrifice that make Eros seem godlike. But here even more than with Affection and Friendship, Lewis finds evidence for his repeated refrain that the natural loves begin to be demons when they begin to be gods.[18] Eros, unless tempered by other loves (especially Charity), 'always tends to turn "being in love" into a sort of religion'.[19] The voice of Eros sounds so much like the voice of a god that 'resistance to his commands feels like apostasy' even if – perhaps especially if – Eros demands violation of morality.[20]

Much of what Lewis has to say about Agape or Charity concerns its redemption of our natural loves: 'Charity does not dwindle into merely natural love but natural love is taken up into, made the tuned and obedient instrument of, Love Himself.'[21] Charity works both to *perfect* and *order* our natural loves. In perfecting our loves, Charity corrects our tendency to hide our own selfish desires under the cloaks of 'affection', 'friendship' and 'being in love'. It also keeps our loves from becoming *inordinate*. '*Inordinate* does not mean "insufficiently cautious". Nor does it mean "too big".'[22] Our loves become inordinate when we love creatures more than God. God, for Lewis, is the Great Rival – a jealous Lover who will rightly demand that if we cannot love *ordinately* we must do what will look like, and sometimes feel like, *hate* (Luke 14.26). As Gilbert Meilaender perspicaciously observes:

> The picture of the natural loves harmoniously perfected by divine love must never blind our eyes to what this may mean in any person's experience. It may mean conflict, rivalry, renunciation, and grief. Rightly used, the natural loves can become means of approach to God, images of the love that must abide in us and move us in every relation. So often, however, they are not rightly used. If the lover is not healthy, neither is the love; they are not easily separated. The only cure is the drastic one of death and rebirth.[23]

Meilaender, in a later essay, elaborates on this observation, noting that Lewis's '*mere* Christian' amalgam of Catholic and Protestant impulses seeks to affirm both the Catholic thought that grace does not destroy, but perfects, nature, *and* the Protestant thought that perfecting nature often feels like putting nature to death.[24]

CULTURAL CONTEXTS OF LEWIS'S VIEWS ON LOVE

Lewis was a great scholar and a gifted writer. He was also a twentieth-century, British, middle-class, late-married male. *The Four Loves* (perhaps especially Lewis's discussion of the vicissitudes of the importance of Friendship) shows that he was well aware that views of love are culturally influenced;[25] certainly he would grant that his own views on love are not immune. To what extent should Lewis's views on love be taken seriously in the twenty-first century? Which among his views are, if not timeless, at least perennially useful? And which of his views have at most sociological or historical interest?

My own view is that Lewis is better taken as a role model than as an oracle or final authority on the subject of love. In order not to be held hostage by the time and culture into which he was born, Lewis sought out wisdom from other times and places. He weighed the views of 'the wise' critically. The scales he used were, of necessity, influenced by his own experience and the culture that shaped him. We ourselves should in turn treat Lewis's views with respect – perhaps honouring him as among 'the wise' – but we should not give him uncritical homage. Part of critical reflection is noting some of Lewis's intellectual debts and also noting what look like some of his personal particularities.

I will briefly note what I take to be Lewis's personal particularities (including those he shared with many of his contemporaries) before turning to a discussion of his intellectual debts.[26] As Ann Loades discusses much more thoroughly in the next chapter of this volume, C.S. Lewis had complicated views on gender that included, but were not limited to, a vivid sense of the fittingness of gender complementarity.[27] This conviction was rooted in what, in Lewis's day, would have been standard interpretations of certain parts of the Bible and was reinforced by his study of myth. It affects not only his discussion of Eros, but his claims about Friendship and, to a lesser extent, Affection. Large parts of late-twentieth-century biblical and theological scholarship have called gender complementarity, as Lewis understood it, into question. Although that scholarship should not be accepted uncritically, it certainly renders controversial what Lewis would have taken as a given. To my mind, Lewis is not at his best or most insightful when he is spinning yarns of the prehistory of male friendship as comradeship in the hunt[28] or depicting men as playing masterful Sky-Father to women's passive Earth-Mother on the marriage bed.[29] For the most part, these sorts of remarks do not deeply mar his otherwise sensible exposition. However, his characterization of Friendship as an affair of 'naked personalities',[30] in which friends are completely incurious and indifferent to the personal details of each others' lives, does seem to be a universalization of his own experience of friendships within almost exclusively male, twentieth-century British intellectual circles into a timeless norm. Most twenty-first-century women and many twenty-first-century men would aver that self-disclosure is an important hallmark of their deepest friendships.[31]

However, much of what Lewis says on the subject of love *is* of lasting value, in no small part because of his ability to give clear and winsome articulation to the best intellectual products of a long tradition. The power of Lewis's writings as a Christian public intellectual lies in his being learned without being pedantic. His views on love are deeply shaped by his study of the classical Graeco-Roman tradition and the dialogue between that tradition and the history of Christian thought and culture. He did not clutter his 'popular' writing with footnotes and name-dropping. He cared far more about saying true things than saying something original. He has many intellectual debts, some more obvious than others.

Certainly one of Lewis's great intellectual debts, particularly on his understanding of love, is to Augustine. He calls Augustine 'a great saint and a great thinker to whom my debts are incalculable'.[32] Lewis's emphasis on the need for love to be *ordered* by what should be our highest love, our love for God, is clearly Augustinian. Lewis's vision in *The Great Divorce* of the *smallness* of hell ('All Hell is smaller than one pebble of your earthly world'[33]) and the lack of substance characteristic of hell's inhabitants is indebted to Augustine's Neoplatonic idea that evil is a privation of being. However large his debts to Augustine, Lewis is willing (with some trepidation) to disagree in the final chapter of *The Four Loves* with what he takes to be Augustine's Stoic 'hangover'. This hangover is the mistake of thinking that if our hearts rest in God we should not give our hearts to anything that we may lose. On the contrary, says Lewis, 'To love at all is to be vulnerable. Love anything, and your heart will certainly be wrung and possibly broken ... The only place outside of Heaven where you can be perfectly safe from all the dangers and perturbations of love is Hell.'[34]

A more subtle influence on *The Four Loves* is exerted by Spenser. That there should be such an influence is unsurprising, given the amount of time that Lewis spent studying him. Lewis's seminal scholarly work on the history of courtly love, *The Allegory of Love*, culminates in a chapter on Spenser's *The Faerie Queene*, where Lewis calls Spenser 'That great mediator between the Middle Ages and the modern poets, the man who saved us from the catastrophe of too thorough a renaissance.'[35] Lewis's earliest published reference to *eros*, *storge* and *philia* as the three natural loves occurs when he notes Spenser's use of this classification.[36] Lewis saw Spenser as the protector of the Christian tradition against the impending secularization inchoate in Renaissance humanism. This may have added to Lewis's sense that this three-fold distinction is part of the perennial wisdom which should be supplemented and redeemed by Christian Charity. Certainly Lewis's concerns about the inflated standing given to Eros, even in modern Christian thinking about the nature of marriage, are part and parcel with suspicions about 'courtly love' or 'passion' he shares with (indeed perhaps learned from) Spenser.

Lewis's views were also formed by his engagement with his contemporaries who were writing on the subject of love. I have already noted (note 18) his debt to Denis de Rougemont. He also is indebted to Simone Weil. Ann Loades observes that Lewis had read Weil's *Waiting for God* and sees it as influencing *A Grief Observed*.[37] There are also certainly echoes of Weil's discussion of what she calls supernatural love of our neighbour in Lewis's characterization of Divine Gift-love.[38] A reader moving from Weil's essay 'Forms of Implicit Love of God' in *Waiting for God* to *The Four Loves* might also be struck with a contrast in the proportionate space they each give to the discussion of neighbour love. Lewis drops brief comments about neighbour love throughout the book[39] but Weil gives this subject much more explicit and sustained attention. This is not because Lewis discounts the importance of love of neighbour. In 'The Weight of Glory' he asserts, 'Next to the Blessed Sacrament itself, your neighbour is the holiest object presented to your senses.'[40] In *The Four Loves*, however, Lewis is much more interested in Charity's role in elevating and redeeming our natural loves than in its role as an independent force that might lead us to put ourselves at risk for a stranger or give sacrificially to the poor.

Though Lewis had significant disagreements with Anders Nygren, he is also influenced by him. While Lewis does not say so explicitly, his opening remarks in *The Four Loves* are critical of Nygren's main thesis in *Agape and Eros*.[41] Nygren had maintained that Agape was the major motif of primitive Christianity and that Eros was the major motif of the Hellenistic world into which Christianity was born. Nygren characterised Eros as a desiring, egocentric love; Eros, according to him, starts with human need and seeks human flourishing. In stark contrast, Nygren characterizes Agape as a love that is not drawn to valued qualities, but is wholly, unconditionally giving – unmotivated by either an apprehension of the worth of the object of love or of any thought of reciprocity. Eros, by which Nygren means not romance but all-desiring love, is always at bottom self-love, even if its object is God. Humans cannot love God without God first giving them supernatural Agape. Christian love is wholly supernatural. Like God's love for us, our Agape for our neighbour should be unconditional and unmotivated by any sense of our neighbour's worth. In a letter written in 1935, Lewis says of Nygren's view, 'I wonder if he is not trying to force on the conception of love an antithesis which it is the precise nature of love, in all its forms, to overcome.'[42]

Lewis's view of the nature of Agape, or 'Charity', is much closer to what Nygren criticizes as Augustine's '*caritas* motif' than to Nygren's '*agape* motif'. Love, on Augustine's view, is always longing; if longing rightly ordered by our longing for God, it is *caritas*. If it is disordered or inordinate longing – longing that treats creatures as more important than the Creator – it is concupiscence. Despite the fact that, etymologically, *caritas* is just the Latin translation of the Greek word *agapē*, Nygren criticized Augustine's concept of *caritas* as a compromise with Hellenism and as an impure amalgam of Agape and Eros.[43] Lewis does at times sound like Nygren ('Divine Gift-love in the man enables him to love what is not naturally lovable'[44]) but more often sides with

Augustine (in, for example, asserting that there is also a Divine Need-love and his insistence that our natural loves are not only God-given but also Godlike in their resemblances to God's love).

LEWIS AND DANTE ON LOVE, ITS
DISTORTIONS AND REDEMPTION

In closing, I will turn to a discussion of Lewis's debts to and differences with Dante. This will allow some examination of the literary embodiment of Lewis's ideas on love in *The Great Divorce* and *Till We Have Faces*.[45] It will also provide an opportunity for further examination of Lewis's '*mere* Christian' amalgam of Catholic and Protestant impulses concerning the relationship between natural love and charity.

Surely no one who has read both Dante's *The Divine Comedy* and *The Great Divorce* could resist noting similarities. A striking difference, however, is the intricate hierarchical structure of Dante's hell, purgatory and heaven compared with the flatness of Lewis's hell and heaven. Dante's hell has *levels* and these levels represent hierarchies of sin. These hierarchies of sin are in turn based on hierarchies among natural loves and their distortions. Dante, following Thomas Aquinas, thinks that distortions of love which are closely connected to appetites are sins that are less damaging to our humanity than distortions of love which are connected to our will or intellect.[46] The lustful are in the upper levels of Dante's hell; betrayers, cold and calculating plotters, are in hell's frozen depths.

Lewis sometimes hints at a vestige of this hierarchical thinking,[47] but his belief that 'no natural feelings are high or low, holy or unholy, in themselves'[48] is reflected in the very structure of his hell and heaven. There are *distances* within both Lewis's hell and his heaven. Hell's inhabitants move further from one another in a perverse attempt to be no one's neighbour. Some inhabitants are much further away than others (not, within the geography of Lewis's fictional space, further from God but from one another). But this seems more a function of how long they have been in hell than of what particular distorted love they exhibit. The heavenly guide, George MacDonald, tells the narrator that the bus has only brought him to the Valley of the Shadow of Life, not to Deep Heaven. Some inhabitants of heaven are much further in and much nearer to God. However, this again seems to be a function of time, not of degrees of virtue.[49] Lewis's 'Catholic sympathies' in both *The Great Divorce* and *The Four Loves* lead him to acknowledge the great and glorious value of the natural loves and to follow Aquinas and

Dante in hoping that our natural loves will not be replaced by Charity but elevated into perfected but still natural loves.[50] But as the structure of his fictional 'afterlife' in *The Great Divorce* emphasizes, his 'Protestant sympathies' lead him to emphasize what Meilaender calls 'a great either – or';[51] either our loves are on the way to being redeemed or they are on the way to perdition.

Having looked at the themes of *The Four Loves* as they are foreshadowed in *The Great Divorce*, it is fitting to end with a brief look at these themes in Lewis's last novel, *Till We Have Faces*.[52] The central character of the book, Queen Orual, displays distorted and possessive Affection for her sister, distorted Friendship for her teacher, and distorted Eros for her second-in-command. She hides these distortions effectively from herself, as she hides what she acknowledges are her distorted physical features from the world by veiling her face.

Orual comes in the end of the novel to an understanding of her own distortions and destructiveness. She finally faces the remedy for her distorted loves: 'Die before you die.'[53] She reaches this understanding through a series of trials and visions. One of these visions depicts her following her once bitterly hated father to the Pillar Room, which had been the strategy centre for their selfish rule within their earthly kingdom. She is instructed to dig through the floor and jump down. Upon doing so she finds herself in yet another Pillar Room. This process is repeated a second and third time, becoming more and more arduous and painful. It is a pivotal process by which she comes at last to face her own twisted nature; the confession of her insight is an anguished wail. This descent mirrors the descent of Dante's pilgrim into deeper and deeper reaches of hell – more and more profound revelations of the depths of his own distorted loves, culminating in their root of prideful self-love and rebellion.

This is also a powerful imaginative depiction of Lewis's reflection in a brief passage in *The Four Loves* on the depth of our pride and the difficulty of really embracing our deep need of grace. We often see ourselves, Lewis says, as making spiritual progress as we move from believing that God must be quite pleased with us to holding our humility up for God's admiration, and from seeing our humility as admirable to congratulating ourselves for our 'clear-sighted and humble recognition that we still lack humility. Thus, depth beneath depth and subtlety within subtlety, there remains some lingering idea of our own, our very own attractiveness'.[54] The passage in *The Four Loves* may invoke a nod of recognition. In *Till We Have Faces*, Lewis invites us to identify with Orual in hopes of generating epiphany. Our hearts are often more effectively tutored by appeals to our imagination than to our intellect. Showing can be more powerful than telling. Like Dante, Lewis uses our imaginations to help us toward an anguished, but hopefully enduring, realization of what our intellect might only be able to bring us momentarily to acknowledge.

C.S. Lewis, both in *The Four Loves* and in his imaginative works, tutors us toward gratitude for God's gift of the natural loves and, most of all, for Christ's sacrificial love which redeems our loves' distortions. Lewis would rejoice if his writings have cooperated with the ongoing work of the Spirit in stripping us of our self-deceptions and bringing us, along with the grace-filled communion of saints, to rest in God, for 'God is love'.[55]

Notes

1 Michael Malanga, '*The Four Loves*: C.S. Lewis's Theology of Love', in Bruce L. Edwards (ed.), *C.S. Lewis: Life, Works, and Legacy. Vol. 4: Scholar, Teacher, and Public Intellectual* (London: Praeger, 2007), 78.

2 FL 9.

3 FL 125–28.

4 The first sentence of chapter 3 was the first sentence of Lewis's original radio addresses. Lewis did not revise the sentence after he added the first two chapters to the book. I am indebted to Peter J. Schakel for this explanation.

5 FL 21.

6 FL 36.

7 FL 8.

8 FL 107.

9 Gilbert Meilaender, *The Taste for the Other: The Social and Ethical Thought of C.S. Lewis* (Grand Rapids: Eerdmans, 1978), 62.

10 FL 23.

11 FL 120.

12 FL 121–22.

13 FL 56.

14 FL 74.

15 For more on this subject, see 'The Inner Ring' (EC 721–28).

16 FL 105.

17 FL 88.

18 This is a saying which Lewis borrows from Denis de Rougemont's *Love in the Western World*, tr. Montgomery Belgion (New York: Harcourt, Brace, 1940). Lewis makes reference to this idea as early as 1942 in a letter to Daphne Harwood (CLIII 511).

19 FL 102.

20 FL 103.

21 FL 122.

22 FL 112.

23 Meilaender, *The Taste for the Other*, 175.

24   Gilbert Meilaender, 'The Everyday C.S. Lewis', *First Things* 85 (Aug.–Sept. 1998), 27–33. Lewis called the idea that love could be 'pure' without being crucified and reborn the great nineteenth-century heresy: see his letter to Owen Barfield, 20 Aug. 1942 (CLII 530).

25   FL 55.

26   Commentators have noted the influence that Lewis's short marriage and the death of his wife had on his discussion of Eros and his poignant remarks about the hope of the resurrection of our natural loves in heaven. I have not treated this topic because of space constraints, but note Ann Loades' observation that 'The last chapter of *The Four Loves*, published in 1960, clearly emerges from the period just before Joy's death, and tells us something about the relationship his marriage had to his religious convictions': 'Some Reflections on C.S. Lewis's *A Grief Observed*', in Cynthia Marshall (ed.), *Essays on C.S. Lewis and George MacDonald* (Lampeter: Edwin Mellen Press, 1991), 34. See also Malanga, '*The Four Loves*', 50.

27   While he consistently maintained that men should be 'heads' within marriages, he also expressed the thought that within professional and social settings, women should be judged on their merits and be allowed to exercise roles suited to their individual gifts (e.g., FL 68, 72). See also 'Interim Report', EC 641.

28   FL 60–61.

29   FL 95–97. Lewis also seems to have shared with many of his contemporaries the assumption that men's libidos were significantly stronger than women's and that women 'simply don't understand' the pressure of sexual appetite on men. See his letter to Mary Neylan, 18 Apr. 1940 (CLII 392–97). His views on homosexuality (FL 57–60) are in part conditioned by the fact that homosexual acts were still illegal in the United Kingdom at the time of his writing *The Four Loves*.

30   FL 67.

31   For further discussion of alternatives to Lewis's views of Friendship and Romantic Love that are less dependent on male hierarchy and gender roles see Caroline Simon, *The Disciplined Heart: Love, Destiny and Imagination* (Grand Rapids: Eerdmans, 1997), chs 4, 5 and 6.

32   FL 110.

33   GD 113.

34   FL 111–12. This theme is treated in several of Lewis's poems. See, for example, 'Joys that Sting', 'Old Poets Remembered', 'As the Ruin Falls', 'Five Sonnets' and 'Love's as Warm as Tears' (CP 122, 123, 123–24, 139–41, 137–38).

35   AOL 360.

36   AOL 339. Lewis also refers to the four Greek words for love in a letter written to his brother Warren, 4 May 1940 (CLII 408).

37   Loades, 'Some Reflections on C.S. Lewis's *A Grief Observed*', 46 n. 3.

38   Simone Weil, *Waiting for God*, tr. Emma Craufurd (New York: Harper and Row, 1951), 146–47.

39   For example, FL 20, 27, 40, 105.

40   'The Weight of Glory', EC 106.

41 Anders Nygren, *Agape and Eros*, tr. Philips S. Watson (London: SPCK, 1953).

42 Letter to Janet Spens, 8 Jan. 1935 (CLII 153).

43 For further discussion of this issue see Simon, *The Disciplined Heart*, 79–86.

44 FL 117.

45 Jerry L. Walls and Peter J. Schakel have more to say about these novels in Chapters 18 and 20 this volume, respectively.

46 See, for example, Virgil's lectures to Dante the pilgrim in *Inferno* (canto 11) and *Purgatorio* (cantos 17 and 18).

47 For example, in a remark like that of his guide in heaven, George MacDonald: 'if the risen body even of appetite is as grand a horse as ye saw, what would the risen body of maternal love or friendship be?' (GD 96).

48 GD 84.

49 In fact among the 'Solid People' (redeemed saints) those who are furthest from God within Lewis's fictional space are the ones who have returned to the outskirts of heaven out of Charity. They are hoping to give those from the bus a last chance to repent.

50 FL 122.

51 Meilaender, *The Taste for the Other*, 104.

52 As Peter J. Schakel has noted, 'It would not be unfair or misleading to call *Till We Have Faces* a development in fiction of the central themes Lewis would spell out a few years later in *The Four Loves*. Each of the four loves ... has an important place in *Till We Have Faces*': Peter J. Schakel, *Reason and Imagination in C. S. Lewis: A Study of 'Till We Have Faces'* (Grand Rapids: Eerdmans, 1984), 27. Karen Rowe goes further, claiming, 'In essence, *The Four Loves* can be read as a commentary on the novel ... In this case showing precedes telling': Karen Rowe, '*Till We Have Faces*: A Study of the Soul and the Self', in Bruce L. Edwards (ed.), *C.S. Lewis: Life, Works, and Legacy. Volume 1: An Examined Life* (London: Praeger, 2007), 136–37.

53 TWHF 291.

54 FL 119.

55 FL 7, quoting 1 John 4.16.

12　On gender

ANN LOADES

For the purposes of what is necessarily merely an introductory essay in reading Lewis on 'gender', the term is to be taken to refer to the relationship of the 'feminine' to the 'masculine' and vice versa. We assume that one cannot be understood without the other. Lewis himself lived through a period of immense change in what we would now call 'gender relationships', and we can draw attention to but a few examples of his views. We need to note also that, given his resistance to the merits and growth of some of the 'social sciences', one cannot imagine that he personally would have been sympathetic to the development of 'gender studies' which took place after his death. In such studies, attention to 'masculinity' is as yet still coming into focus, not least in the study of the Christian tradition in all its complexities.[1]

We can recall, for example, that it was axiomatic in the church of Lewis's baptism, the Church of Ireland, part of the Anglican Communion, that very few were able to take seriously those women who believed themselves to have a vocation to ordination. So whilst women could be baptized, confirmed, forgiven, exchange vows with a male in marriage, receive communion, chrism or a blessing, and like any other baptized person, could baptize someone in extreme circumstances, they would never be able to confirm anyone, pronounce divine forgiveness, celebrate communion, chrismate or bless someone. Whether they could read scripture in public, let alone give an address or preach to a 'mixed' audience, was contentious across different churches, as indeed remains the case in our own time. Only in 1944 was Florence Li Tim-Oi ordained by the Anglican bishop of Hong Kong to serve Christians in China, otherwise bereft of priestly ministry. She ceased to act as a priest in 1948 when her bishop's actions were condemned by his fellow-bishops at the Lambeth Conference, though her ordination was eventually recognized within the Hong Kong diocese in 1970. In due course some provinces of the Anglican Communion accepted the ordination of women to the priesthood, including the Church of England itself in 1992.

The vigour of the debate about the ordination of women in the twentieth century was virtually inevitable given the changes of attitude to gender in other areas of life, such as access to university education. Lewis's mother graduated from Queen's University, Belfast (then the Royal University of Ireland) with honours in 1886, but her son's university experience was confined to Oxford, where women were admitted to BA and MA status only in 1920, and to Cambridge, where, shamefully, women were not granted full degree status until 1948. There were no mixed undergraduate colleges at Oxbridge before the 1970s, and, with only a minuscule number of female dons employed in the few women's colleges, it was rare for them to meet on equal terms with their male colleagues, otherwise than perhaps at a Board of Faculty meeting or at a full-dress dinner party. After his move to Cambridge in 1955, and to his great credit, Lewis commented that he had had 'some tiny share' in changing such traditions in a more equal direction.[2]

University graduates, male and female together, comprised a very small percentage of the British population as a whole in Lewis's day, but the slowly increasing proportion of female graduates was soon connected with a more widespread social change, the right to vote. As a 19-year-old male, able to supply an address, Lewis, like other young men, took it for granted that he could vote in a general election. In February 1918 suffrage was extended to women, within limitations (they had to be over 30 years old, householders or wives thereof, occupiers of property worth at least £5 a year, and university graduates). A decade later, the age for women was lowered to 21, then the 'age of majority'. Nancy Astor in 1919 was the first woman ever to take a seat in the House of Commons, but it was another forty years before women could become members of the House of Lords, the result of the 1958 Life Peerages Act.

Lewis was naturally alert to the implications of these changes which had taken place in his time, though rather antipathetic to those new disciplines which, with hindsight, we can see are germane to understanding what 'feminine' and 'masculine' may mean in any given society, and how male and female children come to embody gender.[3] Lewis drew on resources other than these new social sciences in his genuine concern that all people, regardless of gender, should be educated into the possibilities of having experiences which are held to be generous, fruitful and humane, to make appropriate responses to 'what is the case', to learn what merits reverence or contempt, and this across a spectrum of cultures and religions. It was precisely failure to learn such things which led to what Lewis, in a series of philosophical lectures delivered in 1943, called 'the abolition of man' – that is, the abolition of the sort of person capable of the integration of intellect and emotion, of reason and imagination.[4]

For the benefit of those unlikely to come across his academic lectures, Lewis published the science-fiction novels *Perelandra* (1943) – with its portrayal of the physicist Weston, later 'the Un-man', both callous and cruel to the creatures of the paradise in which he finds himself – and *That Hideous Strength* (1945). In the latter, the male protagonist, Mark Studdock, is easily corruptible precisely because as a 'sociologist' he has not been taught to feel and to think appropriately. Mark is ambitious, obsessed with making his own way, deeply preoccupied with becoming an 'insider', neglectful of his wife Jane, whose life, as well as his own, is put in jeopardy by his actions. When at the end of the novel the wicked are destroyed and the penitent and the good flourish, there is also release and celebration for captive and misused animals of many species. Cruelty and indifference to suffering have no place in Lewis's worldview.

The strength of Lewis's humane convictions, however, did not mean that he found it easy to accept criticism of previously normative values in gender relations even as he so vigorously defended others that he believed were being ignored. But it is worth bearing in mind that although many examples of human behaviour in his various works are indeed problematic, his attention throughout is on how who we are and what we do turns us either towards or away from God. The manner in which men and women enact gender and accordingly interact with one another in gendered ways was, for Lewis, a matter of theological as well as practical and social significance, and perhaps nowhere more importantly seen than in the area of the priestly ministry.

LEWIS ON THE ORDINATION OF WOMEN

In an essay first published in 1948, and subsequently entitled 'Priestesses in the Church?',[5] Lewis informed his readers that he had heard that the Church of England was being advised to declare women capable of priestly orders, though he believed that such a proposal was unlikely to be considered seriously by the authorities. (He may have been thinking of the controversy over the ordination of Florence Li Tim-Oi referred to earlier.) Lewis uses the term 'priestesses' rather than 'priests' and that in itself raises a question in his readers' minds as to whether the word 'priest', which etymologically looks as if it could be gender-neutral or gender-inclusive, is really anything of the kind. For Lewis, 'priest' means a person of male sex and masculine gender.

Lewis advances the claim that ordaining women to the priesthood would be a revolutionary step to take and, in his day, that was arguably the way in which it would most commonly have been perceived. Since his time, however, work by historians has suggested that patterns of male and female participation in Christian ministry have varied, depending on circumstance.[6] Lewis thought that ordaining women would cut us off from the Christian past, whereas one might consider such ordination as being in continuity with it, as well as a timely enrichment of ministry. He also thought it would widen divisions between the Church of England and other churches. To this one might reply that it depends on which churches are being talked about.

Lewis himself may have been particularly concerned about the relationship of the Church of England to the Roman Catholic church, given the undeniably 'Catholic' way in which he characterizes priestly ministry and his own close friendships with Roman Catholics such as J.R.R. Tolkien, Robert Havard and George Sayer, among others. However, it is hard to see how he thought the division between Canterbury and Rome could significantly widen, given that the Vatican already regarded (and still regards) as invalid *all* Anglican ordained ministers – bishops, priests, and deacons, male or female, irrespective of the (then merely potential) ordination of women to the priesthood.

Whereas the ordination of women remains a problem for some inter-denominational relationships it is indispensable for negotiations with others – including for example the Methodist Church in the United Kingdom and the United States, and most Lutherans. And if a fundamental matter of theological principle was at stake, one would have to say that ecclesiastical or ecumenical controversy of a deep-seated kind would simply have to be lived through, in good conscience. For those who support the ordination of women, the theological principle at stake is whether or not Christ both redeemed and represents *all* of humanity, and thus whether women can celebrate that redemption by means of all that is included in the significance of ordination. But Lewis saw another theological issue at stake: the scriptural emphasis upon God's 'masculinity' *vis-à-vis* 'feminine' humanity, images which Lewis understood as pupillary metaphors, inescapably conditioning our thinking, rather than as 'unessential'[7] or magistral metaphors which could be used interchangeably with other images.[8]

Lewis attempted to disarm his critics by saying that he had every respect for those who wished women to be priestesses, thinking them to be sincere and pious and sensible. He acknowledged that women could preach, that they speak truly who speak of women's competence in administration, their tact and sympathy when giving advice, or visiting parishioners, and that women are as capable as men in piety, zeal and learning. He further agreed that in one field after another it had been discovered that women could do very well all sorts of things once supposedly within the competence of men only. There was a shortage of priests and so it would seem obvious, he concedes, to put women on the same footing as men 'here, as in so many other professions'.[9] However, Lewis did not allow such evidence to weigh with him. In his article he pays no attention to those churches which already ordained women in his day and nor does he concern himself with the possible fragmentation of ecclesial ministry given that, even within the Church of England in his own time, women were already undertaking so much of what had hitherto been thought to be a priest's role. The diaconate had been open to women for over eighty years at the time of his writing.[10]

Lewis claims that opposition to the ordination of women (some of it from women, for reasons he does not analyse) springs from no contempt for the female sex as such and that this is 'plain from history'. He appeals to the medieval 'reverence' for the 'Blessed Virgin' as evidence for his point.[11] However, it has been argued most forcefully by Roman Catholic women members of religious orders, though not by them alone, that devotion to the mother of Jesus has often – although not necessarily or even intentionally – involved the devaluing of women. As a historian, Lewis could have usefully reflected on the connections between such devotion to the impossible ideal for women of a woman both Virgin and Mother and arguments for the inferiority of women and their appropriate subservience to men, expressed in quite different societies.[12]

Lewis claims that, despite the highest veneration for Mary in the tradition of the church, there has never been 'anything remotely resembling a sacerdotal office attributed to her'.[13] This is debateable, depending on what might be meant by 'remotely resembling' or 'sacerdotal office', the latter not in itself a significant term for every Christian denomination in any case. And who might qualify to make the attribution? For not only are there at least a few medieval representations of Mary as Virgin Priest, but a tradition of devotion to her as such was lively enough for the Holy Office of the Roman Catholic church to forbid pictures of her in priestly vestments in 1916, and in 1927 to curtail all discussion of the issue.[14]

We can of course agree with Lewis that human salvation indeed depends on Mary's assent to God's action in her in the incarnation, united in nine months of 'inconceivable intimacy with the eternal Word'.[15] We can further acknowledge the symbolic significance attributed to her presence near the crucified one in the Fourth Gospel. That she is absent from the records of the Last Supper presumably implies for Lewis that Christ did not 'ordain' his mother, as indeed some medieval theologians argued, but it is far from clear that Christ's words at that supper amount to the ordination of those present either. Lewis also claims that the Blessed Virgin was absent from the descent of the Spirit at Pentecost, failing to notice that Acts 1.14 has long been interpreted to mean that she was indeed present, as an extensive tradition of iconography reveals. He thus also fails to note what her presence at Pentecost might imply for a discussion of ordination for women as well as for men.

Lewis's problem with women's priestly ordination really lay in the idea of a priest's being a *representative*, 'a double representative, who represents us to God and God to us'.[16] He writes: 'Our very eyes teach us this in church. Sometimes the priest turns his back on us and faces the East – he speaks to God for us; sometimes he faces us and speaks to us for God.' He had no objection to a woman doing the first: 'the whole difficulty is about the second'.[17] Lewis agreed that men and women were equal; indeed, he fully admits that a given man might be considerably *less* holy or *less* charitable than a given woman, and that thus far she might be not just as 'God-like' as a man but much more so. But, he goes on, 'unless "equal" means "interchangeable", equality makes nothing for the priesthood of women'.[18] So the relative virtues of individual men and women are not the point at issue. The point is that, as he sees it, on an imaginative level men more adequately than women qualify to 'speak to us for God' because men better symbolize the truth that God, *vis-à-vis* humanity, is, so to speak, 'masculine'. Or, as Lewis puts it elsewhere: 'on the level of the imagination the masculinity of the Word is almost impregnably entrenched by the six-fold character of Son, Bridegroom, King, Priest, Judge, and Shepherd'.[19] Men may make very bad priests, but at least they are masculine: as such, they symbolically affirm in their own person something of the divine nature which women in their own person cannot symbolically affirm.

One of Lewis's younger contemporaries, the Scottish Episcopalian philosopher Donald MacKinnon, in a 1992 article, rightly objected to this approach to the matter. MacKinnon found the claim that a priest-celebrant must be male both obscure and indeed 'strangely, even alarmingly, uncatholic'.[20] One could not suppose that the visible appearance of the celebrant was central to the Eucharist, such that the 'real presence' of Christ was to be sought neither in the Eucharistic words and action nor in the consecrated elements, but in the observable body of the priest. It was catholic doctrine that Christ represented all humanity, and that could on no account be put in question. It was also catholic doctrine that Christ was 'one with' the Father, as the Fourth Gospel so repeatedly teaches, and that 'in him dwelleth all the fullness of the Godhead bodily' (Col. 2.9). Christ is both fully human and fully divine. In MacKinnon's view, the theology of a priest's necessarily being male in Eucharistic celebration turned priestly ministry into a citadel of masculine authority, prising such celebration out of the whole context of Christ's ministry of reuniting humanity to God and God to humanity.

Lewis must have been familiar with at least some of these points at issue. MacKinnon was hardly inventing them from scratch, though the insistence that only a male can represent Christ at the Eucharist has been given more weight as arguments for the ordination of women have developed, as Roman Catholic critics have made clear.[21] Nevertheless, Lewis proceeded to consider the implications not just of saying that 'a good woman may be like God' but of saying that 'God is like a good woman'. We can agree with him that bowdlerization of the Lord's Prayer or of the doctrine of Trinity is not an option. We can also agree, though not for reasons of which he himself might approve, that it is non-negotiable that the incarnation took a male form, if we think of 'the humility of a non-gendered God who was prepared to come in human, sexual form'.[22] We can also agree that the biblical imagery of Christ as Bridegroom and the church as Bride is valuable as a central image of the relationship between Christ and all the redeemed – the Bride being a collective symbol for all humanity, male and female. But all of this is not necessarily a cause of horror or even of discomfort at the use of female or feminine-related language for God.

Lewis himself knew and in various places quotes from the *Revelations of Divine Love* by Julian of Norwich (1342 – after 1416), a full edition of her work having been published at the beginning of the twentieth century. *Revelations* happens to be the first known book by an English woman. It is also a text of subtle theology, and Julian made divine 'motherhood' central to her exposition of the doctrines of the Trinity, creation, incarnation, Eucharist and salvation. This was not as odd as it seems, given overlooked metaphors and similes in the biblical witness and the richness of the medieval tradition for both men and women.[23] Lewis was of course right to see that Christian symbolism was likely to be reconstrued once women were not only educated in theology but in a position to be able to teach it from a priestly position, though sadly he could not bring himself to see that this could result in an enrichment of the Christian tradition rather than its change in a negative sense.

He writes: 'Christians think that God Himself has taught us how to speak of Him.'[24] Yes, but such teaching, despite Lewis's assumptions, by no means limits speech about God, the divine mystery beyond our apprehension, to the precise terminology given to us in scripture alone, which in any case is more diverse than Lewis admitted, as noted above. Rather, revelation is an ongoing dialogue between God and humanity, developed in a living tradition involving imagination and social growth, which graciously invites our response in humanly inclusive ways, each of which acts as a corrective to every other.[25]

We can also agree with Lewis that our sexual identity is not superficial and that 'one of the things for which sex [i.e. here, biological gender] was created was to symbolize to us the hidden things of God',[26] which Lewis referred to as the 'opaque element' in religion. But the argument does not necessarily lead in the direction he supposed. With some genuine pain, he asserted 'the privilege, or the burden'[27] of representing God which Christianity lays upon his own sex, despite men's obvious inadequacies.[28] He wanted the 'salute' to be given to the uniform (that is, the masculine gender), not to the wearer (that is, the male individual), and claimed that only one 'wearing the masculine uniform can (provisionally, and until the Parousia) represent the Lord to the Church: for we are all, corporately and individually, feminine to Him'.[29] We may question whether being male or female can be analogous to wearing a 'uniform', and propose rather that the 'uniform' is the authority given to the ordained person by the church, and thus represented in Eucharistic vestments, regardless of biological gender. Later in his life, Lewis indeed recognized with respect to Queen Elizabeth II's coronation that she represented 'humanity called by God to be His vice-gerent and high priest on earth' – a clear case of saluting the uniform rather than the wearer, as it were.[30]

In the case of ordination, Lewis thought that when men made bad priests it was at least in part because they were 'insufficiently masculine', with the same point to be made about bad husbands and bad male partners in a dance. The latter case could be remedied by diligent attention at dancing classes, but the other two could not be remedied by calling in 'those who are not masculine at all'.[31] It is far from clear what he means either by men being 'insufficiently masculine' or women being 'not masculine at all', as if these were clear and unambiguous identities related only to biology. Nor is it clear that being a priest, a husband or a partner at a dance are not significantly dissimilar, rather than so similar that identifying them as similar-in-masculinity adds weight to his case. Being a priest, a husband or a partner in a dance might each be seen differently if not understood in terms of a total exclusion of the 'feminine' to which, at the end of the day, Lewis was not committed.

The primary difficulty here is that Lewis had his own 'theology' of gender which is perhaps more imaginative metaphysics than sober theology: he writes that, in the church, 'we are dealing with male and female not merely as facts of nature but as the live and awful shadows of realities utterly beyond our control and largely beyond our direct knowledge. Or rather, we are not dealing with them but (as we shall soon learn if we meddle), they are dealing with us.'[32] That here it was his imagination, rather than his theological thinking, which motivated his approach to this question is also indicated when he confesses: 'Without drawing upon religion, we know from our poetical experience that image and apprehension cleave closer together than common sense is here prepared to admit.'[33] We therefore turn more briefly to his imaginative and theological works in order to gain further insight into Lewis's understanding of gender.

LEWIS ON GENDER IN FICTION AND THEOLOGY

Lewis belonged to the tradition in Christianity which took paganism seriously for what it might reveal to us indirectly of the Christian God. In *That Hideous Strength* the planetary 'gods' descend, including masculine Mars, feminine Venus and, interestingly, Mercury, who appears to represent an aspect of both masculinity and femininity at once. At any rate, Lewis writes:

> In Viritrilbia [Mercury] and Venus and Malacandra [Mars] were represented those two of the Seven genders which bear a certain analogy to the biological sexes, and can therefore be in some measure understood by men. It would not be so with those who were now preparing to descend [Saturn and Jupiter]. These also doubtless had their genders, but we have no clue to them. These would be mightier energies: ancient eldils [planetary angels], steersmen of giant worlds which have never from the beginning been subdued to the sweet humiliations of organic life.[34]

In the previous novel in the trilogy, *Perelandra*, Ransom sees in Mars and Venus 'the real meaning of gender' – 'a reality, and a more fundamental reality than sex' – the latter being 'merely the adaptation to organic life of a fundamental polarity which divides all created beings'.[35] These two 'gods' whom Ransom sees are biologically 'sexless', yet still masculine and feminine respectively.

Lewis does not explain what he means by those five of the 'Seven genders' which have not manifested themselves in 'organic life', nor does he attempt to reconcile this larger number with the 'fundamental polarity' of the later passage. His principal symbolic concern is Venus. Whereas the novel had begun with Jane Studdock's analysis of her failing marriage to Mark, Jane learns both from her own encounter with the 'terrestrial Venus' (ch. 14, part 2) and then from 'the Director', Ransom (ch. 14, part 5), that her understanding of marriage must be transformed. It is not simply that 'there might be differences and contrasts all the way up, richer, sharper, even fiercer, at every rung of the ascent',[36] but that she has been resisting the (divine) 'masculine' to which all are required to surrender. The Director says to her that 'The male you could have escaped, for it exists only on the biological level. But the masculine none of us can escape. What is above and beyond all things is so masculine that we are all feminine in relation to it.'[37] She recognizes that she herself is to be 'remade' (ch. 14, part 6) and likewise her husband Mark realizes that just as Jane had failed in the humility of a wife, more important for him was his own penitence for having failed to show her the humility of a lover (ch. 17, part 7). He then, like his wife earlier, sees the terrestrial Venus, a woman 'divinely tall, part naked, part wrapped in a flame-coloured robe', who holds open for him the door of the lodge in which Jane later joins him. Mark and Jane together come under the influence of feminine Venus in order that they may the more truly meet the masculine Maleldil (the Second Person of the Trinity).

Although Lewis once wrote that 'comparative evaluations of essentially different excellencies are in my opinion senseless',[38] the problem remains that because he associates femininity with creatureliness, necessarily inferior to God, he ran into difficulties when the comparative values of the 'different excellencies' were to be expressed not merely socially, where he affirms basic equality, but, as we have seen, in the church as well. His reason, expressed in a memorable passage on 'The Divine Goodness' in *The Problem of Pain*, was that 'we are only creatures: our role must always be that of patient to agent, female to male, mirror to light, echo to voice. Our highest activity must be response, not initiative.'[39] We experience the love of God as surrender to his demand, conformity to his desire. This may raise severe difficulties for men, given that Lewis thinks that the deficiencies of men mean that they are not masculine enough. He does not make clear how to overcome the problem of the way men are to relate to God if they, on one hand, must strive to become sufficiently assertively 'masculine' while, on the other hand, becoming appropriately receptively 'feminine' as part of broader humanity. And to argue thus for the receptivity of all creatures to God, with even their response being made possible by divine gift, ironically requires that 'receptivity' be detached from feminine gender if women are not to be deemed inferior to men, as creatures are to God.

Lewis may actually have been more critical than he explicitly indicates of the type of masculinity inherent in the images he uses of the pro-active, demanding, vocal agent. Lewis also valued something else in the Christian tradition which offered him a different masculinity: namely, his understanding of Christ himself in his reflections on Ephesians 5–6 and one of the analogies for human interaction deployed there, which captures something of what he believed about the importance of forgiveness and self-sacrifice in human life. His understanding of Christ offered a most significant alternative to the masculinity of violence, intimidation, self-seeking and manipulative behaviour of which he was rightly critical.[40]

We cannot attend here in detail to Lewis's portrayal of the loving, self-denying, endlessly crucified Christ – which indeed has both positive and negative aspects.[41] However, it is understandable that, given his late marriage to Joy Davidman and knowing that she was mortally ill, Lewis would stress primarily the Christ-likeness of a husband who gave a sick wife unwearying but never paraded care. Even so, the normative mutuality of give-and-take cannot be a predominantly one-sided matter in human relationships, as persons might well discover in a church which lives from Christ's resurrection and is nourished by the sacraments, for which Lewis of course argues. Women and men alike may be graced to develop the needed virtues which they possess in different measure so as to enhance the other. Both may be Christ-like if either is to be. As Lewis had written, home life 'has its own rule of courtesy – a code more intimate, more subtle, more sensitive, and, therefore, in some ways more difficult, than that of the outer world'[42] – and that courtesy was to be learned in Christian life as well.

CONCLUSION

The mention of home life leads us to some closing reflections taken from Lewis's own domestic experience. Towards the end of his brief marriage, Lewis discovered that, although Joy was so grievously ill, in her courage she gave to him at least as much as he gave to her – not to mention her love of and care for his brother, Warren, as well as her own two sons. Joy died in 1960, and in Lewis's remarkable memoir of bereavement, *A Grief Observed*, we see that something of a late revolution has occurred in his thinking on these matters, a revolution that – while coming close to the end of his life – is perhaps all the more impressive and commendable for that. It shows that Lewis was capable of recasting many of the themes and topics discussed above, in the light of new thought and new emotional experience. I conclude with these words:

> [W]e did learn and achieve something. There is, hidden or flaunted, a sword between the sexes till an entire marriage reconciles them. It is arrogance in us to call frankness, fairness and chivalry 'masculine' when we see them in a woman; it is arrogance in them, to describe a man's sensitiveness or tact or tenderness as 'feminine'. But also what poor warped fragments of humanity most mere men and mere women must be to make the implications of that arrogance plausible. Marriage heals this. Jointly the two become fully human. 'In the image of God created He *them*.' Thus, by a paradox, this carnival of sexuality leads us out beyond our sexes.[43]

Notes

1　D.J.A. Clines, 'Paul, the Invisible Man', in S.D. Moore and J. C. Anderson (eds), *New Testament Masculinities* (Atlanta: Society of Biblical Literature, 2003), 181–92.

2　In an essay comparing Cambridge with Oxford, he says of Oxford: 'Until quite lately – I think I may claim some tiny share in breaking down the tradition – it was unlikely you would meet your female colleagues anywhere except at the Board of Faculty or at a full dress dinner party' ('Interim Report', EC 641).

3　See M. S. Van Leeuwen, *A Sword between the Sexes? C.S. Lewis and the Gender Debates* (Grand Rapids: Brazos Press, 2010). See also her contributions to the *Christian Scholar's Review* 'Colloquium Issue: C.S. Lewis on Gender', 36:4 (Summer 2007).

4　For a sympathetic and critical reconsideration of *The Abolition of Man*, see J.R. Lucas, 'The Restoration of Man', *Theology* 98 (1995), 445–56.

5　'Priestesses in the Church?', EC 398–402; repr. also in L. Bouyer *Woman in the Church* (San Francisco: Ignatius Press, 1979), tr. M. Teichart, with an epilogue by Hans Urs von Balthasar.

6　For example, C. Methuen, 'Women with Oversight: Evidence from the Early Church', in J. Rigney and M.D. Chapman (eds), *Women as Bishops* (London: Mowbray, 2008), 72–91, and G. Macy, *The Hidden History of Women's Ordination: Female Clergy in the Medieval West* (Oxford: Oxford University Press, 2008).

7　'Priestesses in the Church?', EC 401.

8 This distinction between kinds of metaphor is outlined in his essay 'Bluspels and Flalansferes: A Semantic Nightmare', SLE 251–65.

9 'Priestesses in the Church?', EC 399.

10 It is arguable that to be consistent in excluding women from the priesthood, Lewis should also have argued that women should be debarred from participation in any form of public office or leadership role. See S.W. Sykes, 'Richard Hooker and the Ordination of Women to the Priesthood', in J.M. Soskice (ed.), *After Eve: Women, Theology and the Christian Tradition* (London: Marshall Pickering, 1990), 132.

11 'Priestesses in the Church?', EC 399.

12 See e.g. E.A. Johnson, *Truly Our Sister: A Theology of Mary in the Communion of Saints* (London: Continuum, 2000).

13 'Priestesses in the Church?', EC 399.

14 See the material in T. Beattie, *God's Mother, Eve's Advocate: A Marian Narrative of Women's Salvation* (London: Continuum, 2003), 144–49.

15 'Priestesses in the Church?', EC 399.

16 'Priestesses in the Church?', EC 400.

17 'Priestesses in the Church?', EC 400.

18 'Priestesses in the Church?', EC 401.

19 'Neoplatonism in Spenser's Poetry', SMRL 155.

20 D.M. MacKinnon, 'The *Icon Christi* and Eucharistic Theology', *Theology* 95 (1992), 109–13.

21 See J. Wijngaards, 'Women Bishops? Views in the Roman Catholic Church, Official and Otherwise', in Rigney and Chapman (eds), *Women as Bishops*, 31–42.

22 E. Storkey, 'The Significance of Mary for Feminist Theology', in D.F. Wright (ed.), *Chosen by God: Mary in Evangelical Perspective* (London: Marshall Pickering, 1989), 198.

23 C.W. Bynum, *Jesus as Mother: Studies in the Spirituality of the High Middle Ages* (Berkeley: University of California Press, 1982). See also Wijngaards, 'Women Bishops?', 39.

24 'Priestesses in the Church?', EC 400.

25 E.A. Johnson, *She Who Is: The Mystery of God in Feminist Theological Discourse* (New York: Crossroad, 1993). See also D. Brown, *Tradition and Imagination: Revelation and Change* (Oxford: Oxford University Press, 1999) and *Discipleship and Imagination: Christian Tradition and Truth* (Oxford: Oxford University Press, 2000).

26 'Priestesses in the Church?', EC 400.

27 'Priestesses in the Church?', EC 400.

28 In 'Membership' (EC 332–40), Lewis made the case for democracy – egalitariansm – as a defence against one another's cruelty, listing fathers, husbands and priests in particular, and the abuse of authority 'of man over beast'. He viewed with the 'strongest disapproval any proposal to abolish the Married Women's Property Act', which secured to married women property and earnings acquired after marriage (EC 337).

29 'Priestesses in the Church?', EC 402.

30 Letter to Mary Willis Shelburne, 10 July 1953 (CLIII 343).

31 'Priestesses in the Church?', EC 402.

32 'Priestesses in the Church?', EC 402.
33 'Priestesses in the Church?', EC 401.
34 THS 325.
35 Per 186.
36 THS 315.
37 THS 316. Lewis writes about the splendours of the 'trans-sexual' life for both men and women in his imaginative portrayal of heaven in *Miracles* (164).
38 DI 20.
39 POP 39; cf. FL 95ff. and Lewis's observations on the 'divine joke' of human sexuality, in which he uses the metaphors of 'Sky-Father and Earth-Mother' as images for intercourse in which the husband may enact 'the dominance of a conqueror or a captor' and the woman 'a correspondingly extreme abjection and surrender'. For more on the 'Earth-Mother/Sky-Father' distinction and the feminine understood symbolically as 'garden', see FL 95; 'Must Our Image of God Go?', EC 67; PPL 49; THS 71, 304; AGO 53. Throughout Lewis's works, Nature is gendered as 'she', occasionally as 'it', but never as 'he'.
40 POP 33; FL 121ff.
41 Some of his comments are, indeed, deeply regrettable, such as his use of the story of King Cophetua and the beggar maid, e.g. POP 36; FL 97–98.
42 'The Sermon and the Lunch', EC 341–45.
43 AGO 42–43.

13 On power

JUDITH WOLFE

In recent years, C.S. Lewis has been publicly criticized for using his children's fiction to propagate a particular kind of Christianity, one built on a 'rigid hierarchy of power' that negates personal responsibility. For journalist Polly Toynbee, this rigidity is embodied in the Narnian world 'of obedient plebs and inferior folk eager to bend at the knee to any passing superior white persons – even children'.[1] For author Philip Pullman, this hierarchical structure is inimical to *story* as such, which for him is inherently concerned with growth towards maturity and responsibility. The test case, for Pullman, is Lewis's (supposed) final mention of Susan Pevensie:

> [I]n *The Last Battle*, notoriously, there's the turning away of Susan from the Stable (which stands for salvation) because 'She's interested in nothing nowadays except nylons and lipstick and invitations. She always was a jolly sight too keen on being grown-up'. In other words, Susan, like Cinderella, is undergoing a transition from one phase of her life to another. Lewis didn't approve of that.[2]

In fact, according to Pullman, the entire ending of *The Last Battle*, which involves the death of all the characters with whom the story opens, is a betrayal of story-telling:

> To solve a narrative problem by killing one of your characters is something many authors have done at one time or another. To slaughter the lot of them, and then claim they're better off, is not honest storytelling: it's propaganda in the service of a life-hating ideology [in which] Death is better than life; boys are better than girls; light-coloured people are better than dark-coloured people ... [I] detest the supernaturalism, the reactionary sneering, the misogyny, the racism, and the sheer dishonesty of his narrative method.[3]

One aim of Pullman's *His Dark Materials* trilogy is to make the 'life-hating ideology' that drives (or rather, stunts) Lewis's stories explicit as the foil of his own story. Pullman's deity ('the Ancient of Days') is a petty, evil God, an impostor who merely pretends to have created the world, and who is so disgusted with its inhabitants that he tries to impose on them a repressed and stifled existence, lasting eternally. Pullman's story is of the quest to destroy this character; to re-enact the Fall as a necessary and positive step towards personal responsibility.

But this conception of God is not obviously a step beyond Lewis. In his 1919 poetic cycle, *Spirits in Bondage,* published twelve years before his Christian conversion, Lewis passionately invokes a similar vision of heroism in the face of a hostile deity:

> Come let us curse our Master ere we die,
> For all our hopes in endless ruin lie.
> The good is dead. Let us curse God most High.
> ...
> O universal strength, I know it well,
> It is but froth of folly to rebel;
> For thou art Lord and hast the keys of Hell.
> Yet I will not bow down to thee nor love thee,
> For looking in my own heart I can prove thee,
> And know this frail, bruised being is above thee.
> Our love, our hope, our thirsting for the right,
> Our mercy and long seeking of the light,
> Shall we change these for thy relentless might?
> Laugh then and slay. Shatter all things of worth,
> Heap torment still on torment for thy mirth –
> Thou art not Lord while there are Men on earth.[4]

Lewis's vision here turns on the conviction that God is merely the maker of material nature, not of our minds: these remain free, and may rise above God's petty tyranny. His journey towards theism in the late 1920s is motivated by the reluctant recognition of this position as incoherent, and the conclusion that human reason, desire and moral intuition must have their ultimate source in the same God as nature has.[5]

However, Lewis's adoption of a theistic position does not change his emotional response to that Maker as manifest to human beings primarily as a brute, oppressive force. His poem 'Caught', written at this time, encapsulates this mood:

> You rest upon me all my days
> The inevitable Eye,
> Dreadful and undeflected as the blaze
> Of some Arabian sky;
> …
> Oh, for but one cool breath in seven,
> One air from northern climes,
> The changing and the castle-clouded heaven
> Of my old Pagan times!
> …
> But you have seized all in your rage
> Of Oneness. Round about,
> Beating my wings, all ways, within your cage,
> I flutter, but not out.[6]

CHRISTIANITY AND POWER

The watershed in Lewis's understanding of power, moderating what he regarded as the temperament of 'an extreme anarchist',[7] was his conversion from theism to Christianity, with its counter-intuitive yet central theological doctrine of one God in three Persons. For Lewis, this doctrine implied that the concept of 'power' was not, as he had previously thought, paradigmatically defined by the sway of a monolithic God over his exposed and helpless creatures, but rather by the relationship between eternal Father and co-eternal Son, which is a hierarchically structured relationship of love. In it, each Person subsists by continually giving himself away to the other: 'From before the foundation of the world [the Son] surrenders begotten Deity back to begetting Deity in obedience.'[8] God the Father, conversely, 'glorifies the Son' and bestows on him 'the name that is above every name' (Phil. 2.9).

This 'living, dynamic activity of love, which has been going on in God forever',[9] is also the principle of the entire creation: 'From the highest to the lowest, self exists to be abdicated and, by that abdication, becomes the more truly self, to be thereupon yet the more abdicated, and so forever.'[10] Hierarchical structure, in other words, far from necessarily being external to (and imposed upon) a person's identity, is the condition of personhood as such, and is reciprocal in its workings: 'To be high or central means to abdicate continually: to be low means to be raised: all good masters are servants: God washes the feet of men.'[11]

Lewis describes this complex idea through the image of a dance. In *Mere Christianity*, he describes God as being 'not a static thing ... but a dynamic, pulsating activity, a life, almost a kind of drama [or] dance.'[12] This dance, patterned by a dynamic hierarchy of surrender and receipt, is not an activity confined to the Trinity, but opens out to all creation. In fact, it is the very point of human life that 'the whole dance, or drama, or pattern of this three-Personal life is to be played out in each one of us: or (putting it the other way round) each one of us has got to enter that pattern, take his place in that dance'.[13] Lewis describes glorified humanity as a heavenly game of self-surrender:

> When [the golden apple of selfhood] flies to and fro among the players too swift for eye to follow, and the great master Himself leads the revelry, giving Himself eternally to His creatures in the generation, and back to Himself in the sacrifice, of the Word, then indeed the eternal dance 'makes heaven drowsy with the harmony'.[14]

But this (ultimately mystical) Christian vision of power or hierarchy as a constitutive principle of personhood is immediately complicated by two factors: Lewis's theological understanding of fallenness and his appropriation for theological purposes of one particular literary-historical model of hierarchy.

POWER AND FALLENNESS

The first factor, which determines the entirety of Lewis's pragmatic engagement with the subject of power, is human fallenness. As *The Abolition of Man* and its fictional counterpart, *That Hideous Strength*, make clear, the correct exercise of power requires a common submission and directedness towards a shared good (and, ultimately, God). But Lewis believes the essence of the Fall to be precisely the turning away from this directedness and a turning instead towards love of power for its own sake, i.e. towards the untruth that human beings are self-sufficient, that they can be 'like God' in power, rather than like him in willing self-abandonment.[15] A consequence, for Lewis, is the necessity of *equality* as a protection from one another's sinful arrogation of power for its own sake. Lewis's use of 'equality' here is strongly weighted. Categorizing it as a purely 'quantitative term' expressing the equivalence of two numerical values, Lewis insists that the term cannot be mapped onto the infinite variety of human persons without entailing, whether consciously or not, their reduction to mere quantitative units.[16] Equality is thus not a good in itself; it is legitimate only as a 'legal fiction' describing the political or legal status, but never the essential or original nature, of a person.[17]

This understanding of equality as a 'legal fiction' necessary to protect human beings (as well as animals and the environment) from human fallenness determines Lewis's whole political, social and environmental thought. His essay 'Membership' makes his reasoning explicit:

> I believe that if we had not fallen ... patriarchal monarchy would be the sole lawful government. But since we have learned sin, we have found, as Lord Acton says, that 'all power corrupts, and absolute power corrupts absolutely'. The only remedy has been to take away the powers and substitute a legal fiction of equality. The authority of Father and Husband has been rightly abolished on the legal plane, not because this authority is in itself bad (on the contrary, it is, I hold, divine in origin) but because Fathers and Husbands are bad. Theocracy has been rightly abolished not because it is bad that learned priests should govern ignorant laymen, but because priests are wicked men like the rest of us. Even the authority of man over beast has had to be interfered with because it is constantly abused.[18]

Lewis's sharp distinction between the legal and political status of persons on the one hand, and their spiritual nature (which desires hierarchy) on the other, encourages a preference, already characteristic of his thought, for the private over the public. For Lewis, legal and political structures are there only to allow people to 'get on with life':

> All political power is at best a necessary evil: but it is least evil when its sanctions are most modest and commonplace, when it claims no more than to be useful or convenient and sets itself strictly limited objectives. Anything transcendental or spiritual, or even anything very strongly ethical, in its pretensions is dangerous and encourages it to meddle with our private lives. Let the shoemaker stick to his last.[19]

This valorization of the private sphere does not imply individualism: human beings, on Lewis's understanding, are created for community. But the kind of community engendered by an ontological rather than a merely juridical understanding of equality is either a social contract between fundamentally isolated individuals or a collective in which no one must excel. Both, to Lewis, are a distortion of reality and in his fiction both are held, in a typically blunt manner, to be associated with hell. In *The Screwtape Letters*, a senior devil extols hell's aim of absorbing each human will into that of the 'Father Below' like a drop into an ocean (a conception contrasting favourably, in his view, with God's distasteful wish to raise 'creatures whose life, on its miniature scale, will be qualitatively like his own').[20] In *The Great Divorce*, the Intelligent Man who instructs the narrator at the bus stop describes the hellish Grey Town as a sprawling wasteland of streets deserted by people too quarrelsome to live together, who continually move farther and farther apart. The remedy, he proposes, is to lay 'a proper economic basis' for 'community life' by creating conditions of scarcity, to be moderated and regulated by market and police forces.[21]

In Lewis's view, collectivism and individualism, by distorting the nature of human personhood and community, also undermine their own ideals. He warns that unless citizens realize that their legal and political equality is merely 'medicine', not their sustenance, merely 'clothing', not their living body, they will always be susceptible to false political hierarchies, particularly totalitarianism. Therefore Lewis maintains that all relationships which are governed by love, and so transcend the allure of power for its own sake, should embrace hierarchical order – especially friendships, familial relationships, learning communities, and the church: 'Hierarchy within can alone preserve egalitarianism without ... For spiritual nature, like bodily nature, will be served; deny it food and it will gobble poison'.[22]

Lewis's distrust of political power within the state extends to his attitude to relations between countries and peoples (both terrestrial and, hypothetically, extra-terrestrial). *Contra* the claims of Toynbee, Pullman and others, he has a strong distaste for racism of any kind. The 'racism' arguably implicit in his portrayal of the Calormenes in *The Horse and His Boy* and *The Last Battle* is a literary Orientalism suitable to the romance genre in which Lewis is writing, rather than a political or anthropological view. Though this no doubt has its own problems, it is a distinct stance.

In *The Four Loves*, Lewis sharply distinguishes between a healthy patriotism, which is essentially literary in kind – a love for one's province, or country, as *home*, or an ennobling admiration for the heroic tales of the past *as stories* – and patriotism as a prosaic belief in the absolute superiority of one's nation: a conviction which 'on the lunatic fringe ... may shade off into that popular Racialism which Christianity and science equally forbid'.[23] In 'Religion and Rocketry', Lewis compares the likely behaviour humans will exhibit towards alien races, should we ever meet them, with the appalling behaviour Westerners have exhibited towards indigenous peoples:

> We know what our race does to strangers. Man destroys or enslaves every species he can. Civilised man murders, enslaves, cheats and corrupts savage man. Even inanimate nature he turns into dust bowls and slagheaps ... [I]f ever we meet rational creatures which are not human ... we shall, if we can, commit [against them] all the crimes we have already committed against creatures certainly human but differing from us in features and pigmentation.[24]

Lewis's sharply distinguished, and continuously balanced, assessments of human power relations in their ideal and practical forms are mirrored in his analyses of human interactions with animals and the environment. He derives an ideal understanding of humanity's role *vis-à-vis* fauna and flora from the divine injunction to 'have dominion' (Gen. 1.28), read through the lens of his Trinitarian understanding of power. As God is to Christ, Christ to humanity, man to woman, head to body, so (*mutatis mutandis*) humans are to animals.[25] The significance of this analogy is broad and startling: it implies that human interaction with animals is not merely a casual encounter (or interference) of one species with another, but always 'either a lawful exercise, or a sacrilegious abuse, of an authority by divine right'.[26] The criterion for the correct practice of that authority is implied in its analogical definition: '[M]an was made to be the priest and even, in one sense, the Christ, of the animals – the mediator through whom they apprehend so much of the Divine splendour as their irrational nature allows'.[27] Consequently, as man is to be understood only in his relationship to God, so animals are to be understood only in their relation to man and, through man, to God: the 'natural' animal is not the wild animal but the tame one.[28] Imaginative realizations of this distinctive understanding animate much of Lewis's fiction: the roles of animals as 'jesters, servants and playfellows' in St Anne's-on-the-Hill[29] and Perelandra, the dignified position of the Talking Beasts of Narnia under their rightful rulers, and so forth.

Like human relationships, the relationship between humans and animals is ultimately determined by their common directedness towards God, which implies, for Lewis, that though humans may have dominion over animals, they also remain inexhaustible mysteries to us in their reflection of God's creativity and purposefulness. (In this connection Lewis talks specifically of the role of fauna and flora to be sources of metaphor and symbol.) This mystery – the fact that they are not mere material, meaningless 'Nature' – describes the absolute limit of human power over fauna and flora. The exploitation of the environment, the vivisection of animals (to which Lewis was passionately opposed[30]), and other forms of treating the natural world with less than the respect and reticence due to their mystery, reduces not only them, but also the one who manipulates them. Lewis writes in *The Abolition of Man*:

> We reduce things to mere Nature *in order that* we may 'conquer' them. We are always conquering Nature, because 'Nature' is the name for what we have, to some extent, conquered. The price of conquest is to treat a thing as mere Nature. Every conquest over Nature increases her domain. The stars do not become Nature till we can weigh and measure them: the soul does not become Nature till we can psycho-analyse her. The wresting of powers *from* Nature is also the surrendering of things *to* Nature.[31]

From seeing animals in this way, it is a short step to reducing our own species to the level of nature. But once we take that final step, Lewis contends, 'the whole process is stultified, for this time the being who stood to gain and the being who has been sacrificed are one and the same'.[32] What will be left are 'Conditioners' manipulating their subjects and descendants at will, but driven themselves by mere appetite. The discussion concludes in the same assertion with which Lewis's thought about power began: 'A dogmatic belief in objective value is necessary to the very idea of a rule which is not tyranny or an obedience which is not slavery.'[33]

ONE MODEL OF HIERARCHY

The second factor complicating Lewis's Christian understanding of power – complicating precisely because Lewis is not, arguably, sufficiently aware of it – is the affinity (but not identity) of his vision with the 'hierarchical model' which he examines from a literary-critical vantage-point in *A Preface to Paradise Lost, English Literature in the Sixteenth Century* and *The Discarded Image*. Lewis describes this 'hierarchical model' as the guiding cosmological model of 'the ancient orthodox tradition of European ethics' from Aristotle to Milton and beyond.[34] It posits a physical and metaphysical hierarchy or 'chain' of being, beginning with God and ending with unformed matter, whose ontologically fixed degrees of value determine the moral rights and obligations of each:

> Everything except God has some natural superior; everything except unformed matter has some natural inferior. The goodness, happiness, and dignity of every being consists in obeying its natural superior and ruling its natural inferiors. When it fails in either part of this twofold task we have disease or monstrosity in the scheme of things until the peccant being is either destroyed or corrected. One or the other it will certainly be; for by stepping out of its place in the system (whether it step up like a rebellious angel or down like an uxorious husband) it has made the very nature of things its enemy. It cannot succeed.[35]

In his 'Prolegomena' lectures to medieval and Renaissance literature, Lewis describes this model as a 'discarded image' which we can no longer accept 'as true', though it was, when accepted, a source of 'profound satisfaction' and 'a great deal of … strength' for medieval art and literature.[36] His own vision of spiritual hierarchy postulates not a quasi-scientific 'chain of being', but rather an 'analogy of love' between the relationships of God the Father and God the Son, Christ and humanity, father and child, husband and wife, and ruler and ruled.[37]

But while the two versions of hierarchy are logically independent, they are nevertheless not easily separated in Lewis's writings. A telltale passage comes near the beginning of 'Equality':

> I don't think the old authority in kings, priests, husbands, or fathers, and the old obedience in subjects, laymen, wives, and sons, was in itself a degrading or evil thing at all. I think it was intrinsically as good and beautiful as the nakedness of Adam and Eve. It was rightly taken away because men became bad and abused it … Legal and economic equality are absolutely necessary remedies for the Fall, and protection against cruelty.[38]

Explicitly, Lewis is drawing a contrast between the conditions of pre- and postlapsarian humanity, grounded in belief in a historical Fall.[39] But when he talks sweepingly about 'the old authority in kings, priests, husbands, or fathers', who later 'became bad and abused it', his imagination outruns his doctrinal belief, towards a Golden Age familiar to classical and post-classical myth, but not so obviously acceptable to canonical Christianity.[40] A similar conflation, in this case of natural law ethics and a Romantically inflected hierarchical model, is (as I have argued elsewhere) at work in *The Abolition of Man*.[41]

Lewis himself occasionally shows some unease about this ill-defined relationship between the 'hierarchical model' and his own theological vision of hierarchy. At the end of 'Christianity and Literature', after expounding this vision at length, he hesitates:

> Now that I see where I have arrived some doubt assails me. It sounds suspiciously like things I have said before, starting from very different premises … Have I mistaken for the 'vision' the same old 'transitory being' who, in some ways, is not nearly transitory enough?[42]

This complicated relationship to the 'hierarchical model', as well as the first complicating factor of Lewis's theological vision – human fallenness – converge on a prioritization of *story* over *essay* as the medium of his positive engagement with hierarchy. It is accordingly to power in Lewis's fiction that we now turn.

POWER IN LEWIS'S FICTION

Lewis's stories are didactic in the sense in which he uses the term in *The Abolition of Man*: that is, they offer visions of the good which elicit imaginative or emotional responses preceding or complementing rational deliberation. In the present case, Lewis's stories facilitate an imaginative appreciation of his theological vision of hierarchy, while circumventing the need for a direct confrontation between this vision and particular political structures or scientific models.

A striking example is the divinely appointed rule of the Pevensie children over Narnia, a land created not (as Earth in the biblical account) for humans, but for Talking Beasts and non-human creatures out of Greek and Norse mythology.[43] This transposition of the idea of kingship, out of political reality (where it is ineradicably marked by the vices provoked by absolute power of one man over another) into a fictional realm whose ontological structure and relative moral purity permit a righteous kingly rule, enables an imaginative appreciation of certain values which Lewis considers essential to being human, but which are largely inaccessible through our own 'remedial' political structures and demythologized science: courtesy, grandeur, justice and magnanimity, as well as their counterparts, humility, awe, joyful submission and thankfulness. More generally, by portraying the Good in all its attractiveness and splendour in the figure of Aslan (and, to a lesser extent, in other characters), Lewis seeks to kindle in his readers a love and reverence for the Good which they may then sustain in the ordinary world, where its proper splendour is often hidden.

This strategy has both strengths and weaknesses. Most immediate among the latter is the fact that it leaves as a separate question, which the fiction itself does not and arguably cannot address, how such an imaginative appreciation is to be transposed into the ordinary world. Secondly (and perhaps more controversially), it consequently leaves Lewis partially vulnerable to attacks like Toynbee's, who claims not only that Lewis's stories may contain political statements, but that they inescapably do so: that for Lewis to ignore the real-life parallels that can be drawn to his Calormenes and subservient animals is to entertain a self-delusion that originates in – and perpetuates – precisely the kind of prejudice and insensitivity she deplores. This criticism in turn exposes a specifically theological weakness in Lewis's author-ial strategy, namely that in constructing visions of glorified human-ity, Lewis claims a viewpoint beyond the epistemological (rather than merely practical) corruption occasioned by the Fall. He himself criticizes this arrogation by some of the writers of sixteenth-century 'Golden Literature', which in some ways represents the acme of a liter-ary tradition based on the 'hierarchical model'.[44] Lewis's own, similar strategy may suggest a greater dependence on such a model than is easily overcome.

However, I would wish to argue that in his mature fiction of the early 1950s and beyond, Lewis transforms these weaknesses through an increasingly self-reflexive handling of the fact that his visions – played out in worlds manifestly removed from the ontological make-up of ours – are explicitly projections *beyond* the world, and so arouse in their readers a longing they do not themselves claim to fulfil.

As a consequence, the process of reading Lewis's stories always (and increasingly self-reflexively) involves a subsequent setting aside or 'dis-carding' of the visions they contain. This is conditioned both by the fact that these visions are, in an important sense, less real than ordinary life, and by the more painful fact that, being created and consumed by sinful beings, they remain to some extent, as Lewis himself acknowledged, part of the 'Old Man' which 'must be crucified before the end'.[45] Lewis references both conditions when he ends his most extended reflection on glorified humanity, the sermon 'The Weight of Glory', with the sober reminder: 'Meanwhile the cross comes before the crown and tomorrow is a Monday morning.'[46] On that and every morning, what counts pri-marily is not the speculative vision he has invoked so eloquently, but the everyday, faithful following of Christ, 'the great Captain'.

This necessary renunciation of Lewis's images – their acknow-ledgement as no more than images, themselves incapable of fulfilling that which they promise – is not an activity marginal to the experience of reading Lewis's fantasy, but as crucial to it as it is crucial to the very fact of being human in a hierarchical universe such as that in which Lewis believes. The iconographic shaping and iconoclastic discarding of images is grounded in the very creation of human beings 'in the image of God'.[47] This distinction implies, among other things, that humans are not, at their deepest level, self-reflective but God-reflective and will consequently be and know themselves fully only when they encounter God, their source and model, Face to face.[48] For Lewis, part of the task of becoming human, taking one's place in the hierarchy of being, is to acknowledge precisely this relationship of dependence.[49]

But perhaps the most difficult part of such an acknowledgement is that it requires dependence on a power not yet revealed, or hope for a fulfilment 'that is never fully given – nay, cannot even be imagined as given – in our present mode of subjective and spatio-temporal experience', but remains, in this life, provisional, an object of eschatological hope.[50] The Old Man must be surrendered before the New Man becomes visible. Lewis dramatizes this necessary discarding of one's own image time and again: in the man who surrenders the lizard of his lust to death in *The Great Divorce*, and witnesses it turn into a mighty stallion; in Eustace's 'undragoning'; in *Mere Christianity*'s Obstinate Tin Soldiers and its statues in the sculptor's shop.

But the most complete realization of this idea, on multiple levels, is *Till We Have Faces*. The entire first part of the novel represents Orual's 'book' of her life, brought before the gods in complaint against their treatment of her. It is only when, in the second part, this 'book' dissolves in her hand, forcing her to realize that she is not the author of her life or its meaning, but merely a character in the hands of a masterful storyteller who can interweave the themes of her life and Psyche's in ways too magnificent for her imagination, that she becomes truly herself. Lewis's stories, at their best, help their readers on their Christian pilgrimage by constituting both reflections, however tarnished, of the glory he would have them hope for, and exercises in the acknowledgement of the nature of images, and so of ourselves: 'Our whole destiny seems to lie in ... being as little as possible ourselves, in ... becoming clean mirrors filled with the image of a face that is not our own'.[51] When this comes to pass, 'each soul, we suppose, will be eternally engaged in giving away [to its fellow-creatures] that which it receives ... Its union with God is, almost by definition, a continual self-abandonment – an opening, an unveiling, a surrender of itself'.[52]

Notes

1   Polly Toynbee, 'Narnia Represents Everything that Is Most Hateful about Religion', *Guardian*, 5 Dec. 2005.
2   Philip Pullman, 'The Dark Side of Narnia', *Guardian*, 1 Oct. 1998. In fact, Susan does not appear in *The Last Battle* at all. She is not turned away from salvation, but rather is left alive in England and 'perhaps she will get to Aslan's country in the end – in her own way' (Lewis's letter to Martin Kilmer, 22 Jan. 1957, CLIII 826).
3   Pullman, 'The Dark Side of Narnia'.
4   From '*De Profundis*', *Spirits in Bondage* (1919), repr. CP 179–80; cf. 'Satan Speaks', CP 181.
5   Lewis discusses this matter, both biographically and philosophically, in many places; see e.g. his autobiography, *Surprised by Joy*, ch. 20; M chs 2–5; '*De Futilitate*', EC 669–81; AMR 281.
6   'Caught', CP 129; originally published untitled in PR 186–87.
7   NP 6.
8   POP 140. About the Holy Spirit, the Third Person of the Trinity, Lewis writes: 'The union between the Father and Son is such a live concrete thing that this union itself is also a Person' (MC 148–49); 'The Father eternally begets the Son and the Holy Ghost proceeds: deity introduces distinction within itself so that the union of reciprocal loves may transcend mere arithmetical unity or self-identity' (POP 139).
9   MC 148.
10 POP 140.
11 M 128.
12 MC 148.
13 MC 149–50. For more on Lewis's understanding of the Trinity as 'a kind of dance', see Chapter 7 in this volume.
14 POP 141.
15 See MC II.3; cf. 'The descent to hell is easy, and those who begin by worshipping power soon worship evil' (AOL 188).
16 See especially 'Membership', EC 332–40; also *Miracles*, where he uses the phrase 'flat repetitive equality' (M 128).
17 See 'Equality', EC 666–68.
18 'Membership', EC 337; cf. 'Willing Slaves of the Welfare State' (EC 746–51) and 'Lilies that Fester', where Lewis writes: 'I fully embrace the maxim … that "all power corrupts". I would go further. The loftier the pretensions of the power, the more meddlesome, inhuman, and oppressive it will be … Thus the Renaissance doctrine of the Divine Right [of kings] is for me a corruption of monarchy; Rousseau's General Will, of democracy; racial mysticisms, of nationality' (EC 372).
19 'Lilies that Fester', EC 372.
20 SL 45.
21 GD 21.
22 'Equality', EC 668.
23 FL 29.
24 'Religion and Rocketry', EC 234.

25 See 'Christianity and Literature', EC 414–15; POP 127. The biblical source texts for this catena of analogical relationships include 1 Cor. 11.3 and Eph. 5.22–25.

26 POP 126. For more about Lewis's understanding of the relationship of the sexes, see Chapter 12 in this volume.

27 POP 66; cf. 127.

28 POP 126. See his letter to Evelyn Underhill, 16 Jan. 1941 (CLII 459–60).

29 THS 378.

30 For more on this topic, see Lewis's essays 'Vivisection' (EC 693–97) and 'The Pains of Animals' (EC 187–96); also Andrew Linzey, 'C.S. Lewis's Theology of Animals', *Anglican Theological Review* 80 (1988), 60–81.

31 AOM 43.

32 AOM 43.

33 AOM 44.

34 PPL 73. The 'hierarchical model' in its cosmological dimension is also described as 'the Great Chain of Being'; the standard introduction remains A.O. Lovejoy's book of the same title (Cambridge, MA: Harvard University Press, 1936). The model in its ethical dimension is discussed illuminatingly in Charles Taylor's *Sources of the Self: The Making of the Modern Identity* (Cambridge: Cambridge University Press, 1989), chs 1–2. The probable origin of this model in Neoplatonism remains a subject of debate.

35 PPL 73–74.

36 DI 12.

37 The term 'analogy of love' is Hans Urs von Balthasar's. For an overview, see Joseph Palakeel, *The Use of Analogy in Theological Discourse* (Rome: Editrice Pontificia Università Gregoriana, 1995).

38 'Equality', EC 666.

39 See further e.g. Lewis's chapter on 'The Fall of Man' in POP (55–76).

40 Lewis draws an explicit parallel between the Judaeo-Christian notion of the Fall and the 'Stoic conception of the Golden Age' in 'Modern Man and His Categories of Thought' (EC 616).

41 See Judith E. Tonning, 'A Romantic in the Republic: A Few Critical Comments on *The Abolition of Man*', *The Chronicle of the Oxford University C.S. Lewis Society* 5:1 (2008), 27–39.

42 'Christianity and Literature', EC 419.

43 See LWW ch. 8 and MN ch. 10; cf. Gen. 1.1–31.

44 Of Hooker's *Laws of Ecclesiastical Polity*, for example, Lewis writes: 'Sometimes a suspicion crosses our mind that the doctrine of the Fall did not loom quite large enough in [Hooker's] universe' (EL 460–1).

45 POP 137.

46 'The Weight of Glory', EC 105.

47 Gen. 1.27.

48 Important biblical source texts for this idea are 1 Cor. 13.12 and 1 John 3.2.

49 This hierarchical, 'mirroring' society that Lewis describes as ideal for humanity is precisely the one explicitly rejected by Mary Daly in the conclusion to *Beyond God the Father* (Boston: Beacon Press, 1973);

see the excerpt titled 'The Looking Glass Society', in Ann Loades (ed.), *Feminist Theology: A Reader* (London: SPCK; Louisville, KY: Westminster John Knox Press, 1990), 189–92.

50 PR 15.
51 'Christianity and Literature', EC 416.
52 POP 139.

14 On violence

STANLEY HAUERWAS

It is not easy to criticize a writer who has done so much good as C.S. Lewis. Yet I must here write critically because I am to address his views concerning violence and war. I am a pacifist. Lewis was not. Indeed, not only was he not a pacifist, he argued strongly *against* pacifism and in defence of the idea that some wars may be just. During the Second World War he gave a talk to the Oxford Pacifist Society explaining his position, an address which was later published as the (justly famous) essay, 'Why I Am Not a Pacifist'.[1] I will try to show that his arguments against pacifism are inadequate, but I also want to suggest that he provides imaginative resources for Christians to inhabit a very different form of Christian non-violence, a form practically unknown to Lewis himself, but with which I think he might have had some sympathy.[2]

LEWIS AND WAR

Before turning to Lewis's arguments against pacifism I think it important to set the context for his more formal reflections on war by calling attention to his own experience of armed conflict. Born in 1898, Lewis fought in World War I and gave talks to the Royal Air Force during World War II. It never seriously occurred to him that there could be a genuine, reasonable, non-violent alternative to war. War was simply a fact of life. Moreover, as we shall see, for Lewis the claim that war is a fact of life is not only an empirical generalization, but a claim about the way things necessarily are. In Lewis's view, war is a fact of human existence that we must accept if we are to be rational.

Lewis, however, was anything but an enthusiast on behalf of war. It would probably be correct to say he was more fatalist than enthusiast. With respect to the Great War, he tells us in *Surprised By Joy* that as a young student he did not 'plume' himself on his decision to serve when he reached military age (being Irish, he was not subject to conscription). He had simply resolved to volunteer because, it seems, he could not conceive what else an honourable gentleman might do. However, having made that fateful decision, he thought himself absolved from taking any further notice of the war. It was as if he was saying to his country, 'You shall have me on a certain date, not before. I will die in your wars if need be, but till then I shall live my own life. You may have my body but not my mind. I will take part in battles but not read about them.'[3] Or, as he put it in his sermon 'Learning in War-time', 'A man may have to die for his country, but no man must, in any exclusive sense, live for his country.'[4]

Lewis duly signed up and was commissioned as a second lieutenant in the Somerset Light Infantry. In November 1917, on his nineteenth birthday, he found himself at the front in France near the village of Arras. Strongly averse to being part of any 'collective', he was surprised to discover he did not dislike the army as much as he thought he might. He did not mean that he did not find life in the army detestable and war at best an 'odious necessity', but the frank recognition by all concerned that you were not supposed to like the army meant there was an honesty about the situation which Lewis found refreshing. War was a tribulation, but it was a tribulation you could bear because it did not disguise itself as a pleasure.[5]

Lewis was, of course, lucky to survive. Soon after arriving at the front he contracted 'trench fever', which required a three-week hospitalization, during which time he read a volume of essays by G.K. Chesterton, a writer whom he would later fault for being 'enchanted' by war, when war in reality was anything but enchanting.[6] He returned to the front only to be wounded by shrapnel in April 1918. Lewis's war had come to an end after actively serving on the front line for about three and a half months. There are, however, 11,000 British soldiers buried in a cemetery in Étaples not far from where Lewis served. He was not to forget them.[7]

Like many who survived the Great War, Lewis had no time for the sentimental glorification of battle. He tells us he 'came to know and pity and reverence' the ordinary men with whom he served. He had a particular fondness for his sergeant, a man named Ayres, who was killed by the same shell that wounded Lewis. He even describes himself as 'a puppet' benignly moved about by Ayres so that the ridiculous and painful position of a raw lieutenant issuing orders to a seasoned sergeant was turned into 'something beautiful'. Ayres became for him 'almost like a father'.[8]

That war is capable of producing such close relationships does not mean that Lewis was ever tempted to think war a 'good thing'. In a moving passage he recounts some of what he witnessed: 'the horribly smashed men still moving like half-crushed beetles, the sitting or standing corpses, the landscape of sheer earth without a blade of grass'.[9] This was a life so cut off from the rest of his experience that, to the older Lewis reflecting upon it nearly forty years later, it seemed almost to have happened to someone else. These images, he said, showed rarely and faintly in his memory.[10]

But as World War I faded from view and World War II neared, Lewis could be quite impatient with those who entirely forgot the true horror of armed conflict. Asked whether he would enter his name in a list of people who would serve 'in the next war', he replied, 'That depends Sir on who it is against and what it is about',[11] and when, in 1939, he heard an Anglican priest pray, 'Prosper, O Lord, our righteous cause', he 'protested against the audacity of informing God that our cause was righteous ... a point on which He may have His own view ... I hope it's quite like ours, of course: but you never know with Him.'[12] This protest notwithstanding, Lewis would later write in 'Learning in War-time': 'I believe our cause to be, as human causes go, very righteous, and I therefore believe it to be a duty to participate in this war. And every duty is a religious duty, and our obligation to perform every duty is therefore absolute.'[13]

In another letter occasioned by the approach of World War II, he confessed that his memories of the Great War had haunted his dreams for years. Military service, he observed, 'includes the threat of *every* temporal evil: pain and death, which is what we fear from sickness; isolation from those we love, which is what we fear from exile: toil under arbitrary masters, injustice and humiliation, which is what we fear from slavery ... I'm not a pacifist. If it's got to be it's got to be. But the flesh is weak and selfish and I think death would be much better than to live through another war.'[14]

The complexity of Lewis's attitude toward the war is made explicit in *The Screwtape Letters*. The demon Screwtape warns his nephew Wormwood from thinking that the European war is necessarily good for their diabolical cause. To be sure, the war will involve a good deal of cruelty and unchastity, but it will also lead many to have their attention diverted from themselves to values and causes higher than the self. Screwtape observes that 'the Enemy' (God) may disapprove of many of those values and causes, but war at least has the benefit from the Enemy's perspective of reminding humans that they are not going to live for ever.[15]

Nor should Wormwood, Screwtape advises, rely too much on the generalized hatred the war engenders against Germans. The English, who at one moment say that torture is too good for their enemies, turn out to be more than willing to give tea and cigarettes to the first German pilot who turns up at their door after they have shot him down.[16] Far more promising is to encourage those faced with war to identify their patriotism or pacifism with their faith in God. This is particularly useful when dealing with pacifists because they will be tempted to identify ending the war with Christianity and thereby forget that they have another destiny.[17]

Lewis thought war horrible, but not the worst thing that could happen to us. To kill or to be killed in war is not murder. Rather, war is a species of punishment that may require our death or the death of the enemy, but we must not hate or enjoy hating those we kill.[18] Punishment, regrettably, is necessary in this fallen world to restrain evil and maintain the moral order. He even suggests that if in World War I some young German and he had simultaneously killed each other in battle and then met again the moment after death, neither of them 'would have felt resentment or even any embarrassment. I think we might have laughed over it.'[19]

Although not professionally concerned with teaching about or writing on the philosophical tradition of 'just war theory', Lewis was a close reader of Augustine, Aquinas, Richard Hooker and many others who addressed this matter. He could not help, therefore, but have considerable understanding of the ethical conversation about what makes a war just. There are hints throughout his discussions of war that he thought it should be a last resort, declared by a lawful authority, a defensive rather than an imperialistic endeavour, that the aims of the war be limited, that there be some realistic chance of success, and that there be a willingness on the part of the combatants to take responsibility for their actions so that civilians will be properly protected.[20] But just as important for Lewis, as is clear from his description of the laugh he and the German soldier might have shared, was his hope that at the end of a war reconciliation and magnanimity would be possible between former enemies.

Darrell Cole argues, therefore, that informing Lewis's understanding of war was an understanding of the kind of person necessary to make a war just. Cole observes that too often advocates of just war forget that those who would sustain a war intended to be just must be formed by a particular set of virtues.[21] Lewis rightly thought only a just people would be capable of fighting a just war. His ideal was the knight – 'the Christian in arms for the defence of a good cause'[22] – who could go to war and at once be fierce but meek. That is the perspective Lewis brought to his engagement with pacifism. If war was necessary, equally there was 'the necessity of chivalry'.[23] In other words, 'If it's got to be it's got to be.' A seemingly innocent remark, but an axiom that is at the heart of how he understood moral rationality. His argument against pacifism nicely illustrates that contention.

WHY LEWIS WAS NOT A PACIFIST

It was some time in 1940 that Lewis gave his talk 'Why I Am Not a Pacifist' to the Pacifist Society in Oxford. Lewis here not only develops his most considered case for the 'facticity' of war, but does so by first making clear how he understands the character of moral reason in general. He thus begins by asking, 'How do we decide what is good or evil?'[24]

The usual answer to that question, Lewis observes, is some appeal to the conscience. Such an answer does not mean, however, that this is the end of the matter, because conscience can be changed by argument. 'Argument' is but another name for 'reason', which according to Lewis involves three main elements: (1) reception of facts to reason about, (2) the direct and simple intuitive act of perceiving self-evident truths, and (3) the art and skill of 'arranging the facts so as to yield a series of such intuitions which linked together produce a proof of the truth or falsehood of the propositions we are considering'.[25]

Lewis suggests that to correct error in our reasoning involves the first and third elements. Particularly important is the role authority plays in the reception of facts because most of what we reliably believe is based on authority. We are, moreover, right to rely on the authority of our common sense because it reflects the law that constitutes our nature and that we did not need to be taught. Thus Lewis believed that, taking the race as a whole, we rightly think the idea of decent behaviour is obvious to everyone. That does not mean there are not differences between moralities but that such differences have never amounted to anything like a total difference.[26]

Lewis therefore bases his case against pacifism on natural law grounds he believes are enshrined in the common conscience of our humanity. He is quite clear that all three elements of reason are also found in conscience, but the difference is that the unarguable intuitions of conscience are much more likely to be corrupted by passion in matters of good and evil than when considering questions of truth and falsehood. That is why authority is so important for checking our grasp of the facts. Our judgements as to right and wrong are a mixture of unarguable intuitions and arguable processes of reasoning or submission to authority. Accordingly nothing is to be treated as an intuition unless it is such that no good man has ever dreamed of doubting it.

Therefore Lewis rules out any presumption by a pacifist that their disavowal of killing can be based on an intuition that taking life is always wrong. A person may think they should not kill by appealing to an authority, but not to an intuition. The former is open to argument but the latter is not. Pacifists who would base their position on such an intuition have simply excommunicated themselves from the human race. Lewis does not think, however, that most pacifists base their position on such an intuitive ground.

He begins, therefore, systematically to characterize and then critique the arguments he understands pacifists to make. He opens by observing that all agree that war is very disagreeable, but pacifists seem to hold the view that wars do more harm than good. Lewis argues that such a view is speculative, making it impossible to know what might count as evidence for such a conclusion. Lewis concedes that rulers often promise more than they should but that is not a valid argument that no good ever comes from war. In fact Lewis asserts that history is full of useful as well as useless wars.

The pacifist case, moreover, seems to be committed to the idea that we can do good to and for some without harming others. But what Lewis calls 'the law of beneficence'[27] means that we must do good to some particular people at some particular time, thus making it impossible to avoid helping some in preference to others. It is certainly true, Lewis acknowledges, that the lesser violence and harm is to be preferred but that does not mean that killing X or Y is always wrong or can be avoided.

Nor can it be shown that war is always a greater evil. Such a view, Lewis argues, seems to imply a materialistic ethic, that is, the view that death and pain are the greatest evils. But surely Christians cannot believe that. Only people parasitic on liberal societies can afford to be pacifists, believing as they do that the miseries of human suffering can be eliminated if we just find the right cures. But Lewis contends it is a mistake to think we can eradicate suffering *tout court*. Rather we must 'work quietly away at limited objectives': real progress is made by those with discrete aims such as the abolition of the slave trade, or prison reform, or factory acts, or a cure for tuberculosis, 'not by those who think they can achieve universal justice, or health, or peace'.[28]

Nor can the pacifist case be made by appeals to authority. The special human authority that should command our conscience, Lewis argues, is that of the society to which we belong – which for Lewis was, of course, the United Kingdom of Great Britain and Northern Ireland. British society has decided the issue against pacifism through figures such as Arthur and Aelfred, Elizabeth and Cromwell, Walpole and Burke. Also standing against the British pacifist is the literature of his country, represented by, among others, the *Beowulf* poet, Shakespeare, Johnson and Wordsworth. Lewis concedes that this social authority is not final, but, being indebted to it by birth, upbringing and education, the pacifist should accord it due respect.

Not only the specific authority of the United Kingdom but the authority of all humanity is against the pacifist. To be a pacifist means we must part company with Homer, Virgil, Plato, Aristotle, Cicero and Montaigne, with the sagas of Iceland and Egypt. Lewis declines to engage with those who would appeal to 'a belief in Progress'[29] to out-weigh such voices. He will not argue with them because he and they do not share enough in common to have an argument. But, crucially, he is willing to argue with those who would dismiss the authority of human-ity on grounds of the authority of the Divine.

Those that appeal to divine authority do so almost exclusively by appeal to certain sayings of Christ. But in so doing, Lewis argues, they pass over the interpretive authority of the Thirty-Nine Articles, Thomas Aquinas and St Augustine. For each of these authorities main-tained it lawful for Christians at the command of the magistrates to serve in wars. The whole pacifist case, therefore, rests on a doubtful interpretation of the dominical saying, 'Resist not evil: but whoso-ever shall smite thee on thy right cheek, turn to him the other also' (Matt. 5.39).

Lewis acknowledges that a pacifist interpretation of this text is pos-sible, that is, that the text seems to impose a duty of non-resistance on all men in all circumstances. He argues that the text means what it says, but with an unspoken reservation of obvious exceptions that the hearer would understand without being told. Thus, confronted by a homicidal maniac attempting murder against a third party, we must come to the aid of the innocent. According to Lewis, Christ simply did not mean that his call not to resist evil would apply to those with the duty to protect the public good. How otherwise could we explain his praise of the Roman centurion?

Lewis ends his case by considering the possibility of 'a warping pas-sion' that naturally inclines people towards pacifism when the choice to take up arms involves 'so much misery'. He acknowledges that moral decisions do not admit of certainty, so pacifism may well be right. But he concludes: 'it seems to me very long odds, longer odds than I would care to take with the voice of almost all humanity against me'.[30]

WHY LEWIS SHOULD HAVE BEEN A PACIFIST

I have spelled out Lewis's arguments against pacifism not only in an effort to be fair to him but because he gives voice to what many assume are the knockdown arguments that tell against any account of Christian non-violence. I hope to show, however, that his case against pacifism is not persuasive. It is not persuasive first and foremost because he made little effort to understand the most defensible forms of Christian pacifism.

As far as one can tell from his text he seems to think pacifism can be equated with a general disavowal of war. Pacifism is, of course, a stance against war, but it makes all the difference how that stance is shaped by more constitutive practices. Lewis seems to have assumed that pacifism is rightly identified with liberal forms of pacifism – that is, the view that war is so horrible it has got to be wrong. Liberal paci-fists often, as Lewis's critique presupposes, think war must be some kind of mistake or the result of a conspiracy because no right-thinking human being could truly believe war to be a 'good thing'. Such a view may seem naïve but it was a very common position held by many after World War I.[31] Lewis, therefore, had a far too easy target for his critique of pacifism.

What Lewis does not consider, an avoidance I fear that goes to the heart of not only his understanding of pacifism but of his account of reason and Christianity, is that Christian non-violence does not derive from any one dominical saying but from the very character of Jesus' life, death and resurrection. Such an account of Christological non-violence John Howard Yoder identifies as the pacifism of the messianic commu-nity. Christian non-violence must be embodied in a community that is an alternative to the world's violence. Accordingly, Jesus' authority is expressed not only in his teachings or his spiritual depth, but in 'the way he went about representing a new moral option in Palestine, at the cost of his death'.[32] Christians are therefore non-violent not because we believe that non-violence is a strategy to rid the world of war, but because non-violence is constitutive of what it means to be a disciple of Jesus.[33]

To be sure, such an account of non-violence draws on an eschato-logical understanding of the relation of the church to the world which is largely foreign to Lewis's theology. Lewis, as is clear from his appeal to common sense, assumes a strong identification between what it means to be a Christian and what it means to be a human being. Throughout his work Lewis emphasized the difference that being a Christian makes for what it means to believe in God, but how he understood that difference did not deeply shape his thinking about war. I think he failed to draw out the implications of his theological convictions for war because of his conviction that a natural law ethic was a sufficient resource for addressing moral questions such as this.

Lewis's flatfooted interpretation of 'resist not evil' nicely illustrates his inability to recognize the difference Christ makes for the transformation of our 'reason'. He dismisses any accounts of how to read the passage that might be constructed through historical criticism because he has learned as a scholar of literature that such methods are no way to read a text.[34] But Lewis's suggestion that those hearing Jesus' words were 'private people in a disarmed nation' and, therefore, would have not thought 'Our Lord to be referring to war', is as nice an example as one could wish for the kind of speculative reading associated with historical criticism.[35]

Lewis's account of practical reason in 'Why I Am Not a Pacifist' drew on his general view that 'prudence means practical common sense, taking the trouble to think out what you are doing and what is likely to come of it'.[36] The problem is not that his account of the three elements of reason is wrong, but rather his failure to see – at least in this instance – how reason and conscience must be transformed by the virtues. For we do not come to see 'facts' just by looking; we come to see the world rightly because we have been formed by habits, that is, the virtues, that enable us to see, for example, how the just person sees justice.[37]

Lewis's view thus seems odd given his claim that every moral judgement involves facts, intuitions and reasoning, but also requires a regard for authority commensurate with the virtue of humility. That seems exactly right – but then I cannot help but wonder why Lewis does not include as authorities for the shaping of practical reason for Christians the lives of the martyrs, and in particular the life of Christ, who are the prime exemplars of this very virtue.

In 'Learning in War-time' Lewis observes that before he became a Christian he did not realize that after conversion his life would consist in doing most of the same things he had done prior to his conversion. He notes that he hopes he is doing the same things in a new spirit, but they are still the same things. There is wisdom in what he says because we rightly believe that what it means to be a Christian is what God has created us all to be. Therefore there is some continuity between the natural moral virtues and the theological virtues – but Lewis is wrong to think that what he is doing is 'the same thing'. It cannot be exactly the same thing because what he 'does' now is part of a different narrative, and hence a different community.

Pacifists, at least pacifists shaped by Christological convictions, can agree with most of the arguments Lewis makes in 'Why I Am Not a Pacifist'. We have no stake in arguments that try to ground pacifism on an immediate intuition that the killing of a human being is an absolute evil. We believe, however, that we were not created to kill, so we will not be surprised that those who do not count themselves Christians may also think it rational to be a pacifist. But Christian pacifism does not appeal to such general human intuitions for its justification.

Nor is Christian pacifism grounded in claims about the 'disagreeable' character of war. Any serious moral conviction may entail quite disagreeable consequences. So Lewis is quite right that we simply cannot know whether wars do more harm than good. Lewis, even after rightly identifying the speculative character of questions concerning whether war has a good or bad result, says it seems to him that history is full of useful wars. I assume, however, he does not mean that observation to be a justification for war. For if he did so it would have the speculative character which he rightly criticized the pacifist for assuming.

Lewis was quite right, moreover, to suggest that it is a mistake to try to eliminate evil *qua* evil. Much better is the attempt to work away at limited objectives. Such is the work of non-violence. Christian exponents of non-violence believe war has been ended at the cross, making it possible in a world of war for Christians to do the small and simple things that make war less likely. So the refusal to go to war is the condition necessary to force the wider world to consider possibilities that would not otherwise exist.

And Lewis is also right to criticize liberal pacifists for underwriting the presumption that death and pain are the greatest evils we encounter. Indeed, Christological pacifism is determined by the conviction that there is much for which it is worth dying. In particular those shaped by the presumptions of Christological pacifism assume it is better to die than to kill. Thus, Lewis correctly reminds us in 'Learning in War-time' that the state of war is no different from the situation we face every day: that is, we face death. The only difference war makes is to help us remember we are destined to die.

Nor do pacifists have reason to disagree with Lewis's concern that the innocent be protected from homicidal maniacs. But there are non-violent and non-lethal alternatives to protect innocent people from unjust attack. The Dutch unwillingness to give up the Jews and the people of Le Chambon-sur-Lignon's resistance are prime examples of such alternatives. It is, moreover, quite a leap from using force to stop a homicidal manic to justifying war. At best Lewis has given a justification for the police function of governing authorities. But war is essentially a different reality from the largely peaceable work of the police.

Lewis's strongest argument against pacifism is quite simply that war is a 'fact' of life. We cannot imagine a world without war. How would we have the resources to read Homer, Virgil, Plato, Montaigne if we have disavowed war? War must remain a permanent possibility because without war we will lack the resources to sustain lives of gallantry. Michael Ward, I think, well sums up Lewis's most determinative position about war by characterizing Lewis's basic view as the attempt to sustain an ethic of chivalry. Lewis well knew that the innocent suffer in war, but you cannot alleviate the suffering of the peasant by banishing the knight.[38]

HONOUR VERSUS LOVE: IMAGINING CHRISTIAN NON-VIOLENCE

Lewis's view of the imaginative power of war for making our lives morally significant is not lightly to be dismissed. I suspect that such an account is what compels many to think it unthinkable to disavow war. Yet I also believe that the Gospel, as Lewis often argued, requires us to think the unthinkable by refusing to assume that the way things are is the way things have to be. To be able to conceive a world without war would have been the kind of imaginative challenge befitting an imagination like that of C.S. Lewis.

In his wonderful sermon 'Learning in War-time' Lewis struck what I take to be a note for such an understanding of non-violence by insisting that war does not create a new situation of crisis to which all activities must be subordinated. In this sermon, delivered in 1939, Lewis exhorts his mostly Oxford undergraduate listeners not to allow the coming war to prevent them from pursuing knowledge and the recognition of beauty, or trying to see God in the work of peace. The intellectual life, Lewis observes, may not be the only road to God, nor the safest, but it is the road they have been given. Failure to take that road would ultimately be to make war more likely.

Lewis advises the students who must begin their work in a time of war not to let their lives be subject to the frustration of not having time to finish. He observes that no one in war or out of war ever has time to finish. According to Lewis, 'a more Christian attitude, which can be attained at any age, is that of leaving futurity in God's hands. We may as well, for God will certainly retain it whether we leave it to Him or not.'[39] But that is exactly the stance that makes it possible to have the patience to sustain the work of non-violence.

To a large extent, the Narnia Chronicles are war-determined stories. I do not think Lewis could have written well or truthfully if he had tried to avoid the reality of war. Christians are after all in a battle with 'the world, the flesh, and the devil'. Lewis rightly did not want Christians to think we do not live in a dangerous world. I wish, however, that Lewis had imagined what it might have meant for the conflicts that make those books so readable to have been fought non-violently. There are hints, however, that Lewis's imagination could see alternatives to war.

Consider, for example, the story of Reepicheep, who, at first sight, seems an unlikely example in support of non-violence. This honour-obsessed 'martial mouse'[40] is one of Lewis's most militaristic creations in the most war-centred of the Narnia Chronicles, *Prince Caspian*. After the great battle in which he has fought bravely, Reepicheep, who has had his wounds healed by Lucy, bows before Aslan. In the process he discovers, because he has difficulty keeping his balance, that he has lost most of his tail.

He is confounded, explaining to Aslan that 'a tail is the honour and glory of a mouse', which prompts Aslan to say: 'I have some-times wondered, friend, whether you do not think too much of your honour.'[41] Reepicheep defends himself, noting that, given their small size, if mice did not guard their dignity some might take advantage of them. But what finally moves Aslan to act is that all the other mice have drawn their swords to cut off their tails as well so that they will 'not bear the shame of wearing an honour which is denied to the High Mouse'.[42]

Despite his high estimation of the tradition of honour and chivalry, Lewis was not prepared to afford it the highest place: 'To the perfected Christian the ideal of honour is simply a temptation. His courage has a better root, and, being learned in Gethsemane, may have no honour about it. But to the man coming up from below, the ideal of knighthood may prove a schoolmaster to the ideal of martyrdom.'[43] Aslan thus restores Reepicheep's tail not for the sake of his honour and dignity, but 'for the love that is between you and your people, and still more for the kindness your people showed me long ago when you ate away the cords that bound me on the Stone Table'.[44] For surely Aslan's martyrdom on that very Table exemplifies the selfless love and service God has given to the world in Christ, and which thus makes possible a community of love to provide an alternative to violence.[45] Lewis, though a man of war, could, I believe, see that.

Notes

1 'Why I Am Not a Pacifist,' EC 281–93.
2 For an earlier, very different, and more positive essay on Lewis's relevance for the ethical imagination, see my 'Aslan and the New Morality', in *Vision and Virtue: Essays in Christian Ethical Reflection* (Notre Dame, IN: University of Notre Dame Press, 1981), 93–110.
3 SBJ 128.
4 'Learning in War-time', EC 582.
5 SBJ 152.
6 'Talking about Bicycles', EC 691.
7 See Alan Jacobs, *The Narnian: The Life and Imagination of C.S. Lewis* (New York: HarperOne, 2006), 72.
8 SBJ 157.
9 SBJ 157.
10 SBJ 157.
11 AMR 292.
12 Letter to his brother, Warren Lewis, 10 Sept. 1939 (CLII 272).
13 'Learning in War-time', EC 581.
14 Letter to Dom Bede Griffiths, 8 May 1939 (CLII 258). There is a passage in 'Why I Am Not a Pacifist' that is almost identical, except that there Lewis observes that war threatens every evil 'except dishonour and final perdition, and those who bear it like it no better than you would like it' (EC 292).
15 SL 32.
16 SL 36.
17 SL 42.
18 Space does not permit me to discuss the portrayal of Ransom's fight against the Un-man in *Perelandra*, an episode in which Lewis does seem to admit a justifiable role for hatred (Per 143).
19 MC 105.
20 For example, his letter to the editor of *Theology*, 27 Feb. 1939 (CLII 250–52). See also his letter to Dom Bede Griffiths, 5 Oct. 1938 (CLII 233–34); letter to Stephen Schofield, 23 Aug. 1956 (CLII 782); also his essays 'Private Bates' (EC 604–06) and 'Is English Doomed?' (EC 434–37).
21 Darrell Cole, 'C.S. Lewis on Pacifism, War and the Christian Warrior', *Touchstone: A Journal of Mere Christianity* 16:3 (Apr. 2003); available at <www.touchstonemag.com/archives/issue.php?id=59>.
22 MC 104.
23 'The Necessity of Chivalry', EC 717–20.
24 'Why I Am Not a Pacifist', EC 281.
25 'Why I Am Not a Pacifist', EC 282.

26   See further e.g. MC 17 and the appendix on 'the Tao' in *The Abolition of Man* (AOM 49–59).

27   'Why I Am Not a Pacifist', EC 286; cf. AOM 51–52 for more on 'special beneficence'.

28   'Why I Am Not a Pacifist', EC 288.

29   'Why I Am Not a Pacifist', EC 289.

30   'Why I Am Not a Pacifist', EC 292.

31   There are, of course, diverse forms of liberal pacifism. John Howard Yoder provides a helpful analysis of different forms of pacifism in his *Nevertheless: Varieties of Religious Pacifism* (Scottdale, PA: Herald Press, 1992).

32   Yoder, *Nevertheless*, 134.

33   For a fuller account and defence of this claim see John Howard Yoder, *The Politics of Jesus* (Grand Rapids: Eerdmans, 1995) and my *Against the Nations* (Notre Dame, IN: University of Notre Dame Press, 1992).

34   'Why I Am Not a Pacifist', EC 290–92.

35   'Why I Am Not a Pacifist', EC 291. For my own interpretation of Matt. 5.39, see my commentary on Matthew (*Matthew*, Grand Rapids: Brazos Press, 2006), 58–73.

36   MC 71.

37   Gilbert Meilaender's essay elsewhere in this volume (Chapter 9) suggests that Lewis did indeed accept this understanding of virtue ethics in AOM.

38   Michael Ward, *Planet Narnia: The Seven Heavens in the Imagination of C.S. Lewis* (New York: Oxford University Press, 2008), 95.

39   'Learning in War-time', EC 585.

40   PC 73.

41   PC 177.

42   PC 178.

43   'Christianity and Culture', EC 80.

44   PC 178.

45   Michael Ward provides a helpful analysis of *Prince Caspian* in his book *Planet Narnia* (93–99). He interprets Aslan's response to Reepicheep primarily as a rebuke suggesting that 'Martyrdom, not knighthood, is the summit of Martial achievement and contains no worldly dignity or honour, only crucifixion-like shame that must be "despised" (Heb. 12:2). In *Prince Caspian* Lewis gives us three martyrs, that is, three characters who witness to the truth and suffer for it: Caspian's Nurse, Dr. Cornelius, and Lucy Pevensie' (97).

15   On suffering

MICHAEL WARD

A few days after the Great War Armistice, C.S. Lewis wrote to his father from the army depot where he was convalescing from battle injuries:

> As to the great news which is uppermost in our minds, I can only echo what you have already said. The man who can give way to mafficking at such a time is more than indecent – he is mad. I remember five of us at Keble, and I am the only survivor: I think of Mr Sutton, a widower with five sons, all of whom have gone. One cannot help wondering why.[1]

A veteran of the trenches, Lewis knew something of what Siegfried Sassoon called 'the hell where youth and laughter go'.[2] He had witnessed 'horribly smashed men still moving like half-crushed beetles, the sitting or standing corpses'.[3] His own wounds came from a mortar that exploded in his trench during the Battle of Arras, killing the man next to him and spattering Lewis with metal, parts of which he carried around in his body for the rest of his life.

But it was not just the trauma of the First World War that Lewis had suffered by the time of the Armistice. He had lost his mother when he was nine and then endured a deeply disturbing period at school under a sadistic headmaster who was later certified insane. All these experiences, taken together, meant that before he was twenty years old, Lewis had been subject to pains that many people would be unlikely to encounter in a lifetime.

How did he respond to these and his later sufferings? A popular view of Lewis, propagated in large part through the 1994 feature film *Shadowlands*, is of a man emotionally numbed by the early loss of his mother, but all too willing to inform his lecture audiences that 'pain is God's megaphone to rouse a deaf world' – a line from his 1940 book *The Problem of Pain*.[4] The death of his wife suddenly ejects him from the safety-net of these easy answers about the soul-making effects of suffering. He becomes willing to face pain, real pain, detestable and serving no apparent moral or spiritual purpose, because the pain of loss, so he has learned, is 'part of' the happiness of love. He can't have one without the other.

Shadowlands is a powerful and moving film. However, the account it gives of Lewis's experience of suffering and his reflections thereon, even allowing for poetic licence, bears scant resemblance to the real picture.

In order properly to understand Lewis's views on suffering we need to set them in a context larger than his relationship with Joy Gresham, a relationship which spanned in total only eight years from their first meeting in 1952 until her death in 1960. In particular, we need to look at the period between the end of the Great War and Lewis's conversion to Christianity in 1931. It was during these years, I would argue, that the foundational principles of Lewis's perspective on the problem of pain were laid down. It is the spiritual crisis of 1931, not the personal loss of 1960, that provides the key to an accurate interpretation of this subject.

FROM ARRAS TO WHIPSNADE

Lewis gave vent to the hurt and confusion of his wartime experiences in his first publication, a cycle of lyrics called *Spirits in Bondage* (1919). In '*De Profundis*', he suggests that God, if he exists, must be uninterested in the fate of man. A particularly bleak poem is 'Ode for New Year's Day', which includes the lines:

> Nature will not pity, nor the red God lend an ear.
> Yet I too have been mad in the hour of bitter paining
> And lifted up my voice to God, thinking that he could hear
> The curse wherewith I cursed Him because the Good was dead.[5]

The collection ends with sixteen poems of 'Escape' that look for release from the brutality and meaninglessness of material existence into a realm of beauty and hope, the 'Country of Dreams'[6].

The paradox of cursing God for the death of the Good came home to Lewis in 1924 when he read Bertrand Russell's 'A Free Man's Worship'. He noted in his diary that Russell failed to face 'the real difficulty', namely that 'our ideals are after all a natural product, facts with a relation to all other facts, and cannot survive the condemnation of the fact as a whole. The Promethean attitude would be tenable only if we were really members of some other whole outside the real whole: which we're not.'[7]

Awareness of this 'fallacy', as Lewis called it, entered his literary-critical reflections too. Around this time we find him criticizing Thackeray for being too completely negative: 'He finds meanness in all things but he does not show us any "light by which he has seen that darkness".'[8] Pessimism, to be credible, must give an account, Lewis thought, of how the universe, otherwise meaningless, has given rise to a species which can detect its meaninglessness. How can the river flow higher than its source? How does a blind chaos yield beings who think they can see?

As he explored these questions, he was working on his second publication, a long narrative poem called *Dymer* (1926). Opposite the title page he placed an epigram from the Elder Edda: 'Nine nights I hung upon the Tree, wounded with the spear as an offering to Odin, myself sacrificed to myself.' *Dymer* is not a Christian poem, but it clearly plays with Christian themes of sacrifice and resurrection in telling its own peculiar story. Near the end of the poem when 'hope and purpose were cut short', Dymer is left unsupported, 'wailing: "Why hast Thou forsaken me?"'.[9] The cry is an indication of where Lewis's reflections on suffering were leading him.

It was to take Lewis another five years before he was prepared to call himself a Christian, and there is not space to retell that movement here, but there are two aspects of his conversion which are especially relevant to a consideration of his understanding of suffering.

The first aspect is its focus on the cross and resurrection. As is well known, a crystallizing moment in his conversion was a conversation he had with J.R.R. Tolkien and Hugo Dyson in Addison's Walk in the grounds of Magdalen College, Oxford. In recounting this conversation, Lewis explained that it had largely been concerned with something 'very mysterious', namely 'the centre of Christianity', the death of 'Someone Else (whoever he was) 2000 years ago'.[10] Christian accounts of Christ's death had always, up to this point, seemed to Lewis 'either silly or shocking'; he had 'ridiculed' the traditional formulations, 'propitiation' – 'sacrifice' – 'the blood of the Lamb'. Tolkien and Dyson showed Lewis that if he met the idea of divine sacrifice in a pagan myth, he had no objection to it. Quite the reverse: 'if I met the idea of a god sacrificing himself to himself (cf. the quotation opposite the title page of *Dymer*) I liked it very much and was mysteriously moved by it'. Again, the idea of a god such as Balder or Adonis or Bacchus who somehow dies and revives, 'similarly moved me provided I met it anywhere *except* in the Gospels'.[11]

Tolkien and Dyson encouraged Lewis to view Christianity as a 'true myth', to be approached with imagination as well as with the abstract intellect. Lewis began to accept that 'the actual incarnation, crucifixion, and resurrection' of Christ might well amount to 'a language more adequate' than any other and that mere 'doctrines' about it were 'less true'. Was this the ultimate expression of reality? Insofar as the universe was comprehensible, was it most fully comprehensible within the terms of this Christ story, a story about one man's sufferings in Palestine, in the year 33, under a Roman procurator called Pontius Pilate? Lewis was not quite prepared to call himself a Christian following this conversation, but he was on the very brink.

The other important aspect of his conversion was the *way* he perceived it as happening; the means by which Lewis came to his new beliefs were as important as, and indeed connected to, the beliefs themselves. The path that Lewis travelled was one which is perhaps best described as capitulation or resignation, even humiliation: he was a fish hooked by an angler; he was a chess-player put into checkmate by a Grand Master; he was a mouse caught by a cat.[12]

In other words, he 'was decided upon'; he was 'the object rather than the subject in this affair'.[13] This relinquishing of his own will had been long in the making; Lewis had not found it easy because he identified his besetting sin as pride: 'Depth under depth of self-love and admiration. Closely connected with this is the difficulty I find in making even the faintest approach to giving up my own will.'[14] A few months later and he returns to the theme: 'we have got to die', and until we learn to die to ourselves 'we shall get this kind of suffering again and again'.[15] He writes about how he tends to confuse imaginative or aesthetic appreciation of spiritual progress with actual progress, how he keeps dreaming that he has woken, only to find himself still asleep in bed. In this connection he quotes George MacDonald: 'Unless you unclose your hand you will never die & therefore never wake. You may think you have died and even that you have risen again: but both will be a dream.'[16] This 'MacDonald conception of death – or, to speak more correctly, St Paul's' becomes a recurrent object of meditation for Lewis.[17] In a closely related vein of thought, he studies *Hamlet* intensively, focusing on its 'prevalent sense of death' and on 'the extraordinary graciousness and lovableness of H[amlet] himself'.[18]

Years later, in an address to the British Academy, Lewis remarked that 'the subject of *Hamlet* is death' and that 'any serious attention to the state of being dead, unless it is limited by some definite religious or anti-religious doctrine, must, I suppose, paralyse the will by introducing infinite uncertainties and rendering all motives inadequate. Being dead is the unknown *x* in our sum. Unless you ignore it or else give it a value, you can get no answer.'[19]

Lewis knew, intellectually and imaginatively, that the Christ story gave death 'a value'. Hamlet might have described death as 'the undiscovered country, from whose bourn / No traveller returns', but Christ was supposed to be the one traveller who had both discovered and successfully returned from that bourn. However, Lewis found that he could not believe this to be a historical event and a relevant spiritual truth by sheer exertion of his own will. The final stage of his conversion was mysterious. He believed that a strange and beautiful gust of wind in Addison's Walk was the Holy Spirit.[20] And finally, during a journey to Whipsnade Zoo when he became prepared for the first time to admit that 'Jesus Christ is the Son of God', the change happened not through any great exercise of will or storm of emotion, but naturally, almost indiscernibly, like 'when a man, after long sleep, still lying motionless in bed, becomes aware that he is now awake'.[21] In contrast to his earlier desire to 'escape' from the troubles of this life by dying into a 'Country of Dreams', Lewis became 'awake' by focusing his attention on Christ, the archetypal innocent sufferer, the true dying and rising god. His aim was no longer oneiric fantasy, but the waking reality of carrying one's cross, as Christ commanded, and, in imitation of Christ, enduring that suffering, despising its shame, passing through death in his company, and so joining the eternal life of the Trinity.

Having arrived at these beliefs in 1931, Lewis had established, philosophically, religiously and existentially, his basic approach to the question of suffering which would shape the rest of his life. Naturally and inevitably, he found himself engaged in an ongoing process of testing and deepening the principles described above as he began to live out his Christian faith, but there was, I would argue, no crucial change in his perspective on suffering after the date of his conversion. He had moved from 'the logic of speculative thought into what might perhaps be called the logic of personal relations'.[22] He would spend the second half of his life exploring these relations and writing about them in his various works. Suffering is a subject which recurs repeatedly throughout much of his corpus, but I think there are four principal places where Lewis elects to make it his main theme: not only *The Problem of Pain* and *A Grief Observed*, but also his poem sequence called 'Five Sonnets' and his final Chronicle of Narnia, *The Last Battle*. Since I have written extensively about *The Last Battle* elsewhere,[23] I will confine my comments to the first three titles just listed.

THE PROBLEM OF PAIN

Lewis's first work of non-fiction Christian apologetics is popularly thought to be summarizable by reference to the line quoted above: 'it [pain] is His [God's] megaphone to rouse a deaf world'.[24] It is certainly true that the book has something to say about what we might call the educative or purgative effects of suffering, but such purgative effects are not where the book starts, nor where it ends. The book is best summarized, I would argue, by reference to its epigraph, a line from MacDonald: 'The Son of God suffered unto death, not that men might not suffer, but that their sufferings might be like His.'[25] Christ's passion becomes a recurrent reference point throughout the book[26] and is interestingly recontextualized in the final chapter as part of Lewis's discussion of the intra-Trinitarian life, as we shall see below.

Having struck the keynote of the whole work with this epigraph, Lewis then opens with a thumbnail sketch of the development of Christianity before proceeding to discussions of divine omnipotence and goodness and of human goodness corrupted into wickedness by freely made choices that cannot be self-reversed. Only in the sixth chapter, more than halfway through the book, does he begin to address some of the possible lessons that may in certain circumstances be learnt from an experience of suffering. He lists three. First, suffering may show 'bad men' where they are wrong, that their prideful, self-centred attitude to life does not 'answer'.[27] Second, it may show all people, the 'good' no less than the 'bad', that their lives are not their own and that self-sufficiency is not an option.[28] Third, it may show people where they are consciously choosing the good, because it is only when moral choice is made in the teeth of natural desires (e.g. the desire to avoid pain) that people can fully know that they are choosing from disinterested motives.[29] In the remainder of the book, Lewis advances a number of further propositions which he regards as relevant, including the belief that tribulation, though it may be turned to positive effect, should nevertheless be avoided and relieved where possible.[30] He introduces the theme of divine justice and God's eradication of evil from the universe by means of that freely chosen self-negation called hell. A speculative chapter on animal suffering follows. The book ends with a discussion of eternal beatitude and participation in the divine life.

Lewis's friend, the philosopher and theologian Austin Farrer, regarded *The Problem of Pain* as deficient at an elementary level because he thought that Lewis conceived of pain exclusively as 'a moral instrument'. Farrer wished to maintain that, on the contrary, 'When under suffering we see good men go to pieces we do not witness the failure of a moral discipline to take effect; we witness the advance of death where death comes by inches.'[31]

Farrer, I think, has paid insufficient attention to the MacDonald epigraph and the associated references to the crucifixion which run throughout the book: they provide the basic context within which the arguments of *The Problem of Pain* are propounded. Lewis's starting-point is not that pain is 'related to the will of God as an evil wholly turned into a moral instrument', as Farrer asserts.[32] Rather, his starting-point is a man who was stripped and tortured on a false charge and who, in his final agony, having been deserted by his friends, did indeed 'go to pieces'. There was nothing 'moral' about the crucifixion of Christ. As Lewis puts it: 'not only all natural supports, but the presence of the very Father to whom the sacrifice is made deserts the victim'.[33] This suffering is so intense that it leaves the sufferer completely disorientated, without any awareness of purpose or moral value but only questioning why God has abandoned him. However, as Lewis proceeds to say, Christ's 'surrender to God does not falter though God "forsakes" it'.[34] The reason for saying that Christ's surrender did not falter is that Christ returned from death's 'bourn' – he was vindicated on the third day, and this vindication ultimately allows for a complete reinterpretation of his sufferings. It is essential, though, that this *re*interpretation of the events of Good Friday does not get entangled with the initial interpretation of them. Considered in their own terms, without reference to subsequent events, the sufferings experienced by Christ on the cross constitute precisely that 'full involvement of the reasonable soul in a random and perishable system' which Farrer thinks that Lewis did not allow for.[35] In what other way would Christ's sufferings have been seen than as random and meaningless on the Friday of his death, and the Saturday of his lying in the tomb? Without reference to the events of Easter, Christ's passion gives off only 'the odour of death';[36] it is quite unlike being made 'perfect through suffering'.[37] If knowledge of the resurrection is allowed prematurely to interfere with our understanding of the cross we have not properly understood the cross. We have not, as it were, heard the 'lived language', we have not encountered the 'true myth' in which events happen consecutively and only consecutively. Instead, we have stepped out of the story and treated it as a kind of allegory, translating it into abstract categories of 'sacrifice' or 'propitiation' that may be valuable in their own way but that are 'less true' than the terms within which the story was experienced by its original participants – those terms which we must learn to 'trace'.[38]

It is interesting that, of all scriptural verses, the one that appears in Lewis's works more than any other, by a large margin, is the cry of dereliction (Ps. 22.1; Matt. 27.46; Mark 15.34).[39] Although Lewis certainly believed that, considered in a certain light, 'pain is God's megaphone to rouse a deaf world', his more fundamental belief was that pain is Christ's agony beneath a deaf sky. The very nub of his faith was in a Christ who experienced Godforsakenness.

The miracle of the resurrection is that it shows Godforsakenness to be redeemable, reinterpretable,[40] and in the final chapter of *The Problem of Pain*, Lewis again quotes MacDonald, this time speaking of how the Eternal Word

> gives Himself in sacrifice; and that not only on Calvary. For when He was crucified He 'did that in the wild weather of His outlying provinces which He had done at home in glory and gladness'. From the foundation of the world He surrenders begotten Deity back to begetting Deity in obedience.[41]

Lewis is here not quite introducing suffering into the immanent Trinity, but he comes close. Earlier in the book he twice describes God as impassible,[42] but in the final chapter, with this notion of the Second Person's eternal obedience to the Father as a mode of surrender which *becomes* suffering when undertaken in the 'outlying provinces,' Lewis puts forward one of the most interesting aspects of his theodicy. Suffering remains an evil, alien to the heart of God, yet suffering entered into freely as self-giving allows us, Lewis suggests, to 'touch a rhythm not only of all creation but of all being', for self-giving is 'absolute reality', the inner law of God's own Trinitarian nature.[43]

However, although self-giving (of which Christ's crucifixion is the supreme example) is a recurrent reference point throughout *The Problem of Pain* and the context within which Lewis expects us to hear all his arguments, it is not, I think, the most striking thing about the book and so it is hardly a surprise that the deliberately challenging 'megaphone' image has stuck in readers' minds instead. Lewis was still learning his craft as an apologist when he wrote this book and its awkward shifts of gear, its sudden brakings, stallings and accelerations, mark this out as easily his least adroit venture into the field. And the curious thing is that Lewis seems to realize that what he is trying to write will prove insufficient. Some lines in the preface are illuminating in this regard:

> for the ... task of teaching fortitude and patience I was never fool enough to suppose myself qualified, nor have I anything to offer

my readers except my conviction that when pain is to be borne, a little courage helps more than much knowledge, a little human sympathy more than much courage, and the least tincture of the love of God more than all.[44]

Pain is much more than a problem to be addressed by means of 'know-ledge', that is, by ratiocination. Intellectual 'answers', even where they seem plausible, are of little practical value in the furnace of actual suf-fering. If a writer is to teach anything about 'fortitude and patience' and 'the love of God', which are the resources more needful when coping with real pain, Lewis believes, the better way to do so is by imitating the 'language more adequate' provided by the Christ story and to retell that story in various ways. We do not have space to look at how Lewis attempted to imitate the Christ story in the way he lived his own life, but we can at least look at two places where, in his writings, he *depicts* a lived, Christian response to suffering.

'FIVE SONNETS'

To many people, the question to be asked when it comes to a con-sideration of suffering is not 'Is there a purpose in my pain?' but 'Why on earth would you even imagine that that question is worth asking? Is it not obvious that suffering is meaningless and that God is either evil or impotent or non-existent?' In the midst of suffering we often wish to say, as the grief-stricken Lewis of *Shadowlands* says, 'It's a bloody awful mess and that's all there is to it.' There is a numbness and a bewilder-ment and an anger in sorrow. This can be compounded by a realization that others, whom one might expect to be sharing one's grief, are begin-ning to 'recover'. Lewis addresses this point in the opening stanza of his 'Five Sonnets'[45]:

> You think that we who do not shout and shake
> Our fists at God when youth or bravery die
> Have colder blood or hearts less apt to ache
> Than yours who rail. I know you do. Yet why?[46]

He goes on to suggest that there are two ways of coping with loss. The first way is to explain it by finding 'someone to blame', someone whom one can hold responsible and therefore with whom one can be legitim-ately angry: 'Anger's the anaesthetic of the mind, | It does men good, it fumes away their grief.' The other way is less obvious and more pain-ful. This second way involves sinking intentionally into the depths of one's sorrow, letting it pull one down so far that one can actually begin to tread in a master's footsteps. Here the master is not, to begin with, Christ, but one of Christ's disciples, Dante. Dante's path through hell is the route that Lewis holds up here for imitation: 'Down to the frozen centre, up the vast | Mountain of pain, from world to world, he passed.' This latter method is 'unearthly', a realization that mundane categories of avoidance or blame or explanation are inadequate:

> Of this we're certain; no one who dared knock
> At heaven's door for earthly comfort found
> Even a door – only smooth endless rock,
> And save the echo of his cry no sound.
> …
> Far better to turn, grimly sane, away.
> Heaven cannot thus, Earth cannot ever, give
> The thing we want. We ask what isn't there
> And by our asking water and make live
> That very part of love which must despair
> And die and go down cold into the earth
> Before there's talk of springtime and re-birth.[47]

The 'very part of love which must despair' is the part which believes that this world is the true and final location of our loves and hopes. It is not so, Lewis argues. Rather, the right way of proceeding is to 'Ask for the Morning Star and take (thrown in) | Your earthly love'. The Morning Star is, of course, a scriptural title of Christ.[48] Only by seeking first for Christ, who in turn seeks the Father's will, can one's mundane expectations find their proper place. This is deeply frustrating to human creatures who are disposed to think that, since they find themselves alive on Earth, Earth must be their home. This, Lewis suggests, is our fundamental, albeit entirely natural, mistake, and

> if we once assent
> To Nature's voice, we shall be like the bee
> That booms against the window-pane for hours
> Thinking that way to reach the laden flowers.

Then comes the closing stanza:

> 'If we could speak to her,' my doctor said,
> 'And told her, "Not that way! All, all in vain
> You weary out your wings and bruise your head,"
> Might she not answer, buzzing at the pane,
> "Let queens and mystics and religious bees

Talk of such inconceivables as glass;
The blunt lay worker flies at what she sees,
Look there – ahead, ahead – the flowers, the grass!"
We catch her in a handkerchief (who knows
What rage she feels, what terror, what despair?)
And shake her out – and gaily out she goes
Where quivering flowers stand thick in summer air,
To drink their hearts. But left to her own will
She would have died upon the window-sill.'[49]

The problem of pain, Lewis seems to be suggesting here, is that it presents itself as one thing (the frustration of our will) when in fact it is another thing (the requirement that our will should be surrendered into God's hands). For as long as we treat only the presenting symptoms, we will not recognize the issue at stake. That is to say, progress can be made only when utter realism sets in, when the full diagnosis of our disease is acknowledged: that we are mortal, destined for another world than this. The route that needs to be taken is 'That long way round which Dante trod.' And that long way round 'seems a crazy stair' to our natural way of thinking. The last thing one would expect to be the way out of pain is more pain. Yet this is Lewis's answer: the only true consolation 'for one bereavement, makes us more bereft' because it bereaves us of all our merely natural hopes. The consolation comes by asking for 'the Morning Star' who did not refuse the cup of suffering but rather said, 'Not my will but thine be done.'[50] By following Christ's example and accepting pain in all its terrible forsaking of our earthly hopes, toiling up its 'vast mountain', one shares spiritually in his crucifixion and therefore also, eventually, in the spirit of his resurrection: 'from world to world he passed'. It is a deeply disorientating experience and Lewis uses two images of disorientation to communicate this.

The first is by means of the allusion to the *Divine Comedy*. In Dante's case, at the end of his journey through the Inferno, he climbed down from Lucifer's shoulders to his waist, and then assumed he would descend even further, down his legs, but in fact found that, once he had passed the midpoint, he actually began going upwards, that the route from his waist to his feet was really an ascent. He had 'passed the centre of gravitation', as Lewis puts it in his discussion of this passage.[51] What was 'down' miraculously turns out to be 'up'.

The other image of disorientation is the window, which the bee cannot see. The bee is imagined dismissing the idea of invisible glass as one of those 'inconceivables'. All it can see is 'the flowers, the grass', symbols of love, growth, peace, on the other side of the pane. Lewis likened Christ to a window ('he that hath seen me hath seen the Father'[52]) and had an interest in the symbolic uses of vitrification.[53] Christ is a stumbling-block to those who do not receive him; he frustrates the very thing he enables – one's vision of God – unless one consents to be spiritually wrapped in his graveclothes (symbolized here by the handkerchief encasing the bee). The process of being so wrapped is not painless. On the contrary, 'who knows | what rage she feels, what terror, what despair?' But it is the only way out of the blunting, confusing cycle which pain otherwise gives rise to.

Whether the 'message' of this poem convinces the reader intellectually is not really pertinent. It is not presented as an intellectual argument, like *The Problem of Pain* was. It is a vision of experience communicated by means of symbol and story. We are not meant to ratiocinate and thereby assess the plausibility of a case, but to feel and thereby gain a hint of the meaningfulness of what Lewis believes to be a spiritual reality. For many readers, I suspect, the image of the bee buzzing anxiously inside a handkerchief will be a far more powerful, and certainly a more memorable, expression of the 'old Christian doctrine of being made "perfect through suffering"'[54] than the battery of arguments and reasons that Lewis marshals in *The Problem of Pain*.

A GRIEF OBSERVED

In *A Grief Observed* Lewis re-presents the Christ story in yet another way: a first-hand journal of bereavement. The extent to which *A Grief Observed* is raw, unassimilated emotion and the extent to which it is organized as a purposive, rhetorical construct is not a question I can here address.[55] However, I will refer to the author as N.W. Clerk, not C.S. Lewis, since that better reflects the pseudonymous nature of the book that was actually published in 1961.

The first mention of God notes his absence: 'where is God? ... go to Him when your need is desperate ... and what do you find? A door slammed in your face, and a sound of bolting and double bolting on the inside. After that, silence. You may as well turn away.'[56] As Lewis put it in 'Five Sonnets': 'Far better to turn, grimly sane, away.'[57] And there are other echoes of the poem in the journal, including Clerk's confession that 'I cannot even see her face distinctly in my imagination ... I have a ghastly sense of unreality' (compare 'The face we loved appears | Fainter each night, or ghastlier, in our dreams');[58] his admission that reunion with the beloved dead 'pictured entirely in earthly terms' must be a cheat ('no one who dared knock | At heaven's door for earthly comfort found | Even a door');[59] his anger hurled at God that makes him 'feel better for a moment' ('Anger ... does men good, it fumes away their grief').[60] The reliance on Dante in 'Five Sonnets' is repeated in the very closing words of *A Grief Observed*, a quotation from the *Paradiso*: 'Then she turned to the eternal fountain.'[61]

I draw out these parallels not in an effort to suggest that *A Grief Observed* was simply a re-run of sentiments previously expressed and therefore not genuinely felt in the moment. I point them out to indicate that the anguish and the questions caused by bereavement, as expressed through the persona of Clerk, are not unprecedented experiences for Lewis. He has felt them before. *A Grief Observed* is not the sudden discovery that the 'intellectual' answers offered in *The Problem of Pain* are insufficient; it is qualitatively the same discovery as has been made on many prior occasions, both before and after 1940.

However, although the *quality* may reflect previous episodes of questioning and pain, the *degree* to which Clerk takes them is indeed unprecedented. As so often, there is a reference to the cry of dereliction, except, this time, Christ's question from the cross is itself interrogated. Twice Clerk drags his mind to Christ's sense of forsakenness and twice he turns away: '"Why hast thou forsaken me?" I know. Does that make it easier to understand? ... Almost His last words may have a perfectly clear meaning. He had found that the Being He called Father was horribly and infinitely different from what He had supposed. The trap, so long and carefully prepared and so subtly baited was at last sprung, on the cross.'[62]

The questioning even of the cry of dereliction is a sign of the depths of misery which Clerk is sounding. But these moments occur in chapters 1 and 2. In chapter 3, when Clerk is beginning finally to turn his mind to God as a primary consideration, a change comes: 'Something quite unexpected has happened. It came this morning early. For various reasons, not in themselves at all mysterious, my heart was lighter than it had been for many weeks.'[63] The interesting thing about this heart-lightening is what it follows, what has been described in the immediately preceding paragraphs, where Clerk is questioning whether it is ever allowed for one sufferer to bear the burdens of another. The answer he gets is: 'It was allowed to One, we are told, and I find that I can now believe again, that He has done vicariously whatever can be so done. He replies to our babble, "You cannot and you dare not. I could and dared."'[64] It is after this moment that Clerk finds he 'can now believe again'.

But *how* is it that he can now believe again? This is the mysterious thing. No explicit explanation is given and, as so often in Lewis, this is deliberate: as he says elsewhere, 'what the reader is made to do for himself has a particular importance'.[65] It seems that Clerk has come to a realization that his love for his wife is not, after all, absolute or utterly pure. In asking himself whether he could have borne her burdens, he says, 'But one can't tell how serious that bid is, for nothing is staked on it. If it suddenly became a real possibility, then, for the first time, we should discover how seriously we had meant it.'[66] And as he imagines himself into this hypothetical situation he apparently concedes that he does not mean it so very seriously. His self-love will, regrettably, trump his love for his wife. He is a weak man whose love for his wife is tragically but truly unable to accomplish what it wants to accomplish. He would not and could not dare to bear her suffering. And this realization is humiliating. Not only has she died; now he sees that his love for her is not immortally strong. All supports fall away. He plunges down at last, after two false starts, into true dereliction. That is to say, he can now share in Christ's cross and therefore in his rising. It is the same pattern that Lewis had traced in his conversion in 1931 and repeatedly thereafter throughout his Christian life: 'Go down to go up – it is a key principle. Through this bottleneck, this belittlement, the highroad nearly always lies.'[67]

CONCLUSION

This discussion of Lewis's thoughts on suffering has barely scratched the surface. Not only has it omitted to treat of *The Last Battle*, it has not even mentioned the numerous other works in which suffering is an important theme or subject;[68] it has also, perforce, focused on Lewis's treatment of emotional, psychological and spiritual pain as opposed to sheer physical pain. Nevertheless, we have seen some of the contours of Lewis's approach. At the most basic and obvious level, suffering is an evil to be avoided and a burden to be relieved. At a slightly higher level, suffering may sometimes be understood as educative or purgative in various ways. Higher still, suffering is a kind of cross to be endured in fellowship with Christ, and a horror that only the miracle of resurrection can rightly interpret. Highest of all, suffering is a mode of self-abdication that in a fallen manner somehow mirrors an *un*fallen pattern enjoyed eternally within the life of God. And yet there can be no mirroring, for God 'has no opposite'.[69] Lewis wrote in his posthumous final work:

> 'He came down from Heaven' can almost be transposed into
> 'Heaven drew earth up into it', and locality, limitation, sleep,
> sweat, footsore weariness, frustration, pain, doubt and death, are,

from before all worlds, known by God from within. The pure light walks the earth; the darkness, received into the heart of Deity, is there swallowed up. Where, except in uncreated light, can the darkness be drowned?[70]

Notes

1   Letter to his father, Albert Lewis, 17? Nov. 1918 (CLI 416–17).
2   Siegfried Sassoon, 'Suicide in the Trenches', in *The War Poems of Siegfried Sassoon* (London: Faber & Faber, 1983), 119.
3   SBJ 157.
4   POP 81.
5   'Ode for New Year's Day', CP 174.
6   'Death in Battle', CP 223.
7   AMR 281.
8   AMR 286.
9   NP 82.
10 Letter to Arthur Greeves, 18 Oct. 1931 (CLI 976).
11 Letter to Arthur Greeves, 18 Oct. 1931 (CLI 977).
12 SBJ 169; 173, 177; 182.
13 'Cross-Examination', EC 553.
14 Letter to Arthur Greeves, 30 Jan. 1930 (CLI 879).
15 Letter to Arthur Greeves, 18 Aug. 1930 (CLI 926–27).
16 Letter to Arthur Greeves, 15 June 1930 (CLI 906).
17 Letters to Arthur Greeves, 22 Sept. 1931 (CLI 970) and 1 Oct. 1931 (CLI 975).
18 Letter to Arthur Greeves, 22 Sept. 1931 (CLI 971).
19 'Hamlet: The Prince or the Poem?', SLE 100. For more on this, see my 'The Tragedy is in the Pity: C.S. Lewis and the Song of the Goat', in T. Kevin Taylor and Giles Waller (eds), *Christian Theology and Tragedy: Theologians, Tragic Literature, and Tragic Theory* (Aldershot: Ashgate, forthcoming, 2011).
20 See George Sayer, *Jack: C.S. Lewis and his Times* (San Francisco: Harper & Row, 1988), 134.
21 SBJ 189.
22 'On Obstinacy in Belief', EC 215.
23 Michael Ward, *Planet Narnia: The Seven Heavens in the Imagination of C.S. Lewis* (New York: Oxford University Press, 2008), ch. 9.
24 POP 81.
25 POP p. vi.
26 See pp. 37, 49, 67, 72, 74, 77, 90–92, 99, 101, 108, 116, 137, 140, 141.
27 POP 78–83.
28 POP 83–86.
29 POP 86–92.
30 POP 98–102.
31 Austin Farrer, 'The Christian Apologist', in Jocelyn Gibb (ed.), *Light on C.S. Lewis* (London: Geoffrey Bles, 1965), 40.

32   Farrer, 'The Christian Apologist', 40.

33   POP 91.

34   POP 91.

35   Farrer, 'The Christian Apologist', 41.

36   2 Cor. 2.16.

37   Heb. 2.10.

38   Letter to Arthur Greeves, 18 Oct. 1931 (CLI 976) POP 92.

39   See AMR 186; AT 154–55; CLIII 250, 567, 963, 1550, 1559; 'The Efficacy
      of Prayer', EC 241; FL 111; GMA 18; LTM 46–47; Per 140; ROP 106; SL
      47; THS 337; 'The World's Last Night', EC 45.

40   As Lewis has MacDonald say in *The Great Divorce*: 'That is what mor-
      tals misunderstand. They say of some temporal suffering, "No future
      bliss can make up for it," not knowing that Heaven, once attained, will
      work backwards and turn even that agony into a glory' (GD 62).

41   POP 140.

42   POP 35, 38. See also 'Petitionary Prayer: A Problem without an Answer',
      EC 197–205; LTM ch. 9. For a brief defence of divine impassibility, see my
      'Theopaschitism', in Ben Quash and Michael Ward (eds), *Heresies and
      How to Avoid Them* (London: SPCK and Peabody, MA: Hendrickson,
      2007), 59–69.

43   POP 140.

44   POP pp. vii–viii.

45   CP 139–41. Never published in Lewis's lifetime, the sonnets were writ-
      ten some time in the mid-1940s; see his letter to Sheldon Vanauken, 5
      June 1955 (CLIII 617).

46   'Five Sonnets', I, 1–4 (CP 139).

47   'Five Sonnets', III, 1–4, 8–14 (CP 140).

48   2 Pet. 1.19; Rev. 22.16.

49   'Five Sonnets', V, 1–14 (CP 141).

50   Matt. 26.39, 42, 44 cf. POP 101.

51   'On Science Fiction', EC 454.

52   'Must Our Image of God Go?', EC 66, quoting John 14.9.

53   See Ward, *Planet Narnia*, 289 n. 57.

54   POP 93, quoting Heb. 2.10.

55   But see George Musacchio, 'Fiction in *A Grief Observed*', *SEVEN: An
      Anglo-American Literary Review* 8 (1987), 73–83.

56   AGO 7.

57   'Five Sonnets', III, 8 (CP 140).

58   AGO 15, 20; 'Five Sonnets', IV, 7–8 (CP 141).

59   AGO 23; 'Five Sonnets', III, 1–3 (CP 140).

60   AGO 35; 'Five Sonnets', I, 7–8 (CP 139).

61   Dante, *Paradiso* 31, 93; cf. Lewis's letter to Sheldon Vanauken, 5 June
      1955 (CLIII 616).

62   AGO 8, 26.

63   AGO 38–39.

64   AGO 38.

65   'Imagery in the Last Eleven Cantos of Dante's *Comedy*', SMRL 81.

66   AGO 38.

67 M 116.
68 For example, *Till We Have Faces* and ch. 6 of *The Four Loves*, to name but two.
69 POP 142.
70 LTM 73.

Part III

Writer

16 *The Pilgrim's Regress* and *Surprised by Joy*

DAVID JASPER

Both as a Christian and as a writer C.S. Lewis provokes divided opinions and perhaps never more so than in two accounts of his conversion to Christianity, *The Pilgrim's Regress: An Allegorical Apology for Christianity, Reason and Romanticism* (1933) and *Surprised by Joy* (1955). My focus in this essay will be not so much with the theological destination of these narratives (although I touch on this occasionally), but rather with two subsidiary themes. One is the manner of the description of the journey – Lewis's rhetoric.[1] The other is that Romantic longing which drives the journey and which provokes hermeneutical and interpretative questions that remain important for our understanding of Romanticism and its place in the religious quest.

Conversion to Christianity for Lewis, in both *The Pilgrim's Regress* and *Surprised by Joy*, seems largely an intellectual process and an individual one at that. But more important than any intellectual conclusions that he comes to is Lewis's persistent exploration of the theme of 'joy' lying at the heart of both these works, emanating from that 'private' Romanticism which he was to speak of (in the *Regress*) as being located in 'a particular recurrent experience which dominated my childhood and adolescence and which I hastily called 'Romantic' because inanimate nature and marvellous literature were among the things that evoked it'.[2]

In his 1943 preface to the third edition of the *Regress*, Lewis indicates that he would now eschew the obscurity of the term 'Romanticism', and indeed he does eschew it when he comes to write *Surprised by Joy*, preferring there simply to call it 'joy': an experience of inconsolable longing which he describes as the 'central story of my life', originating even before he was six years old. He also sometimes calls it *Sehnsucht*,[3] the German word deliberately conveying the complex Romantic notion which Lewis distinguishes from both happiness and pleasure, for *Sehnsucht* is, rather, an 'unsatisfied desire which is itself more desirable than any other satisfaction'.[4] The deep yearning which is at the heart of 'joy' is profoundly expressed in the poetry of Hölderlin in German and Wordsworth in English. And just as in Hölderlin's 1802 poem *'Heimkunft'* ('Homecoming') it is not the arrival itself but the journeying and the joyful anticipation which are the true homecoming, so likewise in George MacDonald's *Phantastes* (1858) – which, as is clear in *Surprised by Joy*, was such a central and formative text for Lewis[5] – Fairyland is not so much the goal of the traveller's quest as the location of the spiritual journey which itself enables the quester to perceive something of the truth in God.

The title of *Surprised by Joy* is taken not from Lewis's wife's name (though she cannot be entirely absent from it, as they were married only months after the publication of the book) but from the first line of a sonnet by Wordsworth, which is actually a lament for his recently deceased daughter.[6] It, too, is a poem of longing in which the poet's love for his daughter calls her to his mind – a momentary joy in loss. Joy, for Lewis, is an experience of being drawn by the 'visionary gleam'[7] that is at the heart of another of Wordsworth's poems, 'Ode: Intimations of Immortality' (1807). Like Wordsworth, for whom heaven lay about him 'in his infancy', Lewis looks back on his childhood through a profoundly literary life.[8] He cannot even recount his first experience of joy without importing into it a later, learned, literary gloss:

> As I stood beside a flowering currant bush on a summer day
> there suddenly arose in me without warning, and as if from a
> depth not of years but of centuries, the memory of that earlier
> morning at the Old House when my brother had brought his toy
> garden into the nursery. It is difficult to find words strong enough
> for the sensation which came over me; Milton's 'enormous bliss'
> of Eden (giving the full, ancient meaning to 'enormous') comes
> somewhere near it.[9]

Lewis's literary descriptions of joy are in many ways a continual, deliberate reconstruction of his early visions, a process that may be the key at once to his popularity as a writer and to his insistently rhetorical and intellectual constructions in adulthood which, I will argue, both convey and obscure the form of his personal understanding of Christianity.

THE PILGRIM'S REGRESS

Lewis himself later admitted to what he described as the 'needless obscurity' and 'uncharitable temper' of *The Pilgrim's Regress*.[10] In this, Lewis's first post-conversion book, written explicitly as an allegory, a young man named John sets out from his childhood home of Puritania in search of an Island (representing joy or *Sehnsucht*) which he has glimpsed in a vision. In this search he encounters many other characters and obstacles, learns many lessons, and finally returns to his homeland – yet changed. The journey and the quest of this book continue to haunt the reader, even if the final goal of Lewis's Christianity itself finally fails to attract or persuade. The attainment of John's visionary Island in the *Regress* is finally an unlearning of the many things both cultural and intellectual which he had encountered and gathered through the journey of his life. As the reviewer in *The Times Literary Supplement* observed:

> It is impossible to traverse more than a few pages of the allegory without recognizing a style that is out of the ordinary; and 'Oxford' should be diagnosed from the neatness with which the extravagances of psycho-analysis are hit off in the eighth chapter of the third Book, and the essentials of Hegelianism packed into a nutshell in the last four chapters of the seventh. Moreover, when John, the pilgrim-hero of this 'Regress', begins to find the way to salvation he is inspired to break into fragments of song ... revealing a poetic gift that may rightly be called arresting.[11]

Thus, although the book ends in a regress, a return from worldly sophistication to childlike longing, which is inevitably a kind of loss, yet, 'as my dream ended, and the voice of the birds at my window began to reach my ear (for it was a summer morning)',[12] joy is reborn even in life's sorrow.

When Lewis wrote *The Pilgrim's Regress*, penned with extreme rapidity during a two-week holiday in Ireland in September 1932, he was already working on his study of courtly love and the allegorical method in the medieval tradition, *The Allegory of Love* (1936), and this text, I suggest, provides the essential rhetorical backdrop to the *Regress*. In *The Allegory of Love*, he argues that 'we cannot speak, perhaps we can hardly think, of an "inner conflict" without a metaphor; and every metaphor is an allegory in little'.[13] In chapter 2 of this work, Lewis distinguished between, on the one hand, archetypal metaphors, representing 'what is immaterial in picturable terms', and, on the other, 'allegory'.[14] The use of the former he calls 'sacramentalism or symbolism', while the latter is a process of invention from abstraction:

> The difference between the two can hardly be exaggerated. The allegorist leaves the given – his own passions – to talk of that

which is confessedly less real, which is a fiction. The symbolist
leaves the given to find that which is more real.[15]

The intellectualism underlying the invention of the allegorical, thus
understood, was brusquely dismissed by Coleridge at the beginning of
the nineteenth century in his Lay Sermon, *The Statesman's Manual*
(1816): 'Now an Allegory is but a translation of abstract notions into
a picture-language which is itself nothing but an abstraction from the
objects of the senses; the principal being more worthless than its phan-
tom proxy, both alike unsubstantial, and the former shapeless to boot.'[16]
Lewis somewhat shared Coleridge's low view of the intellectualism of
allegory, acknowledging that it was natural to prefer the symbolic to
the allegorical. The latter, he conceded, could easily turn into a 'disease
of literature' if the equivalences were 'purely conceptual' and failed to
'satisfy imagination as well'.[17]

Both kinds of metaphors, allegorical and archetypal, are present in
The Pilgrim's Regress. The problem is that, in this early work, the par-
ticularity of the allegorical and the universality of the archetypal metaphor are confused and their connection unclear. On the one hand we have
the tightly drawn allegories of historical figures such as Spinoza, Hegel,
Kant, Marx and Freud, while on the other we have 'John' the pilgrim,
who is partly C.S. ('Jack') Lewis and partly Everyman. This disjunction
lends a disharmony to the voice of the narrator, Lewis's dreamer, a vari-
ance of distance which leaves the reader caught between the suspension
of disbelief and intellectual deciphering. Herein may lie a clue as to the
difference between *The Pilgrim's Regress* and its predecessor in so many
ways, Bunyan's *The Pilgrim's Progress* (1678, 1684), for Bunyan simply
set out to write a tract or a sermon, not a work which was part tract,
part spiritual autobiography, and part philosophical polemic.

Bunyan's Christian journeys through a world that is immediately
recognizable, the characters whom he meets being at once archetypical
and, in the encounter, utterly individual and real. In the words of Walter
Allen, 'They come alive in their speech, and come alive immediately',[18]
and, as such, they immediately serve Bunyan's purpose in the reader's
un-selfconscious response. Now Bunyan's purpose is unequivocally
theological, and thus without apology his religious allegory is woven
into the imaginative universe of his reader. In contrast to the glorious
conclusion of part I of Bunyan's allegory (with its reminder of hell even
in the penultimate sentence), it is difficult to know precisely where,
theologically, *The Pilgrim's Regress* leaves us, for John and his friend
Vertue are still analysing their situation even as they return to Puritania,

more concerned with their own achievements it seems than with the visionary Island as, somewhat unpleasantly, 'Vertue invented doggerels to [the old fiddler's] tunes to mock the old Pagan virtues in which he had been bred.'[19]

When the *Regress* was originally written, Lewis appears to have had an elite intellectual readership in mind, capable of picking up the philosophical, theological and cultural references.[20] It was for the wartime third edition that he added explanatory headlines to each page to assist a wider audience, which actually provide a distracting and highly uneven commentary to the text. They serve merely to highlight the hermeneutical problem for the reader, caught often between three levels of response to the voice of the narrator, the headlines and the already unstable allegory, sometimes ludicrous, as in the conversation and pastimes of the sons and daughters of Wisdom in book 7, or simply incoherent, in the case of the archetypal figure of Mother Kirk (designated in the headlines as 'Traditional Christianity'[21] but at other times as the Landlord's 'daughter-in-law',[22] that is, the Bride of Christ).

A helpful sidelight on the difficulties that I find in *The Pilgrim's Regress* is provided, rather ironically, in Lewis's essay entitled 'The Vision of John Bunyan'.[23] If my own view of the intellectual and theological character of Lewis's Christianity remains rather negative, then his own of John Bunyan's was no less critical. At the end of the essay Lewis writes: 'Part of the unpleasant side of *The Pilgrim's Progress* lies in the extreme narrowness and exclusiveness of Bunyan's religious outlook.'[24] That having been said, one also has to acknowledge that the invitation to read and interpret the story (both Bunyan's and Lewis's) is all-important, accepting the gravity of its metaphors and images as they speak to our own longings and visions beyond the limits of theological particulars. Lewis puts it succinctly when he suggests that for Bunyan (and we in our turn as readers might say the same for the *Regress*), 'the telling of such a story would have required on merely artistic grounds to be thus loaded with a further significance, *a significance which is believed only by some, but can be felt (while they read) by all*, to be of immeasurable importance'.[25]

It is, perhaps, significant that the *Regress* is actually not Lewis's first attempt to explain what he means by 'Joy'. In April 1922, while still an atheist, he wrote a poem entitled 'Joy',[26] and in the diary he kept between 1922 and 1927 he repeatedly recounts having the experience itself.[27] He tried again in prose after his conversion, and finally in the spring of 1932 in another, unfinished poem.[28] The pursuit of joy was, indeed, the central quest of his life, finally defined for him in Christianity, though its form remains supremely within the literary imagination. Lewis himself was at times almost painfully aware of this, reflecting in 1930 that it is possible 'to confuse an aesthetic appreciation of the spiritual life with the life itself',[29] and wondering at the conclusion of *The Four Loves* (1960), 'God knows, not I, whether I have ever tasted this love. Perhaps I have only imagined the tasting.'[30] Such imagining, he muses, is a danger for the intellectual and literary scholar in the capacity easily to 'imagine conditions far higher than any we have really reached'. Through the imagination it is, perhaps, only possible to reach out in an ultimate 'unawareness' in a dreaming through an uneasy cognition of God who is absent: '*To know* that one is dreaming is to be no longer perfectly asleep.'[31]

The roughly realized territory of *The Pilgrim's Regress* in some ways anticipates the more completely imagined fictional worlds of Perelandra, Narnia and Glome (the mythic kingdom of *Till We Have Faces*). Here he is just beginning to find his mode of public Christian teaching, here rough indeed yet still, at times, attractive and even (perhaps) persuasive.

SURPRISED BY JOY

In the years between the publication of *The Pilgrim's Regress* and *Surprised by Joy* Lewis became a cult figure, a Christian phenomenon, while remaining a mildly eccentric professor of Renaissance literature lodged within the ancient heart of English academia. Massively learned, though extraordinarily resistant to shifts in twentieth-century culture, he is remembered far more for his brief, popular exercises in Christian apologetics and for his works of fantasy fiction than for his solid academic achievements, chief among which, perhaps, is *English Literature in the Sixteenth Century, Excluding Drama* (1954).

This substantial, even magisterial, contribution to The Oxford History of English Literature (volume IV) provides a key to our reading of *Surprised by Joy* (as well as to his other 'autobiographical' work, *A Grief Observed* (1961)) because it serves to raise our awareness of both his interest in rhetoric and his powers as a rhetorician. The reviewer in *The Times Literary Supplement* (7 Oct. 1955) likens the reading of *Surprised by Joy* to the excitement of encountering a thriller which holds us by its strange oddity:

> the tension of these final chapters holds the interest like the close
> of a thriller. Nor is this lessened by the fact that the spiritual

experiences here recorded follow – intellectually, at least – no common pattern. Few other Christians can have been convinced by just such a strategy; few ever could be. God moves, indeed, in a mysterious way, and this book gives a brilliant account of one of the oddest and most decisive end-games He has ever played.[32]

At the same time, two pages on Renaissance rhetoric in Lewis's *English Literature in the Sixteenth Century* suggest his own peculiar absorption as a scholar in a literary art that is, he wrote, 'the greatest barrier between us and our ancestors'.[33] To start with, Lewis informs us, rhetoric is the embodiment of the continuity of an ancient European tradition, 'older than the Church, older than the Roman Law, older than all Latin literature, it descends from the age of the Greek Sophists', as the 'darling of humanity'.[34] And it is an art for which we now, in the twentieth century, have no sympathy. Yet the Renaissance schoolboy of the sixteenth century was saturated in it, not only granting him a remarkable range of knowledge, but a form of knowledge in which 'high abstractions and rarified artifices jostled the earthiest particulars ... The mind darted more easily to and fro between that mental heaven and earth: the cloud of middle generalizations, hanging between the two, was then much smaller. Hence, as it seems to us, both the naïvety and the energy of their writing. Much of their literary strength ... is bound up with this. They talk something like angels and something like sailors and stable-boys'.[35]

This description tells us a great deal about Lewis the writer. In *Surprised by Joy* we encounter precisely such a mind, often arcane and archaic, and one which revels in the story, inventing worlds which he himself inhabits and in which the extraordinary, the abstract and the intellectual suddenly emerge from the most simple and everyday and even childish. In *The Pilgrim's Regress* he has not yet mastered the rhetoric, nor hidden it after the manner of all good rhetoric. Thus, as they talk, John and Vertue are now angels in their conversation, now 'stable-boys' – but their two manners are imperfectly mixed. In their early talks before they reach the House of Wisdom they speak like Bunyan's lively characters. Later, Lewis allows them to adopt the sophisticated literary style of Boethius's *Consolation of Philosophy*, a *prosimetrum* – that is, a form of prose alternating with verse that has its origins in Greek philosophical writings.[36]

But in the later *Surprised by Joy*, the rhetoric is perfectly concealed within the fabric of the text. Almost from the beginning of the book he establishes a 'persona' for himself as narrator, creating of himself a literary figure with something of an austere remoteness and 'a certain distrust or dislike of emotion as something uncomfortable and embarrassing and even dangerous'.[37] This allows a perspective on others behind which he can conceal himself and build other characters with a judgement hidden within the literary and alluring tropes of irony, litotes (understatement) and caricature.[38] Thus the reader is led by a firm voice that acts persuasively, even when what is being said is confusing or otherwise unacceptable, as Lewis now masterfully employs the rhetoric that in the *Regress* is as yet unformed and unstable.

How, then, do we read its narrative – the question of hermeneutics? I suggest that the key lies in Lewis's absorption in sixteenth-century literature and classical rhetoric, particularly at the time of writing *Surprised by Joy*.[39] If *The Pilgrim's Regress* was informed by his thinking for *The Allegory of Love*, then the later work is informed by *English Literature in the Sixteenth Century* and in particular its very concern for the ancient rhetorical art. It could be said that Lewis's success as a Christian writer and apologist might be explained, to a degree at least, by his success as a rhetorician. It might help account for both his extraordinary popularity and the deep suspicion in which, simultaneously, he is held by many, as an apologist and a Christian thinker. Nor need the presentation of rhetoric always imply negative characteristics and dubious motives. Aristotle, to whom Lewis refers in his work on the sixteenth century,[40] defends in his *Rhetoric* the capacity of the rhetorician to sustain moral purposes, and, more especially, the potential of rhetoric to be heuristic, enabling us to discover rather than distort the facts.

The preface to *Surprised by Joy* employs well-tried devices of rhetoric to disarm and situate the reader, and to establish an appropriate hermeneutical milieu. Lewis begins with a clear statement of why he is writing (not on his own initiative), and to assure the reader that his book will rectify common misconceptions (without actually stating what they are): 'This book is written partly in answer to requests that I would tell how I passed from Atheism to Christianity and partly to correct one or two false notions that seem to have got about.'[41] Importantly, Lewis is careful to assert what the book is *not*; it is not a general autobiography, nor 'Confessions' in the manner of St Augustine or Rousseau. It is the much more limited 'story of my conversion'.[42] This immediately slants the reading as there is, undeniably, a great deal of autobiographical material presented, which we then read 'with a purpose' – all being offered in the context of explaining his conversion and experience of 'joy'. Second, Lewis carefully anticipates his critics, admitting the crime of 'subjectivity' and smiling with full recognition at those of his readers for whom this kind of writing is unbearable. Like all good rhetoricians he is always one step ahead:

> The story is, I fear, suffocatingly subjective; the kind of thing I have never written before and shall probably never write again. [Both these claims are highly questionable!] I have tried so to write the first chapter that those who can't bear such a story will see at once what they are in for and close the book with the least waste of time.[43]

Thus his disparagers are left out in the cold, and we who remain can proceed in good company.

The element of complicity is crucial. Walter Nash, in his book *Rhetoric: The Wit of Persuasion*, suggests that

> It is indeed the point of rhetoric to have designs on an audience, or a victim; and the purpose of these designs is not wholly to persuade, as may be commonly supposed, but rather to involve the recipient in a conspiracy from which there is no easy withdrawal. In rhetoric there is always an element of conspiracy; it can be magniloquent, or charming, or forceful, or devious, but whatever its manner it seeks assiduously to involve an accomplice in its designs.[44]

Is this what is happening in *Surprised by Joy*, and an explanation, in part at least, of the uncritical, even adoring, character of sections of Lewis's readership? From an early age Lewis presents himself as a clever man, bookish and serious, and within this persona (which may be largely true, though that is not the point) he distracts, teases and flirts with his readers. He can get away with making some pretty questionable claims, but we still revel in his wonderful prose: for example, in the Dickensian gothic of his 'concentration camp' first school, with its Wackford Squeers of a master, the worst of his teachers,[45] just as we do in his characterization of more revered schoolmasters like Kirk (the 'Great Knock'), who 'had been a Presbyterian and was now an Atheist'.[46]

But this is not to conclude with simple cynicism. It may help to explain why, from a literary perspective, Lewis divides his readers, but his skill in rhetoric does not necessarily undermine his honesty, still less his effectiveness, as an apologist. As one reviewer of *Surprised by Joy* put it (although one wonders if she had read the first page of the book, on which Lewis specifically distinguished his work from the *Confessions*): 'This is an almost agonizingly personal book: it is the conversion of a pure romantic, and it is as completely convincing as are the conversion stories of Augustine and Newman.'[47]

ALLEGORY, METAPHOR AND SYMBOL

Finally, then, we are brought back to the role of allegory, metaphor and symbol in Lewis's work in the linking of the particular and the general, the specific and the universal, the mundane and the Romantic. Certainly Lewis in the two works which we are considering must be described as a 'didactic' writer, though at the same time the polemic of his fiction and autobiographical narratives must be understood as not only a rhetorical tool (which it is), but also an imaginative construct.[48] As an admitted 'Romanticist', Lewis looks back to Coleridge's writings on the imagination, and in particular to the crucial thirteenth chapter of the *Biographia Literaria* (1817), with its distinction between the primary and secondary imagination.[49] In this the elements of the primary imagination, as 'a repetition in the finite mind of the eternal act of creation in the infinite I AM', are, in the secondary imagination, 'dissolved, diffused and dissipated' in the process of image-making – a Coleridgean process which Lewis (following his friend J.R.R. Tolkien) adapted and developed in the context of the reader's 'willing suspension of disbelief'[50] in the creative process through the theory of 'sub-creation'.[51] This is described succinctly by Kath Filmer:

> the story-maker becomes the 'sub-creator' of a secondary world into which the reader's mind may enter. While the reader is thus 'present' in the secondary world, he 'believes' in it. Should disbelief arise, Tolkien adds, 'the spell is broken; the magic, or rather art, has failed. You are then out in the Primary World again, looking at the little abortive Secondary World from outside' ... The belief aroused by a writer's imaginative and artistic skill is a positive state, rather than the negative state suggested by Coleridge.[52]

Through metaphor and symbol it is precisely this 'secondary world' into which the rhetoric ushers the reader in both *The Pilgrim's Regress* and *Surprised by Joy*, with different degrees of success. In describing himself, his own beliefs and conversion, Lewis, in a sense, becomes a victim of his own bookishness. For, entering this world, just as when we enter the worlds of the novels of Jane Austen or Charles Dickens, we can forgive and perhaps even forget Lewis's old-fashioned and donnish eccentricity as we follow his 'character' in its odd, moving, individualistic journey into Christianity – a journey both Romantic and mundane:

> And John said, 'I thought all those things when I was in the house of Wisdom. But now I think better things. Be sure it is not for

nothing that the Landlord has knit our hearts so closely to time and place – to one friend rather than another and one shire more than all the land.'[53]

I was driven to Whipsnade one sunny morning. When we set out I did not believe that Jesus Christ is the Son of God, and when we reached the zoo I did ... Wallaby Wood, with the birds singing overhead and the bluebells underfoot and the Wallabies hopping all round one, was almost Eden come again.[54]

When the spell is broken, we step outside his world, recognizing its allurements, its dramatic and symbolic attractions. Countless readers are happy to have been so enchanted, while others are puzzled by what they consider the ultimate incoherence of his claims.

Perhaps for Lewis, the bookish dreamer and compulsive reader, the very narrative – the sheer experience of being inside a story – is always more important than the conclusion of it. He knew that he had inherited from his father a 'fatal bent towards dramatisation and rhetoric'[55] and believed in any case that it was not possible 'for any one to describe himself, even in prose, without making of himself, to some extent, a dramatic creation'.[56] In the preface to the third edition of *The Pilgrim's Regress* he states his rhetorical purpose clearly: 'I was attempting to generalise, not to tell people about my own life.'[57] But by the end of both *Regress* and *Joy* his reader takes that for granted because, by then, he or she has so entered into the character of 'John' or of C.S. Lewis, 'the most dejected and reluctant convert in all England',[58] that the narrative has also become his or her story and its confirmation. The seductions of rhetoric have conspired against us and we have become its accomplices – or not.

The manner in which Lewis composed these works constitutes an invitation to every reader to identify with the protagonist and thus for his story to become particular to each reader. It is Lewis's capacity to succeed in this which secures his status within Christian literature of the twentieth century. In the two conversion narratives which are the subject of this chapter we see him learning his craft as a writer and a Christian apologist from early attempt to mature assurance.[59]

Notes

1   For more on Lewis's rhetoric see Gary L. Tandy, *The Rhetoric of Certitude: C.S. Lewis's Nonfiction Prose* (Kent, OH: Kent State University Press, 2009) and James T. Como, *Branches to Heaven: The Geniuses of C.S. Lewis* (Dallas: Spence Publishing, 1999).

2   PR 12.

3   SBJ 12.

4   SBJ 20.

5   SBJ 144–46.

6   Catherine, the poet's second daughter, born 6 Sept. 1808, died 5 June 1812.

7   SBJ 190.

8   Lewis distinguishes his own approach somewhat from Wordsworth's in his sermon 'The Weight of Glory'. There he argues that Wordsworth made a mistake in locating joy in certain moments in his own past and that, if he had returned to those moments, he would have found that even then the joy they communicated was only a reminder of something further back (EC 98). Cf. Lewis's poem 'Leaving Forever the Home of One's Youth' (CP 245).

9   SBJ 18–19.

10   PR 9.

11   Quoted in Walter Hooper, *C.S. Lewis: A Companion and Guide* (London: HarperCollins, 1996), 184–85.

12   PR 250.

13   AOL 60.

14   AOL 44–45.

15   AOL 45. Lewis's friend Owen Barfield makes a similar distinction in his book *Poetic Diction*, between the 'unitive metaphor' which is *'given, as it were, by Nature'*, and the 'analytic metaphor' whereby an individual 'register[s] as thought' a relationship: *Poetic Diction*, 2nd edn (London: Faber & Faber, 1952), 102–03. See further Doris T. Myers, *C.S. Lewis in Context* (Kent, OH: Kent State University Press, 1991), 11–13.

16   Samuel Taylor Coleridge, *The Statesman's Manual. Lay Sermons*, in *The Collected Works*, vol. VI. ed. R.J. White (Princeton: Princeton University Press, 1972), 30.

17   AOL 268–69.

18   Walter Allen, *The English Novel: A Short Critical History* (Harmondsworth: Penguin, 1958), 32.

19   PR 247.

20   See Lionel Adey, *C.S. Lewis: Writer, Dreamer and Mentor* (Grand Rapids: Eerdmans, 1998), 110; Kathryn Ann Lindskoog, *Finding the Landlord: A Guidebook to C.S. Lewis's 'The Pilgrim's Regress'* (Chicago: Cornerstone Press Chicago, 1995), pp. xxvi–xxvii.

21   PR 98.

22   PR 100.

23   'The Vision of John Bunyan', SLE 146–53.

24   SLE 152.

25   SLE 152–53 (emphasis added).

26   CP 243.

27   AMR 48, 297–98, 317, 328.

28   Hooper, *C.S. Lewis: A Companion and Guide*, 181–82.

29   Letter to Arthur Greeves, 15 June 1930 (CLI 906).

30 FL 128.
31 FL 128 (Emphasis added).
32 Quoted in Hooper, *C.S. Lewis: A Companion and Guide*, 193.
33 EL 61.
34 EL 61.
35 EL 62.
36 See V.E. Watts's introduction to Boethius, *The Consolation of Philosophy*, tr. V. E. Watts (Harmondsworth: Penguin, 1969), 19–20; also Myers, *C.S. Lewis in Context*, 23.
37 SBJ 9.
38 The term 'alluring' I draw from D.J. Enright's fine book on irony, *The Alluring Problem* (Oxford: Oxford University Press, 1986). The point which I am making is somewhat different, assuming a literary calculation on Lewis's part as a writer, from John Wain's description of Lewis's self-portrait in *Surprised by Joy* as 'a wooden dummy' which 'bears the individual features of no living man' (John Wain, 'A Great Clerke', in James Como (ed.), *Remembering C.S. Lewis: Recollections of Those Who Knew Him* (San Francisco: Ignatius Press, 2005), 152–63) and also from Michael Ward's analysis of Lewis's rhetorical purposes in *Surprised by Joy* ('C.S. Lewis', in Andrew Atherstone (ed.), *The Heart of Faith: Following Christ in the Church of England* (Cambridge: Lutterworth Press, 2008), 121–30).
39 *Surprised by Joy* was published almost exactly twelve months to the day after *English Literature in the Sixteenth Century* (EL, 16 Sept. 1954, SBJ 19 Sept. 1955).
40 EL 271, 319–21.
41 SBJ 7.
42 SBJ 7.
43 SBJ 7–8.
44 Walter Nash, *Rhetoric: The Wit of Persuasion* (Oxford: Basil Blackwell, 1989), 1.
45 SBJ 24–39.
46 SBJ 113.
47 Anne Fremantle in *Commonweal* 63 (3 Feb. 1956), quoted in Hooper, *C.S. Lewis: A Companion and Guide*, 193.
48 See Kath Filmer, 'The Polemic Image: The Role of Metaphor and Symbol in the Fiction of C.S. Lewis', in Bruce L. Edwards (ed.), *The Taste of the Pineapple: Essays on C.S. Lewis as Reader, Critic and Imaginative Writer* (Bowling Green, OH: Bowling Green State University Popular Press, 1988), 149–65.
49 See Samuel Taylor Coleridge, *Biographia Literaria*, ed. James Engell and W. Jackson Bate (London: Routledge & Kegan Paul, 1983), I, 304.
50 *Biographia Literaria*, II, 6.
51 Lewis discusses Coleridge's distinction between Phantasy and Imagination in ch. 7 of *The Discarded Image*, arguing that he turned the medieval nomenclature upside down.
52 Filmer, 'The Polemic Image', 150. Filmer is referring to J.R.R. Tolkien, 'On Fairy Stories', in C.S. Lewis (ed.), *Essays Presented to Charles*

Williams. (Grand Rapids: Eerdmans, 1981; 1st publ. 1947), 60–61, and also M 137n.

53   PR 249.
54   SBJ 189–90.
55   SBJ 36.
56   PH 10.
57   PR 21.
58   SBJ 182.
59   For some of the initial ideas for this essay I am indebted to a fine, unpublished Ph.D. thesis by Hsiu-Chin Chou, 'The Problem of Faith and Self: The Interplay between Literary Art, Apologetics and Hermeneutics in C.S. Lewis's Religious Narratives' (Glasgow University, 2008).

17   The Ransom Trilogy

T.A. SHIPPEY

C.S. Lewis's Ransom Trilogy sprang, on the personal level, from a conversation and a coincidence.

The conversation was with his friend Tolkien, and though Lewis has left no record of it, Tolkien mentions it no fewer than five times in his published *Letters*, with convincing consistency.[1] According to Tolkien, what happened was that Lewis said to him, 'If they won't write the kind of books we want to read, we shall have to write them ourselves.' They agreed accordingly 'each to write an excursionary "Thriller" ... discovering Myth', one about space travel and one about travel in time, and the toss of a coin gave time to Tolkien and space to Lewis. The results of the agreement were very different. Lewis had finished his first 'excursionary thriller', *Out of the Silent Planet*, by November 1937, when he submitted it to J.M. Dent and it was rejected. Tolkien then stepped in and used his influence with the publisher Stanley Unwin, who had by this time accepted *The Hobbit*, to reconsider his friend's work, which duly appeared in 1938, with its two sequels in 1943 and 1945. Lewis attempted to repay the favour by working 'plugs' for Tolkien's projected time-thriller into the postscript to *Out of the Silent Planet* and the preface to *That Hideous Strength*, but Tolkien's efforts to fulfil their agreement only appeared many years later and unfinished, as 'The Lost Road' and 'The Notion Club Papers' in volumes 5 and 9 of the twelve-volume *History of Middle-earth* edited by Christopher Tolkien.

Unlike the conversation, the coincidence can be fairly precisely dated, to February 1936, though both must have happened at about the same time. Another Oxford friend, Hugo Dyson, persuaded Lewis to read Charles Williams's *The Place of the Lion* (1931), third in what was to be a sequence of seven 'occult thrillers' by Williams. Lewis, very impressed, wrote Williams a fan letter, but before he posted it received one from Williams. The latter worked for Oxford University Press and as part of his duties had been reading the proofs of Lewis's first major academic work, *The Allegory of Love*, which moved him to write in terms of similar appreciation. The coincidence of simultaneous discovery and mutual admiration led to a friendship which lasted the nine years till Williams's death, but it also opened Lewis's eyes to a new possibility: one could write a work inspired by recondite learning (in both cases essentially Neoplatonic learning), but still use the style and method of popular fiction. With this discovery, and prompted also by the agreement with Tolkien, Lewis was launched on a career of ever-accelerating production and success.

INTELLECTUAL ORIGINS

The intellectual origins of the Ransom Trilogy are much more various,[2] and it would be mere guesswork to try to say which came first or which were most important – especially in view of Lewis's own remarks on the unexpected nature of literary inspiration.[3] However, even before the start of chapter 1 of *Out of the Silent Planet* Lewis inserted a note saying gracefully that, in spite of apparently 'slighting references' in the text, he would be sorry 'if any reader supposed he was too stupid to have enjoyed Mr. H.G. Wells's fantasies or too ungrateful to acknowledge his debt to them'. One may still think that however much he enjoyed them, Lewis did not agree with them. Despite his earlier disclaimer, the portrait near the end of *That Hideous Strength* of the half-educated cockney pontificator Horace Jules is recognizably based on Herbert Wells, by the 1940s no longer a writer of fiction but a disseminator of grandiose universal surveys like *An Outline of History* (1920), or ill-informed political prophecies like *The Shape of Things to Come* (1933). *Out of the Silent Planet* is certainly similar in structure and in some details to Wells's *The First Men in the Moon* (1901), but solidly opposed ideologically.[4] In both works men from Earth embark on a space voyage, encounter the inhabitants of the Moon or Mars, clash with them, further encounter the planetary ruler, return with difficulty to Earth, lose their ship or have it destroyed. Moreover, Wells's characters Cavor and Bedford are more or less parallel to Lewis's Weston and Devine – respectively inventor and exploiter – but Lewis's pair are explicitly identified as evil, while there is a third figure, Ransom, to oppose them. In the end the real clash is between Weston and the Oyarsa (or planetary Intelligence) of Mars, and the view Weston puts forward, which is one of aggressive and amoral evolutionism, is decisively mocked and rejected. Very near the start of Wells's *The War of the Worlds* (1898) the narrator states, 'The intellectual side of man already admits that life is an incessant struggle for existence', and there is no sign that this was not Wells's view also. Lewis's Oyarsa, however, at one point says very firmly that when, millions of years ago, the idea of a Wellsian invasion of Earth did occur to some of his people on Mars, who were 'well able to have made sky-ships',[5] he stopped them, curing some, killing others. Lewis repeatedly stressed his own distinction between real science and what he called 'scientism',[6] the ill-informed misapplication of scientific theories to social, moral and political issues in forms such as 'social Darwinism' and 'Creative Evolution', and Wells, brilliant writer though he was (to begin with), was an arch-exponent of such views.

Lewis had another and more positive goal in writing, and that was to challenge modern cosmology and offer an alternative view of the universe. The biologist J.B.S. Haldane (a close parallel to Wells in his evolutionism and his belief in state direction of science) reviewed the Ransom Trilogy in 1946 under the scornful title 'Auld Hornie, FRS',[7] and remarked there that integrating the cosmological theories of antiquity and Christianity with what was actually known had been 'a slight strain' for Dante and 'harder' for Milton, while 'Mr. Lewis finds it impossible'. Haldane knew little about Dante or Milton, but he did have a point: some things are now known beyond any possibility of refutation, and they may well conflict with ancient ideas well entrenched in literature. Writers have their own ways of dealing with that, however. Milton, for instance, describing the effects of the Fall of Humanity in *Paradise Lost* (10, 668–80), carefully wrote in two alternative explanations of Earth's ecliptic tilt, the one suitable to the old geocentric cosmology, the other as demanded by the new solar-centred Galilean model. Lewis, surely aware of this fact, noted in his posthumously published work *The Discarded Image* that the old Model (the capitalization is his) 'was not totally and confidently abandoned till the end of the seventeenth century', i.e. some decades after Milton.[8] Meanwhile Tolkien, faced with a contradiction between his imagined 'Silmarillion' cosmology and the common knowledge of his time, invented a more poetic reconciliation. In his account the world is indeed round now, but this is a result of the reshaping of the world after the Fall of Númenor. No one thereafter can sail directly across the sea to the Undying Lands, for 'All roads now are bent', but some believe that 'a Straight Road still must be'.[9] The idea of 'bending' as a result of the Fall was important to Lewis too, though he took it morally rather than geographically. But like Milton and Tolkien, and in much more detail than either of them, he too meant to reconcile cosmologies.

This was an important matter to Lewis for most if not all of his adult life, and arguably underlies all of his fictional inventions, including

Narnia.[10] His love of what he called 'the Medieval Model' of the universe appears as early as 1935 in the poem 'The Planets', but reaches its clearest expression in *The Discarded Image*. There he repeatedly asks the modern reader to try to imagine the universe 'turned inside out', not so as to re-establish Earth as the centre (something no longer intellectually possible), but instead to remove the idea of Earth as the only warm and habitable spot in an abyss of cold, dark vacuum.[11] At the end of *Out of the Silent Planet* Ransom writes, 'If we could even effect in one per cent of our readers a change-over from the conception of Space to the conception of Heaven, we should have made a beginning'.[12] In the main body of the story that change-over occurs when Ransom – shanghaied into a spaceship and on his way to unknown terrors – feels ecstasy instead of fear. Instead of the dark and cold he expected, he finds colour and radiance in which he basks:

> Stretched naked on his bed, a second Danaë, he found it night by night more difficult to disbelieve in old astrology: almost he felt, wholly he imagined, 'sweet influence' pouring or even stabbing into his surrendered body.[13]

Lewis explained the technical meaning of 'influence' elsewhere,[14] but note that while Ransom only 'almost' feels it, he nevertheless 'wholly' imagines it. The whole of the Ransom Trilogy is set within the constraints of modern astronomy, or at least the astronomy of Lewis's time (spaceships; 'canals' or canyons on Mars; Venus as a water-world). But within those constraints a place has been made also for 'old astrology'.

One can see further that Tolkien's statement that both writers were to aim at 'discovering Myth' was precisely accurate, and that both men kept to it. In all three parts of the Ransom Trilogy a myth is either discovered to be literally true or is re-enacted: the Fall of the Angels (*Out of the Silent Planet*); the Fall of Humanity (*Perelandra*); the destruction of the Tower of Babel (*That Hideous Strength*). Tolkien's time-travel thriller would have done the same for the Atlantis myth, and Tolkien may well have correctly identified the governing myth of Lewis's 'Dark Tower' fragment as being that of the descendants of Seth and Cain.[15]

OUT OF THE SILENT PLANET

The mythical and astrological ideas of the Medieval Model which Lewis most obviously incorporated into *Out of the Silent Planet* were these: first, that each of the planets known to the Medieval Model has

its own presiding genius, or Oyarsa; second, that these are readily identifiable with the pagan deities (e.g. Malacandra's Oyarsa is identifiable
with the Roman Mars and the Greek Ares; Perelandra's Oyarsa with
Venus and Aphrodite). However, making them into deities was simple
human error, for the Intelligences themselves are well aware that they
are the creatures and devoted servants of the One God of Christianity –
with, however, one exception, for Lewis's most original speculation
was to declare that the presiding Intelligence of Earth is Satan. That is
why Earth is 'the silent planet', cut off from the everlasting harmony of
the planetary and stellar spheres, not the warm centre surrounded by
dark vacuum of the modern imagination, but the universe's cold dregs,
its inhabitants a prey to demonic temptation and delusion, in a word,
'fallen' – though not beyond salvation.

A critical term is the word 'bent'. Satan is 'the bent eldil [angel]',
and the Oyarsa of Mars says that while Satan has 'only bent' Weston,
he has 'broken' Devine, 'for he has left him nothing but greed'.[16] The
implication is that no one, not even Satan, was evil from the beginning.
Everyone, humans and even devils, once had and perhaps still has the
option of 'going straight'. Evil comes about when people take a wrong
option or direction, and all his life Lewis showed unusual interest in
the moment when people (understandably, even forgivably) go wrong.
The trouble is, they then persist in their error, and as presented by both
Lewis and Tolkien turn into 'wraiths' – 'wraith' derives from the word
'writhe', to twist or bend. In *Out of the Silent Planet* Weston has not
yet become a total wraith, for ruthless, bullying and murderous though
he is, his drive is based on a kind of love, though it is love for abstractions (Man, Life, Destiny) which he has himself created. The Oyarsa
notes that one of the devices of Satan is to make people break all laws,
even the greatest, in the service of one of the lesser, in this case 'love of
kindred';[17] and Lewis is here using fiction to present a diagnosis. Satan
or no Satan, he thought that 'bending' was exactly what was going on
in his own world and time. The real danger was not mere cynical gold-
seekers like Devine, but idealists like Weston – or Wells and Haldane
and a whole gallery of clever fools, with their support for Stalin and
their conviction that ends justify means, even if the ends include genocide. Weston certainly intends to inflict genocide on Mars, but in the
late 1930s, as Lewis was writing, genocide on Earth was not far off.
Like astronomy and astrology, myth and reality were not impossibly
distinct.

Besides its moral argument and cosmological speculation, *Out
of the Silent Planet* contains a substantial element of science-fiction

travelogue. Lewis attempted to imagine interplanetary travel, gave an image of Mars which stressed the 'perpendicular theme' (everything from plants to mountains and even waves seems impossibly tall), and in chapter 17 suddenly showed Ransom seeing Earthmen as the Malacandrians see them, impossibly short, thick, stumpy. His conversation about eldils with Augray the *sorn* – one of the three intelligent species Ransom finds on Mars, all and especially the *hrossa* lovingly described – leaves him feeling the universe has been turned 'rather oddly inside out',[18] but this, as he notes, is something he is getting used to.

PERELANDRA

There is an element of similarly joyous invention in the sequel but *Perelandra* is markedly more severe, more argumentative. *Perelandra* is clearly a reprise of books 4 and 9–10 of *Paradise Lost*, the basic idea being that both God and Satan have sent emissaries to Venus, where Satan's emissary Weston (now demonically possessed) means to tempt the Lady, Venus's counterpart of Eve, to repeat the original sin of disobedience to God and so create another Fall. Ransom is there to stop him. The core of the work is a long debate between the two in chapters 7 through 10, as the one tries to convince the Lady that she should disobey the one prohibition which God has laid on her, and the other urges her to obedience.

It is impossible here to give any detailed account of this debate, into which Lewis poured not only his own interpretations of Milton, which he was developing at the same time in a second major academic work, *A Preface to Paradise Lost* (1942), but also his views on free will, sin and human psychology. One could, however, make a start by noting the connection between Venus as Lewis imagines it, a water-world in which the near-human inhabitants live on floating islands, and the prohibition imposed on the Lady and her Adam-counterpart husband, which is never to spend a night on the Fixed Lands in the middle of the world-ocean. They live on the wave, and the moving wave as opposed to the Fixed Land is the dominant image of plot and of debate. When he arrives and struggles onto an island, Ransom encounters one strange thing after another, all of them welcome. A balloon-fruit quenches his thirst; a bubble-tree gives him a refreshing shower; a bread-berry feeds him, with the added delight of occasionally encountering one with a red heart which is especially savoury. Each time Ransom feels an urge to repeat the experience, or to pick out the 'red-heart' berries only, but something warns him not to because, Ransom concludes, this 'itch to have things over again' is perhaps 'the root of all evil'.[19] Isn't that supposed to be money, he asks himself? But perhaps money is a defence against chance and change, something which 'would provide the means of saying *encore* in a voice that could not be disobeyed'.[20] By contrast, the Lady in her unfallen state is happy to ride the wave: whatever comes to her, she accepts as good. Dwelling on the Fixed Land would be at once to reject the will of God, to try to impose her own will on events, to start down the path of pride and cupidity. The Satanic Weston's temptation of the Lady starts by suggesting that perhaps (just as a speculation) she might consider whether God does not really, in his heart, mean her to show independence by going against his will, and not just accepting whatever he sends.

The argument is never decisively settled, for it comes to Ransom that the matter has to be decided physically, by unarmed combat between himself and Weston, whom he now sees as the Un-Man. This could be seen as an evasion by Lewis, though one should remember – Ransom mentions it several times – that this is a book written in wartime, when the fate of the world was being settled not by debate but by guns and bombs and torpedoes: neither Lewis nor Tolkien was a pacifist, and both were veterans. However, the most macabre aspect of *Perelandra* is its presentation of what one might call 'psychic decomposition' in Weston. When he first appears he is recognizably the blustering scientist of *Out of the Silent Planet*, aggressive but still human. But he has switched from physics to biology and become a believer in Creative Evolution, and so a devotee of 'the Life-Force', a worshipper of 'Spirit'[21] – and this ends with him being indeed possessed by a spirit, but a diabolical one. For much of the book Weston is the Un-Man, in effect Satan, though a far less glamorous Satan than any of the imaginations of Marlowe or Milton or Goethe. But every now and then a trapped Weston seems to break out, begging for help. In a horrific passage near the end Weston voices his terror of death, and gives a glimpse of what Ransom calls 'The Empirical Bogey … the great myth of our century',[22] which leads only, in Weston's imagining, to a Homeric or pre-Homeric belief in a meaningless universe in which conscious life is a mere flicker, a thin layer over existential horror. That is what the devils do to us, Ransom concludes. Just as they frightened the narrator at the start of the novel with thoughts they put in his brain, so they project panic and despair via the Un-Man as he wanders in the strange underworld of Venus. But this underlying panic and despair, the result (Lewis suggests) of a Godless worldview, is perhaps what drove Weston down his path of aggression and domination, what first began to make him 'bent'.

THAT HIDEOUS STRENGTH

The third volume in the trilogy, *That Hideous Strength*, is markedly different from its predecessors, more than twice the length of the other two put together, set on Earth and so without any 'travelogue' element, in modern terms fantasy rather than science fiction. It is also much more crowded. For most of its length *Perelandra* contained only three characters, Ransom, Weston and the Lady, and *Out of the Silent Planet* not many more. *That Hideous Strength* by contrast seems to have too many. The basic conflict in the story is between a new Dark Power, which Lewis labels satirically as N.I.C.E., the National Institute for Co-ordinated Experiments, state-run science secretly controlled by Earth's devils, and a 'fellowship' directed by Ransom, who has now become (with obvious allusion to the Grail legends) both 'the Pendragon' and 'Mr Fisher-King'. This fellowship, like Tolkien's more famous one, has nine members, but most readers of the novel might be hard put to remember them all. Ransom is the leader, Jane Studdock is the vital seer who can locate the re-awakened Merlin for them, MacPhee takes the role of sceptic and Ivy Maggs adds social breadth, Cecil Dimble is a vehicle for academic theory while his wife contributes a dash of practicality – but what, one might wonder, are the roles of Grace Ironwood and Arthur and Camilla Denniston? The first has a suggestive name, the other two might well be hangovers from Lewis's abandoned 'Dark Tower' romance,[23] but none of them really functions in the story other than incidentally. Meanwhile Belbury, the stronghold of the N.I.C.E., is even more packed with characters: Mark Studdock, Jane's straw-man husband, Wither the Deputy Director, Devine from *Out of the Silent Planet* reimagined as Lord Feverstone, Frost and Filostrato and Straik and Jules, Cosser and Steele and Hardcastle and O'Hara. Some of them are striking portraits, notably Straik the mad parson and Professor Frost, paired by name and power with Wither, but one wonders sometimes quite what satirical target they are aimed at. A third locus in the novel is Bracton College, a little world of academic manoeuvring with its own extended cast, notably Sub-Warden Curry and Busby the Bursar. Lewis put twenty years' experience of 'office politics' into the collegial scenes: the opening account of the College meeting with its cunningly rigged agenda is a gem. But where, one might again wonder, is the core of this atypically sprawling narrative?

A strong indication of Lewis's thinking is given by his third major academic work, which he was researching as he wrote *That Hideous Strength – English Literature in the Sixteenth Century, Excluding Drama*

(1954). The book's dull title is belied by an extraordinarily original and contrarian opening chapter, 'New Learning and New Ignorance'. Here Lewis argues that the Renaissance was not, as popularly supposed, a period in which rational science broke free of medieval superstition, but an era in which magic and science were seen as alternative and equally practicable routes to power. In *That Hideous Strength* the N.I.C.E. is attempting to reunite the two methods, an attempt eventually frustrated by the return of Merlin from the past, with his older and more natural magic, which allows him to be a channel for the planetary deities: the eldils from outside intervene to counter the bent eldils of Earth. It is, however, science (or scientism) which Lewis saw as the threat to his own society, because behind it there lay an urge towards power and a conviction that it must be grasped. 'Man has got to take charge of man', says Feverstone,[24] and though he himself remains essentially venal, his rhetoric is repeated elsewhere in the novel by other figures who have deeper beliefs – for instance Filostrato, the Italian professor with his conviction that Nature should be erased as untidy; Straik, who seems to be expecting the Apocalypse; and Frost, with his determination that 'The human race is to become all Technocracy'.[25] Tracing the intellectual origins of any of these figures to the real world of 1945 would be a separate exercise, and such references as Lewis gives have usually, a lifetime later, lost all resonance. Nevertheless some of Lewis's targets remain utterly familiar, including the growth of bureaucracy and the corruption of language.

This latter was a concern to Lewis for much of his life, expressed notably by Screwtape and through the discussion of 'verbicide' in *Studies in Words*.[26] It provides the novel's dominating myth in the final re-enactment of the Tower of Babel, as the N.I.C.E.'s programme (like Weston's manifesto in the first novel) is reduced to gibberish. Lewis's point, though, is that the kind of language the N.I.C.E. uses always *was* gibberish, a kind of Higher Nonsense at first adopted deliberately by clever men to delude less clever ones, but slowly poisoning their minds till that becomes the way they actually think. Mark Studdock dramatizes the process. In chapter 6 he is shown writing up false accounts of the Edgestow riots, first in *Times*-leader style (authoritative, self-flattering, using Latin tags), and then tabloid-style (with much simpler language, still self-flattering, but aggressively sarcastic), and he knows as he is doing it that he is telling lies. But can he stop? Again and again we see him resorting to his familiar comfortable rhetoric in the face of obvious facts, for his education has given him nothing else to use; his mind contains 'hardly one rag of noble thought, either Christian or

Pagan'.[27] One of the dominant images of the twentieth century has been 'the hollow man', and if in Studdock the hollowing is well under way, in Wither the Deputy Director it has become complete. His rhetoric is so abstract, so impersonal, so full of qualifications and grammatical loops, that no one can ever work out exactly what he is saying – except that it is laden with veiled threat. Since he never gives a clear instruction he can never be blamed for failure, but all his subordinates know that at any moment they may be demoted, dismissed, have their careers ruined, be charged with murder, executed, or handed over to the torture chambers of the N.I.C.E.'s institutional police. The way in which the ground is cut from under Mark Studdock's feet is, on a larger scale, just like the way the agenda is rigged for the Bracton College meeting. That is the way bureaucrats exert power. Wither knows what he is doing, for at one point he notes Professor Frost trying the same tricks on him, and with icy politeness remarks that such 'modes of oblique discipline' should be reserved for 'our inferiors'.[28] But he too eventually knows no other way to talk. When he does for the first time feel a crack in his own self-created 'mental machine', all he can say is 'God bless my soul!'[29] But the words ironically mean nothing, for he has emptied words of meaning. The point is rubbed in very memorably in the fantastic mode by Mark's repeated visions of Wither as a genuine 'wraith', detached from his own body,[30] but one might say that 'wraithing' is something that can happen to anyone in sober reality. When Ransom's fellowship discusses the moral justice of the destruction of the University of Edgestow as well as the N.I.C.E. at Belbury, Arthur Denniston says the dons deserved it: they preached the doctrines of power and amorality which the N.I.C.E. put into practice, and the fact that they never meant them just shows once again the fatal separation of words and meaning. There is a poetic justice in the curse of Babel which falls on them, which Merlin sums up in his triumphant cry, '*Qui verbum Dei contempserunt, eis auferetur etiam Verbum hominis*' ('They that have despised the Word of God, from them shall the word of man also be taken away').[31]

Merlin remains the most strikingly original figure in *That Hideous Strength*, with his importation of a medieval *magia* which Lewis insisted, in *English Literature in the Sixteenth Century*, was palpably different from the *goeteia* of the Renaissance. One of the most attractive features of the novel is indeed the little lectures which Cecil Dimble occasionally gives about Arthurian Britain, about magic and the *longaevi*, about Logres and Britain, even about Celticity, which have had (one suspects) a considerable effect on the many later retellers of the Arthurian story. The wisdom-contest between Merlin and Ransom in chapter 13 is another gem, which incidentally allows Lewis to reintroduce some cosmological speculation about the two sides of the Moon – once again 'turned inside out', for it is the side we cannot see that actually 'looks to Deep Heaven'[32] – and to deploy his unrivalled grasp of non-classical Latin. A similar gem is the opening account of Bragdon Wood, with its brief pastiches of medieval lyric, Elizabethan polemic and anti-Cromwellian rudeness. However, for all Lewis's formidable learning, which so often gives his writing an unmatched depth of suggestion, one may close by noting his charitable and essentially non-elitist rescue of the wretched Studdock. Studdock is glib, shallow, weak, half-educated, without inner resources of learning or character, and under severe pressure from Professor Frost, who seems determined to turn him into a disciple and then, one fears, into some sort of spiritual food like Screwtape with his nephew Wormwood. Nevertheless in the end the worm turns. Told by Frost to trample and insult a crucifix, Studdock has no logical reason not to do so. He has no belief in Christ, does not believe he exists to be insulted. But just as Puddleglum, under the deluding spell of the Witch in *The Silver Chair*, says 'I'm on Aslan's side even if there isn't any Aslan to lead it',[33] so Mark decides to 'go down with the ship'. What he actually says is 'It's all bloody nonsense, and I'm damned if I do any such thing',[34] and unlike Wither's 'God bless my soul!' a few pages earlier, this time the words are literally, if unintentionally, true. Studdock has in fact invented for himself what Tolkien called 'the theory of courage', and which he located in Norse myth: the Norse gods are doomed to defeat by the monsters, but the heroes do not see in that any reason for changing sides. He is also supported by a sense – created in him by ricochet, so to speak, from the Belbury 'training' – of the Straight and the Normal, which he cannot articulate, and which Lewis probably could not either. But (Lewis might have said) you do not need to read the recipe to appreciate the cake.

CONCLUSION

It has to be conceded that many of Lewis's concerns and intentions in the Ransom Trilogy have passed beyond recall. His anxiety about the dangers of 'Creative Evolution' proved unnecessary: not even Richard Dawkins believes in that any more. The Chestertonian idea of 'Christian Distributism' which makes a brief appearance as 'Distributivism' in connection with Arthur Denniston has been largely forgotten, at least under that name,[35] and Lewis's views on the nature of Christian marriage are probably unacceptable to almost everyone – though it should be noted that the common accusation that he was a misogynist has been subtly countered by Monika Hilders, who points out Lewis's deliberate presentation of a 'feminine heroic' in contrast to the traditional masculine one.[36] Real-life space travel gave a great boost to science-fiction writers, but not in ways Lewis approved;[37] his wish to convert readers from the conception of space to the conception of heaven has not been fulfilled.

Nevertheless one may go back to Tolkien's memory of the agreement by which he and Lewis were to write stories 'discovering Myth'. It is the characters *in* the stories who 'discover' myth. The readers of the stories *are exposed* to it, and here there can be no doubt of Lewis's success. More people now owe their understanding of the Fall of Man to *Perelandra* than to any formal works of theology, even Lewis's. Neoplatonism would not have so much as a toehold on the modern imagination if it were not for Lewis's fiction, and to a lesser extent Williams's and Tolkien's.[38] His image of Babel has provided a powerful corrective (echoed by other writers of fantasy and science fiction such as George Orwell and Ursula Le Guin) to the plague of bureaucratic and academic 'babble' which, unlike 'Creative Evolution', does remain a clear and present danger. To return to Wells, with whom Lewis started his trilogy, while Wells in *The Island of Dr Moreau* centred his story on the claim that the old myths of Circe and Comus were simply wrong, irrelevant, to be inverted, and in *The Time Machine* showed the Time Traveller turning his back on the great dead library to look for something more useful than old books, Lewis answered him discursively, and eventually satirically. He brought the myths and the wisdom of the ancients back. Without him they would have a far less evident presence in the contemporary world.

Notes

1 *Letters of J.R.R. Tolkien*, ed. Humphrey Carpenter with the assistance of Christopher Tolkien (London: Allen & Unwin, 1981), 29, 209, 342, 347, 378. See further John D. Rateliff, '*The Lost Road, The Dark Tower,* and *The Notion Club Papers*: Tolkien and Lewis's Time Travel Triad', in Verlyn Flieger and Carl F. Hostetter (eds), *Tolkien's Legendarium: Essays on the History of Middle-earth* (London: Greenwood Press, 2000), 199–218.
2 Studies of the Ransom Trilogy include David C. Downing, *Planets in Peril: A Critical Study of C.S. Lewis's Ransom Trilogy* (Amherst, MA: University of Massachusetts Press, 1992); Jared Lobdell, *The Scientifiction Novels of C.S. Lewis: Space and Time in the Ransom*

Stories (Jefferson, NC: McFarland, 2004); and Sanford Schwartz, *C.S. Lewis on the Final Frontier: Science and the Supernatural in the Space Trilogy* (New York: Oxford University Press, 2009).

3   Lewis stated repeatedly that his fictions began, not with ideas, but with mental images: e.g. 'All seven of my Narnia books, and my three science fiction books, began with seeing pictures in my head': 'It All Began with a Picture', EC 529.

4   Parallels and contrasts are pointed out in detail by Doris T. Myers, *C.S. Lewis in Context* (Kent, OH: Kent State University Press, 1994), 39–47.

5   OSP 163.

6   See for instance his 'A Reply to Professor Haldane', OTOW 97–109.

7   Published in *The Modern Quarterly* for Autumn 1946, cited here from <www.marxists.org/archive/haldane/works/1940s/oncslewis.htm>,p.2, accessed 12 Aug. 2008. For Lewis's reply see n. 6 above. Haldane may well have realized that *Out of the Silent Planet* was in part a response to speculations put forward in his *On Possible Worlds and Other Essays* (1927).

8   DI 13: though not published till 1964, the book was based on a course of lectures given 'more than once at Oxford' (DI p. vii), i.e. before Lewis moved to Cambridge in 1955.

9   J.R.R. Tolkien, *The Silmarillion*, ed. Christopher Tolkien (George Allen & Unwin, 1977), 281.

10   As argued in Michael Ward, *Planet Narnia: The Seven Heavens in the Imagination of C.S. Lewis* (New York: Oxford University Press, 2008).

11   See, for example, DI 74, 99, 111, 116.

12   OSP 180.

13   OSP 34.

14   DI 103–10; cf. 'De Audiendis Poetis', SMRL 1–17.

15   See his letter to Christopher Tolkien, 24 Dec. 1944, in *Letters of J.R.R. Tolkien*, 105. The importance of this 1944 comment is stressed by Jonathan Himes, 'The Allegory of Lust: Textual and Sexual Deviance in *The Dark Tower*', in Jonathan B. Himes (ed.) with Joe R. Christopher and Salwa Khoddam, *Truths Breathed through Silver: The Inklings' Moral and Mythopoeic Legacy* (Newcastle upon Tyne: Cambridge Scholars Publishing, 2008), 51–80.

16   OSP 162.

17   OSP 161.

18   OSP 109.

19   Per 42.

20   Per 43.

21   Per 84.

22   Per 151.

23   Camilla is the name of one of the 'doubled' characters in the 'Dark Tower' fragment; see DT 17–91, *passim*. Possibly she and her husband in *That Hideous Strength* were at one time imagined as the true, rescued Camilla of 'Dark Tower', and (one of) her rescuer(s). See further Lobdell, *The Scientifiction Novels of C.S. Lewis*, 62ff.

24   THS 42.

25   THS 259.

26   Discussed at more length in Myers, *C.S. Lewis in Context*, 72–112, and in my 'Screwtape and the Philological Arm: Lewis on Verbicide', in Himes (ed.), *Truths Breathed through Silver*, 110–22.

27   THS 185.

28   THS 265.

29   THS 332.

30   For example, THS 250, 332.

31   THS 351.

32   THS 273.

33   SC 156.

34   THS 337.

35   But see e.g. E.F. Schumacher, *Small is Beautiful: Economics as if People Mattered* (New York: Harper & Row, 1973) and Jennifer Swift, 'The Original Distributists Have Much to Say that is Still Relevant 80 Years On', *The Tablet*, 1 Aug. 2009, 6–7.

36   Monika Hilders, 'The Foolish Weakness in C.S. Lewis' Cosmic Trilogy: A Feminine Heroic', *SEVEN: An Anglo-American Literary Review* 19 (2002), 77–90.

37   Three later poems, from the 1950s – 'Prelude to Space', 'Science Fiction Cradlesong' and 'An Expostulation' – show Lewis's unease about space programmes and (much) conventional science fiction. Some writers, notably James Blish in *A Case of Conscience* (1958), Walter M. Miller Jr. in *A Canticle for Leibowitz* (1959), and Mary Doria Russell in *The Sparrow* (1996) and its Sequel, *Children of God* (1998), have followed Lewis's blending of science fiction with theology: see further John Clute *et al.* (eds), *The Encyclopedia of Science Fiction* (London: Orbit, 1993), 716–17.

38   The best account of Neoplatonism in the Fantasy literature of both the ancient and modern worlds is Ronald Hutton, *Witches, Druids and King Arthur* (London: Hambledon, 2003); see esp. pp. 9off. and the whole of ch. 7, 'The Inklings and the Gods' (215–37).

18 *The Great Divorce*

JERRY L. WALLS

In *A Preface to Paradise Lost* (1942), C.S. Lewis notes that the divine laughter directed at Satan in John Milton's epic poem has offended some readers. Lewis defends the laughter, however, and judges it a mistake to think that Satan should have licence to rant and posture on a cosmic scale without arousing the comic spirit: 'The whole nature of reality would have to be altered in order to give such immunity, and it is not alterable. At that precise point where Satan ... meets something real, laughter *must* arise, just as steam must when water meets fire.'[1]

This comment portends the central themes in a more popular and widely read book Lewis published four years later, namely, *The Great Divorce*. Written as a reply to *The Marriage of Heaven and Hell* by William Blake, Lewis's title encapsulates his essential message that Blake's imagined marriage is doomed from the start by the nature of unalterable reality. The divorce Lewis reckons 'great' is not the tragedy of putting asunder what God has joined together, but rather the futile, and in some ways comic, attempt to marry what cannot possibly be united. He terms it a 'disastrous error' to believe that 'reality never presents us with an absolutely unavoidable "either – or"', or to imagine 'that mere development or adjustment or refinement will somehow turn evil into good without our being called on for a final and total rejection of anything we should like to retain'.[2]

Lewis's strategy for exposing and refuting this error is to write a fantasy (in which Lewis himself appears as the first-person narrator) about characters in hell who take a bus ride to heaven and are invited, indeed implored, to stay. As creatively imagined by Lewis, hell is depicted not by means of conventional images (e.g. fire and brimstone), but in the form of an infinitely expanding, depressing Grey Town, and heaven is described as a glorious sunlit meadow ('the Valley of the Shadow of Life') with great mountains ('Deep Heaven') shining in the distance. Most of the characters are willing to stay in heaven only on their own terms, all of which are variations of the disastrous error stated above. Lewis insists that he is not interested in speculation about the 'conditions'[3] of the afterlife, but only in showing more clearly 'the nature of the choice'[4] that leads either to heaven or to hell. Nevertheless, he does present us with an intriguing and suggestive eschatological vision of these two ultimate destinations. In what follows, I shall look at each of these in turn, and discuss conceptual issues raised by Lewis's fantastic voyage.

HEAVEN

'Heaven is reality itself.'[5] This wonderfully concise definition is offered in the narrative by George MacDonald, the nineteenth-century Scottish writer whose works so profoundly affected Lewis, and whom Lewis honours by placing him in heaven and by giving him the role of Lewis's personal guide (Beatrice to his Dante, if you like). This suggestive definition implies that reality is far more expansive and remarkable than we could ever guess from our present limited experience. Shortly after arriving in heaven, the narrator relates that he 'had the sense of being in a larger space, perhaps even a larger *sort* of space' than he had ever known before, and that he had 'got "out" in some sense which made the Solar System itself seem an indoor affair'.[6]

MacDonald first appears several chapters later when the narrator is deeply distraught by the question of whether the Ghosts from hell really can stay in heaven, or whether it is all an elaborate hoax. The claim that heaven is reality itself is perhaps the most fundamental reason why there can be nothing deceptive about it. Indeed, earlier in this passage, MacDonald had described what happens to the saved as 'the opposite of a mirage. What seemed, when they entered it, to be the vale of misery turns out, when they look back, to have been a well; and where present experience saw only salt deserts, memory truthfully records that the wells were full of water.'[7] The climax of salvation is a fully truthful experience of reality shorn of all misleading appearances. Heaven thus becomes retrospective, so that when good has reached its full flower, it transforms agonies into glories even as it turns deserts into gushing wells. MacDonald explains that this means the blessed will be able truly to say, 'We have never lived anywhere except in Heaven.'[8]

Now the claim that 'heaven is reality itself' is hardly obviously true, for the simple reason that there are many conceivable ways that reality could be constituted such that a truthful experience of it might better be described as hell. So what is it about the very essence of reality that makes it heaven? We receive further insight a page or so later in a passage where MacDonald is characterizing the fundamental essence of the choice of those who go to hell. He invokes Milton's famous line ascribed to Satan, 'Better to reign in hell than serve in heaven', and then goes on to elaborate: 'There is always something they prefer to joy – that is, to reality.'[9] So the equation of heaven with reality is taken a step further in the equation of reality with joy.

But we still have not arrived at the deepest explanation of why ultimate reality should be joy. Perhaps the best clue we have in this book is in a later chapter that features one of the most radiant of the saints in heaven, namely, Sarah Smith, a woman of no earthly reputation who has attained immortal splendour by a life of extraordinary love. She is accompanied by a host of Bright Spirits who sing a song in her honour. The first lines of the song are both striking and revealing: 'The Happy Trinity is her home: nothing can trouble her joy.'[10]

The phrase 'Happy Trinity' calls to mind Lewis's discussion of this distinctive picture of God in *Mere Christianity*. There Lewis points out that the popular truth that God is love in his very essence is an implicitly Trinitarian claim, for if God did not contain more than one Person, he could not have been love before he created the world. Indeed, Lewis claims that the most important thing to know about the relationship between the Persons of the Trinity is that it is a relationship of love: 'The Father delights in His Son; the Son looks up to His Father.'[11] Lewis goes on to elaborate on this delightful relationship of love with colourful and appealing images, describing God as 'a dynamic, pulsating activity, a life, almost a kind of drama. Almost, if you will not think me irreverent, a kind of dance.'[12] He proceeds shortly thereafter to emphasize that only by taking our place in that dance can we find the happiness for which we were created.

This illumines what it means to say that Sarah Smith is at home in the Happy Trinity and why her happiness is so profound and secure. The bedrock reality is the Three-Personed God, whose delighted love is an unquenchable source of vitality, joy and pleasure. To be at home in such a reality is heaven indeed.

The claim that heaven is reality itself is, moreover, an emphatic rejection of the common notion that heaven is a state of mind. Elsewhere, Lewis blamed this popular fiction for the fact that the specifically Christian virtue of hope has in our time grown so cold and listless.[13] Connected with this error, he believed, were misleading pictures of 'Spirit'. Whereas it is proper to think of ghosts as shadowy 'half-men', Spirit should not be imagined this way: 'If we must have a mental picture to symbolise Spirit, we should represent it as something *heavier* than matter.'[14]

In keeping with these convictions, Lewis depicts the saints in heaven as decidedly more real than their ghostly counterparts from hell. Indeed, it is painful for the Ghosts even to walk on the grass in heaven because they are so insubstantial: 'Reality is harsh to the feet of shadows.'[15] By contrast, the solid saints are so constituted that heaven is their natural habitat: they can frolic in the grass and romp in the river. They have become accustomed and adapted to reality in such a way that they experience – enter into – the love and joy that is the essence of the heavenly life. In this condition, their happiness is forever secured against the delusions that sustain the ongoing existence of hell. As the bright spirits sing in praise of Sarah Smith: 'Falsehoods tricked out as truths assail her in vain: she sees through the lie as if it were glass.'[16]

HELL

These words from the paean to Sarah Smith are an excellent entry point for a definition of hell, which could be described as a losing battle against reality. Recall Milton's famous line quoted above. Immediately following that reference to *Paradise Lost*, MacDonald elaborates: 'There is always something [those in hell] insist on keeping even at the price of misery. There is always something they prefer to joy – that is, to reality.'[17] This latter sentence, as previously noted, is significant for its equation of reality with joy. So if heaven is reality, and reality is joy, then hell is the loss of reality and consequently the loss of joy.

Whereas Lewis (in the voice of MacDonald) emphatically rejects the notion that heaven is merely a state of mind, he warmly embraces this as a description of hell. Early in the fantasy we learn that the Grey Town is ever expanding and why this is so. Its inhabitants inevitably quarrel and are constantly moving farther and farther apart. This is easy for them, because all they need to build a new house is to think it. Indeed, in hell 'you get everything you want (not very good quality, of course) by just imagining it'.[18] This contrasts sharply with heaven, where everything is for the asking – but real, not imaginary. Real things are the gift of God, the ultimate reality, and can be had by no other means than through him. No such constraint exists in hell, where undisciplined desires create an unreal world, suited to the fancies of its denizens. But evil desires are at war with joy, so that even though in some sense the damned get what they want, they are left empty and frustrated. What they want is to be happy on their own terms, but that is impossible, so strictly speaking they do not get what they want after all, even though the Grey Town endlessly adapts and expands to their wishes.

It is crucial to underscore that the choice of hell as Lewis under-stands it is a free one in a very strong sense. Near the end of the book, MacDonald asserts that freedom is 'the gift whereby ye most resemble your Maker and are yourselves parts of eternal reality'.[19] A couple of lines later, free choices are characterized as ones 'that might have been otherwise'.[20] And in one of the most often quoted passages in the book, MacDonald says,

> 'There are only two kinds of people in the end: those who say to God, "Thy will be done," and those to whom God says, in the end, "*Thy* will be done." All that are in Hell choose it. Without that self-choice there could be no Hell. No soul that seriously and constantly desires joy will ever miss it.'[21]

The last line just quoted highlights one of the most fascinating aspects of Lewis's view of hell and also rejects a popular picture of it. It is often thought that hell is populated with persons who would gladly repent and go to heaven if they could, but their desire to repent is a futile one because God will no longer accept their repentance and allow them into heaven. On this popular picture, they are held in hell against their wishes. Countering this picture, Lewis recorded his conviction in another famous line (this one from *The Problem of Pain*): 'that the damned are, in one sense, successful, rebels to the end; that the doors of hell are locked on the *inside*'.[22]

Now the interesting implication of this claim is that sinners in hell could, at least in principle, repent and be saved. In *A Preface to Paradise Lost*, Lewis notes that the way of repentance is closed to the devils in Milton's poem. Moreover, Lewis observes that the 'poet very wisely never allows the question "What if they *did* repent?" to become actual'.[23] By striking contrast, especially if Milton was wise to repress the question, Lewis allows it to become actual with respect to the Ghosts from the Grey Town. Although most of them refuse to repent, they are all urged to do so with the clear promise that they can indeed stay in heaven if they are willing to give up the things that are keep-ing them out. For a start, their feet will harden and they can begin to enjoy walking on the heavenly grass as they progress to deeper levels of redeemed transformation.

Yet, strictly speaking, Lewis does not suggest there is a way out of hell into heaven. To the question of whether this is possible, MacDonald replies: 'It depends on the way ye're using the words. If they leave that grey town behind it will not have been Hell. To any that leaves it, it is Purgatory.'[24]

In one of the most memorable encounters in the book, a Ghost with a red lizard on his shoulder (apparently representing the Ghost's besetting sin of lust) chooses to repent and leave the Grey Town behind, and is immediately and dramatically transformed in such a way that he can finally be at home in heaven and delight in being there. This takes place after a prolonged struggle between his enslaved will and a bright angel who offers him redemption – but only at the cost of killing the lizard. The exchange between this Ghost and the angel highlights the essential role of freedom in the moral and spiritual transformation required to remain in heaven. The angel will not, indeed cannot, kill the lizard without the permission of the Ghost: 'I cannot kill it against your will. It is impossible.'[25]

The fact that the doors of hell are locked on the inside is also emphasized by the manner in which the saints do everything possible, short of overriding their freedom, to save the Ghosts from the Grey Town. In so far as the Ghosts retain any sort of foothold in reality that might allow them to be saved, hope remains. This is illustrated by an old woman who is given to excessive grumbling. Lewis the narrator thinks she is just a silly, garrulous person who is an unlikely candidate for damnation. But MacDonald explains that the question is whether she is still a grumbler or merely a grumble: 'If there is a real woman – even the trace of one – still there inside the grumbling, it can be brought to life again.'[26] But if not even a trace remains of a real woman, there is nothing personal left that can come to terms with reality and thereby be saved: 'What is cast (or casts itself) into hell is not a man: it is "remains".'[27]

Given the equation of reality and joy, it is hardly surprising that joy is the primary vehicle through which the saints in heaven attempt to persuade the Ghosts to embrace reality. Again and again throughout the narrative, the bright Spirits are described in terms of joy, mirth, merriment and laughter. The appeal of this joy is obviously powerful, and yet it is possible to prefer something to joy and to resist its radiant attraction. Perhaps the most telling instance of this again involves Sarah Smith, of whom it is said that there is enough joy in her little finger 'to awaken all the dead things of the universe into life'.[28] This claim makes all the more remarkable the encounter she has with a dwarfish Ghost named Frank who turns out to be her husband. The dwarfish figure assumes that she must have been sad without him, and is clearly disappointed to learn that she has been perfectly happy and that he has no more power to make her miserable. She urges him to give up his resentments and his desire to cause pain: 'the invitation to all joy, singing out of her whole being like a bird's song on an April evening, seemed to be such that no creature could resist it'.[29] And yet resist it he does, although at points this is almost more than he can manage. The narrator doubts that he 'ever saw anything more terrible than the struggle of that Dwarf Ghost against joy'.[30]

One of the weapons Frank vainly brandishes in his struggle is a misguided appeal to love. He assumes that if his wife loves him, she must need him, and it is this sense of need that he attempts to exploit. In *The Four Loves*, Lewis recognizes what he calls 'Need-love' as a genuine form of love. One of the central themes of that book is that all of the natural loves are vulnerable to corruption, and when corrupted they become forms of hatred and abuse.[31] Need-love, as this scenario demonstrates, is easily twisted and abused. In heaven, however, there are no unsatisfied needs, and thus no possibility of abusing love in the way Frank attempts. His struggle against true love is as futile and self-destructive as his struggle against joy. To 'succeed' in this struggle means ultimate loss and final defeat.

The great positive truth that Lewis wants to highlight is that 'No soul that seriously and constantly desires joy will ever miss it'.[32] The negative counterpart to this truth is that any soul that seriously and constantly resists and refuses joy will lose it. And yet, such is the perversity and irrationality of choosing evil that those who do so actually imagine they have gained something better: 'Better to reign in hell than serve in heaven.' As Sarah Smith attempts to reason with Frank, urging him to stay, he continues to cling to the notion that she is doing so because it will hurt her if he does not: '"Ah, you can't bear to hear it!" he shouted with miserable triumph.'[33]

The phrase 'miserable triumph' perhaps encapsulates as well as anything the perverse illusion of the damned. This is as close to happiness as they are capable of coming. They may be 'almost happy', but having rejected joy – that is, reality – they can never know the real thing. Their 'triumphs' leave them in misery and whatever advantages they almost gain fade into nothingness. Indeed, as Frank persists in his struggle against joy, he grows smaller and eventually disappears altogether. Frank's individual fate is a reflection of what is true of hell generally.

Despite their best intentions, many writers, including Christians, have depicted evil in such a way that it appears more fascinating and colourful than goodness. C.S. Lewis is not one of them. As he describes evil and its ultimate stronghold, it appears neither strong nor worth holding onto. To the contrary, it is exposed as impotent and shadowy, a pretender that must inevitably and decisively lose in its bid to unseat reality. The ultimate philosophical reason for this lies in the traditional

Augustinian view that evil is at best a parasite, a perversion of the good that has no independent claim to reality: 'Bad cannot succeed even in being bad as truly as good is good.'[34]

ISSUES AND INFLUENCE

There are a number of fascinating issues raised by Lewis's account of heaven and hell. There is hardly space to explore any of them in detail, but I will sketch five such issues, giving the most space to the final three, which have received considerable attention in recent literature. That Lewis's work remains a rich and suggestive resource for the ongoing discussion of these topics is shown by the fact that it continues to inspire the work of others as well as incite criticism.[35]

First, difficult theological and pastoral issues are raised by the scene involving a mother named Pam whose son Michael was taken away from her by God partly in order to remedy her inordinate maternal love.[36] The inordinacy of Pam's love resides not in that she has too much love for her son but in that, first, her love for Michael exceeds and outranks her love for God, and second, it is, in fact, a rather selfish love. She does not love God first and foremost, and wants to use God simply as a means to get to Michael, so that Michael can satisfy her emotional needs. She is another illustration of Lewis's conviction that the natural loves become demons when they are made gods. While Lewis is likely correct about this general point, it is more doubtful to claim that God deals with such disordered loves by taking the lives of persons who are the objects of that love. It is well known that Lewis drew similar conclusions about his own lack of true faith and love when his own wife died, and he felt that God had taken her partly in order to demolish his 'house of cards' and consequently purify his faith.[37] The theological conundrums as well as emotional anguish he wrestled with in his own experience perhaps indicate that he should have been more cautious about suggesting that God deals with disordered love in this fashion.[38]

Second, it is not clear how to square Lewis's notion that the saved were always in heaven, and the damned were always in hell, with his dynamic view of freedom and character formation. He clearly believes we are free in a very strong sense, that our choices are undetermined, that the choices we make could have been otherwise, and that how we in fact choose shapes our character. Moreover, it is not a single choice that determines our character, but a long series of choices, and if these choices had been different, they would have produced a very different outcome.[39] Near the end of the book, MacDonald notes that 'every attempt to see the shape of eternity except through the lens of Time destroys your knowledge of Freedom'.[40] Whether time is real here or only a lens is not altogether clear, so the tension between his view of eternity and the reality of freedom remains unresolved.

Third, universal salvation apparently remains a possibility in Lewis's view although he cautions (through the mouth of MacDonald, who had strong universalist sympathies[41]) that to teach universalism as true is to fall prey to the misguided temptation to see eternity apart from the lens of time.[42] Moreover, to complicate matters, there are passages in his writings which suggest that the damned will finally be annihilated, such as when Frank, the Dwarf Ghost, simply vanishes as he struggles against joy. Elsewhere, Lewis describes hell as '"the darkness outside," the outer rim where being fades away into nonentity'.[43] His depiction of hell in these terms is part of his answer to the objection that the saved could not truly rejoice in heaven while some were languishing in hell.[44]

Jonathan Kvanvig has charged that Lewis's position on this matter is incoherent because, on the one hand, his position implies annihilationism (the belief that unrepentant sinners are eventually destroyed rather than being subjected to everlasting punishment), while on the other hand, he overtly rejected it. Lewis wrote: 'people often talk as if the "annihilation" of a soul were intrinsically possible. In all our experience, however, the destruction of one thing means the emergence of something else. Burn a log, and you have gases, heat and ash.'[45] Not only is Lewis's position internally inconsistent, according to Kvanvig, but his argument against annihilation is flawed. In the first place, his claim that every change involves a change of something into something else is incompatible with the Christian doctrine of creation *ex nihilo*, according to which God created the world out of nothing. Second, he contends that Lewis made the mistake of confusing what is possible according to scientific law with what is possible in the broader logical or metaphysical sense. The scientific law that says mass and energy must be conserved in a closed system does not rule out the metaphysical possibility that God has power to destroy the entire created order – including individual human souls.[46]

Fourth, one of the most provocative passages in *The Great Divorce* challenges a classic argument against the doctrine of an everlasting hell, an argument that has received renewed attention and fresh formulation in the contemporary debates about eschatology. The argument, which goes back at least to the nineteenth-century theologian Friedrich Schleiermacher, contends that the damnation of even a single person would make it impossible for anyone else to experience perfect happiness. To be perfectly happy, the argument insists, persons must be fully sanctified in such a way that they have deep and genuine love for all persons. Such persons, shaped by a profound sense of inclusive and empathetic love, could not be completely happy if they knew that some were shut up in misery and excluded from the fellowship of heaven. In short, the eternal co-existence of heaven and hell amounts to a fundamental incompatibility, so if Christians want to hold to the doctrine of perfect blessedness, they must give up the doctrine of an eternal hell.

The essence of this argument is advanced by the narrator, who feels that Sarah Smith should have been more touched by the misery of her husband, even if it was self-inflicted. In reply, MacDonald acknowledges that such a stance sounds merciful, but he goes on to point out that something much more sinister is lurking behind it: '[t]he demand of the loveless and the self-imprisoned that they should be allowed to blackmail the universe: that till they consent to be happy (on their terms) no one else shall taste joy: that theirs should be the final power: that Hell should be able to *veto* Heaven'.[47] A few lines later, he lays out logically exclusive options on this matter and says we must choose which we prefer: 'Either the day must come when joy prevails and all makers of misery are no longer able to infect it: or else for ever and ever the makers of misery can destroy in others the happiness they reject for themselves.'[48]

Contemporary advocates of universalism insist we need a third option. The first option above, they argue, is impossible if the saved are truly transformed by love, and the second is intolerable. Therefore, the only way that heaven can truly be heaven is if everyone ends up there and none are finally excluded from the perfect fellowship of eternal love and joy. It may be argued in reply that the primary obstacle to universal salvation is human freedom, and that it is this sometimes perverse reality that presents us with the two options above. A number of contemporary universalists, however, do not see this as an insurmountable problem. They contend that God can, in fact, save everyone without overriding freedom, or that, if necessary, God should override freedom in order to secure the great good of universal salvation and the unsullied happiness that this would make possible.[49] For those who are dubious about these moves to defend universalism, Lewis's argument is a valuable resource for responding to the claim that heaven and hell are simply incompatible.

Fifth and finally, Lewis's book as a whole is most relevant to another argument against the doctrine of eternal hell that has been advanced with considerable force in the contemporary debate, namely, that the doctrine is incoherent and therefore not even possibly true. Thomas Talbott, the best-known proponent of this challenge, contends that there is no intelligible account of why anyone would choose evil to the degree necessary for damnation. Of course, Lewis addresses this difficulty by sketching numerous characters who, following Milton's Satan, prefer something else to serving in heaven. Much of the power of the book lies in the fact that through these vignettes he makes this choice psychologically and morally plausible. In my own work on hell, I have drawn on Lewis's characters to answer Talbott's challenge and to show that there is a coherent and intelligible account of the decisive choice of evil that results in eternal damnation.[50]

Talbott has charged, however, that Lewis – and I, following him – fall into incoherence in the attempt to defend the claim that eternal hell could be freely chosen:

> According to Lewis, it is an objective truth that union with the divine 'nature is bliss and separation from it is horror'.[51] But if it is an objective truth, even as it is an objective truth that a hand placed on a hot stove will burn badly, then an important question arises: how could anyone, rational enough to qualify as a free moral agent, choose an eternity of horror over an eternity of bliss, or actually prefer hell to heaven? … In the face of such questions as these, Lewis backs away from the idea of an objective horror and begins talking as if it were all a matter of perspective.[52]

I have argued that the ability to deceive ourselves in this fashion and maintain the illusion that hell is preferable to heaven is an essential component of the moral freedom to choose God or not. Talbott takes exception to this, replying that one cannot 'escape the charge of incoherence here by appealing, as Walls and Lewis both do, to an illusion that in effect takes the hell out of hell, at least as far as the damned are concerned'.[53]

The charge that Lewis takes the hell out of hell is a strong one. Indeed, the traditional notion of hell as a place of excruciating physical punishment is very much at odds with Lewis's more psychological picture of damnation. If such torment is the essence of hell, Lewis is guilty as charged.[54] Lewis's picture, however, is of a God of love who does everything he can to save all persons, short of overriding their freedom. If God is love in this fashion, then indeed it is more difficult to grasp how and why anyone would be lost. But the loss of a relationship with such a God is enough to make one's existence hell, even if one does so by maintaining the illusion that things are better without him.[55] For those who believe that ultimate reality is heaven, that reality is joy and, that the Trinity is the deepest reason why this is true, Lewis's picture of the clash between persistent evil and unalterable reality, and what is at stake in taking sides, will continue to be credible as well as moving.

Notes

1. PPL 95.
2. GD 7.
3. GD 9.
4. GD 63.
5. GD 63.
6. GD 26.
7. GD 63.
8. GD 62.
9. GD 64.
10. GD 109.
11. MC 148.
12. MC 148. For more on Lewis's conception of the Trinity as a dance, see Paul Fiddes's essay in this volume (Chapter 7).
13. M 166.
14. M 96.
15. GD 40.
16. GD 110.
17. GD 64.
18. GD 21.
19. GD 115.
20. GD 115. In some of his other writings, Lewis seems to hold a different view of freedom. For critical analysis of these issues, see Scott R. Burson and Jerry L. Walls, *C.S. Lewis and Francis Schaeffer: Lessons for a New Century from the Most Influential Apologists of Our Time* (Downers Grove, IL: Intervarsity Press, 1998), 74–80, 98–105.
21. GD 66–67; cf. PPL 99.
22. POP 130; cf. PPL 105.
23. PPL 105.
24. GD 61.
25. GD 92.
26. GD 68; see also 88.
27. POP 113.
28. GD 99.
29. GD 102.
30. GD 106.
31. For more on these themes, see Caroline Simon's piece earlier in this volume (Chapter 11).
32. GD 67.
33. GD 107.

34   GD 113; cf. PPL 66–72.
35   *The Great Divorce* is an extremely popular text among contemporary philosophers of religion interested in the intersection of eschatology and free will, and has been cited in numerous essays. What follows is a sample of some of the issues discussed in this literature.
36   GD 82–87, 95–96.
37   AGO 36–39, 51–52, 67–68.
38   For more on this, see Ann Loades, 'C.S. Lewis: Grief Observed, Rationality Abandoned, Faith Regained', *Journal of Literature and Theology* 3 (Mar. 1989), 107–21.
39   For some of Lewis's comments on character formation and the choices that make us either heavenly or hellish creatures, see MC 79–81, 91–92, 119–20, 191–92. For a vivid statement of the sentiment that even small choices can have large consequences, see his poem 'Nearly They Stood' (CP 116–17), and also SL 64–65.
40   GD 115.
41   See David L. Neuhouser, 'George MacDonald and Universalism', in *George MacDonald: Literary Heritage and Heirs*, ed. Roderick McGillis (Hadlock, WA: Zossima Press, 2008), 83–97.
42   GD 114–15.
43   POP 115.
44   As we shall see below, Lewis addresses this issue somewhat differently in *The Great Divorce*.
45   POP 113.
46   Jonathan L. Kvanvig, *The Problem of Hell* (Oxford: Oxford University Press, 1993), 122. For a recent exploration of annihilationism that briefly refers to *The Great Divorce*, see Paul Griffiths, 'Self-Annihilation or Damnation? A Disputable Question in Christian Eschatology', in Paul J. Weithman (ed.), *Liberal Faith: Essays in Honor of Philip Quinn* (Notre Dame, IN: University of Notre Dame Press, 2008), 83–117.
47   GD 111.
48   GD 111.
49   For an impressive attempt to argue that heaven and hell are incompatible, see Eric Reitan, 'Eternal Damnation and Blessed Ignorance: Is the Damnation of Some Incompatible with the Salvation of Any?', *Religious Studies* 38 (2002), 429–50. See esp. pp. 445–48 for his argument that God can rightly violate human autonomy to secure universal salvation. Marilyn McCord Adams is another noted philosopher who has argued that there is no problem if God needs to override freedom to save all. See her *Horrendous Evils and the Goodness of God* (Ithaca, NY: Cornell University Press, 1999), 47–49, 103–04, 157. Other philosophers have argued for 'theistic compatibilism', the claim that, even if God ultimately determines all of our choices and actions, we might nevertheless have as much freedom as traditional theism requires us to have. If so, then an omnipotent God could save everyone without violating anyone's freedom. For a recent defence of this position by a philosopher who is agnostic on the issue of universalism, see T.W. Bartel, 'Theistic Compatibilism: Better Than You Think', in T.W. Bartel (ed.),

Comparative Theology: Essays for Keith Ward (London: SPCK, 2003), 87–99.

50 See my *Hell: The Logic of Damnation* (Notre Dame, IN: University of Notre Dame Press, 1992), 113–38, esp. 123, 126.

51 SBJ 185.

52 Thomas Talbott, 'Freedom, Damnation, and the Power to Sin with Impunity', *Religious Studies* 37 (2001), 429.

53 Talbott, 'Freedom, Damnation, and the Power of Sin', 429–30. For a defence of the claim that freedom involves the power to deceive ourselves, see Walls, *Hell: The Logic of Damnation*, 129–33. I have replied to Talbott's essay in my 'A Hell of a Choice: Reply to Talbott', *Religious Studies* 40 (2004), 203–16. The same volume of this journal includes Talbott's response, 'Misery and Freedom: Reply to Walls' and my counter-argument, 'A Hell of a Dilemma: Rejoinder to Talbott', *Religious Studies* 40 (2004), 217–24, 225–27.

54 Part of my critique of Talbott is that he cannot coherently maintain as severe a picture of hell as he claims. His view of hell as ever-increasing misery is part of what underwrites his claim that all will eventually repent and be saved. For further discussion of Lewis's account, see Wayne Martindale, *Beyond the Shadowlands: C.S. Lewis on Heaven and Hell* (Wheaton, IL: Crossway Books, 2005).

55 It is worth noting that in *The Great Divorce* there are hints and threats that when the Sun finally rises in heaven, it will set in hell, with frightful consequences for hell's inhabitants: 'no one wants to be out of doors when that happens' (23; see also 24, 62, 117). Though it is not the main thrust of the book, this imagery suggests the reality of a Final Judgement to be feared by the impenitent. For further examination of this issue, see Joel Buenting (ed.), *The Problem of Hell: A Philosophical Anthology* (Burlington, VT: Ashgate, 2010).

19 The Chronicles of Narnia

ALAN JACOBS

C.S. Lewis was a lifelong reader of fairy tales and children's stories, though his repertoire was limited and he returned repeatedly to his roster of favourites: George MacDonald, Kenneth Grahame, Beatrix Potter, E. Nesbit. As a middle-aged man he wrote, 'When I was ten, I read fairy stories in secret and would have been ashamed if I had been found doing so. Now that I am fifty I read them openly. When I became a man I put away childish things, including the fear of childishness and the desire to be very grown up.'[1]

So shameless was he in this matter that, in a scholarly lecture, he used Beatrix Potter to illustrate the theme of disobedience in *Paradise Lost* ('It is, after all, the commonest of themes; even Peter Rabbit came to grief because he *would* go into Mr. McGregor's garden'[2]); and in a learned discourse on friendship he invoked not just Aristotle but also *The Wind in the Willows* ('the quaternion of Mole, Rat, Badger and Toad suggests the amazing heterogeneity possible between those who are bound by Affection'[3]).

That he would choose to write children's books of his own, however, has surprised some. He was a bachelor for most of his life and had no children of his own, nor did those closest to him discern any particular affection for or interest in children. I cite these facts because they are commonly thought relevant, and yet it is not clear in Lewis's case that they are. He said he turned to writing children's stories to meet some need of his own – but a need he didn't understand. 'I am not quite sure', Lewis wrote in 1952, when most of the Narnia books were completed, 'what made me, in a particular year of my life, feel that not only a fairy tale, but a fairy tale addressed to children, was exactly what I must write – or burst.'[4] He suggests that the children's story 'permits, or compels you to leave out things I wanted to leave out. It compels you to throw all the force of a book into what was done and said. It checks what a kind, but discerning critic called "the expository demon" in me.'[5] But of course this demon could have been

265

checked by the writing of sonnets or sestinas as well. Why children's books?

ORIGINS AND DEVELOPMENT OF THE SERIES

One reason is that the stories connect with a mental image that had been in Lewis's mind since his youth: 'The *Lion* all began with a picture of a Faun carrying an umbrella and parcels in a snowy wood. This picture had been in my mind since I was about sixteen. Then one day, when I was about forty, I said to myself, "Let's try to make a story about it."'[6]

Furthermore, Lewis was thrown into close proximity with children when four schoolgirls were evacuated to his Oxford home at the outbreak of the Second World War – which indeed happened when he was 'about forty'. Probably near the same time Lewis wrote a single paragraph on the back of a piece of paper on which he was writing another story:

> This book is about four children whose names were Ann, Martin, Rose and Peter. But mostly it is about Peter who was the youngest. They all had to go away from London suddenly because of the Air Raids, and because Father, who was in the army, had gone off to the war and Mother was doing some kind of war work. They were sent to stay with a relation of Mother's who was a very old Professor who lived by himself in the country.[7]

Since the story goes no further we cannot know how Lewis at this stage was planning to connect these four children with the Faun in the snowy wood. Only a decade later would he explain – or, perhaps it would be better to say, discover – the nature of that connection: in the summer of 1948 he told Chad Walsh that he was completing a children's book which he had begun 'in the style of E. Nesbit'.[8]

Some who have written about Lewis's life would see the account I have given so far as insufficient, and neglectful of what they believe to be a major event in Lewis's life: the critique of an argument in his book *Miracles* that was given at Oxford's Socratic Club in February 1948 by the philosopher Elizabeth Anscombe. Lewis immediately recognized the cogency of Anscombe's critique, and later revised *Miracles* accordingly (and in Anscombe's view at least partially successfully). But Humphrey Carpenter and A.N. Wilson believe that Lewis was so devastated by Anscombe's paper that he abandoned Christian apologetics altogether; indeed, Wilson goes so far as to assert that Lewis used the story he began writing to transform Anscombe into a terrifying and monstrous witch. There is nothing that could be called *evidence* for these speculations – especially considering that Lewis continued to have perfectly cordial relations with Anscombe, whose mind he openly admired and who was moreover his fellow Christian – but one can see how they might appeal to those of an especially theatrical turn of mind.[9]

Whatever Lewis was thinking of when he began his children's story in earnest, he was *not* thinking of Aslan, the great lion who became the central figure in *The Lion, the Witch and the Wardrobe* and then in the whole series. As he got into the serious writing of the first Narnia story, he said he 'had very little idea how the story would go'. Somehow the Lion entered the story, for reasons Lewis did not comprehend, and it was only when he 'came bounding into it' that 'He pulled the whole story together, and soon He pulled the six other Narnian stories in after Him'.[10]

Lewis was always at pains to insist that he never originally planned to write a story that would illustrate some Christian theme or doctrine – indeed, he said on more than one occasion, 'I couldn't write in that way at all.' There was nothing Christian about the Narnia stories to begin with: 'that element pushed itself in of its own accord'.[11] In writing his stories, he wished to trust the images that came into his mind. This required him to reject not only the market-driven questions of modern authors and publishers ('What do children want?') but even the more morally sound question of the Christian apologist ('What do children need?'): 'It is better not to ask the questions at all. Let the pictures tell you their own moral. For the moral inherent in them will rise from whatever spiritual roots you have succeeded in striking during the whole course of your life.'[12]

Yet there is reason to believe that Lewis is here overstressing his point. For instance, it couldn't be true that 'they' (the Narnia stories, in the plural) had nothing Christian about them at first – that could only have been true of the first one, and even then only up to a point. Perhaps it is an awareness of this difficulty that leads him to posit two aspects of himself that were at work when he wrote the Narnia books (and others): the Author and the Man. The Author simply responds to the promptings of his own creative mind, taking the images produced therein – fauns with parcels, mighty lions – and weaves them into a story. It is the Man who, looking upon this developing story, as it were from without, sees its events as possible object lessons, discerns the instrumental uses of the story:

> I thought I saw how stories of this kind could steal past a certain inhibition which had paralysed much of my own religion in

childhood. Why did one find it so hard to feel as one was told one ought to feel about God or about the sufferings of Christ? I thought the chief reason was that one was told one ought to. An obligation to feel can freeze feelings. And reverence itself did harm. The whole subject was associated with lowered voices; almost as if it were something medical. But supposing that by casting all these things into an imaginary world, stripping them of their stained-glass and Sunday School associations, one could make them for the first time appear in their real potency? Could one not thus steal past those watchful dragons? I thought one could. That was the Man's motive. But of course he could have done nothing if the Author had not been on the boil first.[13]

This picture of a bifurcated Lewis – the purely imaginative Author consorting uneasily with, though always preceding, the ideological Man – is a curious one, and not wholly convincing. Is it really possible that the Man could be so reliably passive, so sure to remain out of the way until the Author's imaginative 'boiling' was well under way and therefore powerful enough to overcome any interference from this Man – otherwise known as 'the Expository Demon'[14]?

Lewis always insisted that it was so. In 1954, when he had finished writing the Chronicles (though *The Magician's Nephew* and *The Last Battle* remained to be published), he described his inner world to the Milton Society of America, which was honouring him for his work on the poet. He stressed one point in particular:

> The imaginative man in me is older, more continuously operative, and in that sense more basic than either the religious writer or the critic. It was he who made me first attempt (with little success) to be a poet. It was he who, in response to the poetry of others, made me a critic, and in defense of that response, sometimes a critical controversialist. It was he who, after my conversion led me to embody my religious belief in symbolic or mythopoeic forms, ranging from Screwtape to a kind of theologised science-fiction. And it was, of course, he who has brought me, in the last few years to write the series of Narnian stories for children; not asking what children want and then endeavouring to adapt myself (this was not needed) but because the fairy-tale was the genre best fitted for what I wanted to say.[15]

The 'imaginative man' here is, clearly enough, the Author; the 'religious writer' and the 'critic' comprise the Man.

Such comments, in their frequency and consistency, make it clear that Lewis is deeply aware of his reputation as an apologist for Christianity and (among these Miltonists) an apologist for what he elsewhere called 'old books'. He is for his own taste too often thought a 'controversialist', and he is determined to exempt his Narnia tales from such a context: his stories are stories, not concealed theology or polemic.

Thus also his frequent insistence that he had no plan for the series. In a 1957 letter to an American boy named Laurence Krieg he claimed, 'When I wrote *The Lion* I did not know I was going to write any more. Then I wrote *P. Caspian* as a sequel and still didn't think there would be any more, and when I had done the *Voyage* I felt quite sure it would be the last. But I found I was wrong.'[16] Until recently this was an intriguing letter; but since the publication of Michael Ward's book *Planet Narnia*, it has become for some a troubling one. For Ward has demonstrated beyond any reasonable doubt that each of the Narnia books bears the traits associated, in medieval thought, with one of the seven planets: *The Lion, the Witch and the Wardrobe* with Jupiter, *Prince Caspian* with Mars, *The Voyage of the 'Dawn Treader'* with the Sun, and so on. We shall return to Ward's discovery later, but for now it is enough to note that in each book Lewis worked out the correspondences to the appropriate planetary character with great care.

If we are to reconcile such thorough planning with his letter to Laurence Krieg, we must believe that, having built an entire book out of the imagery of Jupiter, Lewis did not anticipate exploring further planetary riches. So much is plausible; but that after having written a second book into which the character of Mars is deeply woven, and a third in which the imagery of the Sun is richly elaborated, he 'felt quite sure' that he would go no further – surely this puts credulity to a rather strict test. Yet Ward's case for the planetary themes in the novels is iron-clad. Perhaps Lewis returned to each of the first few books to revise them in light of a discovered plan – four were written before the first was published; perhaps by the time he wrote to Laurence Krieg he had forgotten the books' origins; it is not impossible that he misled the boy, though that seems unlikely. There is no way to be sure.

ENTERING NARNIA

A vexed question involves the sequence of the Narnia stories. This is the sequence in which they were originally published:

The Lion, the Witch and the Wardrobe (1950)
Prince Caspian (1951)

The Voyage of the 'Dawn Treader' (1952)
The Silver Chair (1953)
The Horse and His Boy (1954)
The Magician's Nephew (1955)
The Last Battle (1956)

But Lewis sometimes said – in letters to children and in conversation, at the end of his life, with his executor-to-be Walter Hooper – that he preferred a more strictly chronological order.[17] As a result, in 1985 Lewis's publishers reordered the sequence:

The Magician's Nephew
The Lion, the Witch and the Wardrobe
The Horse and His Boy
Prince Caspian
The Voyage of the 'Dawn Treader'
The Silver Chair
The Last Battle

Some have questioned whether Lewis's wishes on this subject were quite as definitive as Hooper has claimed, but I will waive that question here and simply ask: in what order *should* the Narnia books be read?

Any reasonable ordering of the books must have *The Last Battle* as the final story, and must place *Prince Caspian* before *The Voyage of the 'Dawn Treader'*, since the latter is very straightforwardly a sequel to the former. Also, *The Silver Chair* cannot come before either of those books, since one of its main characters, Eustace, appears in *Dawn Treader* as a younger and very different sort of person from the one he is in *The Silver Chair*. Moreover, readers of the series will probably agree that *The Horse and His Boy*, being a largely self-contained story with minimal connection to the others – it is mentioned briefly in *The Silver Chair*, and the Pevensies appear in it briefly as rulers of Narnia – could be stuck into the sequence anywhere except the beginning and end. So the dispute really concerns only one question: should the sequence begin with *The Lion, the Witch and the Wardrobe* or *The Magician's Nephew*?

The argument for *The Magician's Nephew* is simple: since it describes Aslan's making of Narnia, placing it at the beginning yields a biblical, Creation-to-Apocalypse arc for the series. The case for *The Lion* is more complex and much stronger. First of all, though Lewis spoke of altering the order of the books, he also spoke of needing to revise the books in order to remove inconsistencies – and if *Nephew* is read first, there will be many such inconsistencies. For one thing, we are told quite explicitly at the end of *The Lion* that its narrative is 'the *beginning* of the adventures of Narnia'.[18] For another, Lewis tells his readers that the children in *The Lion* do not know who Aslan is 'any more than you do';[19] but of course the readers *would* know Aslan if they had already read *Nephew*. Moreover, much of the suspense in the early chapters of *The Lion* derives from our inability to understand what is happening in the magical wardrobe – but if we have read *Nephew* we will know all about the wardrobe, and that part of the story will become, effectively, pointless. Similarly, one of the delights of *The Lion* is the inexplicable presence of a lamp-post in the midst of a forest – a very familiar object from our world standing curiously in the midst of an utterly different world – and one of the delights of *Nephew* is the unexpected discovery of how that lamp-post got there. Anyone who begins with *Nephew* will lose that small but intense pleasure, the *frisson* of one of Lewis's richest images.

If Lewis really and truly thought that the series was best begun with *The Magician's Nephew*, he was simply mistaken. The original order of publication is the best for any reader wishing to enter Narnia.

GENRE AND TECHNIQUE

The most famous of all English literary portrayals of the realm of Faery is Edmund Spenser's *The Faerie Queene* (1590, 1596) – one of Lewis's favourite works. But in one crucial respect Spenser's epic is an uncharacteristic treatment of its subject: the whole of the narrative takes place *within* the realm of Faery. From the medieval ballad of 'Thomas the Rhymer' to Victorian fairy tales to J.R.R. Tolkien's 'Smith of Wootton Major' (1967) to Susanna Clarke's *Jonathan Strange & Mr Norrell* (2004), the great topic of Faery stories is the interpenetration of worlds, the unpredictably permeable boundaries that allow humans to pass into the realm of Faery and, if they are fortunate, to return again.

The Narnia stories follow this tradition rather than Spenser's model: they focus on boundaries and passages *between* a Faery-like world and ours, which means, in turn, that they are dependent not on strict allegorical correspondences but rather on what Lewis called a 'supposal'.[20] Suppose that there is another realm that overlaps somehow with our own, so that in what appears to be the same space there can be a Queen of England but also a Queen of Faery. Suppose that there are doors into that realm upon which you or I might stumble. Or: suppose that there are wholly other worlds surrounded by wholly other stars, populated by beings with whom we could commune and converse – and suppose that there are doors to *that* realm as well. Further: if you happen to be a Christian, suppose that although that world is in some respects alien to ours it is nevertheless the creation of the same God, who loves and cares for *those* people just as he loves and cares for us? Just *suppose*.

In an allegory, such as Spenser's, the story itself – the procedure of the narrative and the action of characters within it – is purely and evidently fictional, but those wholly imaginary persons and events correspond, more or less strictly, to persons and events in our world. Most stories of Faery, and the Faery-like stories of Narnia, don't function in that way. Lewis imagines that there really could be, in another world that God has made, an Enemy very like the White Witch; but Spenser does not imagine that somewhere there could be a dragon named Error.

Nevertheless, while in general Faery can be as like or unlike our world as a storyteller chooses to make it, Lewis's supposal is constrained by his understanding of what human beings are like and what God is like. As we know from his novel *Perelandra*, Lewis did not believe that if there are sentient and God-conscious beings on other worlds they are necessarily fallen like us; but he did believe that *if* they fell their fall would be like ours – rebellion through disobedience – and that they could only be restored by God's own self-sacrificial initiative. Since God simply *is*, in traditional Christian teaching, Father, Son and Holy Spirit, that set of relations would have to obtain in other words as well: thus Aslan is the son of the great Emperor-Beyond-the-Sea. He does not have to be of the same species as we are, because it is not intrinsic to the Christian narrative that fellowship with God be confined to a single species; but he does have to be able to communicate with us.[21] He need not die on a cross, but he must needs die; a Stone Table does as well. And though the period that his body lies lifeless can vary, he must rise again and by his rising demonstrate that he has defeated the Enemy. Such correspondences necessarily link Narnia and our world, and the regularity and predictability of those correspondences sometimes gives the books the *feel* of allegory.

Moreover, there are clearly allegorical passages, though not whole books, in the Chronicles, chief among them the baptism-like undragoning of Eustace Scrubb in *The Voyage of the 'Dawn Treader'*. No one could plausibly claim that when people habitually sin in Narnia they become dragons, and that when they become penitent they subject themselves to having their dragonish hides torn off by the Lion's claws. The whole episode clearly allegorizes both the effects of habitual sin and the agonizing but life-giving pain that inevitably accompanies true repentance.

Aslan's guidance of Shasta in *The Horse and his Boy* functions similarly, as an evident illustration of the principle that, as William Cowper put it in one of his most famous hymns, 'Behind a frowning providence | [God] hides a smiling face'.

That allegorical elements occasionally creep into the tales should not surprise us, nor should the occasional transference of characters from our (imaginative) world to Narnia, as in the appearance of Father Christmas in *The Lion* or that of Bacchus and Silenus in *Prince Caspian*. All of this is perfectly consistent with, and indeed intrinsic to, Lewis's narrative technique. Which means that these oddities and incongruities are not what Lewis's friend Tolkien thought they were, testimonies to carelessness. 'It really won't do, you know!' Tolkien said to Roger Lancelyn Green. 'I mean to say – *"Nymphs and their Ways, The Love-Life of a Faun"*. Doesn't he know what he's talking about?'[22] For Tolkien that was a rhetorical question: to him there was obviously no place in a 'secondary world' for such quaint jokes. No doubt Tolkien was offended by the very notion that fauns would have books at all.

But Tolkien's response betrayed a certain failure of imaginative sympathy. For in creating so variable and (by Tolkien's standards) inconsistent a world, Lewis was working in a venerable tradition. He was granting himself the same liberties taken by Shakespeare when, in *A Midsummer Night's Dream*, he planted no less English a figure than Puck (Robin Goodfellow) in a forest on the outskirts of Athens, or when, in *The Winter's Tale*, he bequeathed a coastline to Bohemia. Lewis's more direct model may well have been Sir Philip Sidney, whose pastoral romance *Arcadia* (c. 1585) is varied and miscellaneous, alternately comic, tragic and didactic, in a way that Narnia strongly recalls. 'Theoretically we are all pagans in Arcadia,' Lewis wrote in his great history of sixteenth-century literature. 'Nevertheless, Christian theology is always breaking in.' And in Lewis's view this is certainly not an error or an indicator of Sidney's carelessness: rather, such a practice was, in that era, a 'convention ... well understood, and very useful. In such works the gods are God incognito and everyone is in the secret. Paganism is the religion of poetry through which the author can express, at any moment, just so much or so little of his real religion as his art requires.'[23]

Sidney was beyond Tolkien's sphere of interest, and even if he had acknowledged that Lewis was working in this tradition, he wouldn't have liked it. But I think he would have been less inclined to see his old friend as someone who 'doesn't ... know what he's talking about'. Lewis knew very well what he was talking about. He chose a model of fictional composition in which the distance between the 'secondary world' and our own world was not fixed but rather flexible. Thus if he wished to associate the coming of Aslan into Narnia, after long absence, with our world's Christmas, and to do so by hauling Father Christmas into Narnia, he was free to do that; and if later on he wanted to produce a miniature allegory of conversion and penitence, he was free to do that too. He did not share Tolkien's interest in world-making for its own sake; rather he was a kind of *bricoleur*, a happy employer of any literary tools that came to hand. The very variousness that offended Tolkien's sensibilities was a joy to Lewis and has been a delight to many millions of his readers.

DISPUTED SOVEREIGNTY

Lewis once suggested that literary critics are, and have always been, neglectful of 'Story considered in itself'.[24] They have been so focused on themes and images and ideological commitments that they have failed to notice the thing that decisively differentiates stories from articles or treatises. If we then try to consider the seven Narnia stories as a single story, what is that story *about*? I contend that the best answer is *disputed sovereignty*. More than any other single thing, the *story* of Narnia concerns an unacknowledged but true King and the efforts of his loyalists to reclaim or protect his throne from would-be usurpers.

This theme is announced early in *The Lion, the Witch and the Wardrobe*: when the four Pevensies first enter Narnia as a group, their first action is to visit the house of Mr Tumnus. There they discover the house ransacked and a notice of Tumnus's arrest that concludes with the words 'LONG LIVE THE QUEEN!' – to which Lucy replies, 'She isn't a real queen at all.' Immediately after that they meet the Beavers, from whom they learn about Aslan:

> 'Aslan?' said Mr Beaver, 'Why don't you know? He's the King. He's the Lord of the whole wood, but not often here, you understand. Never in my time or my father's time. But the word has reached us that he has come back. He is in Narnia at this moment. He'll settle the White Queen all right.'[25]

So among the first facts established about Narnia are these: it is a realm in which authority is contested, in which the present and visible Queen of This World 'isn't a real queen at all' but rather a usurper, while the rightful King is frequently absent and invisible – but liable to return and assert his sovereignty. One of the key qualities of the Jovian temperament (Jupiter being the planet governing this book, as Michael Ward has explained in *Planet Narnia*) is kingliness. Jupiter is sovereign over all the spheres, and it is therefore fitting that his book is the first in the series.

This theme is repeated in several forms in the later books, and is never wholly absent from them. In *Prince Caspian* the young Prince learns that he is the rightful King of Narnia, whose uncle Miraz has murdered his father and usurped the throne. (One might also note that Caspian is the descendent of Telmarine conquerors of Narnia.) *The Voyage of the 'Dawn Treader'* is prompted by Caspian's search for lords loyal to his father who had been sent away by Miraz, in the course of which he re-establishes his 'overlordship' of the Lone Islands, where Governor Gumpas is shocked to find 'a real, live King of Narnia coming in upon him.'[26] And at the end of the tale, Caspian has to learn a painful lesson about what it means to be that 'real, live King', when he is prevented from abdicating and reminded of his duty to serve his subjects rather than his own personal interests. He must not usurp himself.

Further: in *The Silver Chair* Eustace and Jill are sent to help 'an aged King [Caspian] who is sad because he has no prince of his blood to be king after him. He has no heir because his only son was stolen from him many years ago.'[27] But the greater threat is that the Queen of Underland is bent on conquest of Narnia through the stratagem of putting the crown prince, Rilian, on the throne, as 'king in name, but really her slave'.[28] In *The Horse and His Boy* it is not the Narnian throne but rather that of its neighbour and ally, Archenland, that is threatened, but once again children are called to aid in the restoration of a rightful crown prince and then to serve as he asserts his authority against would-be conquerors and usurpers. In *The Magician's Nephew* we meet Jadis, Queen of Charn, who, having destroyed her own world, now seeks the rule of the just-made world of Narnia; against her and for Aslan two young Londoners, Digory and Polly, align themselves. And *The Last Battle* tells of Shift the Ape, who with Calormene help establishes himself and poor Puzzle the Donkey as substitutes for Aslan, before that world's time is ended and those who loved the true Aslan inherit the new, resurrected Narnian kingdom for ever.

In short: there is a King of Kings and Lord of Lords whose Son is the rightful ruler of this world. Indeed, through that Son all things were made, and the world will end when he 'comes again in glory to judge the living and the dead', though 'his kingdom will have no end', in the words of the Nicene Creed. Meanwhile, in these in-between times, the rulership of Earth is claimed by an Adversary, the Prince of this world.

And what is asked of all Lewis's characters is simply, as the biblical Joshua put it, to 'choose this day' whom they will serve.[29]

THE RULER OF THE HEAVENS

Lewis once told a friend that if he were going to write more than one Narnia tale he had to write three or seven or nine, for 'those are the magic numbers'.[30] They have indeed had a magical effect on the minds of readers, who have discerned in the Narnian tales complex and deeply imbedded allegories of the seven deadly sins, or the seven cardinal virtues, or the seven sacraments of Catholic theology. (This is a selective list.) But in his study *Planet Narnia* Michael Ward has demonstrated that Lewis wove into each Narnia tale the characteristic traits of one of the seven planets of medieval cosmology. That Lewis was deeply interested in this cosmology is evident from his poem 'The Planets', his Ransom Trilogy, and his survey of medieval thought in *The Discarded Image*; this makes it rather surprising that no one before Ward noticed the planetary traits in the Chronicles. But indeed they are there.

The Lion, the Witch and the Wardrobe embodies the festal and kingly spirit of Jupiter, *Price Caspian* the warlike character of Mars; *The Voyage of the 'Dawn Treader'* moves always towards the golden shining Sun; *The Silver Chair*, with its theme of change and its Witch who hides from the Sun, is dominated by the Moon, whose associated metal is silver; the separating and re-forming of the metal mercury matches the events of *The Horse and His Boy*, ruled by the planet of that name; *The Magician's Nephew* is all about creative love, which befits a book governed by Venus; and the end of the old Narnia in *The Last Battle* is presided over by ancient Saturn, who appears in the book as the Time-Giant. This is but a sketch of the major correspondences; each of the books has many more, as Ward is the first to show.

In *The Discarded Image* Lewis explains the medieval idea that the cosmos consists of a series of concentric spheres: 'Each sphere, or something resident in each sphere, is a conscious and intellectual being, moved by the "intellectual love" of God … These lofty creatures are called Intelligences.'[31] It was usually thought that an Intelligence is a very particular kind of angel: a 'creature', but not embodied, and with the single function of being the mover of its sphere.

These are the Oyarsa of the Ransom Trilogy. In *Out of the Silent Planet* the protagonist, Ransom, learns early on that the name of the planet he visits is Malacandra, but he does not yet understand that when he meets the Oyarsa of that planet he is meeting Malacandra itself.

Malacandra is the Intelligence that moves the planetary body that we call Mars, just as Perelandra is the Intelligence that moves the planet we call Venus. And in the third book of the trilogy, *That Hideous Strength*, the Intelligences come to earth and enter Ransom's room, each one bringing an overwhelmingly powerful *mood* – of liveliness or passion or resolution or gloom or festivity – which governs the lesser spirits of the people who are nearby.

Similarly, each of the Narnia tales is a narrative 'body' to which one of the planetary Intelligences gives a spirit; and the characters of each story are governed, or mis-governed, by the ruling spirit of that book. Jovial festivity overwhelms the Pevensies in *The Lion*; the seafarers become radiant in *Dawn Treader*; in *The Magician's Nephew* Uncle Andrew becomes absurdly besotted with that 'dem fine woman', the terrifying giant Queen Jadis. And so on.

Thus Ward has revealed to us the deep structure, as it were, of the Narnian tales – and this structure reinforces once again the theme of sovereignty. For the Intelligences, masterful and terrifying though they are, are but stewards of the Lord God, the only King of Kings. Their power, though vast, is delegated, and they exercise it properly only when they do so in obedience to the divine will. (In the Ransom Trilogy we are told that only the Oyarsa of our own world refused mere stewardship and disputed the sovereignty of God, thus cutting us off from the rest of the Intelligences and making us 'the silent planet'.[32])

In the Narnia tales this theme is worked out not through the behaviour of the Intelligences themselves but through the responses of characters to the planetary moods. The martial atmosphere of *Prince Caspian* gives us not only the valour of Reepicheep but also the *libido dominandi* of Miraz. *The Magician's Nephew* is a virtual anatomy of the major forms of love, which, as Augustine might put it, we see in their disordered and their properly ordered states: the key moment in the book comes when Digory is poised agonizingly between two forms of love, one of which would eventually lead to destructive self-gratification, the other to joyful obedience and real newness of life. Characters are revealed to us through their responses to the planetary influences; and those responses tend to involve the deeply Lewisian themes of obedience and love.

CONCLUSION

A central experience for Lewis was that of *Sehnsucht*, or longing.[33] Lewis thought that this mood of longing could be well or badly used.

Indeed, one could say that, just as joviality is the mood of Jupiter and exhaustion that of Saturn, *Sehnsucht* is the mood of our world: the Silent Planet longs for connection, for a restoration of the music of the other spheres from which we have cut ourselves off. But it is not well understood that Lewis believed also that there are fundamentally different *kinds* of longing – so different that they scarcely deserve the same name.[34]

In his essay 'On Three Ways of Writing for Children', Lewis explores the effects that different kinds of stories have upon children and adults alike – the kinds of desires that the story prompts. 'Does anyone really suppose', he asks, that the lover of fairy tales 'really and prosaically longs for all the dangers and discomforts of a fairy tale? – really wants dragons in contemporary England?'[35] Of course not. By contrast, more realistic stories are far more liable to become 'fantasies' in the clinical sense than fantastic stories are:

> The real victim of wishful reverie does not batten on the *Odyssey*, *The Tempest* or *The Worm Ouroboros*: he or she prefers stories about millionaires, irresistible beauties, posh hotels, palm beaches and bedroom scenes – things that really might happen, that ought to happen, that would have happened if the reader had had a fair chance. For, as I say, there are two kinds of longing. The one is an *askesis*, a spiritual exercise, and the other is a disease.[36]

The phrase 'spiritual exercise' is an important one here, because it calls to mind the *Spiritual Exercises* of Ignatius Loyola. The comparison is instructive, for the success of many of the *Exercises* depends on the meditator's ability to 'see in place', to visualize a spiritual truth and thereby make it more real. Although Lewis considered the specific Ignatian practice of *compositio loci* to be 'not "addressed to my condition"', nevertheless he said that 'images play an important part in my prayers'.[37]

As we saw earlier, Lewis tended to emphasize a strict distinction between the image-making Author and the Man with his extra-literary commitments; my scepticism about that distinction I have based in part on Lewis's own stated belief that 'the moral inherent in [the images that come to one's mind] will rise from whatever spiritual roots you have succeeded in striking during the whole course of your life'. What arose in Lewis's mind when he began to make the Narnian tales may be experienced simply as interesting or beautiful pictures; and in that respect they are certainly worth while as colourful, adventurous, engaging expressions of literary art. But understood more deeply and fully, the Chronicles, with their elaborate complement of images, contribute to an *askesis*, a spiritual exercise. They are a kind of training in how to long, and what and whom to long for.

Notes

1 'On Three Ways of Writing for Children', EC 507.
2 PPL 72.
3 FL 34.
4 'On Three Ways of Writing for Children', EC 510.
5 'On Three Ways of Writing for Children', EC 510.
6 'It All Began with a Picture,' EC 529.
7 Roger Lancelyn Green and Walter Hooper, *C.S. Lewis: A Biography*, revd edn (London: HarperCollins, 2002), 303.
8 Chad Walsh, *C.S. Lewis: Apostle to the Skeptics* (New York: Macmillan, 1949), 10.
9 Humphrey Carpenter, *The Inklings: C.S. Lewis, J.R.R. Tolkien, Charles Williams and Their Friends* (London: HarperCollins, 2006), 217; A.N. Wilson, *C.S. Lewis: A Biography* (London: Collins, 1990), 220. My very different account may be found in *The Narnian: The Life and Imagination of C.S. Lewis* (San Francisco: Harper San Francisco, 2005), 232ff. Michael Ward has made a strong argument that the Narnia books, far from constituting a repudiation of the work Lewis was doing in *Miracles*, are actually a continuation of it by other means: see his *Planet Narnia: The Seven Heavens in the Imagination of C.S. Lewis* (New York: Oxford University Press, 2008), ch 10.
10 'It All Began with a Picture', EC 529.
11 'Sometimes Fairy Stories May Say Best What's To Be Said', EC 527.
12 'On Three Ways of Writing for Children,' EC 513.
13 'Sometimes Fairy Stories May Say Best What's To Be Said', EC 527–28.
14 'On Three Ways of Writing for Children', EC 510.
15 Undated letter to the Milton Society of America (CLIII 516–17).
16 Letter to Laurence Krieg, 21 Apr. 1957 (CLIII 848).
17 Letter to Laurence Krieg, 21 Apr. 1957 (CLIII 847).
18 LWW 171.
19 LWW 65.
20 'The Novels of Charles Williams', EC 572. The only Chronicle set entirely within the sub-created world is *The Horse and His Boy*.
21 Aslan's non-humanity *could* be seen, by the theologically overscrupulous, as heterodox: did not the Cappadocian Fathers argue that what Christ did not assume, he could not heal? And since Aslan does not assume humanity, is he not incapable of healing it? But in Narnia 'humanity' – which in our world is confined to people who look like us (Sons of Adam and Daughters of Eve) – is extended equally to the Talking Beasts. Aslan assumes that *whole* humanity, so he can heal not only lions, but also all the other rational ('Talking') beings of Narnia.

22   Green and Hooper, *C.S. Lewis: A Biography*, 307. Tolkien was referring
     to the draft of LWW that Lewis had read to him. It is possible that *'The
     Love-Life of a Faun'* was Tolkien's own exasperated extrapolation from
     'Nymphs and their ways'. At any rate, *'The Love-Life of a Faun'* does
     not appear among the titles listed in LWW.

23   EL 342.

24   'On Stories', EC 491.

25   LWW 74.

26   VDT 41.

27   SC 28–29.

28   SC 193.

29   Josh. 24.15.

30   Charles Wrong, 'A Chance Meeting', in *Remembering C.S. Lewis:
     Recollections of Those Who Knew Him*, ed. James T. Como (San
     Francisco: Ignatius Press, 2005), 212.

31   DI 115.

32   OSP 110.

33   See David Jasper's essay earlier in this volume (Chapter 16).

34   That the Narnia books are deeply concerned with longing is recognized,
     at least implicitly, by some of the fiercest critics of the series: they tend
     to believe that what Lewis is palpably longing for is a world in which,
     as Philip Pullman has put it, 'Death is better than life; boys are better
     than girls; light-coloured people are better than dark-coloured people;
     and so on. There is no shortage of such nauseating drivel in Narnia, if
     you can face it' ('The Dark Side of Narnia', *Guardian*, 1 Oct. 1998). For
     a more detailed critique, see John Goldthwaite's *The Natural History of
     Make-believe: A Guide to the Principal Works of Britain, Europe, and
     America* (Oxford: Oxford University Press, 1996), 220–44.

35   'On Three Ways of Writing for Children', EC 511.

36   'On Three Ways of Writing for Children', EC 511.

37   LTM 86–87. For more on this subject, see Joseph P. Cassidy's essay
     (Chapter 10) in this volume.

20 *Till We Have Faces*

PETER J. SCHAKEL

Till We Have Faces: A Myth Retold (1956) was C.S. Lewis's last work of fiction, and the one he considered his best.[1] He was disappointed by the initial response to it: some reviews were partially negative and sales were lower than his other books,[2] probably because of its difficulty and its differences from his earlier fiction. It remains the least popular of his fictional works, though it is the most highly praised by literary critics.[3]

BACKGROUND

The book is a retelling of the Cupid and Psyche myth, from the *Metamorphoses*, or *The Golden Ass*, of Lucius Apuleius. Lewis first read the tale in late 1916,[4] and responded by trying to write his own version of it. A diary entry for May 1922 records, 'Tried to work on "Psyche" ... with no success'[5] and in November of that year he was 'thinking how to make a masque or play of Psyche'.[6] A year later his 'head was very full of my old idea of a poem on my own version of the Cupid and Psyche story'; he had by this point already started such a poem twice, 'once in couplet and once in ballad form'.[7]

The story stayed in Lewis's mind, 'thickening and hardening with the years',[8] but if he made other attempts to tell it in poetic form, nothing is known of them. He returned to it in March 1955, when Joy Davidman Gresham (the woman he was to marry the following year) spent a weekend with Lewis and his brother. Lewis and Joy 'kicked a few ideas [for a new book] around', focused on the Cupid and Psyche story, then 'had another whiskey each and bounced it back and forth between us', as she put it in a letter at the time.[9] Lewis drafted a chapter the next day, which he revised after they discussed it, and went on to another chapter. A month later he was three-quarters of the way through, and the book was completed by early July.

In an essay published the following year, Lewis describes the writing process as involving two sides of a writer's being: 'In the Author's mind there bubbles up every now and then the material for a story ... This ferment leads to nothing unless it is accompanied with the longing for a Form. ... When these two things click you have the Author's impulse complete.'[10] The material for this story had been bubbling, or at least simmering, since he was an undergraduate, but attempting to write it as poetry never led to the necessary 'click'. In the blurb he wrote for the dust-jacket of *Till We Have Faces*, Lewis says, 'Last spring what seemed to be the right form presented itself and themes suddenly interlocked.'[11] The triggering point seems to have been giving up his fixed intention of turning Apuleius's tale into a poem, and relating it instead in prose.

But the necessary 'click' also involves content, and the ideas Lewis and Joy tossed back and forth probably included themes as well as form. From the first time he read the story, Lewis says, he knew that 'Apuleius got it all wrong. The elder sister ... couldn't *see* Psyche's palace when she visited her. She saw only rock & heather. When P[syche] said she was giving her noble wine, the poor sister saw & tasted only spring water.'[12] But his understanding of why she could not see was different in 1955 than it had been in 1922 or 1923: 'In my pre-Christian days she was to be in the right and the gods in the wrong.'[13] Lewis in the early 1920s was only just beginning to emerge from his materialistic 'New Look' period and still wanted no 'flirtations with any idea of the supernatural, no romantic delusions'.[14] Thus he believed the elder sister was in the right because there was no palace for her to see and no wine for her to taste.

Seventy-six lines of the early attempts at poetic retelling survive.[15] In them Lewis's aim was to defend the elder sister from the accusation that her envy of Psyche's wealth and good fortune drove Psyche into exile and unhappiness: 'The tale of Psyche is unjustly told | And half the truth concealed by all who hold | With Apuleius'. The true reason Psyche was sacrificed was a superstitious attempt to alleviate drought and famine, but a different version has been handed down, 'poorer stuff | And slander', to protect the members of the tribe who made the decision to sacrifice Psyche. 'Some poetic youth', most likely Psyche's twin brother Jardis, shifted the blame from the tribe to the two elder sisters, accusing them of envying Psyche, 'But all this | Is weighted on one side and told amiss.'

Lewis's early attempts went wrong not just because he didn't have the right form, but also because he didn't have the right theme. The surviving lines focus on human actions, with no room for the gods: 'some strange helper came' and rescued Psyche when she was left on the mountain. Those who have told the story before 'talk of the wind spirit opening wide | His cloudy arms', but it seems clear that the narrator of the poem thinks the true explanation must be more rational and naturalistic.

COMPOSITION: FORM AND SUMMARY

The theme that emerged in 1955, that 'clicked' with the prose fiction form, reverses his earlier approach. Once again, the elder sister is in the wrong and the gods are in the right. The elder sister still can't see the palace or taste the wine, but Lewis recognizes now that that is because 'spiritual things are spiritually discerned'.[16] Psyche's sisters could not have seen the god's palace because they did not believe in divine mysteries. Lewis says that he had always intended to use the elder sister as a first-person narrator,[17] presumably as a reliable speaker, since 'she was to be in the right'. A key idea, as the novel began to crystallize, was making the sister an unreliable narrator. Nearly all of Lewis's other stories are third-person accounts, with the narrator providing a reliable point of view to orient the reader. In *Till We Have Faces*, the older sister, whom Lewis names Orual, writes what she believes to be a scrupulously accurate, truthful account of her life, showing how the gods had treated her unjustly. It is up to the reader gradually to recognize her faults and self-deceptions, without a reliable narrator's help.

Lewis's version of the story is set in an imaginary country, Glome, two or three centuries before the birth of Christ. Myths generally have a vague setting, thus creating a degree of universality. Attention focuses on what happens, not on the specific time and place in which it happens. That is not the case in *Till We Have Faces*: the fictional world is crucial to the effect of the book. In a letter to Clyde Kilby, Lewis called the book 'a work of (supposed) *historical* imagination. A guess at what it might have been like in a little barbarous state on the borders of the Hellenistic world with Greek culture just beginning to affect it.'[18] Doris T. Myers argues that the work is a novel, a combination of historical fiction, providing a credible, detailed depiction of life at the time at which the events were set, and modern fiction, with its narrative approach and characterizations based on twentieth-century psychological paradigms.[19]

Lewis's retelling of the Apuleian myth begins with the death of Orual's mother, after which Orual's father, Trom, the King of Glome, marries a new wife, who dies in giving birth to a baby (Psyche). The unattractive but intelligent Orual loves the beautiful Psyche devotedly, and acts as mother to her, meanwhile neglecting the middle sister,

Redival (who is quite a minor character in Lewis's version). As Psyche becomes a young woman, she is so beautiful that people begin to worship her, instead of worshipping the local nature goddess, Ungit (their equivalent of Venus). After a plague and in the midst of a drought and famine, the Priest of Ungit tells the King that relief will come only if Psyche is sacrificed to Ungit's son, the 'Brute', by being exposed on a mountain, bound to a holy tree. The King complies.

When Orual goes, some time later, to bury Psyche's bones, she instead finds Psyche, in a paradisal valley, across a river, vibrantly alive and yet clothed in what Orual perceives as rags. Psyche invites Orual into her palace, but Orual cannot see the palace or the magnificent robes Psyche says she is wearing – and even Psyche admits she has never seen the husband who gave her the clothes and in whose palace she lives, and who sleeps with her at night. When Orual visits Psyche again, she forces Psyche, by threatening suicide, to light a lamp at night and look at her husband. Orual convinces herself that it is for Psyche's own good, though by this point the reader must recognize that she is intensely jealous at being displaced in Psyche's life by another and excluded from an area of Psyche's existence.

Obeying Orual against her better judgement, Psyche lights the lamp and sees the god in all his divine beauty. He awakens and rebukes her, and she is sent weeping into exile. As Psyche goes, Orual has a dazzling glimpse of Psyche's husband, and hears him say that she, too, 'will be Psyche'. Upon her return to Glome, Orual does not tell the Fox, her Greek tutor and friend, what happened on the mountain, and begins to wear a veil to hide her face and feelings from others. Soon after her return, the King dies and Orual succeeds him. She pours herself into official activities and becomes more and more the Queen (a masculine-like monarch), less and less Orual (a woman and a person), and time goes by swiftly.

Many years later she hears a priest in Essur, a neighbouring country, tell a sacred story about Psyche. Here, within his larger retelling of the myth, Lewis incorporates a smaller retelling of the Cupid and Psyche story as a simple nature myth, with Psyche dying in the autumn and coming back to life in the spring. Orual recognizes it as her own story – but she says the teller got it wrong, because (like Apuleius) he says both sisters visited Psyche, and they could actually see the palace and so became jealous of Psyche. Orual decides to write her own version of the story in order to set the facts straight and to show how unjust the gods have been to her: that is what we have been reading as part I of *Till We Have Faces*. However, in the process of writing, Orual discovers how self-deceived she has been and how she has in fact 'devoured' people, especially Psyche, the Fox, and Bardia, the soldier who has served loyally as her adviser for many years. She decides to escape by committing suicide, but again a god intervenes and stops her, telling her to 'die before you die'.[20] In a series of visions she 'becomes Psyche' by helping Psyche with the seemingly impossible tasks that Psyche must complete. Through all this, Orual learns to think of others, instead of just herself; thus she dies to self, as the god said she must. In the process of learning unselfish love, she becomes beautiful like Psyche and gains salvation.[21]

ORUAL

Lewis took justifiable pride in the development of Orual's character. As he put it in a letter, 'I believe I've done what no mere male author has done before, talked thro' the mouth of, & lived in the mind of, an *ugly* woman for a whole book.'[22] Margaret Hannay accurately describes Orual as 'by far the most fully developed character that Lewis created',[23] a complex, multi-faceted woman who incorporates aspects of Janie Moore (the mother of an army friend, with whom Lewis shared a home for over thirty years) and of Joy Gresham, but also some aspects of Lewis himself.

Like Lewis before his conversion, Orual is caught in a tension between rational discourse and religious belief.[24] The word *believe* is used dozens of times in *Till We Have Faces*, as when Orual says, 'If I'd had my eyes shut, I would have believed her palace was as real as this.'[25] Orual is torn between the teachings of the Fox, a Stoic who attempts to rely on 'Greek wisdom' (reason), and the faith of the old Priest of Ungit, with his devotion to the goddess and his 'understanding of holy things' like rituals and sacrifice. For much of her life Orual denies the existence of the gods or denies their justice and goodness if they do exist. What she eventually must admit is that her resistance to the gods was not an inability to believe in them, but an unwillingness to accept them because she did not want to share Psyche with anyone, not even a god. In his letter to Clyde Kilby, Lewis compares it to what is probably happening in anybody's town at the moment: 'Someone becomes a Christian, or, in a family nominally Christian already, does something like becoming a missionary or entering a religious order. The others suffer a sense of outrage. What they love is being taken from them!'[26]

Lewis used Orual's character to give concrete embodiment to ideas about love which he first sketched out in letters of the early 1940s,[27] then incorporated into *The Great Divorce*,[28] expanded further in numerous letters in the following decade,[29] and published as a book, *The Four Loves*,[30] four years after *Till We Have Faces*. He made the connection explicitly in the letter to Kilby quoted above: 'Orual is (not a symbol but) an instance, a "case", of human affection in its natural condition: true, tender, suffering, but in the long run, tyrannically possessive and ready to turn to hatred when the beloved ceases to be its possession.'

Lewis's ideas are given structure by four Greek words for love. The first three Lewis, in *The Four Loves*, calls the 'natural loves', loves grounded in our human natures: *storgē* (affection), *philia* (friendship), and *erōs* (romantic love). The natural loves are good things, but they are subject to corruption. The comfortableness of *storgē* can decline into insensitivity or rudeness, or its need to give can degenerate into possessiveness and jealousy. *Philia* can lead to a sense of pride because others are excluded from a group of friends. And the exalted emotions that characterize *erōs* can be mistaken for transcendence and turn 'being in love' into a sort of religion. The natural loves are not self-sustaining. Without help, they will become self-centred and eventually slide into unlove and end up as a kind of hatred.

Lewis's central point about love is that in order for the natural loves to remain loves, they must be infused with and transformed by a higher love. The fourth of the Greek words for love is *agapē*, divine love, selfless love. The natural loves, says Lewis, must die in order to live: 'Every natural love will rise again and live for ever in this country [heaven],' George MacDonald says in *The Great Divorce*, 'but none will rise again until it has been buried.'[31] Only *agapē* can save the natural loves from themselves, can make them live. In Christian usage, *agapē* is the selfless love of God for humanity; but by a divine gift, God also enables humans to extend this love to God and other humans.

These ideas are embodied in literary form in *Till We Have Faces*. The story shows how all of Orual's loves turn possessive and destructive: her motherly affection for Psyche (*storgē*), her friendship with the Fox (*philia*), and her sublimated but nonetheless real desire for Bardia (*erōs*) decline until they are no longer actually loves. Bardia's wife touches the heart of the matter when she says to Orual, after Bardia's death, 'I begin to think you know nothing of love'.[32] Orual must admit her failures and recognize how she has treated those who loved her – how she has 'gorged [herself] with other men's lives; women's too'.[33] She must begin to understand that 'a love [like hers] can grow to be ninetenths hatred and still call itself love'.[34] Orual must become able to see herself clearly in order to receive the gift of higher love. For much of her life she has worn a veil, to cover what she is. The veil gives her a public identity as the Queen and allows her to bury her personal self: she has no face, no identity, and thus no way to relate genuinely to a god, or to other people. Only when she removes the veil, confronts her true self, and gains a 'face' can she encounter God, without defences, excuses or pretences, for 'how can [God] meet us face to face till we have faces?'[35] By removing the veil, by dying to self, she becomes able to live for others: 'Never again will I call you mine,' she says to Psyche; 'but all there is of me shall be yours'.[36]

SACRIFICE AND MYTH

Dying to self is a synonym for sacrifice, which is a central motif throughout the work. It appears first in the reference to 'the temple-smell of blood ... and burnt fat and singed hair' that the old priest carries with him: 'The Ungit smell'.[37] Orual's father 'made great sacrifices to Ungit'[38] during the young Queen's pregnancy, to ensure that her child will be male, and sacrifices are made on the evening of the child's birth. These references culminate in the Great Offering which must be made to purge the land, end the plague, and bring the needed rain. The Fox's 'Greek wisdom' dismisses sacrifice. According to him the wood from which a bed is made has no effect on whether the children conceived in the bed will be male or female: 'These things come about by natural causes.'[39] When rain comes, the Fox argues that the Great Offering had nothing to do with it: 'That south-west wind came over a thousand miles of sea and land. The weather of the whole world would have to have been different from the beginning if that wind was not to blow.'[40]

In contrast, the old Priest holds, in a key sentence, that Greek wisdom 'brings no rain and grows no corn; sacrifice does both'.[41] In *Miracles: A Preliminary Study*, Lewis argues that the descent and re-ascent of the corn-king in the nature religions depicts a familiar pattern written all over the world, evident in vegetable life, animal life, and our moral and emotional life: 'Death and Re-birth – go down to go up – it is a key principle.'[42] This is the point of the story told by the priest of Essur, who views the young goddess Psyche as a corn-queen. Orual interrupts him just before he would have said the crucial word: 'Then [in the spring] we take off her black veil, and I change my black robe for a white one, and we offer – '.[43] His next word would have been *sacrifices*.

The corn-king and sacrifice flow naturally into the realm of myth, a central issue in any discussion of *Till We Have Faces* as 'A Myth Retold'. The *Oxford English Dictionary* defines myth as a traditional story, typically involving supernatural beings or forces, which embodies and provides an explanation, especially of causes or origins, for something such as the early history of a society, a religious belief or ritual, or a natural phenomenon. It is myth that Orual in *Till We Have Faces* is referring to when she says there is 'a sacred story' that explains why pigs are an abomination to Ungit.[44] For Lewis, as for his friend J.R.R. Tolkien, myths are of divine origin and convey a deep, universal kind of reality: they constitute 'a real though unfocussed gleam of divine truth falling on human imagination'.[45] Elsewhere, echoing Tolkien, Lewis defines it as a particular kind of story that conveys 'a permanent object of contemplation'.[46] A myth, he says, 'hits us at a level deeper than our thoughts or even our passions, troubles oldest certainties till all questions are re-opened, and in general shocks us more fully awake than we are for most of our lives'.[47]

Myths provide not just intellectual understanding of the truth but a powerful imaginative experience of it. One way to clarify the effect of myth is through a concept Lewis learned from the philosopher Samuel Alexander (1859–1938) that became immensely important to him, the distinction between Contemplation (analysis of something from the outside) and Enjoyment (direct experience of something from the inside).[48] For Lewis, the crucial point is that one cannot do both simultaneously: as soon as we step back to analyse, we lose the immediacy of direct experience. In his essay 'Meditation in a Toolshed', Lewis explains Alexander's technical material more simply, using the metaphor of a beam of sunlight shining through the crack at the top of a toolshed door. One can look at the beam as it enters the toolshed and illuminates specks of dust in the air (contemplate the beam), or one can step into the light so that the beam falls directly on one's eye and look along it (enjoy it) to its source, the Sun, which also illumines the world outside the shed: 'You get one experience of a thing when you look along it and another when you look at it.'[49]

Myths enable readers to enjoy (experience directly) things of permanent value that they otherwise can only contemplate (examine from the outside). As Lewis puts it in his essay 'Myth Became Fact': 'In the enjoyment of a great myth we come nearest to experiencing as a concrete what can otherwise be understood only as an abstraction.'[50] In reading myth, attention should not be on what the myth 'means' (knowledge), but on the 'taste' of reality it offers: 'What flows into you from the myth is not truth but reality (truth is always *about* something, but reality is that *about which* truth is).'[51]

That is the case in *Till We Have Faces*. The opening paragraphs indicate that this story will deal with some of the deep, universal issues that all human beings face: whether gods exist and, if so, what they are like, and why bad things happen to good people. Lewis had contemplated such questions in his expository works, such as *The Problem of Pain*, *Mere Christianity* and *Miracles*, trying to supply answers that would help readers understand what they needed to know. In *Till We Have Faces*, instead of abstract meaning ('Only words, words; to be led out to battle against other words'[52]), Lewis offers an imaginative experience which gives readers a taste of reality. Orual's defence of her life is, at a deeper level, a search for a hidden God.

Kallistos Ware writes that, in common with the Orthodox tradition, Lewis 'was acutely conscious of the hiddenness of God, of the inexhaustible mystery of the Divine'. He calls this the *leitmotif* of *Till We Have Faces*.[53] Michael Ward argues that this insight is applicable to Lewis's general theological vision; his continual emphasis is God's unperceived omnipresence and proximity: 'The major feature of his spirituality is the exercising of Enjoyment consciousness in order to experience that hidden divinity.'[54] Thus in *Till We Have Faces* Orual complains that the gods do not show themselves, do not give signs, and speak only in riddles.[55] Similarly, in searching for Psyche, Orual and Bardia come upon 'the secret valley of the god'.[56] The words of the Priest of Ungit sum up the theme well: 'The gods … dazzle our eyes. … Holy places are dark places. … Holy wisdom is not clear and thin like water, but thick and dark like blood.'[57]

Myth is the perfect way to deal with the hidden divinity. By setting the story before the time of Christ, Lewis eliminates the possibility of addressing Christianity directly. He hides what is in fact a central theme. But he does include oblique references that anticipate Christianity, through lines such as 'It's only sense that one should die for many'[58] and 'I wonder do the gods know what it feels like to be a man'.[59] More importantly, the emphasis on sacrifice in the story, both in the pagan worship of Ungit and the personal sacrifices of the characters, points toward the sacrifice of Christ. Christ, as Lewis wrote in *Miracles*, 'is like the Corn-King because the Corn-King is a portrait of Him'.[60] The events in Glome, set before the birth of Christ, anticipate Christ's coming: 'The very thing which the Nature-religions are all about seems to have really happened once'.[61] The reader shares Orual's experience: as she searches for the hidden God, so the reader is searching for the role of Christianity in this supposedly pre-Christian story.

The role of Christianity comes through subtly but distinctly in the motif of sacrifice. Orual thinks of sacrifices as empty rituals: 'The duty of queenship that irked me most was going often to the house of Ungit and sacrificing.'[62] She follows the Fox in denying the efficacy of the religious sacrifices, and she does not recognize the other kinds of sacrifice that are evident all around her. They are evident in the self-sacrificial attitudes of Psyche, as she risks her own health to bring healing during the plague, and of the Fox and Bardia, who selflessly spend their lives for the sake of Glome and Orual, its Queen. They are evident in Orual herself, although she is totally unaware of them, as she devotes herself to her people and her country and then performs Psyche's tasks for her. In his letter to Kilby, Lewis calls Psyche 'an instance of the *anima naturaliter Christiana* [a soul by nature Christian]': 'She is in some ways like Christ not because she is a symbol of Him but because every good man or woman is like Christ. What else could they be like?'[63] Orual also in some ways is like Christ. But she needs to grow more Christ-like by learning the importance of the universal 'principle of *Vicariousness*': 'Everything is indebted to everything else, sacrificed to everything else, dependent on everything else.'[64] It is this principle, 'very deep-rooted in Christianity',[65] that brings Christian theology into *Till We Have Faces* in ways that are less direct, but deeper and more subtle, than in some of Lewis's earlier stories.

Orual started her journey wanting answers, but in the end she finds not answers but the reason why her doubts and questions were not answered: 'I know now, Lord, why you utter no answer. You are yourself the answer. Before your face questions die away. What other answer would suffice?'[66] In many cases, readers come to Lewis's works looking for answers and explanations. Perhaps one reason *Till We Have Faces* is his least popular story is that it doesn't provide either answers or explanations. Instead, it enables readers, by imaginatively identifying with Orual, to taste the reality she experiences. When Orual stood in the god's palace without being able to see it, Psyche said, 'Perhaps ... you too will learn how to see'.[67] And Orual does learn how to see – the story ends with a series of dreams or visions or 'seeings'.[68] Likewise readers must learn how to see what they are shown by the myth, shown – or enabled to taste – what the essence of Christianity is, and not simply told what it is about.

Notes

1   Lewis said of it, 'I think it much my best book' (CLIII 873; cf. CLIII 1040, 1148, 1181, 1214); 'It's my favourite of all my books': quoted in Charles

Wrong, 'A Chance Meeting', in *Remembering C.S. Lewis: Recollections of Those Who Knew Him*, ed. James T. Como (San Francisco: Ignatius Press, 2005), 206; cf. 212.

2   'To judge by reviews and sales, it is my biggest failure yet': letter to Herbert Palmer, 17 Nov. 1957 (CLIII 897; cf. CLIII 808, 812, 829, 835, 836, 1040, 1148, 1181). Lewis was being overly harsh. Of 15 contemporary reviews I have seen, only five express reservations (generally that the second part is less successful than the first), but even those (with the exception of the *New Yorker*'s) find much to praise.

3   An exception to the almost uniformly positive critical assessments of the book is Sally A. Bartlett, 'Humanistic Psychology in C.S. Lewis's *Till We Have Faces*: A Feminist Critique', *Studies in the Literary Imagination* 22:2 (Fall 1989), 185–98. She argues that although Lewis's psychological understandings of his characters are sound, the solutions he offers for their emotional crises would not work in our world.

4   Letters to Arthur Greeves, 28 Jan. and 13 May 1917 (CLI 268, 304–05).

5   AMR 30. He had better success the next day (AMR 31).

6   AMR 142.

7   AMR 266.

8   Letter to Jocelyn Gibb, 29 Feb. 1956 (CLIII 715).

9   The quotations are from a letter by Joy Davidman Gresham to William Gresham, 23 Mar. 1955, published in *Out of My Bone: The Letters of Joy Davidman*, ed. Don W. King (Grand Rapids: Eerdmans, 2009), 242.

10 'Sometimes Fairy Stories May Say Best What's To Be Said', EC 526.

11 Lewis includes this blurb in a letter to Jocelyn Gibb, 29 Feb. 1956 (CLIII 715).

12 Letter to Katharine Farrer, 2 Apr. 1955 (CLIII 590). See also his diary entry for 9 Sept. 1923 (AMR 266).

13 Letter to Christian Hardie, 31 July 1955 (CLIII 633).

14 SBJ 162.

15 'The Lewis Papers: Memoirs of the Lewis Family, 1850–1930', vol. VIII, pp. 163–67, now in the Wade Collection, Wheaton College, Illinois. The fragments have been published as 'On Cupid and Psyche' in Don W. King, *C.S. Lewis, Poet: The Legacy of His Poetic Impulse* (Kent, OH: Kent State University Press, 2001), 269–71.

16 'Transposition', EC 273, alluding to 1 Cor. 2.14.

17 Letter to Christian Hardie, 31 July 1955 (CLIII 633). The surviving fragments of the poetic version are narrated in the third person, perhaps because they are introductory segments.

18 Letter to Clyde S. Kilby, 10 Feb. 1957 (CLIII 830).

19 Doris T. Myers, *Bareface: A Guide to C.S. Lewis's Last Novel* (Columbia, MO: University of Missouri Press, 2004), 3–4. But cf. Mara E. Donaldson, 'Orual's Story and the Art of Retelling: A Study of *Till We Have Faces*', in *Word and Story in C.S. Lewis*, ed. Peter J. Schakel and Charles A. Huttar (Columbia, MO: University of Missouri Press, 1991), 157–70.

20 TWHF 291.

21 For discussions of themes and narrative strategies, see Peter J. Schakel, *Reason and Imagination in C.S. Lewis: A Study of 'Till We Have Faces'* (Grand Rapids: Eerdmans, 1984), available online at <http://hope.edu/

academic/english/schakel/tillwehavefaces/index.html>, and the chapter on *Till We Have Faces* in Charles A. Huttar's forthcoming book *'This Will Never Do': C.S. Lewis's Reworking of Literary Traditions.*

22   Letter to Mary Willis Shelburne, 4 Mar. 1956 (CLIII 716).

23   Margaret Patterson Hannay, *C.S. Lewis* (New York: Ungar, 1981), 125.

24   'Dark idolatry and thin enlightenment at war with each other and with vision': letter to Jocelyn Gibb, 29 Feb. 1956 (CLIII 715).

25   TWHF 150.

26   Letter to Clyde S. Kilby, 10 Feb. 1957 (CLIII 831).

27   See CLII 408, 464, 511, 530, 616–17.

28   GD *passim.*

29   See CLII 788, CLIII 119, 247, 393, 428.

30   See Caroline J. Simon's discussion earlier in this volume (Chapter 11).

31   GD 88–89.

32   TWHF 275.

33   TWHF 275.

34   TWHF 277.

35   TWHF 305.

36   TWHF 316–17.

37   TWHF 19.

38   TWHF 21.

39   TWHF 18.

40   TWHF 93.

41   TWHF 58.

42   M 116.

43   TWHF 255.

44   TWHF 216.

45   M 138 n. In contrast to Lewis and Tolkien, twentieth-century anthropologists and psychologists typically offer naturalistic or structuralist explanations of the development of myths. Lewis jabs at such explanations by having Arnom, the new Priest of Ungit, 'talk like a philosopher about the gods' (243), as when he answers Orual's question 'who is Ungit?' by saying 'she signifies the earth, which is the womb and mother of all living things' (281–82).

46   EIC 43–44. Tolkien says that mythical stories talk about 'permanent and fundamental things': 'On Fairy-Stories', in *Essays Presented to Charles Williams*, ed. C.S. Lewis (Oxford: Oxford University Press, 1947), 77.

47   GMA p. xxxii.

48   Lewis's fullest and clearest explanation can be found in SBJ, 205–07.

49   'Meditation in a Toolshed', EC 608.

50   'Myth Became Fact', EC 140.

51   'Myth Became Fact', EC 141.

52   TWHF 319–20.

53   Kallistos Ware, 'God of the Fathers: C.S. Lewis and Eastern Christianity', in *The Pilgrim's Guide: C.S. Lewis and the Art of Witness*, ed. David Mills (Grand Rapids: Eerdmans, 1998), 56, 58.

54   Michael Ward, *Planet Narnia: The Seven Heavens in the Imagination of C.S. Lewis* (New York: Oxford University Press, 2008), 227.

55 TWHF 142–43, 159, 258–59.
56 TWHF 109.
57 TWHF 58.
58 TWHF 69.
59 TWHF 74.
60 M 119.
61 M 118. A turning point in Lewis's return to Christianity occurred when an atheist, T.D. Weldon, said to him one evening, 'Rum thing, ... all that stuff of Frazer's about the Dying God. Rum thing. It almost looks as if it had really happened once' (SBJ 211). That later became the central point in 'Myth Became Fact': 'The heart of Christianity is a myth which is also a fact. The old myth of the Dying God, *without ceasing to be myth*, comes down from the heaven of legend and imagination to the earth of history. It *happens* – at a particular date, in a particular place' (EC 141).
62 TWHF 243.
63 Letter to Clyde S. Kilby, 10 Feb. 1957 (CLIII 830). The Latin is from Tertullian's *Apology* 17, 6.
64 M 122.
65 M 122.
66 TWHF 319.
67 TWHF 130.
68 TWHF 319.

21 Poet

MALCOLM GUITE

The range and depth of Lewis's engagement with poetry as a scholar and critic is undisputed. *The Allegory of Love* and *A Preface to Paradise Lost* continue to serve as widely read authoritative guides to understanding and enjoying the best of medieval and Renaissance poetry. Their style, lucidity and sheer wealth of illustration give glimpses of a richly furnished mind, passionate about both the substance and technique of poetry. Lewis's own efforts as a poet, by contrast, are barely known and have received little scholarly attention. There is only one substantial book on his verse[1] and a small tally of articles or chapters in the massive secondary literature on Lewis. In the best of these, which contains fine analyses of a number of Lewis's poems, Charles Huttar writes: 'By age 30 it appears Lewis had ... settled for the rank, in poetry, of a minor figure. Barring a major revolution in taste, he will never be accorded a higher position.'[2]

The time has come to revisit this judgement, made many years ago, and to look afresh at Lewis's poetic output. Was this great exponent of the art of poetry in others himself only a minor versifier? In this chapter I propose to revise our assessment of Lewis by re-examining his supposed antipathy to T.S. Eliot and modernism, which has hitherto excluded him from consideration as a successful modern poet, and by re-reading his poetry in four other contexts which have assumed new importance in the years since his death and which may hint at just such a 'revolution of taste' as Huttar bars from the reckoning.

First, however, we need to make clear the variety and extent of Lewis's compositions in verse. Lewis wrote poetry, both lyric and narrative, throughout his life. The two volumes published in his lifetime were *Spirits in Bondage: A Cycle of Lyrics* (1919) and the long narrative poem *Dymer* (1926, reissued 1950). Many of his lyrics were published in journals, often under pseudonyms. Some were also published as part of his allegorical work, *The Pilgrim's Regress*. The lyrics were collected and published posthumously in 1964 and in a second, expanded edition, which included the whole of *Spirits in Bondage*, in 1994; and some, though not all, of his considerable body of narrative verse is gathered in *Narrative Poems* (1969). Some poems not collected in any of these places are to be found scattered through the three volumes of his collected letters and others are now available in the appendices to Don W. King's study, *C.S. Lewis: Poet*. A few remaining works, mostly very minor, but including his translation of the first four books of the *Aeneid*, are still to be published.

So it is only in the last few decades that we have had a chance to look through the whole range (or very nearly the whole range) of his output and make an evaluation, and the range is indeed astonishing. The lyrics cover everything from poetry of the Great War tinged with the influence of Yeats and the French symbolists to satiric verse and epigrams modelled on Horace and Juvenal, rumbustious pieces in the manner of Chesterton, delicate elegies, complex metrical experiments, and imaginative pseudo-pagan panegyrics set alongside chastened meditative examples of classic Christian *examen*. The range of the narrative verse is just as wide. *Dymer* is an emblematic self-made myth of rebellion, death and resurrection written in nine cantos of rhyme royal. *The Queen of Drum* is five cantos of mixed metres strangely combining contemporary political comment on the rise of fascism with a profound meditation on the place of Faerie and hence the role of imagination in both religious and public life. There is a long fragment of Arthurian verse called *Lancelot* which is perhaps too indebted to Tennyson to exhibit Lewis's greatest powers, and then a very fine poem in 742 lines of alliterative verse, entitled by its editor *The Nameless Isle* and dealing at depth and in rich symbolism with the reconciliation and concord of the divided powers of reason and imagination, such a central theme to all Lewis's work, as we shall discuss further below. King's study also includes a fascinating fragment of a long narrative autobiographical poem modelled on Wordsworth's *Prelude*. All these require a much more thorough reassessment and re-reading than space here allows, especially in light of the substantial cultural changes that have occurred since Lewis's death. Developments in economics, science and ecological awareness, as well as changes in the way we appreciate poetry and the role we see for imagination in modelling all our knowledge, mean that we are now in a position to appreciate the prophetic element in Lewis's work and see him more as a prescient foreshadower of our current concerns than merely as a medieval scholar who had locked himself in fantasies of the past. In the rest of this essay I shall sketch out some of the lines of enquiry such a thoroughgoing reassessment might pursue.

As noted above, I suggest five particular contexts in which we might come to revaluate Lewis's poetry and its place in the wider canon of twentieth-century verse: (1) Eliot and modernism; (2) war poetry; (3) Yeats and Irish writing; (4) ecological consciousness and protest; and finally (5) the contemporary debate between reason and imagination as ways of knowing. For this last context we will read him in company with his fellow Inklings, paying attention especially to their effort to discern and embody meaning in new mythic and imaginative structures, which they called 'mythopoeia' and which was at the heart of all their endeavours.

LEWIS, ELIOT AND MODERNISM

Readers of Lewis's *Collected Poems* are confronted on the first page by a poem called 'A Confession' which at first blush seems little more than one long petulant dig at Eliot and in particular at 'The Love Song of J. Alfred Prufrock',[3] with Lewis taking the blunt persona of the 'common man', a persona that served him well in apologetics but does not suit his verse:

> I am so coarse, the things the poets see
> Are obstinately invisible to me.
> For twenty years I've stared my level best
> To see if evening – any evening – would suggest
> A patient etherised upon a table;
> In vain. I simply wasn't able.[4]

It's not a good start and not the opening Lewis probably would have chosen for his collected poems if he had been able to publish them in his lifetime. It sets up the reader to look for an obstinate belligerence which is just the caricature of Lewis held in literary circles and much of the wider academic world. It is made worse by the fact that sensitive readers of Eliot's verse know perfectly well that Eliot's simile is intended to suggest Prufrock's interior state and not to describe the sunset, something Lewis himself also knew.[5]

This brash opening to *Collected Poems* might suggest that 'Eliot and modernism' is a context from which Lewis has deliberately excluded himself, yet it is the most important context for a thoughtful reassessment of his poetry. It is well known that Lewis was not persuaded by the revolution in poetic technique and sensibility ushered in by *Prufrock and Other Observations* in 1917 and that he made Eliot and his poetry the locus and symbol of those aspects of the 'modern' world he was trying to oppose and criticize. It is equally well known that he had a number of public academic disputes with Eliot as a critic, particularly about Milton's place in the canon, but also about the modernist dismissal of Romanticism. Lewis blamed I.A. Richards as a theorist, and Eliot as a poet, for an attack on 'stock responses' (Richards's term) which, for Lewis, undermined the very heart and purpose of European poetry.[6] But this is only one half of the story, for Lewis and Eliot later came to know one another well, reconciling many of their differences and finding a great deal in common through, but also beyond, their common conversion to the Christian faith. George Watson goes so far as to say that Lewis's initial 'bitter campaign against literary modernism was radically misconceived. It took no account of T.S. Eliot's dedicated Anglicanism, not far distant from Lewis's, or of the deep traditionalism of Eliot's own sense of the past. Lewis and Eliot were adversaries who might almost have been blood brothers'.[7]

This idea needs to be pursued a little further. Lewis has been marginalized as a poet as a direct consequence of his self-distancing from literary modernism, which was the central path of the best of his contemporary poets, but when we actually look at the modernist agenda, and particularly at Eliot's own criteria for effective, original poetry, we can see that Lewis himself was engaged in similar tasks with a success that can be judged by just those criteria. In 'Tradition and the Individual Talent',[8] Eliot wrote that the modern poet must write with awareness

> not only of the pastness of the past, but of its presence; the historical sense compels a man to write not merely with his own generation in his bones, but with a feeling that the whole of the literature of Europe from Homer and within it the whole of the literature of his own country, has a simultaneous existence and composes a simultaneous order ... No poet, no artist of any art, has his complete meaning alone ... [W]hat happens when a new work of art is created is something that happens simultaneously to all the works of art which preceded it.[9]

This important passage, so formative for the poetry of the twentieth century, gives us some key ideas for reading and understanding Lewis as a modern (in spite of himself).

Lewis certainly had the historical sense of which Eliot speaks. He lived and breathed poetry from Homer onwards, knew much of most major poets by heart and his work in both poetry and prose is rich with allusions to and echoes of the whole European canon. Whilst he begins his poetic career, as Eliot did, with pastiche and archaism, he rapidly progressed to a more mature and nuanced conversation with poets of the past. In a poem such as 'The Turn of the Tide',[10] for example, he has a sustained conversation with Milton's 'Ode on the Morning of Christ's Nativity', not simply echoing it, but reimagining and re-creating it in contemporary idiom. Indeed, Huttar has argued that 'The Turn of the Tide' takes its point of departure from Lewis's own debate with Eliot about how far and in what ways modern poets can be influenced by Milton without being corrupted by imitation of his style.[11]

Eliot's notion of literature forming a simultaneous order in which each new writer reveals significance and meaning in previous writers is also helpful as we approach Lewis's poetry. I will argue below that the work of the Great War poets, the achievements in Irish poetry in the years since Lewis's death, and the emergence of a literature of ecological awareness have all changed the way in which we are now able to read Lewis. As Eliot argued, the past is 'altered by the present as much as the present is directed by the past'.[12]

Another of Eliot's key ideas is that the poet serves the work rather than giving vent to his private personality or perspectives. So Eliot writes of the ideal poet: 'What happens is a continual surrender of himself as he is at the moment to something which is more valuable. The progress of an artist is a continual self-sacrifice, a continual extinction of personality.'[13] Lewis would have agreed completely and this is indeed what he was arguing in *The Personal Heresy*.[14]

Another substantial and common concern between Lewis and the modernists resided in the arena of myth and mythic structure. Eliot, Pound and Joyce were not, as Lewis supposed, ignoring or denigrating the great myths of the ancient world in a search for merely modern novelty. They worked with myth not as a surface 'poetical decoration' but as a substantial, artistically formative inner structure, as Joyce does with *Ulysses* and Eliot with the mythic structure of the Fisher-King in *The Waste Land*. Now this is just what Lewis himself was doing and his late prose masterpiece, *Till We Have Faces*, is just such a reworking of mythic material to express contemporary insights and dilemmas.

Lewis's disagreement with the modernists was less about the importance of poetry itself within the wider tradition than it was about form and prosody. Lewis wrongly blamed Eliot for the departure of English poetry from rhyme and metre and its apparent suspicion of beauty and pleasure. He attacked Eliot when what he was really objecting to was undisciplined *vers libre*. But that battle is over and need not be fought again on either side. The vogue for 'free verse' associated with the name of Eliot is already at an end; witness Geoffrey Hill's mastery of the sonnet, and Derek Walcott's revival of *terza rima*.[15] Such developments make Lewis's defence of traditional forms look in some respects more like the work of a pioneer than a nostalgic sideshow.

However, the final and most important sense in which Lewis and Eliot were 'adversaries who might almost have been blood brothers' is in their common concern for the nature of language itself, its limits and possibilities and the poet's responsibilities in developing and deepening the way we use it:

> 'Since our concern was speech, and speech impelled us
> To purify the dialect of the tribe ...'

These words from 'Little Gidding',[16] which Eliot imagines himself sharing with Dante, would also apply equally to a conversation between Eliot and Lewis (who, incidentally, also had in common a love of Dante as the supreme poet and guide of other poets[17]). It is instructive to compare the places in their poetry where Eliot and Lewis address the problems and possibilities of language in similar terms. For both of them the key is in the relation between Word and words, between the Logos (the Johannine *Creator*: transcendent, unfragmented, the meaning behind all meaning) and the many and derivative words of the *creature* (fragmented and constantly needing to be remade).

In 'Burnt Norton', for example, Eliot writes about the difficulties of using time-bound language in the face of the eternal:

> Words strain,
> Crack and sometimes break, under the burden,
> Under the tension, slip, slide, perish,
> Decay with imprecision, will not stay in place,
> Will not stay still.
> ...
> The Word in the desert
> Is most attacked by the voices of temptation...[18]

These are precisely Lewis's own concerns. In 'The Country of the Blind',[19] a parable poem that strangely anticipates Seamus Heaney's experiments in *The Haw Lantern*,[20] Lewis revisits the cliché that 'In the country of the blind, the one-eyed man is king' and suggests rather that the one-eyed man would be made a pariah in that country, always misunderstood because he would have no words for his experience, would have to speak metaphorically, but the metaphor itself would be evacuated of its meaning. It is as if he

> Knew too much to be clear, could not explain. The words –
> Sold, raped, flung to the dogs – now could avail no more.[21]

Like Eliot, Lewis acknowledges the difficulties inherent in the use of language but does not despair. They both allow language to bear witness to its own inadequacies and to point beyond itself. So Eliot adds in parenthesis at the height of 'The Dry Salvages':

> These are only hints and guesses,
> Hints followed by guesses …[22]

Lewis finds hope in a language that acknowledges its limitations and leads into silence, as in the moving conclusion to 'The Apologist's Evening Prayer':

> Thoughts are but coins. Let me not trust, instead
> Of Thee, their thin-worn image of Thy head.
> From all my thoughts, even from my thoughts of Thee
> O Thou fair silence, fall and set me free …[23]

And he expresses a similar hope in 'Footnote to All Prayers':

> all men are idolaters, crying unheard
> To a deaf idol, if Thou take them at their word.
> Take not, oh Lord, our literal sense. Lord, in Thy great
> Unbroken speech our limping metaphor translate.[24]

Both poets wanted language to bring us to its own brink and both use words which carry an urgency impelling us beyond themselves.[25]

A fuller study of Lewis's long and complex relations with Eliot – personal, poetic and critical – might well serve to relocate Lewis closer to the mainstream of modern English verse, which Eliot's practice and theory did so much to channel and direct and from which Lewis has wrongly been thought to have excluded himself.

LEWIS AS A WAR POET

Like Wilfred Owen and Siegfried Sassoon, and indeed like his future friend, J.R.R. Tolkien, Lewis saw active service in the Great War. Unlike Owen and Sassoon, Lewis has never been regarded formally as one of 'the War Poets', even though he wrote and published many poems inspired by his wartime experiences. Once again we can now look back and see things differently. Recent work by T.A. Shippey and John Garth[26] has shown conclusively how much of Tolkien's supposedly 'uninfluenced' fantasy writing was a deeply felt response to his time in the trenches and can be read with new understanding as 'war poetry'. Lewis should also be regarded as one of the group that Shippey calls 'traumatised authors'.[27] He deals directly with his war experience in *Spirits in Bondage*, indirectly in *Dymer*. 'French Nocturne (*Monchy-Le-Preux*)' is a good example of the direct approach and also shows the young Lewis, strongly atheist at that point and deeply suspicious of easy poeticisms, deploying just the kind of symbolist poetic technique that Eliot had used in 'Prufrock' two years earlier, in which 'exterior' landscape is given symbolic rather than naturalistic colouring and becomes an emblem of the poet's own dislocated sensibility:

> The pale, green moon is riding overhead.
> The jaws of a sacked village, stark and grim,
> Out on the ridge have swallowed up the sun,
> And in one angry streak his blood has run,
> To left and right along the horizon dim.[28]

Though 'horizon dim' is an awkward inversion too redolent of Victorian 'poeticism', the rest of this verse is strikingly modern. The image of sunset as a long thin streak of blood is uncannily like the image implicit in Eliot's evening 'spread out against the sky | Like a patient etherised upon a table',[29] and is deployed for much the same purpose. 'Nocturne' ends on an entirely bleak note: the Moon, so long the symbol of hope or beauty for poets, is just 'a stone', and as for dreaming poets and their humanity,

> What call have I to dream of anything?
> I am a wolf. Back to the world again
> And speech of fellow brutes that once were men.
> Our throats can bark for slaughter: cannot sing.[30]

After *Spirits in Bondage* came *Dymer*. It is vitiated by archaisms and lapses into Parnassian poetic diction forced on him by the decision to sustain the whole thing in rhyme royal, and also weakened, for some readers, by the obscurity of the self-made myth that forms its plot.[31] However, it was a vehicle through which, in passages of lyric intensity, he was able to embody some of the most dreadful images of the war, rather as Tolkien was later to embody imagery of the trenches in the landscape of the Dead Marshes of Middle-earth. For example, this description of the wasteland in which Dymer's last battle takes place:

> It was a ruinous land. The ragged stumps
> Of broken trees rose out of endless clay
> Naked of flower and grass: the slobbering humps
> Divided the dead pools. Against the grey
> A shattered village gaped.[32]

Lewis has been neglected as a war poet but has a claim to be read and anthologized alongside the better-known names, and this is beginning to happen. He is included, for example, in the recent anthology of Irish war poetry, *Earth Voices Whispering*.[33]

LEWIS, YEATS AND THE IRISH TRADITION

This anthology brings us to the next frame within which to assess Lewis's poetic achievement. Recent work on Lewis has come more and more to see him as an Irish writer,[34] to see that his sense both of landscape and language arise as much out of his County Down childhood and lifelong visits to the land of his birth as from the Oxford where he lived following his matriculation into the university in 1917.[35] His attitude to Yeats is a useful touchstone here, as well as shedding further light on Lewis's approach to modernism.

In a letter to his Belfast friend Arthur Greeves, in which the young Lewis discovers Yeats for the first time as an 'unknown' poet, he writes: 'I have here discovered an author exactly after my own heart, whom I am sure you would delight in, W.B. Yeats. He writes plays and poems of rare spirit and beauty about our old Irish mythology.'[36] This is fascinating both because it locates Lewis's own early poetic efforts, which have equally the graces and the faults of the Celtic Twilight movement, and also because it shows his strong literary and imaginative identification with Ireland: '*our* Old Irish mythology'. Later in Lewis's poetic development, Yeats puts in another appearance as the magician in *Dymer*.[37] Dymer first senses his approach in lines which glance a little at Yeats's 'Isle of Innisfree' with its 'bee-loud glade':

> he heard the noise of bees
> And saw far off, in the blue shade between
> The windless elms, one walking on the green.[38]

More interesting still is the prose preface Lewis wrote 24 years later when *Dymer* was republished. Having apologized for making the

Yeats-like magician one of the villains in the story, he goes on to pay this tribute to Yeats, which also tells us a great deal about Lewis's perspective on his own poetic theory and practice:

> Since his great name comes before us let me take the opportunity of saluting his genius; a genius so potent that having first revivified and transmuted the romantic tradition which he found almost on its deathbed (and invented a new kind of blank verse in the process) he could then go on to weather one of the bitterest literary revolutions we have known, embark on a second career, and, as it were with one hand, play most of the moderns off the field at their own game.[39]

There is a great deal to ponder here. It is a good assessment of Yeats, but I wonder if it is also a confession of Lewis's own failed ambitions. Certainly *Dymer* was an attempt in Lewis's own terms to revivify and transmute the Romantic tradition, but if Lewis's attempt failed in verse it more than succeeded in his later prose romances. It is interesting that he praises Yeats for metrical innovation, for it is in the matter of his intense love of metrics, prosody and verbal dexterity, his obsession with varieties of rhyme (half, slant, internal and oblique), that Lewis is arguably at his most Irish.

Readers of poems like 'A Metrical Experiment' and 'Two Kinds of Memory' will be struck by the effects, sometimes dazzling but more often subtle and unnoticed on first reading, of his sound-patterning. It goes far beyond ordinary end-stopped rhyme, summoning all the possibilities of echo and allusion, of that parley between hope and memory which is inherent in rhyme itself, of what Lewis calls that 'sport that mingles | Sound with senses, in subtle pattern, | Words in wedlock.'[40] Huttar has a fine analysis of some of these, pointing out that well over one quarter of the poems in his posthumously collected poems 'exemplify his fascination with the most unlikely ways in which words might echo one another'.[41]

Lewis can be compared fruitfully with a number of contemporary Irish poets (Michael Longley for his considered and affectionate classicism; Seamus Heaney for craft, form, music and an attention to the particular which only subtly reveals itself to be emblematic of the universal; Derek Mahon for the terse satiric voice that lifts unexpectedly into elegy), but in this matter of prosody, of sheer craft and attention to the sound of poetry, the closest comparison is with Paul Muldoon.[42] In his 1998 Clarendon Lectures,[43] Muldoon draws our attention to Swift's coinage of the half-rhyme as distinctively 'Irish rhyme', by which he means a readiness to rhyme words like *dean* and *gain* that 'seems to go with a certain Irishness of idiom'.[44]

These resemblances are interesting in light of Lewis's own correspondence with other poets on the subject. He was an admirer of Ruth Pitter's work and in correspondence with her he confesses, 'I am enamoured of metrical subtleties – not as a game: the truth is I often lust after a metre as a man lusts after a woman',[45] an idea which would delight Muldoon, for whose work the interplay between verbal and erotic tension is central. Reflecting on this consonance in technique between Lewis and Muldoon, Adam Crothers, an Irish poet currently researching Muldoon's prosody, comments: 'T.S. Eliot suggests that the ghost of iambic pentameter haunts all lines of English poetry; it seems that the time-travelling ghost of Muldoonian end rhyme haunts Lewis's verse.'[46]

LEWIS, BARFIELD AND DEEP ECOLOGY

The fourth frame through which we can continue our re-evaluation of Lewis's poetic achievement is that of ecological consciousness, prophecy or protest. For all the differences that he and Barfield hammered out in their 'Great War',[47] Lewis remained convinced of Barfield's thesis that modern humanity had lost a primary, participative consciousness and that our current mode of consciousness has led to a crisis of meaning for ourselves and our environment.[48] Both Barfield and Lewis believed that this tragic alienation from nature could be overcome, though in different ways. For Barfield it would come from the Christian 'evolution of consciousness'; for Lewis it would come with a catastrophic death and rebirth of humanity and nature centred in and patterned on the death and resurrection of Christ. Both men, though, wanted to use the power of language to make that 'felt change of consciousness' as Barfield defined it in *Poetic Diction*,[49] to begin to effect changes for the better now.

Readers of poems like Lewis's 'The Future of Forestry' will recognize an early voice of ecological protest and perhaps be put in mind of Larkin's fine poem 'Going, Going':

> I thought it would last my time –
> The sense that, beyond the town,
> There would always be fields and farms,
> Where the village louts would climb

Such trees as were not cut down;
…
For the first time I feel somehow
That it isn't going to last,

That before I snuff it, the whole
Boiling will be bricked in
Except for the tourist parts –
First slum of Europe: a role
It won't be hard to win,
With a cast of crooks and tarts.

And that will be England gone…[50]

So Larkin in 1972, but as early as 1938 Lewis had written:

How will the legend of the age of trees
Feel, when the last tree falls in England?
When the concrete spreads and the town conquers
The country's heart; when contraceptive
Tarmac's laid where farm has faded,
Tramline flows where slept a hamlet
And shop-fronts, blazing without a stop from
Dover to Wrath, have glazed us over?[51]

But whereas Larkin's poem is a querulous one-off (and, moreover, commissioned by the Department of the Environment), it is not so with Lewis. Behind Lewis's poems of protest lies a profound exploration of just those altered modes of consciousness which are called for by contemporary exponents of 'deep ecology'; in verse as well as prose Lewis is unsurpassed at suggesting these. In 'The Adam at Night', for example, he tries to imagine and express Barfield's notion of an original or unfallen human participation in a wider cosmic consciousness, suggesting a reintegration of the inner microcosm of human perception and consciousness with the outer macrocosm of natural phenomena, in language which strongly anticipates the first flowering of deep ecology in the writings of the counter-culture in the 1960s:

he would set ajar
The door of his mind. Into him thoughts would pour
Other than day's. He rejoined Earth, his mother.
He melted into her nature.[52]

In 'Pan's Purge' Lewis expresses in verse something very like the scenario that would be suggested years later by James Lovelock in the Gaia hypothesis and *The Revenge of Gaia*.[53] The poem begins:

> I dreamt that all the planning of peremptory humanity
> Had crushed nature finally below the foot of man ...

But then the reaction comes and Nature, personified here as Pan rather than Gaia, 'came, with sleet and shipwreck, for the doom of man'.[54] So, from speculation about early consciousness, through warnings of present danger, to personal attempts at suggesting the new modes of knowing and feeling we need in order to respond to our environmental crisis, Lewis as a poet is in advance of his times and profoundly relevant to ours.[55]

THE INKLINGS AND MYTHOPOEIA

This leads us to the final context in which to reconsider Lewis's achievement. Lewis and Barfield were profoundly aware of the deep and interrelated crises of spiritual meaning on the one hand, and of environmental catastrophe on the other, which are the legacy of the twentieth century. Their great project, together with some of the other members of the Inklings, notably Tolkien and Charles Williams, was to heal the widening split between outer and inner, rational and imaginative, microcosm and macrocosm.[56] They aimed to do so by using the power of poetic language in verse and prose to effect a 'felt change of consciousness', to heighten and deepen our awareness by re-enchanting the disenchanted, by remythologizing a demythologized world.[57]

Lewis had discerned the key symptom of the twentieth-century crisis, a paralysing split between reason and imagination, because he found it in the depths of his own psyche. He expressed it thus in prose, reflecting not only on the divided state of his own mind but also that of the wider culture:

> Such then was the state of my imaginative life; over against it
> stood the life of my intellect. The two hemispheres of my mind
> were in the sharpest contrast. On the one side a many-islanded sea
> of poetry and myth; on the other a glib and shallow 'rationalism'.
> Nearly all that I loved I believed to be imaginary; nearly all that
> I believed to be real I thought grim and meaningless.[58]

This bifurcation of vision between reason and imagination is also the subject of one of his best poems, 'Reason', written probably in the late 1920s or early 1930s, the first fourteen lines of which run as follows:

Set on the soul's acropolis the reason stands
A virgin arm'd, commercing with celestial light,
And he who sins against her has defiled his own
Virginity: no cleansing makes his garment white;
So clear is reason. But how dark, imagining,
Warm, dark, obscure and infinite, daughter of Night:
Dark is her brow, the beauty of her eyes with sleep
Is loaded, and her pains are long, and her delight.
Tempt not Athene. Wound not in her fertile pains
Demeter, nor rebel against her mother-right.
Oh who will reconcile in me both maid and mother,
Who make in me a concord of the depth and height?
Who make imagination's dim exploring touch
Ever report the same as intellectual sight?[59]

There are a number of remarkable things going on in this poem. First is the sense of inner space, of height and depth in the psyche itself. The soul, the inner Athens, has its heights, its Acropolis, but also depths and caves. Second, there is the bodying forth of the soul's distinct powers of reason and imagination in the form of the two goddesses, Athene and Demeter. This is no glib classical allusion in the eighteenth-century manner, but a symbolic reimagination of the inner self in which more than personal, perhaps more than human, powers are at work, and it is highly significant that both these powers are figured as feminine, for the plea in lines 11–12 ('Oh who will reconcile in me both maid and mother, | Who make in me a concord of the depth and height?') subtly summons the echoes of its own answer. These lines point and give new significance to the paradox of incarnation which is at the heart of the integrative faith which Lewis was on the cusp of embracing when he wrote this poem. The pagan goddesses must be *either* maid *or* mother, but the Virgin Mary, in whom their numina is subsumed for Christian devotion, is *both* maid *and* mother. In and through her '*Ecce ancilla Domini*', the archetypal assent of all faith, Christ the reconciler comes into the world, the one who not only reconciles man to God and time to eternity, but is also in himself the concord of all 'breadth, and length, and depth, and height' (the language of the poem surely glances at Eph. 3.17–19). However, these are of course anticipatory echoes only; the poem as it stands witnesses to an impasse and points to a hoped-for 'concord' which has not yet arrived. When it arrives, if it arrives, then and only then – in the words of the closing couplet – will the poet be able to say 'and not deceive, | Then wholly say, that I BELIEVE.'[60]

The way Lewis found out of this impasse was at once spiritual, theological and literary, and it brings us to the heart of both his Christian belief and his poetic theory and practice. In the person of Jesus Christ he sees the relinking of the dimensions of our divided being. Lewis's great task at a personal and devotional level was obedient and humble reintegration of his rational and imaginative powers under the guidance of the shaping and creative Word of God incarnate in Christ, but this became also his vocation as a writer. There is no place in his poetic theory for false 'originality', for a fragmented or privatized vision, because the task of the poet, as he sees it, is not simply to comment privately on our present disintegration of sensibility but to learn afresh the profound and given, unfallen 'stock responses' to all that is 'given' of God. Because Christ is the Logos who is himself a *mimesis* (imitation) of the Father, so a return to poetic *mimesis* can become a kind of *imitatio Christi*.[61]

CONCLUSION

Lewis has sometimes been dismissed as archaic and eccentric, but in retrospect his efforts in poetry, as in other fields, are much more contemporary, much more keenly directed to the crises of modernity, than he has been given credit for. There are many and complex links between his work and that of his two great contemporaries, Yeats and Eliot. He is not perhaps a great poet in the same sense that they are, but he is a great deal better than the long neglect of his verse would imply. There is an internal coherence between all his efforts in every field. Taken together these efforts constitute an attempt at the redemptive reintegration of reason and imagination, the broken modes of our being and knowing. His poetry thus deserves to be reread, more widely studied, and anthologized. It is the concentrated epitome of a timely, and as yet incomplete, project of reintegration.

Notes

1 Don W. King, *C.S. Lewis, Poet: The Legacy of His Poetic Impulse* (Kent, OH: Kent State University Press, 2001).
2 Charles A. Huttar, 'A Life-long Love-affair with Language', in Peter J. Schakel and Charles A. Huttar (eds), *Word and Story in C.S. Lewis* (Columbia, MO: University of Missouri Press, 1991), 86.
3 T.S. Eliot, 'The Love Song of J. Alfred Prufrock', in *Collected Poems 1909–1962* (London: Faber & Faber 1974), 13.
4 CP 15.
5 See Huttar, 'A Life-long Love-affair with Language', 94–97.
6 See, for instance, PPL 54–58.

7   George Watson, 'The High Road to Narnia', *American Scholar*, Winter 2009, 89–95.

8   First published in *The Egoist* in September 1919, the same year Lewis published *Spirits in Bondage*.

9   *Selected Prose of T.S. Eliot*, ed. Frank Kermode (London: Faber & Faber, 1975), 38–39.

10   CP 63.

11   See Charles Huttar, 'C.S. Lewis, T.S. Eliot, and the Milton Legacy: The Nativity Ode Revisited', *Texas Studies in Literature and Language* 44 (Fall 2002), 324–48.

12   Eliot, *Selected Prose*, 39.

13   Eliot, *Selected Prose*, 40.

14   PH 4.

15   See Geoffrey Hill, *Tenebrae* (London: Faber & Faber, 1978) and Derek Walcott, *Omeros* (London: Faber & Faber, 1990).

16   Eliot, *Collected Poems*, 218.

17   'In his essay on Dante, Mr Eliot says that he thinks the last canto of the Paradiso "the highest point that poetry has ever reached". I think the same': 'Shelley, Dryden, and Mr Eliot', SLE 203.

18   Eliot, *Collected Poems*, 194.

19   CP 47–48.

20   Seamus Heaney, *The Haw Lantern* (London: Faber & Faber, 1987); see poems such as 'From the Frontier of Writing' and 'From the Canton of Expectation'.

21   CP 48.

22   Eliot, *Collected Poems*, 213.

23   CP 143.

24   CP 143.

25   In Lewis's case a good example is 'At the Fringe of Language', the final chapter of *Studies in Words*.

26   T.A. Shippey, *J.R.R. Tolkien: Author of the Century* (London: HarperCollins, 2001); John Garth, *Tolkien and the Great War: The Threshold of Middle-earth* (London: HarperCollins, 2003).

27   Shippey, *J.R.R. Tolkien, Author of the Century*, p. xxxi.

28   CP 168.

29   Eliot, *Collected Poems*, 13.

30   CP 168.

31   See George Sayer, 'C.S. Lewis's *Dymer*', *SEVEN: An Anglo-American Literary Review* 1 (1980), 94–116.

32   NP 87.

33   *Earth Voices Whispering: An Anthology of Irish War Poetry, 1914–1945*, ed. by Gerald Dawe (Belfast: Blackstaff Press, 2009).

34   For example, Ronald W. Bresland, *The Backward Glance: CS Lewis and Ireland* (Belfast: Institute of Irish Studies, The Queen's University of Belfast, 1999).

35   For the emotional wrench of this and other transitions see 'Leaving Forever the Home of One's Youth' (CP 245) and 'Angel's Song' (CP 121).

36   Letter to Arthur Greeves, 5 June 1914 (CLI 59).

37 Lewis makes explicit the connection between the magician and Yeats in his preface to the 1950 edition of *Dymer*; see NP 6.

38 NP 54.

39 NP 6

40 'The Planets', CP 26.

41 Huttar, 'A Life-long Love-affair with Language', 87.

42 This is not to say that Muldoon and Lewis would agree with one another about life or theology but that they both have the same serious playfulness with language and passion for form.

43 Paul Muldoon, *To Ireland, I* (Oxford: Oxford University Press, 2000).

44 Muldoon, *To Ireland, I*, 116.

45 Letter to Ruth Pitter, 10 Aug. 1946 (CLII 735).

46 Personal correspondence with the author.

47 For an account of this important exchange of ideas see Lionel Adey, *C.S. Lewis' 'Great War' with Owen Barfield* (Victoria, BC: English Literary Studies, University of Victoria, 1978; new edn, Wigton, Cumbria: Ink Books, 2000).

48 For more on Barfield's theories of consciousness, see *Poetic Diction: A Study in Meaning* (1st publ. 1928; 2nd edn, London: Faber & Faber, 1952) and *Saving the Appearances: A Study in Idolatry* (London: Faber & Faber, 1957), and for a collection of essays on the implications of these theories for our current crises of ecology and meaning see *The Rediscovery of Meaning, and Other Essays* (Middletown, CT: Wesleyan University Press, 1977).

49 Barfield, *Poetic Diction*, (2nd edn), 178.

50 Philip Larkin, *High Windows* (London: Faber & Faber, 1974), 21–22.

51 'The Future of Forestry', CP 75.

52 CP 59.

53 James Lovelock, *The Revenge of Gaia: Why the Earth is Fighting Back – and How We Can Still Save Humanity* (London: Penguin, 2007).

54 CP 19.

55 For an exploration of these themes in Lewis's fiction, see Matthew Dickerson and David O'Hara, *Narnia and the Fields of Arbol: The Environmental Vision of C.S. Lewis* (Lexington, KY: University Press of Kentucky, 2006).

56 For a compelling account of the extent to which the Inklings collaborated, see Diana Glyer, *The Company They Keep: C.S. Lewis and J.R.R. Tolkien as Writers in Community* (Kent, OH: Kent State University Press, 2007).

57 Space precludes a fuller analysis of the many instances of Lewis's 'poetic prose', the places in prose works where he rises to more than ordinarily ordered and heightened language to great effect. For an interesting discussion of the heightened prose in *Perelandra* and the way Ruth Pitter rendered it into verse, see King, *C.S. Lewis, Poet*, ch. 9 and app. 1.

58 SBJ 138.

59 CP 95.

60 CP 95.

61 See 'Christianity and Literature', EC 411–20.

Bibliography

Principal works by C.S. Lewis

The Abolition of Man (Glasgow: Collins, 1984 [1943]).

The Allegory of Love: A Study in Medieval Tradition (Oxford: Oxford University Press, 1958 [1936]).

All My Road Before Me: The Diary of C.S. Lewis, 1922–1927, ed. Walter Hooper (London: HarperCollins, 1991).

Arthurian Torso (London: Oxford University Press, 1948).

Boxen: The Imaginary World of the Young C.S. Lewis, ed. Walter Hooper (London: Collins, 1985).

Collected Letters, Volume I, ed. Walter Hooper (London: HarperCollins, 2000).

Collected Letters, Volume II, ed. Walter Hooper (London: HarperCollins, 2004).

Collected Letters, Volume III, ed. Walter Hooper (London: HarperCollins, 2006).

The Collected Poems of C.S. Lewis, ed. Walter Hooper (London: Fount, 1994).

The Dark Tower and Other Stories, ed. Walter Hooper (London: Collins, 1977).

The Discarded Image (Cambridge: Cambridge University Press, 1964).

English Literature in the Sixteenth Century, Excluding Drama (Oxford: Clarendon Press, 1954).

Essay Collection, ed. Lesley Walmsley (London: HarperCollins, 2000).

An Experiment in Criticism (Cambridge: Cambridge University Press, 1961).

The Four Loves (Glasgow: Collins, 1991 [1960]).

George MacDonald: An Anthology (San Francisco: HarperCollins, 2001 [1946]).

The Great Divorce: A Dream (Glasgow: Collins, 1982 [1945]).

A Grief Observed (London: Faber & Faber, 1966 [1961]).

The Horse and His Boy (Glasgow: Fontana Lions, 1980 [1954]).

The Last Battle (Glasgow: Fontana Lions, 1981 [1956]).

Letters, ed. W.H. Lewis (London: Geoffrey Bles, 1960), revd edn, ed. Walter Hooper (London: Fount, 1988).

The Lion, the Witch and the Wardrobe (Glasgow: Fontana Lions, 1982 [1950]).

The Magician's Nephew (Glasgow: Fontana Lions, 1981 [1955]).

Mere Christianity (Glasgow: Collins, 1990 [1952]).

Miracles: A Preliminary Study (London: Geoffrey Bles, 1947).

Miracles: A Preliminary Study, revd edn (Glasgow: Collins, 1980 [1960]).

Narrative Poems, ed. Walter Hooper (London: HarperCollins, 1994).

Of This and Other Worlds, ed. Walter Hooper (London: Collins, 1982).

Out of the Silent Planet (London: Pan, 1983 [1938]).

Perelandra (London: Pan, 1983 [1943]).

The Personal Heresy. A Controversy (London: Oxford University Press, 1965 [1939]).

The Pilgrim's Regress: An Allegorical Apology for Christianity, Reason and Romanticism (Glasgow: Fount, 1980 [1933]).

Prayer: Letters to Malcolm (London: Collins, 1983 [1964]).

A Preface to Paradise Lost (Oxford: Oxford University Press, 1984 [1942]).

Present Concerns: Ethical Essays, ed. Walter Hooper (Glasgow: Collins, 1986).

Prince Caspian: The Return to Narnia (Glasgow: Fontana Lions, 1981 [1951]).

The Problem of Pain (Glasgow: Collins, 1983 [1940]).

Reflections on the Psalms (Glasgow: Collins, 1984 [1958]).

Rehabilitations and Other Essays (London: Oxford University Press, 1939).

The Screwtape Letters (Glasgow: Collins, 1982 [1942]).

Selected Literary Essays, ed. Walter Hooper (Cambridge: Cambridge University Press, 1969).

The Silver Chair (Glasgow: Fontana Lions, 1981 [1953]).

Spenser's Images of Life, ed. Alastair Fowler (Cambridge: Cambridge University Press, 1967).

Studies in Medieval and Renaissance Literature, ed. Walter Hooper (Cambridge: Cambridge University Press, 1966).

Studies in Words (Cambridge: Cambridge University Press, 1960).

Surprised by Joy: The Shape of My Early Life (Glasgow: Collins, 1982 [1955]).

That Hideous Strength: A Modern Fairy-tale for Grown-ups (London: Pan, 1983 [1945]).

Till We Have Faces: A Myth Retold (Glasgow: Collins, 1985 [1956]).

Undeceptions: Essays on Theology and Ethics, ed. Walter Hooper (London: Geoffrey Bles, 1971). Known as *God in the Dock* in the United States.

The Voyage of the 'Dawn Treader' (Glasgow: Fontana Lions, 1981 [1952]).

Principal works on C.S. Lewis

Adey, Lionel, *C.S. Lewis' 'Great War' with Owen Barfield* (Wigton, Cumbria: Ink Books, 2002).

  C.S. Lewis: Writer, Dreamer and Mentor (Grand Rapids: Eerdmans, 1998).

  'Medievalism in the Space Trilogy of C.S. Lewis', *Studies in Medievalism* 3 (1991), 279–89.

Anscombe, G.E.M., 'Reply to Mr C.S. Lewis's Argument that "Naturalism" is self-refuting', in *Collected Philosophical Papers. Vol. II: Metaphysics and the Philosophy of Mind* (Minneapolis: University of Minnesota Press, 1981), 224–32.

Atherstone, Andrew (ed.), *The Heart of Faith: Following Christ in the Church of England* (Cambridge: Lutterworth Press, 2008).

Avis, Paul, *God and the Creative Imagination: Metaphor, Symbol and Myth in Religion and Theology* (London: Routledge, 1999).

Baggett, David, Gary R. Habermas, and Jerry Walls (eds), *C.S. Lewis as Philosopher: Truth, Goodness and Beauty* (Downers Grove, IL: IVP Academic, 2008).

Barbour, Brian, 'Lewis and Cambridge', *Modern Philology*, 94:4 (May 1999), 439–84.

Barfield, Owen, *Owen Barfield on C.S. Lewis*, ed. G.B. Tennyson (Middletown, CT: Wesleyan University Press, 1989).

Poetic Diction: A Study in Meaning, 2nd edn (London: Faber & Faber, 1952).

Barrington-Ward, Simon, 'The Uncontemporary Apologist', *Theology 68* (1965), 103–08.

Bartlett, Sally A., 'Humanistic Psychology in C.S. Lewis's *Till We Have Faces: A Feminist Critique*', *Studies in the Literary Imagination* 22:2 (Fall 1989), 185–98.

Bennett, J.A.W., *The Humane Medievalist: An Inaugural Lecture* (London: Cambridge University Press, 1965).

Beversluis, John, *C.S. Lewis and the Search for Rational Religion*, 2nd edn (Amherst, NY: Prometheus Books, 2007).

Bresland, Ronald W., *The Backward Glance: C.S. Lewis and Ireland* (Belfast: Institute of Irish Studies, 1999).

Campbell, David C., and Dale E. Hess, 'Olympian Detachment: A Critical Look at the World of C.S. Lewis's Characters', *Studies in the Literary Imagination*, 22:2 (Fall 1989), 199–215.

Cantor, Norman F., *Inventing the Middle Ages: The Lives, Works, and Ideas of the Great Medievalists of the Twentieth Century* (Cambridge: Lutterworth Press, 1991).

Carnell, Corbin Scott, *Bright Shadow of Reality: C.S. Lewis and the Feeling Intellect* (Grand Rapids: Eerdmans, 1974).

Carpenter, Humphrey, *The Inklings: C.S. Lewis, J.R.R. Tolkien, Charles Williams, and Their Friends* (London: HarperCollins, 2006).

Christensen, Michael J., *C.S. Lewis on Scripture: His Thoughts on the Nature of Biblical Inspiration, the Role of Revelation, and the Question of Inerrancy* (Nashville: Abingdon, 1989).

Cole, Darrell, 'C.S. Lewis on Pacifism, War, and the Christian Warrior', *Touchstone: A Journal of Mere Christianity 16:3* (Apr. 2003); available at <www.touchstonemag.com/archives/article.php?id=16-03-045-f>.

Como, James T., *Branches to Heaven: The Geniuses of C.S. Lewis* (Dallas: Spence Publishing, 1999).

(ed.), *Remembering C.S. Lewis: Recollections of Those Who Knew Him* (San Francisco: Ignatius Press, 2005).

Cuneo, Andrew P., 'Selected Literary Letters of C.S. Lewis' (unpubl. D.Phil. diss., University of Oxford, 2001).

Cunningham, Richard B., *C.S. Lewis: Defender of the Faith* (Philadelphia: Westminster Press, 1967).

Daigle, Marsha A., 'Dante's *Divine Comedy* and the Fiction of C.S. Lewis' (unpubl. Ph.D. diss., University of Michigan, 1984).

Derrick, Christopher, *C. S. Lewis and the Church of Rome: A Study in Proto-ecumenism* (San Francisco: Ignatius Press, 1981).

Dickerson, Matthew, and David O'Hara, *Narnia and the Fields of Arbol: The Environmental Vision of C.S. Lewis* (Lexington: University Press of Kentucky, 2006).

Dorsett, Lyle, *Seeking the Secret Place: The Spiritual Formation of C.S. Lewis* (Grand Rapids: Brazos Press, 2004).

Downing, David C., *Into the Region of Awe: Mysticism in C.S. Lewis* (Downers Grove, IL: InterVarsity Press, 2005).

    Planets in Peril: A Critical Study of C.S. Lewis's Ransom Trilogy (Amherst, MA: University of Massachusetts Press, 1992).

Duriez, Colin, *J.R.R. Tolkien and C.S. Lewis: The Story of Their Friendship* (Stroud: Sutton Publishing, 2003).

Edwards, Bruce L. (ed.), *C.S. Lewis: Life, Works and Legacy*, 4 vols (Westport, CT: Praeger, 2007).

    (ed.), *The Taste of the Pineapple: Essays on C.S. Lewis as Reader, Critic and Imaginative Writer* (Bowling Green, OH: Bowling Green State University Popular Press, 1988).

Edwards, Michael. 'C.S. Lewis: Imagining Heaven', *Literature and Theology* 6 (June 1992), 107–24.

Foster, Brett, 'An Estimation of an Admonition: The Nature of Value, the Value of Nature, and The Abolition of Man', *Christian Scholar's Review* 27 (1998), 416–35.

Fowler, Alastair, 'C. S. Lewis: Supervisor', *Yale Review* 91 (2003), 64–80.

Freshwater, Mark Edwards, *C.S. Lewis and the Truth of Myth* (Lanham, MD: University Press of America, 1988).

Friesen, Garry L., 'Scripture in the Writings of C.S. Lewis', *Evangelical Journal* 1 (1983), 17–27.

Gibb, Jocelyn (ed.), *Light on C.S. Lewis* (London: Geoffrey Bles, 1965).

Gilchrist, James K., '2nd Lieutenant Lewis', *SEVEN: An Anglo-American Literary Review* 17 (2000), 61–77.

Glover, Donald E., *C.S. Lewis: The Art of Enchantment* (Athens, OH: Ohio University Press, 1981).

Glyer, Diana Pavlac, *The Company They Keep: C.S. Lewis and J.R.R. Tolkien as Writers in Community* (Kent, OH: Kent State University Press, 2007).

Graham, David (ed.), *We Remember C.S. Lewis: Essays and Memoirs* (Nashville: Broadman & Holman Publishers, 2001).

Green, Garrett, *Theology, Hermeneutics, and Imagination* (Cambridge: Cambridge University Press, 2000).

Green, Roger Lancelyn, and Walter Hooper, *C.S. Lewis: A Biography*, revd edn (London: HarperCollins, 2002).

Gresham, Douglas, *Lenten Lands: My Childhood with Joy Davidman and C.S. Lewis* (London: HarperCollins, 1988).

Guite, Malcolm, *Faith, Hope and Poetry: Theology and the Poetic Imagination* (Aldershot: Ashgate, 2010).

Guroian, Vigen, *Tending the Heart of Virtue: How Classic Stories Awaken a Child's Moral Imagination* (Oxford: Oxford University Press, 1998).

Haldane, J.B.S., 'Auld Hornie, F.R.S.', *Modern Quarterly* (Autumn 1946), 32–40.

Harries, Richard, *C.S. Lewis: The Man and His God* (London: Collins, 1987).

Hauerwas, Stanley, 'Aslan and the New Morality', *Religious Education* 67:6 (Nov. 1972), 419–29.

Hilders, Monika, 'The Foolish Weakness in C.S. Lewis's Cosmic Trilogy: A Feminine Heroic', *SEVEN: An Anglo-American Literary Review* 19 (2002), 77–90.

Himes, Jonathan B. (ed.), with Joe R. Christopher and Salwa Khoddam, *Truths Breathed through Silver: The Inklings' Moral and Mythopoeic Legacy* (Newcastle upon Tyne: Cambridge Scholars Publishing, 2008).

Holmer, Paul, *C.S. Lewis: The Shape of His Faith and Thought* (New York: Harper & Row, 1976).

Hooper, Walter, *C.S. Lewis: A Complete Guide to His Life and Works* (San Francisco: HarperCollins, 1996).

Howard, Thomas, *C.S. Lewis, Man of Letters: A Reading of His Fiction* (Worthing, Sussex: Churchman Publishing, 1987).

Huttar, Charles A., 'C.S. Lewis, T.S. Eliot, and the Milton Legacy: The Nativity Ode Revisited', in *Texas Studies in Literature and Language*, 44:3 (Fall 2002), 324–48.

(ed.), *Imagination and the Spirit* (Grand Rapids: Eerdmans, 1971).

Jacobs, Alan, *The Narnian: The Life and Imagination of C.S. Lewis* (New York: HarperCollins Publishers and London: SPCK, 2005).

Jeffrey, David Lyle, 'C.S. Lewis, the Bible, and Its Literary Critics', *Christianity and Literature* 50 (2000), 95–109.

Keefe, Carolyn (ed.), *C.S. Lewis: Speaker and Teacher* (London: Hodder & Stoughton, 1971).

Kerby-Fulton, Kathryn, '"Standing on Lewis's Shoulders": C.S. Lewis as Critic of Medieval Literature', *Studies in Medievalism*, 3:3 (Winter 1991), 257–78.

Kilby, Clyde S., *The Christian World of C.S. Lewis* (Grand Rapids: Eerdmans, 1968).

and Marjorie Lamp Mead (eds), *Brothers and Friends: The Diaries of Major Warren Hamilton Lewis* (New York: Ballantine Books, 1982).

King, Don W., *C.S. Lewis, Poet: The Legacy of His Poetic Impulse* (Kent, OH: Kent State University Press, 2001).

Kort, Wesley, *C.S. Lewis: Then and Now* (New York: Oxford University Press, 2001).

Lewis, W.H., *Brothers and Friends: The Diaries of Major Warren Hamilton Lewis*, ed. Clyde S. Kilby and Marjorie Lamp Mead (San Francisco: Harper & Row, 1982).

'The Lewis Papers: Memoirs of the Lewis Family, 1850–1930', 11 vols, Wade Center, Wheaton College, Wheaton, IL (unpubl.).

Linzey, Andrew, 'C.S. Lewis's Theology of Animals', *Anglican Theological Review* 80 (1998), 60–81.

Loades, Ann, 'C.S. Lewis: Grief Observed, Rationality Abandoned, Faith Regained', *Journal of Literature and Theology* 3 (1989), 107–21.

Lobdell, Jared, *The Scientifiction Novels of C.S. Lewis: Space and Time in the Ransom Stories* (Jefferson, NC: McFarland, 2004).

Lucas, J.R., 'The Restoration of Man', *Theology* 98 (1995), 445–56.

Manlove, C.N., *C.S. Lewis: His Literary Achievement* (London: Macmillan, 1987).

The Chronicles of Narnia: The Patterning of a Fantastic World (New York: Twayne, 1993).

Marshall, Cynthia (ed.), *Essays on C.S. Lewis and George MacDonald* (Lampeter: Edwin Mellen Press, 1991).

Martin, Thomas L. (ed.). *Reading the Classics with C.S. Lewis* (Grand Rapids: Baker Academic, 2000).

Martindale, Wayne, *Beyond the Shadowlands: C.S. Lewis on Heaven and Hell* (Wheaton, IL: Crossway Books, 2005).

Mastrolia, Arthur, *C.S. Lewis and the Blessed Virgin Mary* (Lima, OH: Fairway Press, 2000).

Matthews, Kenneth, 'C.S. Lewis and the Modern World' (unpubl. Ph.D. diss., University of California, Los Angeles, 1983).

McGillis, Roderick (ed.), *George MacDonald: Literary Heritage and Heirs* (New York: Zossima Press, 2008).

Meilaender, Gilbert, *The Taste for the Other: The Social and Ethical Thought of C.S. Lewis*, 2nd edn (Grand Rapids: Eerdmans, 1998).

Menuge, Angus J. L. (ed.), *C.S. Lewis, Lightbearer in the Shadowlands: The Evangelistic Vision of C. S. Lewis* (Wheaton, IL: Crossway Books, 1997).

Miller, Laura, *The Magician's Book: A Skeptic's Adventures in Narnia* (New York: Little, Brown and Co., 2008).

Mills, David (ed.), *The Pilgrim's Guide: C.S. Lewis and the Art of Witness* (Grand Rapids: Eerdmans, 1998).

Milward, Peter, *A Challenge to C.S. Lewis* (London: Associated University Presses, 1995).

Montgomery, John Warwick (ed.), *Myth, Allegory and Gospel: An Interpretation of J.R.R. Tolkien, C.S. Lewis, G.K. Chesterton, Charles Williams* (Minneapolis: Bethany Fellowship Inc., 1974).

Moodie, C.A.E., 'C.S. Lewis: Exponent of Tradition and Prophet of Postmodernism?' (unpubl. D.Th. diss., University of South Africa, 2000).

Morris, Francis J., 'Metaphor and Myth: Shaping Forces in C.S. Lewis's Critical Assessment of Medieval and Renaissance Literature' (unpubl. Ph.D. diss., University of Pennsylvania, 1977).

and Ronald C. Wendling, 'Coleridge and "the Great Divide" between C.S. Lewis and Owen Barfield', *Studies in the Literary Imagination*, 12:2 (Fall 1989), 149–59.

Musacchio, George, 'Fiction in *A Grief Observed*,' in *SEVEN: An Anglo-American Literary Review* 8 (1987), 73–83.

Myers, Doris T., *Bareface: A Guide to C.S. Lewis's Last Novel* (Columbia, MO: University of Missouri Press, 2004).

C.S. Lewis in Context (Kent, OH: Kent State University Press, 1991).

Newell, Roger J., 'Participatory Knowledge: Theology as Art and Science in C.S. Lewis and T.F. Torrance' (unpubl. Ph.D. diss., University of Aberdeen, 1983).

Nicholi, Armand M., Jr, *The Question of God: C.S. Lewis and Sigmund Freud Debate God, Love, Sex, and the Meaning of Life* (New York: Free Press, 2002).

Norwood, W.D., Jr, 'C.S. Lewis' Portrait of Aphrodite', *Southern Quarterly*, 8 (1970), 237–72.

Patrick, James, *The Magdalen Metaphysicals: Idealism and Orthodoxy at Oxford, 1901–1945* (Macon, GA: Mercer University Press, 1985).

Pearce, Joseph, *C.S. Lewis and the Catholic Church* (San Francisco: lgnatius Press, 2003).

Poe, Harry Lee, and Rebecca Whitten Poe (eds), *C.S. Lewis Remembered* (Grand Rapids: Zondervan, 2006).

Purtill, Richard L., *C.S. Lewis's Case for the Christian Faith* (New York: Harper & Row, 1981).

Pyles, Franklin Arthur, 'The Influence of the British Neo-Hegelians on the Christian Apology of C.S. Lewis' (unpubl. Ph.D. diss., Northwestern University, 1978).

Reppert, Victor, *C.S. Lewis's Dangerous Idea: In Defense of the Argument from Reason* (Downers Grove, IL: InterVarsity Press, 2003).

Robson, W.W., *Critical Essays* (London: Routledge & Kegan Paul, 1966).

Rossi, Lee D., *The Politics of Fantasy: C.S. Lewis and J.R.R. Tolkien* (Epping: UMI Research Press, 1984).

Rowse, A.L., *Glimpses of the Great* (Lanham, MD: University Press of America, 1985).

Sayer, George, 'C.S. Lewis's *Dymer*', *SEVEN: An Anglo-American Literary Review* 1 (1980), 94–116.

Jack: A Life of C.S. Lewis, 2nd edn (London: Hodder & Stoughton, 1997).

Schakel, Peter J., *Imagination and the Arts in C.S. Lewis* (Columbia, MO: University of Missouri Press, 2002).

Reason and Imagination in C.S. Lewis: A Study of 'Till We Have Faces' (Grand Rapids: Eerdmans, 1984).

(ed.), *The Longing for a Form: Essays on the Fiction of C.S. Lewis* (Kent, OH: Kent State University Press, 1977).

and Charles A. Huttar (eds), *Word and Story in C.S. Lewis* (Columbia, MO: University of Missouri Press, 1991).

Schofield, Stephen (ed.), *In Search of C.S. Lewis* (South Plainfield, NJ: Bridge Publishing, 1983).

Schwartz, Sanford, *C.S. Lewis on the Final Frontier: Science and the Supernatural in the Space Trilogy* (New York: Oxford University Press, 2009).

Shippey, T.A., *J.R.R. Tolkien: Author of the Century* (London: HarperCollins, 2001).

Smith, Robert Houston, *Patches of Godlight: The Pattern of Thought of C.S. Lewis* (Athens, GA: University of Georgia Press, 1981).

Sprague, Duncan, 'The Unfundamental C.S. Lewis: Key Components of Lewis's View of Scripture', *Mars Hill Review*, 2 (May 1995), 53–63.

Spufford, Francis, *The Child that Books Built* (London: Faber & Faber, 2002).

Swift, Jennifer, 'A More Fundamental Reality than Sex: C.S. Lewis and the Hierarchy of Gender', *Chronicle of the Oxford University C.S. Lewis Society*, S.1 (2008), 5–26.

Taliaferro, Charles, 'A Narnian Theory of the Atonement', *Scottish Journal of Theology* 41 (1988), 75–92.

Tandy, Gary L., *The Rhetoric of Certitude: C.S. Lewis's Nonfiction Prose* (Kent, OH: Kent State University Press, 2009).

Taylor, Kevin T., and Giles Waller (eds), *Christian Theology and Tragedy: Theologians, Tragic Literature, and Tragic Theory* (Aldershot: Ashgate, forthcoming 2011).

Thorson, Stephen, 'Knowing and Being in C.S. Lewis's "Great War" with Owen Barfield', *CSL: The Bulletin of the New York C.S. Lewis Society* 15:1(Nov. 1983), 1–8.

Tonning, Judith E., 'A Romantic in the Republic: Some Critical Comments about The Abolition of Man', *Chronicle of the Oxford University C.S. Lewis Society* 5 (2008), 27–39.

Travers, Michael (ed.), *C.S. Lewis: Views from Wake Forest* (Wayne, PA: Zossima Press, 2008).

Urang, Gunnar, *Shadows of Heaven: Religion and Fantasy in the Writing of C.S. Lewis, Charles Williams and J.R.R. Tolkien* (London: SCM Press, 1971).

van Leeuwen, Mary Stewart, *A Sword Between the Sexes? C.S. Lewis and the Gender Debates* (Grand Rapids: Brazos Press, 2010).

Vaus, Will, *Mere Theology: A Guide to the Thought of C.S. Lewis* (Downers Grove, IL and Leicester: InterVarsity Press, 2004).

Walker, Andrew, 'Scripture, Revelation and Platonism in C.S. Lewis', *Scottish Journal of Theology* 55 (2002), 19–35.

and James Patrick (eds), *A Christian for All Christians: Essays in Honour of C.S. Lewis* (London: Hodder & Stoughton, 1990).

Walsh, Chad, *C.S. Lewis: Apostle to the Skeptics* (New York: Macmillan, 1949).

The Literary Legacy of C.S. Lewis (London: Sheldon Press, 1979).

Ward, Michael, *Planet Narnia: The Seven Heavens in the Imagination of C.S. Lewis* (New York: Oxford University Press, 2008).

Watson, George, 'The Art of Disagreement: C.S. Lewis (1898–1963)', *Hudson Review* 48 (1995), 229–39.

'The High Road to Narnia', *American Scholar*, Winter 2009, 89–95.

Never Ones for Theory? England and the War of Ideas (Cambridge: Lutterworth Press, 2000).

(ed.), *Critical Essays on C.S. Lewis* (Aldershot: Scolar Press, 1992).

White, William Luther, *The Image of Man in C.S. Lewis* (Nashville: Abingdon Press, 1969).

Wielenberg, Erik J., *God and the Reach of Reason: C.S. Lewis, David Hume, and Bertrand Russell* (Cambridge: Cambridge University Press, 2008).

Williams, Rowan, '*That Hideous Strength*: A Reassessment', address to the Oxford University C.S. Lewis Society, 5 Oct. 1988 (audio recording, Wade Center, Wheaton College, Wheaton, IL).

Wilson, A.N., *C.S. Lewis: A Biography* (New York: Norton and London: Collins, 1990).

Wolfe, Brendan, and Judith Wolfe, *C. S. Lewis and the Church* (London: T & T Clark, forthcoming, 2011).

Index

Note: Entries for C.S. Lewis's works are in **bold**.

THE CAMBRIDGE COMPANION TO PURITANISM
edited by John Coffey and Paul Lim (2008)
ISBN 978 0 521 86088 8 hardback   ISBN 978 0 521 67800 1 paperback

THE CAMBRIDGE COMPANION TO ORTHODOX CHRISTIAN THEOLOGY
edited by Mary Cunningham and Elizabeth Theokritoff (2008)
ISBN 978 0 521 86484 8 hardback   ISBN 978 0 521 68338 8 paperback

THE CAMBRIDGE COMPANION TO PAUL TILLICH
edited by Russell Re Manning (2009)
ISBN 978 0 521 85989 9 hardback   ISBN 978 0 521 67735 6 paperback

THE CAMBRIDGE COMPANION TO JOHN HENRY NEWMAN
edited by Ian Ker and Terrence Merrigan (2009)
ISBN 978 0 521 87186 0 hardback   ISBN 978 0 521 69272 4 paperback

THE CAMBRIDGE COMPANION TO JOHN WESLEY
edited by Randy L. Maddox and Jason E. Vickers (2010)
ISBN 978 0 521 88653 6 hardback   ISBN 978 0 521 71403 7 paperback

THE CAMBRIDGE COMPANION TO CHRISTIAN PHILOSOPHICAL
THEOLOGY
edited by Charles Taliaferro and Chad Meister (2010)
ISBN 978 0 521 51433 0 hardback   ISBN 978 0 521 73037 2 paperback

THE CAMBRIDGE COMPANION TO MUHAMMAD
edited by Jonathan E. Brockopp (2010)
ISBN 978 0 521 88607 9 hardback   ISBN 978 0 521 71372 6 paperback

THE CAMBRIDGE COMPANION TO SCIENCE AND RELIGION
edited by Peter Harrison (2010)
ISBN 978 0 521 88538 6 hardback   ISBN 978 0 521 71251 4 paperback

Forthcoming

THE CAMBRIDGE COMPANION TO THE TRINITY
edited by Peter C. Phan

THE CAMBRIDGE COMPANION TO THE VIRGIN MARY
edited by Sarah Boss

THE CAMBRIDGE COMPANION TO BLACK THEOLOGY
edited by Dwight Hopkins and Edward Antonio